Indian Economy and Neoliberal Globalization

This book assesses the effects of globalization and neoliberal economic regimes in low- and middle-income countries, primarily on industries, investment and trade; finance and credit; and employment, gender and development.

The volume – written to honour the rich academic work of the eminent economist Professor C. P. Chandrasekhar – addresses issues which are relevant to emerging economies and their concerns around development, investment, financial planning and adopting new technologies. It analyses the new financial systems and institutions and the dominance of global finance in policymaking in these countries and their effects in the post-pandemic period. It examines the changing contours of finance, trade and labour models and laws in developing countries to assess the risks and concerns of economic crises and challenges. The volume does justice to an assessment of the macroeconomic and developmental implications of neoliberal policies in India while offering an insightful overview of the new economic practices and policies. It also offers suggestions and measures to address concerns regarding banking and global liquidity, reinforce robust strategies for growth in both small and large industries and bring in reform.

This book will be of interest to scholars and students of economics, political economy, finance and trade, development studies and South Asian studies.

P L Beena is Associate Professor at the Centre for Development Studies, Thiruvananthapuram, Kerala, India.

Murali Kallummal is Professor at the Centre for WTO Studies, Indian Institute of Foreign Trade, New Delhi, India.

Santosh Kumar is Associate Professor of Economics in Department of Commerce, Shri Ram College of Commerce, University of Delhi, India.

Indian Economy and Neoliberal Globalization

Finance, Trade, Industry and Employment

Essays in the honor of C P Chandrasekhar

Edited by P L Beena, Murali Kallummal and Santosh Kumar

Routledge
Taylor & Francis Group
LONDON AND NEW YORK

First published 2023
by Routledge
4 Park Square, Milton Park, Abingdon, Oxon OX14 4RN

and by Routledge
605 Third Avenue, New York, NY 10158

Routledge is an imprint of the Taylor & Francis Group, an informa business

British Library Cataloguing-in-Publication Data
A catalogue record for this book is available from the British Library

Library of Congress Cataloging-in-Publication Data
A catalog record has been requested for this book

ISBN: 978-1-032-34713-4 (hbk)
ISBN: 978-1-032-38216-6 (pbk)
ISBN: 978-1-003-34399-8 (ebk)

DOI: 10.4324/9781003343998

Typeset in Sabon
by Deanta Global Publishing Services, Chennai, India

Contents

Figures

Tables

Contributors

Rose Mary K Abraham, Director, Department of Investment and Public Asset Management, Ministry of Finance, New Delhi, India

Somdutta Banerjee, Senior Research Fellow, Centre for WTO Studies, Indian Institute of Foreign Trade, New Delhi, India

P L Beena Associate Professor, Centre for Development Studies, Thiruvananthapuram, Kerala, India

Arpita Biswas PhD Scholar, University of Massachusetts, Amherst, MA, USA

Amrita Goldar Senior Fellow, Indian Council for Research on International Economic Relations, New Delhi, India

Devangana Jha, Assistant Professor, Department of Economics, Maitreyi College, University of Delhi, New Delhi, India

Gautam Kumar Jha, Assistant Professor, PGDAV College (Evening), University of Delhi, New Delhi, India

Murali Kallummal, Professor, Centre for WTO Studies, Indian Institute of Foreign Trade, New Delhi, India

Animesh Kumar, Assistant Professor, Department of Economics, Kamala Nehru College, University of Delhi, New Delhi, India

Santosh Kumar, Associate Professor of Economics, Department of Commerce, Shri Ram College of Commerce, University of Delhi, Delhi, India

Abhijit Mukhopadhyay, Senior Fellow, ORF's Economy and Growth Programme, Observer Research Foundation, New Delhi, India

Bindu Oberoi, Associate Professor, Department of Economics, Indraprastha College for Women, University of Delhi, Delhi, India

S. Krishnakumar, Associate Professor, Department of Economics, Sri Venkateswara College, University of Delhi, New Delhi, India

Smruti Ranjan Sahoo, PhD Scholar, Centre for Development Studies, Thiruvananthapuram, Kerala, India

Jatinder Singh, Assistant Professor, Centre for Research in Rural and Industrial Development, Chandigarh, Punjab, India

Akanksha Pratik Sonker, PhD Scholar, Centre for Economic Studies and Planning, Jawaharlal Nehru University, New Delhi, India

Anjana Thampi, Assistant Professor, O.P. Jindal Global University, Sonipat, Haryana, India

Foreword

Themes of the festschrift, *Indian Economy and Neoliberal Globalization: Finance, Trade, Industry and Employment*, reflect the broad areas of academic research of Prof. C.P. Chandrasekhar in whose honor these essays have been collated. Industrial development in India has always been an abiding interest of his scholarship beginning with his doctoral thesis "*Growth and Technical Change in Indian Cotton Mills*" prepared during the early 1980s. His focus was on technological choice in India's most important consumer industry during a period of its rapid technological and structural transformation. The import substitution, public regulation, public sector and oligopolistic domination of consumer and intermediate sectors were key characterestics of this period.

Prof. Chandrasekhar contributed to the then ongoing debates on the relative industrial stagnation that characterised the indian economic growth since mid-sixties. He emphasised the demand rather than supply constriants on the performances of the industrial sector. He also noted the different phases of industrial growth and the positive impact of import-substituting industrialisation strategy. The analysis of the oligopolistic structure of Indian corporate landscape, highlighted in the early works of Prof. Chandrasekhar, is a theme of his later studies on private corporate sector.

He was not enthusiastic about the potential of new international division of labour contributing to rapid industrialisation of Under Developed Countries (UDCs) (*Imperialism and Industrialisation in the Underdeveloped Countries: On the Significance of the New International Division of Labour, 1983)*. The Stanberg Group argued that the trend towards exports from UDCs can cause a significant shift in industrial production from developed to underdeveloped countries. A shift in the capital was also suggested to take place, leading to the creation of a new international division of labour (NIDL). Prof Chandrasekhar argued with empirical support that though there is a tendency towards a creation of new international division of labour, it cannot provide the reason for increasing unemployment in the developed countries.

The 1980s was also a period of policy changes in the indian industry. The attempts were being made to remove the demand constraints only by giving export orientation to the industries, liberalising the intermediate goods and reforming some of the most archaic industrial regulations. These measures had a positive impact on industrial growth. But the strategy also resulted in aggravation of the twin deficit and ultimately the denouncement of the post-independence period policy regime for a Bank-Fund dictated neo-liberal development strategy. Prof. Chandrasekhar has been a leading critic of these policies not only in the numerous academic papers and books but also in his prolific journalistic articles on related issues.The chapters in this festschrift are related to some of the key issues thrown up by the neo-liberal policies.

The macroeocomics of globalisation has been a continuing theme in Professor Chandrasekhar's work. There are a set of papers in which he explored the nature of the cross-country experience under export-led growth regimes. See for example his paper with Prabhat Patnaik (*Investment, exports and growth: A cross country analysis, 1996*) and ILO paper with Jayati Ghosh (*The Indian economic reform process and the implications of the Southeast Asian crisis, 1999*). The issue of financialisation, liberalisation and macroeconomics of growth has been another continuing thread.

The initial phase of neo-liberal adjustment program emphasised import-liberalisation, market determined depreciation of the currency and fiscal consolidation to stabilise the economy. It was indeed a mini recession created by the public policy. The structural adjustments in different sectors and inflow of foreign capital are expected to lift the economy from the above recession into a path of accelerated growth. The 1990s thus proved to be a period of deceleration in growth which was captured in the book *Market that Failed*, co-authored with Prof. Jayati Ghosh, 2002. Viewed from the vantage point of view of two decades later, it would appear that the book was too pessimistic about the prospects of economic growth in an emerging economy like India under the neo-liberal policy regime.

The macro-economic squeeze of the Indian economy created a vacuum and a space for the private markets to occupy the development financing. Globally, the imbalance in the financial capacities of the north and south has further aggravated the development financing in developing countries. The significant lesson has been that the adoption of market controlled financing lead to the financial crisis. A classic example can be seen in financial crises across the South East Asian countries (1997-98), highlighted in his book *Crisis as Conquest: Learning from East Asia*, co authored with Prof. Jayati Ghosh, 2001. This case of the South-East Asian economic crisis-1997-98, has been a turning point in the debate on the role of global finance in assessing an economy under neo-liberal conditions. The book revealed that the era of globalisation is always characterised by slow growth in the real sector and enhanced volatility in the financial industry. The economies from both the north and south have come to be characterised by an almost addictive dependence on capital mobility. As tracking the global capital movements is difficult, as it is increasingly being held and controlled by the private sector, he stressed the need for increased government controls on capital flows.

Further picking on the Asian Crisis, in a book titled *Continuity or Change? Finance Capital in Developing Countries: A Decade after the Asian Crisis* (2009), he highlights the magnitude and variety of financial institutions and instruments that have emerged in the context of making the system much more complex for tracking and regulation. The era post-Asian Crisis has been characterised by excessive wealth accumulation in fewer and fewer hands, rise in income inequalities and instability in economic growth that has worked to the disadvantages of developing countries. He demonstrated how financial accumulation, working through process of financialisation, has had an adverse impact on public investment and therefore growth.

He highlights that boom in the stock market index is a precursor of financial fragility. It is driven mainly by international finance capital searching for speculative gains even though the real economic sector may be in shamble; suggesting no link with the actual economic performance of the economy. His work on development banking has brought the debate on the relevance of development financial institutions in countries where the industrialisation project has been incomplete. Many countries, including India, are re-establishing the financial institutions for financing big infrastructure projects meant for pushing economic development. Still, the sustainability of such financial institutions remains under question as the State's support in a big way is absent under the pressure of global finance. Global finance has curtailed the State's power in fiscal maneuvering, and the development banks or commercial banks have turned towards domestic and international financial markets for meeting their financial resources. In such a design of a financial structure, it is not easy to carry out operations of the banking sector in the interest of society and sustainable economic development and progress. The process of industrialisation also becomes the victim of such a fragile financial system; therefore, catching up with the developed world may remain a distant dream.

Prof. Chandrasekhar returned to his industrial roots in the recent edited volume *Promise Belied: India's Post Independence Industrialization Experience*, 2015. He discusses the boom created across the industrial sector as part of the LPG strategy resulting in the spurt of imports and rising corporate profitability, leading to increased corporate sector savings and investment and the growth in the service sector. The boom in demand generated credit-based financing for private consumption and housing investment. The capital inflows caused the liquidity needed to sustain the credit financed boom and provided the required foreign reserve to finance the import of goods to dampen price inflation. However, a growth strategy that combines increased liabilities to the rest of the world with an increased indebtedness of the private sector is not sustainable in the long run. The dominance of global finance in the policy affairs of developing countries and its role in causing economic instabilities and widening economic disparity has been an essential element in analysis by economists associated with heterodoxy.

Prof. Chandrasekhar's writings on financial issues such as issues of capital controls, stock market performance, global saving glut, emerging trends in private equity, financial crisis, new banking horizon, banking regulation, and development banking have been remarkable and insightful. For example, his paper on "*Private Equity: A New Role of Finance*", 2007 in Economic and Political Weekly highlights private equity as an instrument to control and acquire the firms in India by foreign capital. We are witnessing an increase in the scale of mergers and acquisitions of domestic firms (assets) by global finance. At the same time, the governments have turned out to be favourable to international players by pushing more and more regulatory changes that facilitate such takeovers.

The process of premature monopolisation resulted in the emergence of business groups named oligopolists or business houses is a feature that has been widely noted in literature. In his paper "*Firms, Markets and State: An Analysis of Indian Oligopoly*", 1999, he points out that liberalisation opened up economic space to new entrants, with unprecedented opportunities for diversification in new areas, characterised by buoyant demand and higher profits. The new entrant strategy affected the traditional oligopolistic structure in two ways- while some groups started restructuring their capabilities and working out new expansion strategies, the others who could not catch up has declined and disintegrated. Unfortunately, before this restructuring could happen, liberalisation policies intervened, making it more difficult for older groups to compete with the prices of imports or the brand names of foreign producers. Thus, while the first restructuring phase was set to deliver a more innovative, internationally competitive oligopoly structure, the second phase threatened to slow down the process. The emerging structure of new corporate oligarchy in India is an issue of immense economic and political importance.

The small scale industrialists have also been at the receiving end. In "*Industrial Policy: Way Ahead*", 2004, he analyses the crisis of the 'disappearing middle segment". He observes that financial institutions and government policies during 1990s were biased to the large scale industries. The small scale sector which supplies goods to large scale industries or depends on them could also be sustained with an appropriate industrial policies and financing strategies by focusing on MSMEs in particular. He further argues for strengthening MSMEs and limiting the foreign investment in import intensive luxury goods producing industries. Such monitoring, according to him, is necessary for moulding India into a major exporter rather than an importer of raw materials.

Apart from his studies on Industrial growth and its financing, the impact of new policies on employment, income distribution, poverty, and gender have been areas of concerns of his research and studies. The demonetization, the haphazard implementation of GST and the mishandling of the Covid 19 have all contributed to make the period from the middle of 2010s a phase of economic deceleration, employment stagnation and immiserisation.

Equaly important as academic papers and books are his prolific and popular articles in Frontline, Business Line, Macroscan, Website of Network

Ideas, New Economic Thinking etc. which are followed and read by researchers, academicians, policymakers across the world. His regular contributions to the HT Parekh Finance Column in the EPW deals with various contemporary and essential developments on the financial horizon of India and the globe.

I want to propose my appreciation and express my good wishes to his students from the Centre for Economic Studies and Planning (CESP) for putting together this present volume. I am also one of his students. When I joined Centre for Development Studies in 1977 for my M.Phil, he was one of the faculty at the Centre. In my academic work as well as political and administrative pursuits, I have immensely benefitted from his writings and personal discussions. Thank you Chandru.

T. M. Thomas Isaac
Honorary Fellow, CDS, Thiruvananthapuram,
Distinguished Fellow, GIFT, Thiruvananthapuram,
Former Finance Minister, Government Of Kerala.

1 Introduction

P L Beena, Murali Kallummal and Santosh Kumar

The postworld war period envisaged the state as an active agent in promoting capitalist development across many developing countries with a set of manoeuvrable autonomous economic policies accompanied by substantial state spending. It was inspired by the experience of industrialised countries that followed the Keynesian demand management model, state planning in the Soviet Union, fear of market failure and concerns of addressing malnutrition and hunger, which often is a result of spontaneous capitalist development (Patnaik, 1995). Such an economic model in the developing world resonates with Keynes's prescient advocacy of local self-determination and national policy experimentation (Bardhan, Bowles and Wallerstein, 2006).

The World Bank and International Monetary Fund (IMF) originated out of the UN Monetary and Financial Conference held at Bretton Woods in July 1944.The Conference came out with a concrete plan for rebuilding the physically and economically devastated world during the Second World War. They emphasised maintaining adequate global demand so that unemployment, which was witnessed during the Great Depression-1929, is not repeated (Stiglitz, 2002). The Bretton Woods Institutions were also convinced with the problems of bad economic outcomes of market dominancy. Hence, they would envisage an active role of the state in demand management across member countries. Such global consensus in academics and practice continued till classical liberalism came back in the 1970s in academics and policymaking (Kotz, 2002). The repackaging of classical liberal economic thought is known as neoliberalism. An unregulated capitalist system characterises this neoliberalism package with a limited role of the state to achieve efficiency and distributional justice. The World Bank and IMF became proponents to implement neoliberalism across the developing countries in the form of a package called 'Macroeconomic Stabilization and Structural Adjustment Programs' or 'Washington Consensus'. Williamson (2008) coined the term Washington Consensus in 1989 in a background paper for a conference on the Brady Plan at the Institute for International Economics. The Brady Plan was announced by Nicholas Brady, the then Secretary of Treasury in the newly formed Bush Administration in 1989 (Vasquez, 1996).

DOI: 10.4324/9781003343998-1

The Brady Plan was a set of debt reduction schemes for debt-ridden countries, mainly Latin American countries. It consisted of economic reforms that incorporated market-oriented economic principles. The Washington Consensus consisted of ten elements: fiscal discipline, re-ordering public expenditure priorities, tax reforms, liberalisation of interest rates, competitive exchange rate, trade liberalisation, foreign direct investment (FDI) liberalisation, privatisation, deregulation, and property rights (Willamson, 2008). The Washington Consensus did not confine itself to the Latin American countries. It became a reality across most developing countries due to the conditional economic support by the World Bank and IMF. The implementation of Washington Consensus across developing countries can also be attributed to the stagnation of protected capitalism in the metropolitan centres in the industrialised countries. Patnaik (1995) argues that any capitalist development strategy in a country requires sustained demand for its products. Hence, the external market becomes essential for a capitalist country growing in protection. It must be this phenomenon that might have caused the implementation of the Washington Consensus in developing countries routed through the World Bank and IMF as the United States had sole veto power in the decision-making process of these institutions.

However, it has been close to four decades that the world has witnessed the 'Structural Adjustment Program and Macroeconomic Stabilisation' with varying degrees across developing countries. Countries around the globe have seen one after another financial crisis since the early 1990s till date. The recent subprime crisis-2008 in the United States has engulfed the whole world, and country-after-country are waiting to come out from this global economic shock. The plan of globalisation that was characterised by a set of economic regimes as part of the Washington Consensus encountered resistance from social and political forces. The limitation of autonomy in the economic policy formulation by the developing countries has been playing a spoilsport role in achieving developmental targets. The implementation of globalisation has not been able to provide efficiency or relief from inequality. At the global level, there have been frequent incidences of unemployment and a sustained rise in income inequality between rich and poor regions.

International Finance and Banking

External and internal financial liberalisation have been an integral part of the economic globalisation strategy of developing countries. It has facilitated the emergence of global finance as the dominant factor which has been determining the course of fiscal and monetary policies of the developing countries across the world. Mckinnon and Shaw model (1973) has served as a guidinglight for the developing countries to move towards deeper financial markets with innumerable financial instruments to trade the rising risk in the liberalised financial sector. But such changes have not led to a stable macroeconomic environment and sustainable financing for economic development objectives. There has been a steep rise in riskier financial instruments such as derivatives, private equities, venture capitals, etc. A boom in the stock markets has accompanied the innovation and proliferation of such instruments. Such a boom in financial instruments and the stock market has been caused by foreign investments (Kallummal 1999, Kallummal 2001, Chandrasekhar 2009).

The rising dominance of global finance is a cause of concern for policymakers as this has made the countries vulnerable because of three reasons: firstly, rising dependency of developing countries on foreign capital; secondly, the rising foreign capital has caused the evolution of many new risky financial instruments in the myopic informational construct; and thirdly, the transition of ownership of domestic assets into foreign hands. According to Chandrasekhar (2009), the international assets of UK-based banks had increased from $1.5 trillion to $5.8 trillion between 1997 and 2006 and international assets of US-based banks increased from $0.74 trillion to $2.6 trillion over the same period. Similar was the situation in the case of non-bank financial entities in advanced countries.[1] In the backdrop of increasingly liberalised and globalised financial systems across the developing countries, international financial flows have led to entanglement due to innovative financial products' layers and the complexities of the financial structure.

The experience in developing countries has been anti-development with the rising dominance of global finance. The liberalised and globalised financial system has led to the demise of financial institutions that were constituted with the purpose of a nationalistic model of economic development with an objective of economic self-sufficiency. Given the difference in the economic development stages of developing and developed countries, the imposition of uniform BASEL Accord has led to harmonisation of banking activities even at the cost of developmental objectives. Many developing countries founded their banking and financial institutions. India has witnessed the rising effect of the dominancy of global finance on its policymaking affairs daytoday after the inception of financial liberalisation in 1991 with the imposition of the Macroeconomic Stabilisation and Structural Adjustment Programs by the IMF. As a result, India has witnessed rising risky financial instruments, dominancy of stock markets, decline of Development Financial Institutions, skewed regional and sectoral distribution of credits, and liberally regulated shadow banks. These strategies of liberalisation caused India to witness possibly a fragile and relatively unproductive financial structure.

Neoclassical economists have been arguing for free trade deals as they promoted investment linkages. The promotion of cross-border investment has been done despite the fact that there are imbalances in the availability of information globally. Systematically encouraging the private sector and discouraging the public sector have been part of the broader liberalisation agenda. The IMF had regulated all forms of current account payments by 1945. Current Account flows broadly relate to financial transactions linked to the process of transfer of physical assets. These include (a) payments for merchandise trade, (b) international services, (c) investment incomes and payments, (d) remittances, and (e) official government transfers. Until the late 1970s, the prime mode of capital account flows happened in official development assistance by the developed countries. Rather than trade flows, it is the other modes of finance that gained prominence from the mid-1970s. Its pace accelerated in the 1980s. When private capital moved from surplus to deficit countries, they needed open capital accounts with assured conditions for free flows. By the mid-1980s, there was also a surge in the private sector–driven FDI by multinational companies. The opening up of global capital markets and establishing stock markets accelerated after countries began adopting the market economy model and liberalised trade flows under the IMF's structural adjustment and the WTO's binding rules. Today's world is more financially integrated than ever before, with inter- and intra-firm transactions made through multiple financial instruments, which criss-cross various borders. Unlike the current account flows, a significant portion of capital account flows is routed through the speculative mechanism of stock markets. The latter is often not in concurrence with the real sector's needs for productive financing investments.

The available sources of detailed investment flows are being sold for a price by a few private consultant firms like S&P Global Market Intelligence, Bloomberg, CNN Money, CNBC, Goldensource and others with shareholder-driven governance and a very high probability of oversight. Thus, while we have ample disaggregated intergovernmental data on international real economy transactions (through the Current Account), there is a lack of similar data for international financial transactions. It creates an imbalance between the functions of governments in monitoring and regulating the activities of production, which in the present day is being carried-out through mainly the private markets using various financial instruments (Kallummal & Francis, 2020).

It is to be mentioned here that the rising dominance of finance capital determining the economic realities across the developing countries which is being accompanied by the uneven bargaining structure of the WTO, which decides the terms of trade for the countries during the globalisation period. Different financial sector issues have been dealt with and also the current conjuncture of how detrimental and destabilising the financial sector has become in developing countries has been assessed in five chapters of this volume.

Trade and Investment Linkages

The debate on the causal linkages between trade, technology and investment has become more pronounced since the 1970s. In the context of FDIs, it has been extensively discussed in the legal and economic literature (UNCTAD, 2009).The neoclassical frameworks provide for an open and effective international growth driven by core leading to a trickle-down effect for the periphery and thereby creating economic growth and development worldwide.

As the capital and technology were mobile for all the production factors, it led to their movement; foreign direct investment became an integral part of the Industrial Policy.

In some situations, the FDI can substitute trade, such as when a firm invests and produces in a foreign country. As efficiency-seeking firms look for the best location, they invest in the form of FDI. Such investments complement the trading of their products. It then led to complex investment and reinvestment networks across the world. It thus was termed global value chains (GVCs). The increasing investment activities and technological flows needed specific legal instruments to protect the rights of investors. Countries negotiated such legal instruments under two frameworks: the Bilateral Investment Treaties (BITs) and the Treaties with Investment Provisions (TIPs); 2,290 BITs and 324 TIPs are in force globally. The first recorded bilateral investment treaty was signed between Germany and Pakistan on 25th November 1959 and has been in force since 28th November 1962 (UNCTAD).[2]Increasingly, such investment treaties have become a means of enforcing unreasonable conditionalities by the developed countries upon the lesser developed countries.

Multilateral treaties were seen as a solution to address some of these concerns. Under the OECD, negotiation began on a multilateral agreement on investment in 1995. However, it failed as France and some other countries withdrew. The WTO reignited the process of negotiations at the first ministerial conference held in 1996 in Singapore.[3] The negotiation continued until the 2004 Doha Ministerial Declaration (Kallummal, 2008). Once again, a multilateral deal was elusive and did not come into force; discussions were put on hold by the General Council as part of the July 2004 Framework Package. However, outside the WTO, the bilateral investment agreements continued to be the only enforcing form of investment treaties. Most of the international investment agreements had contentious provisions. These were in the areas of the investor–state dispute settlement process, the definition of investments (pre vs. post and narrow vs. broad), fair and equitable treatment provisions, expropriation, most favoured nations, and monetary transfer provisions (MTPs). Nearly all of the BITs ignored the obligations, and there was an overwhelming emphasis on the investor's rights. As of 2020, India has signed 86 BITs, of which 8 are in force and 4 are under negotiation. Seventy-four BITs have been terminated. The WTO's (TRIMs) related issues are increasingly becoming a part of the various free and regional trade agreements (RTAs). Many of these RTAs have a separate agreement or a clause on investment issues, the details of which need to be examined, especially in the context of agreements arrived between partners as well as the RTAs between a developed and a developing country. Erosion of the bargaining power is expected to occur if individual RTAs are signed. To understand to what extent the erosion has already happened, we need two kinds of information: firstly, the RTAs and details on investment-related clauses; secondly, what were the multilateral submissions (within WTO framework) – individually or as a group. More and more research from the perspective of developing countries would enable placing linkages between IITs and RTAs in their correct perspective; two chapters in this book focus on these issues in detail.

Knowledge, Industry and State Policy

In India, it was expected that the financial and international trade liberalisation under the WTO regime and subsequent negotiations under Free Trade Agreements (FTAs), Regional Comprehensive Economic Partnership (RCEP), Comprehensive and Progressive Trans-Pacific Partnership will boost the exports and greater integration into GVCs while gaining access to the cheaper imports. However, it is widely argued that such policy changes did not help India to build sustainable industrial growth, investment flows, and trade relations with their partner countries (Beena 2008; Dhar 2021; Francis, 2019), but rather led to a huge manufacturing trade deficit (Nagaraj,2017; Mani 2020; Choudury, 2013, Beena 2014). Such is the case in the Information Technology (IT) sector too, especially after the decision to join the Information Technology Agreement (ITA) under the WTO regime in 1996 (Kallummal 2013, Francis 2019, Dhar 2021). Scholars have also argued that many of the developing countries are experiencing deindustrialisation (Tregenna, 2009) or premature deindustrialisation, including India (Chouduri, 2015). Mazumdar (2015) argued that there has been a marked deindustrialisation after liberalisation as the increase in the share of the private organised sector is on account of growth in non-manufacturing activities.

Following the LPG (liberalisation, privatisation, and globalisation) regime, the Government of India (GOI) initiated programmes like Bharat Net and Digital Saksharta Abhiyan to bridge the digital divide, particularly over the last two decades. In addition to this, the GOI has amended CCI Act, 2011 and implemented National Manufacturing Policy, 2011, New FDI policy, and 'Make in India' policy, 2014, which aimed to encourage the manufacturing industry and improve exports. Such policies were also expected to make the Indian economy, especially industry, more efficient/competitive and transform the economy into a manufacturing hub by removing barriers to the flow of capital and thus mobilising more foreign savings and better technology. This new policy regime has also encouraged the Indian firms to participate in the global production network by investing in any part of the world by mobilising financial resources through internal or external sources (Beena 2018). A significant share of foreign savings has come in portfolio investments instead of FDI. The service sector has attracted many such FDI/portfolio investments (Rao and Dhar, 2018).

Another fallout of such a strategy is that much of such investment entered India by acquiring existing assets owned by domestic firms (Beena 2014; Saraswathy 2018; Rao and Dhar 2021). It is also evident that many of the leading firms in India invested abroad through Greenfield[4] and Brownfield[5]/Cross-Border Mergers and Acquisitions (CBM&As), especially after 2000 (Nagaraj, 2006; Nayyar 2008; Beena 2018).

Although the debate on India's production being uncompetitive across agricultural and manufacturing sectors is ongoing, one of the factors that can enable the reduction of prices of final product and thereby make India's exports competitive is the price of petroleum products. India had primarily followed two principles for setting the price of petroleum products post-independence. The first was the Administered Pricing Mechanism (APM), which was adopted after the oil crisis in the 1970s. APM was based on the cost-plus pricing approach under which the price of refined products was linked to the cost of production. The dismantling of the APM regime and the adoption of the New Exploration Licensing Policy (NELP) marked the beginning of deregulation in the petroleum sector. APM was dismantled to reduce the government's control on petroleum pricing. In contrast, NELP heralded the privatisation of critical segments of the petroleum sector. This book includes four chapters that focus on the developmental issues discussed here.

Labour, Gender and Development

One of the most important developments during the post-economic liberalisation era has been the gradual withdrawal of the state from the economy and the dilution of labour laws to achieve economic efficiency. But the efficiency term has been elusive as the market requires specific optimal conditions in which efficiency can be achieved. India's growth process during the neoliberal regime has been conceptualised by Bhaduri (2014) as 'development by dispossession' and formalised by using a three-sector (corporate, informal, and agricultural/natural resource) model (Nagaraj and Motiram, 2017). It has been widely argued that reforms in India under neoliberalism have been business-friendly rather than market-friendly and the state supports big business against the weak and vulnerable ones, which has led to growing economic inequality (Bhaduri, 2008). Presently, the contribution of the manufacturing sector to GDP is relatively stationary, while the service sector has contributed two-thirds of GDP growth. However, in terms of employment generation, the service sector contributes almost 48 per cent while the agriculture and manufacturing sectors around 40 per cent and 12 per cent respectively. It should also be noted that much of the employment generated in the service sector pertains to the construction sector. In the manufacturing sector, much of the employment generated has been as contractual employment and the quality of such employment is presumed to be relatively low (Joseph and Kakarlapudi, 2019; Joseph et al., 2021). A significant share of employment is also generated in the unorganised/informal sector, making a large section of the labour force vulnerable (Kannan 2017; Unni 2015). The most affected group is women across all social groups. For instance, the Labour Force Participation Rate of Women (LFPR-W) in India is 22 per cent as compared to almost 60 per cent in the case of Europe and well above 60 per cent in East Asia, especially China (Jose, 2021). Following neoliberal economic reforms in India, a narrative has been woven that such reforms would lead to women's empowerment by relaxing the hold of cultural norms and creating economic opportunities, which would then liberate them from violence (Krishnan 2018). However, global economic conditions can contribute to violence against women through the intertwining of private life with public spaces as well as of patriarchy with the material conditions of daily life (Weissman 2007) . One of the chapters in this volume relates spousal violence in India to such intertwining of women's employment and neoliberal reforms. Given the extent and nature of the unemployment scenario in India, some chapters of this volume deal with the issues of labour, gender and employment.

Scope of the Book

Given the above outline of the emergence of neoliberal economic regimes across developing countries, including India, this edited volume in the honour of Prof. C.P. Chandrasekhar attempts to address the issues which are important for not only India but also developing countries from the point of view of emerging developmental concerns. This volume largely covers the areas which have been extensively and intensively researched upon by Prof. Chandrasekhar, whose academic career spans over the last five decades. The chapters are broadly divided into the following four thematic sections: (i) international finance and banking; (ii) international trade and foreign direct investments; (iii) knowledge, industries, and state policy; and (iv) labour, gender and development.

Keeping in mind the emerging dominance of global finance, Chapter 2, 'Is Global Economic Heading towards a Sovereign Debt Crisis' by Abhijit Mukhopadhyay, delves into the global build-up of an unsustainable debt accumulation in the last decade. Post-subprime crisis, international financial markets witnessed a flush of funds due to easy monetary policies of central banks worldwide, especially central banks from the developed countries. This resulted in rising debt accumulation, particularly for low- and middle-income economies. As world output growth remained secular, many of these countries accumulated unsustainable levels of debt. Now when the world is struggling to deal with the COVID-19 pandemic, this threatens to transform into a likely global sovereign debt crisis. However, after international calls to help the affected countries, the G20 countries floated the Debt Service Suspension Initiative (DSSI). This chapter critically assesses performance of the DSSI and other debt-relief measures taken to date. The scope for the

DSSI has remained geographically. limited, as it covers only 73 low-income countries. Many middle-income countries under debt distress are not eligible to avail this facility. The current duration of the moratorium, extended till December 2021, is too short to deal with the problem by the most affected countries. With the apprehension of a future downgrading by international credit rating, many countries are hesitant to participate. A comprehensive debt restructuring plan however would have helped. In the absence of such an initiative, this chapter finds the current efforts inadequate. It has left the developing countries in an economic wobble.

The issue of global liquidity during the globalisation period is further discussed in Chapter 3, 'Global Liquidity and Emerging Market Economies?' by S. Krishnakumar. The chapter discusses the need of collating indicators about the global liquidity and reporting the same to international economic policy centres regularly. The financial stability of the global economy should not be put at risk, and there should be methods to plan in advance and take necessary steps towards pre-empting the occurrence of such a crisis. Exploring the diverse aspects of global liquidity, the Committee on the Governance of Financial Systems of the Bank for International Settlements submitted its report in 2011 (BIS, 2011). Popularly known as the Landau Report, this report distinguishes between global private liquidity and official liquidity. What are the determinants of global liquidity? How have the trends been with respect to global liquidity ever since the global financial crisis? What implications do the swings in global liquidity have on the emerging market and developing economies? These are the questions that Chapter 3 addresses through its different sections. This chapter also attempts to undertake a critical appraisal of the mainstream literature on global liquidity from a post-Keynesian angle, bringing out its implications for emerging markets and developing economies.

Connecting the real sector with that of the financial sector has been challenging, with the policymakers struggling to find actual policy intervention tools. In Chapter 4, 'Our Preoccupation with Speculation and its Consequences for Commodity Derivatives Markets in India', Rose Mary K Abraham has analysed this aspect in the Indian context as she analyses India's derivatives market. Derivatives have been an important phenomenon during the financial liberalisation period, and they have been invented to search for a better price in this informationally myopic world of the financial market. Abraham has captured this dimension of the new financial environment. The chapter brings out that in India, commodity derivatives markets are stated to be 'speculative' and therefore dismissed outright on account of the low quantum of physical deliveries and low level of participation by farmers and other agents. This chapter explores the historical roots of India's preoccupation with such speculative concerns. It outlines the consequences of the same for the development of the market, particularly the agri-derivatives segment. Relying on the government/parliamentary records, the chapter shows that speculative concerns have influenced the regulatory policy over the years. It has resulted eventually negligible in the absence of any price-setting powers despite India being a powerful commodity-producing/consuming nation. The data shows the gradual displacement of agri-segment from being a 52 per cent to 5 per cent market share segment. What has cramped this derivative market segment is not the delivery of commodity per se, but the 'threat of delivery'. But judging a market based on the extent of physical deliveries has left us in a low-level equilibrium trap. Starting from the legal definition in tax laws, the chapter also tries to give new dimensions to our understanding of speculative interest in the derivative market and quantify the same using velocity of money, warehouse capacity usage, open interest to turnover ratio, etc. It shows that delivery in contracts should not be considered as a firm indicator of a successful contract as it is required mainly in illiquid contracts or cornered contracts. The chapter also gives insights for the future conduct of policy regarding ways of participation for government procurement agencies and the integration of spot and derivatives.

Another aspect of the agricultural sector has been analysed in Chapter 5, 'Rural Credit and Growth in Indian Agriculture' by Akanksha Pratik Sonker – the neglect of agriculture by the new financial architecture in terms of volume and uses of credit by the banks. It highlights how India's macroeconomic stabilisation programme curtailed government expenditure as part of a fiscal consolidation strategy. Such a paradigmatic shift reduced the government's support for agriculture, curtailed public expenditure and placed further constraints on public policy related to agriculture. The neoliberal regime weakened the proactive fiscal approach through the instruments of taxation and public spending. The loss of tax- and debt-financed public spending as a principal stimulus to growth was substituted by debt-financed private investment through the provision of credit. These policies have adversely affected growth in the agricultural sector. Due to the adherence to fiscal conservatism, the government has been reluctant to undertake the necessary public investment for rural development and the agriculture sector to restore its viability and enhance the productivity of Indian agriculture. The chapter highlights the changing contours of the banking sector in the post-reform era with centrality to rural credit. It reviews the progress in rural banking and evaluates the composition, nature, and direction of credit flow, especially after the credit surge in 2003–04 and its implications on agricultural growth. The chapter argued that the transformation of rural credit's nature, composition, and distribution in the post-reform era has failed to serve its intended purpose of spurring growth and development in India's agricultural sector and the rural economy. The chapter underscores the limitations of the credit-led growth strategy and warrants a purposive integration of monetary (credit) and fiscal policies (public expenditure) to alleviate the rural distress and the impending agrarian crisis.

Another area of withering state's support has been the industrial finance. Santosh Kumar in Chapter 6, 'Decline of DFIs in India during Post-Financial

Liberalisation', has captured this aspect. The chapter highlights that financial liberalisation in India has caused the withdrawal of the state's financial incentives to the domestic financial institution of national and regional importance and opening up the domestic territories to international finance. It has been accomplished by the introduction of new segments of industrial finance based less on domestic but more on international market forces supported by the financial innovations linking trade to the risk for speculative gains. The chapter highlights that India had established many DFIs to catch up with the industrialised countries for better economic development outcomes. DFIs in India were mostly state-sponsored to fulfil the state's objectives of development with regional and interpersonal economic justice. The established DFIs extended financial assistance for capital formation across a host of industries as per the planned guidelines of the state. Implementation of financial liberalisation principles has led to the emergence of a new financial structure, which has led to economic vulnerability for the DFIs. The chapter shows that the introduction of various financial reforms measures since 1992 has caused the DFIs to either convert into commercial banks or obtain the status of NBFCs or close down. What emerged as alternative sources of industrial finance has not been adequate in addressing the balanced regional industrialisation and sustainable sources of industrial finance. It raises a question mark on the process of financial globalisation as a better economic development model.

Addressing the imbalances which have been discussed previously in terms of Current Account flows and Capital Account flows, in Chapter 7, 'Impact of India's Bilateral Treaties on FDI: A Firm-Level Analysis', Amrita Goldar deals with the contentious issue of whether or not the BITs have positively impacted FDI flows. However, the extent of those BITs in supporting and expanding FDI flows remains unanswered. The actual question about the quality of FDI flows is increasingly being examined. In other words, an investigation is required if, in addition to providing an investment source to the economy, the incoming FDI has generated positive externalities. On the flip side, it should be noted that the above positive impacts on the economy conform to a best-case scenario. FDI flows are not uniform in character and could vary greatly depending upon the FDI home country, the host country's resources, etc. Thus, even though the theory outlines the possible benefits of FDI inflows, the actual benefits that accrue or would accrue to a developing country may differ case-to-case and need to be studied. The chapter examines the influence of legal security provided under the BITs and the quality of FDI flows. The chapter has attempted to investigate the impact of BIT on specific performance indicators of the manufacturing sector in India, focusing on the effects of foreign investment.

Trade and investment are increasingly recognised as mutually reinforcing channels for cross-border activities. FDI generally occurs in tandem with greater international trade integration, reflecting increasing vertical integration and establishing transnational distribution networks. In Chapter 8, 'India's Tariff Jumping FDI: A Case of Overseas Investment Flows under ASEAN-India FTA', Murali Kallummal and Somdutta Banerjee address the rise of FTAs signed globally, which is also being promoted as a panacea with surging FDI flows and opportunities for GVCs as the border tariffs are eliminated. Globally, the surge in FTAs has led the numbers to almost 600 with 52 per cent share of goods alone agreement followed by goods plus services with 47 per cent and only 1 per cent with the service sector liberalisation. The solid theoretical underpinning is that the FTAs enable faster economic growth and development by creating trade and investment linkages. Compared to the world, the pace of economic growth and development of the East and South-East Asian regions was relatively higher. The second section of the chapter suggests that an overall investment sentiment in ASEAN and India is an essential first step. Therefore, an analysis of the total FDI flows is undertaken under two heads to understand the causal links between tariff liberalisation and the expanded market potentials. India's comparative tariff liberalisation was undertaken under its seven dominant FTAs. The country provided the highest market access to goods from SAFTA (LDCs were offered a significant share up to 99 per cent with only 25 products in the exclusion list).Market access conceded by India under the ISFTA is up to 91 per cent and AIFTA 90 per cent, followed by other FTAs. Therefore, an investigation of India's efforts to create GVCs by analysing firm-wise India's OFDI flows to ASEAN ten countries. Trade liberalisation under an FTA has been mainly centred around the elimination of tariffs. India's tariffs were one of the highest in the Asian region. It offered a big market for the ASEAN countries that had by 2010 integrated themselves with the help of FTAs with almost all major manufacturing economies. The chapter, therefore, investigates India's outward investment flows by firms with a view of GVCs creation in the ASEAN markets. Under the AIFTA, tariffs have been eliminated 90 per cent of tariff lines from the applied tariff with an average of 15 per cent in 2020,[6] thereby offering a lucrative market. The analysis of India's FDI flows to the ASEAN market, both descriptive and empirical analysis using the OLS, suggests a negative impact of the FTA elimination and does not support the neoclassical understanding.

Analysis and studies have suggested that the implementation of TRIMs and TRIPs as part of WTO agreements reduced the space for proactive industrial policies for enabling technological progress and development and the diffusion of the same across developing countries (UNCTAD, 2021; Correa 2016 as cited by Francis, p.192, 2019). There is enough evidence to argue that leading firms, especially in the technology-oriented sectors at the global level, have strengthened their market power by acquiring their potential competitors (WIR, 2001). Given this context, an attempt is made in Chapter 9, 'Mergers & Acquisitions and Antitrust Implications: Evidence from the High-Tech Manufacturing Sector' by P L Beena and Smruti Ranjan Sahoo, to analyse the growth pattern of mergers and acquisitions (M&A) in the high-tech industries during the new IPR regime. The chapter tried to explore whether any surge in M&A in these industries has led to any change in market structure, driven out potential competitors and created conditions for appropriating monopoly profit. It has further looked into the price and non-price competitive strategies followed by these industries and the role of M&A in determining price cost margin. It addresses the antitrust issues related to innovation and competition in the competition policy and IPR policy framework. The chapter observed a surge in the growth of M&A in the high-tech industries in India. The leading firms in these industries are engaged in mergers and acquisitions, predominantly horizontal rather than vertical as observed by earlier studies (Beena 2001; 2014). These firms control a significant share of outputs in those industries. These industries were spending relatively more on in-house R&D, advertisement, and marketing and subcontract more jobs, including professional jobs during the new IPR regime. Anti-competitive practices in terms of pricing or abuse of dominance are also visible in these industries. The econometric model did reveal that M&A and other firm-specific variables did have a positive association with price cost margin. The study argues that introducing regulatory mechanisms could address the antitrust implications of M&A, especially in HT industries and start-ups that are small in size, as such acquisitions can change the innovative and competitive dynamics.

The MSME sector is passed through different regulatory regimes to reach its present stage of development. The most significant change in the policy regime was observed in the early 1990s as the government had systematically abolished almost all the protections provided to the industrial sector, including the MSME sector. Analytically, it is expected that the liberal policy regime intensifies the competition and restructures the industrial sector. In Chapter 10, 'Industrialisation and Role of MSMEs in India: With a special Reference to Punjab', Jatinder Singh tries to understand the performance of and challenges faced by the micro, small and medium enterprises in India by taking the case of Punjab state. Using secondary information, results suggest that the MSME sector grew in all the key parameters during the post-reform period. However, the pace of expansion has declined in recent years, as manifested in the falling growth rates and declining share of the MSME sector in national aggregates such as GDP, industrial output, etc. The situation is even worse in the case of Punjab as some of the small units went out of business, and a significant proportion of small-scale units have witnessed a contraction during the last decade. Various factors have contributed to the declining trends, including a low level of technological upgradation, resources constraints, etc. Despite these reverse trends in

are found to be relatively higher for disadvantaged groups. The study hypothesises that these findings could be explained through the backlash effect arising from two sources: the perceived violation of sociocultural norms by employed women and the double burden of reproductive and market work on them.

Notes

1 As of 2020, the UK-based banks held total assets of $5.1 trillion and the US bank held $3.8 trillion.
2 European Union signed in 1957 is the customs union and has some form of International Investment Agreement which predated the Germany and Pakistan Treaty.
3 Also known as new issues dealt with agreements on investment, competition, government procurement, and trade facilitation.
4 Greenfield FDI involves capital movement that helps establishing new enterprises by buying fixed assets, goods, and services and hiring workers in the host country (WIR, 2001).
5 FDI can be in the form of Brownfield if the entry of capital is in the form of merging or acquiring the assets of existing firms which would not create any further capital formation, additional capacity, or employment. When a Brownfiled/CBM&A takes place, it registers as both a sale in the country of a target firm and purchase in the home country of the acquiring firm (WIR, 2001).
6 WTO, accessed on 2 September 2021, https://www.wto.org/english/thewto_e/countries_e/india_e.htm.

References

Bardhan, P., S.Bowles and M.Wallerstein (2006), *Globalization and Egalitarian Redistribution*, Oxford University Press, New Delhi.

Beena, P. L. (2001), 'Intangibles and Finance: Motives and Consequences of Mergers in Indian Corporate Sector', in Banerjee,P. and Richter,F. J. (eds), *Intangibles in Competition and Cooperation: Euro-Asian Perspectives*, Chapter 3, pp. 53–73, Palgrave, London and New York.

Beena, P. L. (2008;2010), 'Limits to Universal Trade Liberalisation: Experience of South Asia in Textiles and Clothing Sector', in AshwiniDeshpande (ed.), *Globalisation and Development: A Handbook of New Perspectives*, pp. 46–66, Oxford University Press, New Delhi.

Beena, P. L. (2014;2018), *Mergers and Acquisitions: India under Globalisation*, Routledge, New Delhi, London, and NewYork.

Beena, P. L. (2018), *Outward FDI and Cross-Border M&As by Indian Firms: A Host Country-Level Analysis*, WP No.479, CDS, Trivandrum.

Bhaduri, A. (2008), 'Predatory Growth', *Economic and Political Weekly*43(16), 10–14.

Bhaduri, A. (2014), 'A Study in Development by Dispossession', Paper presented at the conference on Political Economy of Contemporary India, held at IGIDR. http://www.igidr.ac.in/indiapolecon/conference.php.

Chandrasekhar, C. P. (2009), 'Continuity or Change? Finance Capital in Developing Countries a Decade after the Asian Crisis', in JayatiGhosh and C.P.Chandrasekhar (eds.), *After Crisis: Adjustment, Recovery and Fragility in East Asia*, Tulika Books, New Delhi.

Chaudhuri, S. (2013), 'Manufacturing Trade Deficit and Industrial Policy in India', *Economic and Political Weekly*48(8), 41–50.

Chaudhuri, S. (2015), 'Import Liberalisation and Premature Deindustrialisation in India', *Economic and Political Weekly*50(43), 60–69.

Dhar, B. (2021), 'Explaining India's Trade Performance', in SanjayaBaru (ed.), *Beyond Covid's Shadow: Mapping India's Economic Resurgence*, pp. 204–222, Rupa Publications, New Delhi.

Francis, S. (2019), *Industrial Policy Challenges for India: Global Value Chains and Free Trade Agreements*, Routledge, South Asia Edition, London.

Jose, A. V. (2021), 'New Threats to Paid Employment of Women', in SanjayaBaru (ed.), *Beyond Covid Shadow: Mapping India's Economic Resurgence*, pp. 242–253, Rupa Publications., New Delhi.

Joseph, K. J. and K. K. Kakarlapudi (2019), 'Export-Employment Conundrum in India's Manufacturing under Globalization: In *Search of a Strategic Approach* ', in Sachin Chaturvedi and Sabyasachi Saha (eds.), *Manufacturing and Jobs in South Asia*, pp. 111–152, Springer, Singapore.

Joseph, K. J., K. K. Kakarlapudi, and A. Joseph (2021). 'Deindustrialization and Innovation Under Globalization: An Analysis of India's Catch Up in Manufacturing', *Nova Economia 30*, 1199–1224.

Kallummal, M. (1999), *'Disintermediation' and Private Corporate Financing: An Analysis of the New Issue (Primary) Market in India*, Unpublished PhD Thesis, Jawaharlal Nehru University, New Delhi.

Kallummal, M. (2001), *An Alternative to Investment Promotion in Developing Countries: A Case Study of Indian Primary Market*, RIS Occasional Paper No. 61, Research and Information System for the Non-Aligned and Other Developing Countries, New Delhi.

Kallummal, M. (2008), 'Country Positions and its Implications on Negotiations of Multilateral Framework on Investment: Review of Pre-Cancun Period' (December 12, 2008). https://doi.org/10.2139/ssrn.1315124.

Kallummal, M. (2013), 'Process of Trade Liberalisation under the Information Technology Agreement (ITA): The Indian Experience', CWS Working Paper No. 3, *CWS/WP/200/3*. http://wtocentre.iift.ac.in/workingpaper/Working%20Paper3.pdf.

Kallummal, M. and F.Smitha (2020), 'FDI Screening: Need of the Hour in the Time of Non-transparent capital flows', Economy, Policy Circle, 27th April. https://www.policycircle.org/economy/screening-fdi-need-of-the-hour-in-the-time-of-non-transparent-capital-flows/.

Kannan, K. P. (2017), *Interrogating Inclusive Growth:Poverty and Inequality in India*, Routledge, London.

Kotz, D. M. (2002), 'Globalization and Neoliberalism', *Rethinking Marxism*12(2), 64–79.

Krishnan, K. (2018), 'Gendered Discipline in Globalising India', *Feminist Review* 119(1), 72–88.

Macmillan, R. and R.Gartner (1999), 'When She Brings Home the Bacon: Labor-Force Participation and the Risk of Spousal Violence against Women', *Journal of Marriage and the Family*61(4), 947–958.

Mani, S. (2020), 'Developing India's Mobile Phone Manufacturing Industry', *Economic and Political Weekly*55(19), 50–57.

Mazumdar, S. (2015), 'Monopoly and Indian Industry', in C. P.Chandrasekhar (ed.), *Indian Industrialisation*, Volume 1, pp. 94–125, Oxford University Press, New Delhi.

McKinnon, R. I. (1973), *Money & Capital in Economic Development*, The Brooking Institutions Press, Washington.

Mehta, S. K. (1969), 'Patterns of Residence in Poona, India, by Caste and Religion: 1822–1965',*Demography*6(4), 473–491.

Nagaraj, R. (2006), 'Indian Investment Abroad: What Explains the Boom?', *Economic and Political Weekly*XLI, 4716–4718.

Nagaraj, R. (2017), 'Economic Reforms and Manufacturing Sector Growth: Need for Reconfiguring the Industrialisation Model,' *Economic and Political Weekly*52(2), January.

Nagaraj, R. and S.Motiram (2017), *Political Economy of Contemporary India*, Cambridge University Press., Cambridge.

Nayyar, D. (2008), 'The Internationalisation of Firm from India: Investment, Mergers and Acquisitions', *Oxford Development Studies*36(1), 111–131.

OECD (2002), *Foreign Direct Investment for Development Maximising Benefits, Minimising Costs, Overview*, Organisation for Economic Co-operation and development, OECD Publications Service, Paris, France.

Park, R. E. (1915), 'The City: Suggestions for the Investigation of Human Behavior in the City Environment', *American Journal of Sociology*20(5). 577–612.

Patnaik, P. (1995), *Whatever Happened to Imperialism and Other Essays*, Tulika, New Delhi.

Rao, K. S. C. and B.Dhar (2018), *India's Recent Foreign Direct Investment-An Assessment*, ISID, New Delhi.

Rao, K. C. and B. Dhar (2021), 'Inbound M&As in India, Issues and Challenges', *Antitrust Bulletin*66(2), 158–183 June.

Saraswathy, B. (2018), *The Globalisation of Indian Business: Cross-Border Mergers and Acquisitions in the Indian Manufacturing*, Routledge, London.

Shaw, E. S. (1973), *Financial Deepening in Economic Development*, Oxford University Press, New York.

Singh, K. and B. Ilge, *Rethinking Bilateral Investment Treaties Critical Issues and Policy Choices*.Both Ends, Madhyam and Somo, Amsterdam and New Delhi.

Stiglitz, J. E. (2002), *Globalization and Its Discontents*, Allen Lane, The Penguin Press, London.

Susewind, R. (2017), 'Muslims in Indian Cities: Degrees of Segregation and the Elusive Ghetto',*Environment and Planning* A49(6), 1286–1307.

Tregenna, F. (2009), 'Characterising Deindustrialisation: An Analysis of Changes in Manufacturing Employment and Output Internationally', *Cambridge Journal of Economics* 33(3), 433–466.

UNCTAD (2009), *The Role of International Investment Agreements in Attracting Foreign Direct Investment to Developing Countries*, UNCTAD Series on International Investment Policies for Development, Geneva.

UNCTAD (2021), *Investment Policy Hub*, Last accessed on 4th September . https://investmentpolicy.unctad.org/.

Unni, J. (2015), 'Employment and Industrial Development in India', in C. P.Chandrasekhar (ed.), *Indian Industrialisation*, Volume 1, pp. 229–258, Oxford University Press, New Delhi.

Vasquez, I. (1996), 'The Brady Plan and Market-Based Solutions to Debt Crisis', *Cato Journal*16(2) (Fall), 233–243.

Weissman, D. M. (2007), 'The Personal Is Political—and Economic: Rethinking Domestic Violence', *BYU Law Review* 2007(2), 387–450.

Williamson, J. (2008), 'A Short History of the Washington Consensus', in NarcisSerra and Joseph E.Stiglitz (eds.), *The Washington Consensus Reconsidered: Towards a New Global Governance*, pp. 14–30, Oxford University Press, New York.

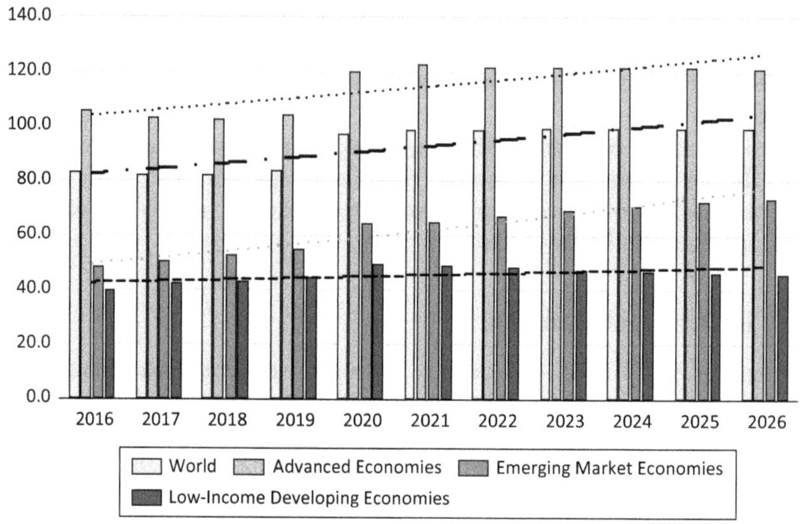

Figure 2.1 Trends in general government gross debt, 2016–26 (as percentage of GDP). All country averages are weighted by nominal GDP converted to US dollars (adjusted by purchasing power parity only for world output) at average market exchange rates in the years indicated and based on data availability. The figures for 2021–26 are projections; these are based on IMF staff assessments of current policies. *Data source:* IMF Fiscal Monitor, April 2021.

serious trouble if there is a global sovereign debt crisis due to widespread defaults. In times of such a crisis, financial resources are likely to be usurped by the advanced economies, which are having a larger external debt burden. In spite of having relatively the lowest debt burdens, low-income economies will lack the wherewithal to tide over that kind of a crisis.

Low-income developing economies have a much lower average term of maturity than any other groupings of countries. Advanced economies (including G7 and G20 countries) and most of the emerging economies have an average term to maturity of their debts of around seven years. Low-income developing economies have an average term to maturity of their debts of less than five years (Figure 2.2). The maturity gap is significant. Shorter duration of loans implies difficulty in repayment.

As a result, the debt to average maturity ratios for low-income countries are relatively at a much higher level than other groupings. These countries have to pay more in relatively shorter time. Emerging economies, both inside and outside G20, have relatively much lower debt to maturity ratios. In other words, low-income economies have relatively much higher cumulative repayment obligations every year than emerging economies. Since overall debt burden is at the highest level for the advanced economies, their debt

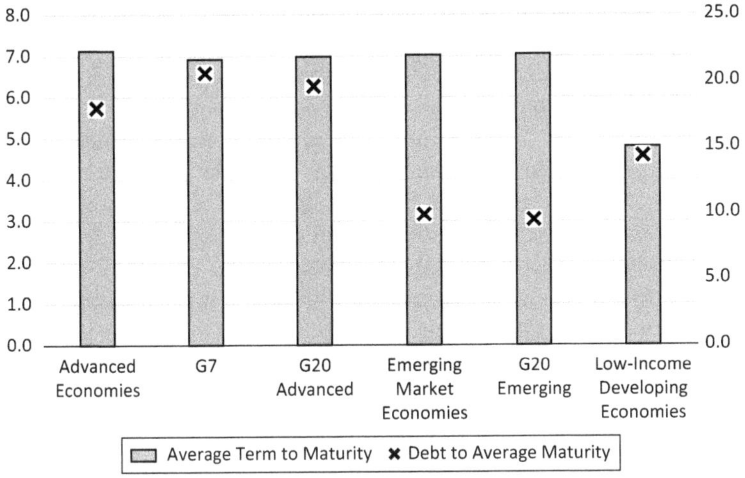

Figure 2.2 Trends in average term to maturity and debt to average maturity (2021). The figures are as in 2021; the average term to maturity is measured in years and debt as percentage of GDP. Debt to average maturity ratio is measured in the secondary axis. Average term to maturity data refers to government securities. *Data source:* IMF Fiscal Monitor, April 2021.

to maturity ratios are also the highest, in spite of having relatively longer average term to maturity. But as mentioned earlier, larger and easier access to global finance is likely to bail them out if there is a debt crisis.

If a global sovereign debt crisis occurs, then low-income developing countries will have much less time to react. Though the size of sovereign debt (as a percentage of GDP) is highest for the advanced countries, these economies are likely to survive through their domestic and international financial resources. However, low-income developing economies are likely to be affected the most, and then defaults and debt crises may follow.

The signs are already there to be seen. There have been seven sovereign debt defaults in 2020. The countries that suffered such a fate are Argentina, Ecuador, Lebanon, Zambia, Belize, and Suriname (twice). The last time these many sovereign defaults happened was in 2012, after the 2008 financial crisis. There were five sovereign defaults, and Greece defaulted twice (Panigrahi, 2021).

Debt Service Suspension Initiative (DSSI)

Lockdowns and restrictions to contain the spread of COVID-19 have resulted in recessionary conditions that may push more than 100 million people into extreme poverty in low-income developing countries. To cushion the debt-related blows to low-income economies, the G20 countries decided to float a Debt Service Suspension Initiative in 2020. There are 73 countries eligible for a temporary moratorium on debt service payments for bilateral loans provided to these countries. Initially, the moratorium under DSSI was offered till 31 December 2020. Later, it has been extended to end-December 2021 (World Bank, 2021).

In November 2020, the "Paris Club"[1] of creditor countries joined this endeavour, and the G20 further endorsed an initiative called Common Framework (CF) for debt treatment beyond the DSSI. CF is established ostensibly to support low-income countries with their potentially unsustainable debt burdens by restructuring and other means.[2]

The DSSI, till now, had limited success in fulfilling its intended objective. With 46 of the total 73 eligible countries participating, the moratorium is requested for debt amounting to USD 5 billion, which is around 10 per cent of the total external debt service (TEDS) scheduled in 2020 for all 73 countries. Full participation, on the other hand, could potentially cover USD 12.2 billion debt in 2020 and another USD 9.25 billion in the first half of 2021 (Jensen, 2021).

However, the prevalence of debt distress and vulnerabilities is not limited to these 73 countries alone, as can be observed in Figures 2.1 and 2.2. Among 105 developing economies, around two-thirds of 73 emerging markets are "non-investment grade" in sovereign credit ratings. Adding 32 low-income developing countries in that grade completes the global base of vulnerable and risky debts. In the period between 2021 and 2025, estimated TEDS payments on external public debt at risk (risky TEDS) will cross USD 598 billion mark for this group of 72 vulnerable countries. Out of this more than USD 598 billion amount, USD 311 billion (more than 50 per cent) debt service payments have to be made to the private creditors (Jensen, 2021).

But the real problem here is that these private creditors are not made part of the DSSI till now. CF has been floated to provide a partial solution to that, as the framework seeks to restructure debt on a case-by-case basis involving all official bilateral creditors. But the fact remains that only 73 DSSI countries are eligible for this framework – leaving out several middle-income vulnerable countries. Chad is the first country to seek debt restructuring under CF in January 2021, followed by Ethiopia and Zambia. Ethiopia sought a flow rescheduling, Chad and Zambia requested debt restructurings with NPV (net present value) reductions (Reuter, 2021).

There are 23 vulnerable countries with USD 387 billion in risky TEDS, which is 65 per cent of the total. The estimated uncovered risky TEDS in 2021 is around USD 87 billion. One-third of the vulnerable countries with two-thirds of the risky TEDS are not covered by the DSSI and CF (Jensen, 2021).

Participation in DSSI remains less than expected among the eligible countries, as quite a few countries are apprehensive of losing access to global financial and debt markets – if there is a subsequent downgrade in ratings. Participation in the DSSI is equated with a potential credit rating

downgrade. The short-term and temporary nature of the moratorium has also not served the broader DSSI purpose well. Along with the absence of private creditors till now, these are the main reasons behind the limited participation.

An Impending Debt Crisis?

The World Bank's International Debt Statistics database provides data for debt accumulation across broad demographic regions and across income levels. High-income countries are excluded, while debt accumulations in low- and middle-income countries are available in the dataset.[3] Similarly, broad region-wise detailed debt accumulation data are available for six developing regions. These are as follows:

1) East Asia and the Pacific
2) South Asia
3) Europe and Central Asia
4) The Middle East and North Africa
5) Sub-Saharan Africa
6) Latin America and the Caribbean

Once again, high-income countries are excluded across all these regions. Four important debt ratios are considered: (a) debt service to exports, (b) external debt stocks to exports, (c) (foreign exchange) reserves to external debt stocks, and (d) external debt stocks to exports.

These ratios across income and geographical classification are used for the analysis. The results are alarming and show that the accumulation of debt started reaching potentially risky levels even before the pandemic started. The pandemic-induced crisis only worsened it further.

For low-income countries, multilateral debt as a percentage to external debt stocks went down from around 40 per cent in 2011 to approximately 35 per cent in 2019. So, the multilateral organisations – including the IMF and the World Bank – provided relatively less credit to these countries in the last decade. Since external debt stocks, as a percentage to exports, increased in this period, it can be inferred that there had been relative rise in other forms of debt, particularly the bilateral ones. Both debt service to exports and external debt stocks to export ratios have risen in this decade for these countries. In contrast, reserves to external debt stocks dwindled (Figure 2.3).

In other words, in low-income countries, external debt burden has gone up but their exports and subsequently forex reserves have steadily declined. While this created the ground for a potential debt crisis, multilateral credit offered to these countries decreased. The fall in multilateral credit indicates multilateral financial institutions' reluctance or hesitation to lend to countries with bad credit ratings or past credit history. So, the reluctance to participate in the DSSI may have a real reason.

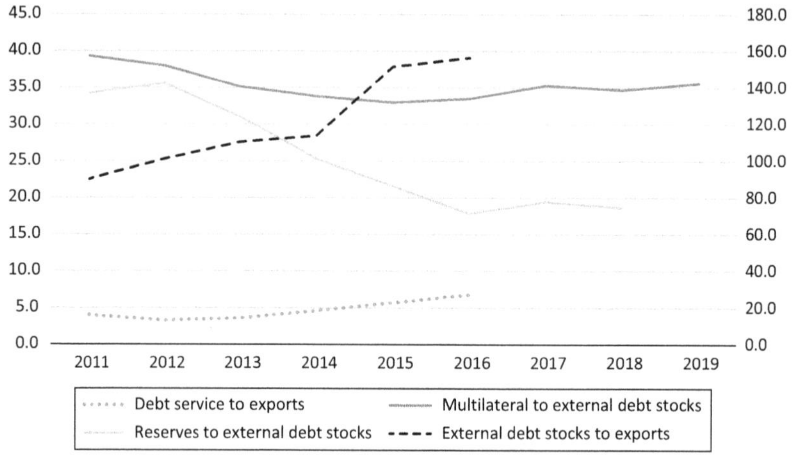

Figure 2.3 Trends in debt ratios of low-income countries (in per cent). Based on available data, some data points are not available. External debt stocks to exports ratio is measured on the secondary axis. *Data source:* International Debt Statistics, 2021, World Bank.

Since the DSSI moratorium has not been extended for a much longer period beyond the end of 2021, the reluctance will increase. Ideally, a primary framework to restructure debt burdens of low-income countries should have been established by now. In the absence of that, it will be increasingly difficult to convince vulnerable countries to participate in the DSSI and the CF.

These countries will be needing more time, if not anything else. But the DSSI extended the moratorium only till December 2021. However, more delay in helping out low-income economies to effectively deal with their mounting external debt burden will simultaneously increase the probability of more future defaults.

Similar trends are visible even for middle-income countries. As the only exception, multilateral credit as a percentage of external debt stocks remained in the range of 8 per cent to 9 per cent during the last decade. However, other ratios follow a similar pattern – while debt service to exports and external debt stocks to exports increased, forex reserves to external debt stocks have plummeted (Figure 2.4).

Therefore, it can be implied that some of these middle-income countries have been experiencing the same pattern of accumulating external debt with dwindling foreign exchange reserves. This is expected to put upward pressure on the debt service ratio, and it did so. This is quite in line with the reporting of the latest data on debt accumulation in the previous section. Though debt accumulation in low-income countries is more in discussion currently, some middle-income countries have become highly vulnerable in the last decade.

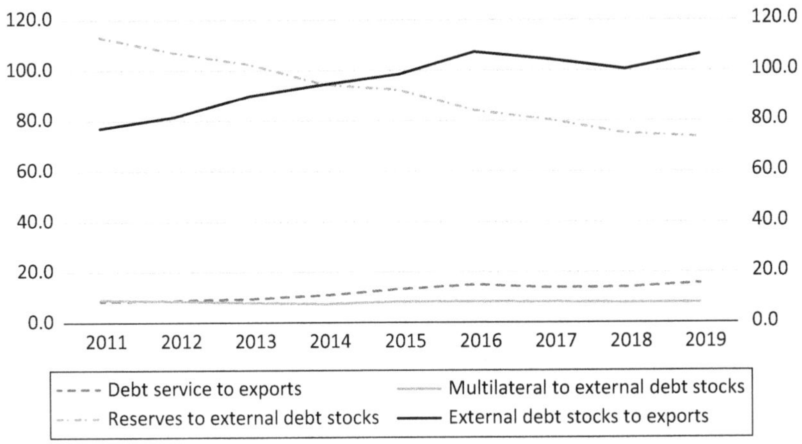

Figure 2.4 Trends in debt ratios of middle-income countries (in per cent). External debt stocks to exports ratio is measured on the secondary axis. *Data source:* International Debt Statistics, 2021, World Bank.

These middle-income economies cannot be part of the DSSI under the current framework, but some of these countries may need support in the immediate future. However, the reluctance to participate in any debt relief programme may emerge for this set of countries as well. The probable reason will be credit rating, once again. Unless apprehension about a downgrade in credit ratings is not addressed, any debt relief programme will suffer from non-participation and subsequent ineffectiveness.

Regional Composition of External Debt

East Asia and Pacific countries show a similar pattern in debt accumulation, like low- and middle-income countries. External debt stocks are on the rise, reserves to external debt stocks are falling, debt service to exports are marginally increasing, and multilateral debts are dwindling in comparison to external debt stocks (Figure 2.5).

The year 2015 presents an interesting kink for this set of countries. External debt stocks to exports decreased, and reserves to external debt stocks ratio increased. This might be a result of overall good export performance in this region. As a result, the rising trend in debt accumulation was reversed for a year. However, this looks like an aberration in this decade. After 2015, rising debt accumulation continued, and foreign exchange reserves – as a ratio to rising external debt stocks – kept on falling again.

Apart from the multilateral financial institutions (like IMF, World Bank, ADB), the advanced economies and a few emerging economies have been the lender or provider of loans and financial aids in the international arena.

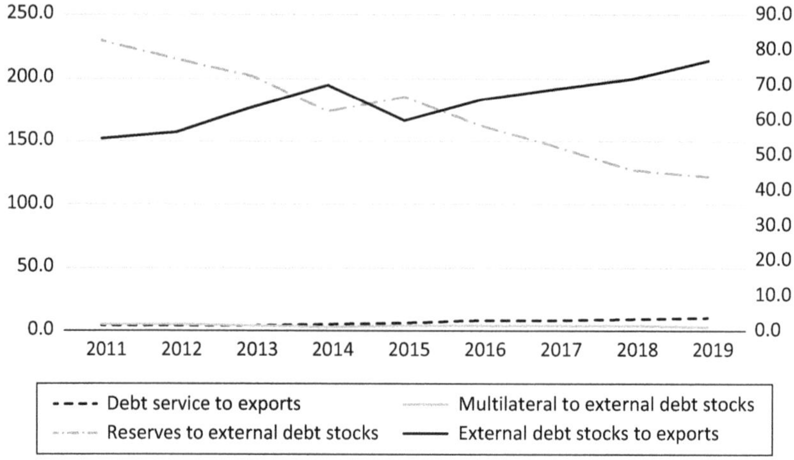

Figure 2.5 Trends in debt ratios of East Asia and Pacific, excluding high-income countries (in per cent). External debt stocks to exports ratio is measured on the secondary axis. *Data source:* International Debt Statistics, 2021, World Bank.

China was also a part of these lenders for quite some time. However, the country changed its role radically as an international lender when in 2013 it proposed the BRI to "improve connectivity and cooperation on a transnational scale" (World Bank, 2018).

This initiative, since then, has drastically changed China's role as an international provider of finance, particularly in infrastructure projects. Western critics have defined the initiative as a part of China's ambition to elevate itself as "the new global power" by using it to create "debt and market traps to reshape international relations in its favour" (Mobley, 2019).

Without going into that broader political debate, it can be safely postulated that China is one of the crucial factors in any international debt relief endeavour in the current juncture, particularly in South-East and South Asia and Africa. Any future outcome will be dependent on the actions taken by the Chinese government about their BRI loan repayment.

Initial focus areas of the BRI have been South-East Asia and South Asia.[4] Later, the initiative has been spread to other regions. There are different estimates of Chinese investment in BRI, varying from USD 1 trillion to USD 8 trillion. These loans primarily are of two forms: concessional loans and preferential buyer's credit. The loans are reportedly provided at higher interest rates than those provided by most multilateral agencies. However, the recipient countries often found the BRI loan norms more flexible than those of other multilateral agencies like IMF and the World Bank. The IMF and World Bank loans invariably come with stricter norms due to conditional imposition of structural reforms (Mobley, 2019).

Early BRI projects were dominantly funded by banks and funds under direct Chinese government control. South-East Asia is a substantial part of East Asia and the Pacific. In this region, Cambodia and Myanmar are good examples of the Chinese BRI approach. Both countries have been recipients of BRI loans for port and road projects for their strategic importance to the region and the ASEAN.[5]

South Asia, as a region, shows some different trends in two of the ratios.[6] Multilateral debt as a percentage to total external debt stocks decreased from 22.7 per cent in 2011 to 16.4 per cent in 2019. External debt stocks to exports have also been increasing. These are similar to broad trends in low- and middle-income countries, but trends in debt service to exports and reserves to external debt stocks ratios are different. Debt service to exports went down to 11.2 per cent in 2019 from a high of 18.1 per cent in 2014. More importantly, reserves to external debt stocks generally had been on the rise since 2013, and it was 63.7 per cent in 2019 (Figure 2.6).

So, the overall figures suggest that the countries in this region experienced a rise in foreign exchange inflow, which may have helped in reducing the relative burden of debt servicing. However, each individual country may have deviations from this overall trend. For example, these debt ratios in India would be different from the debt ratios in Myanmar or Sri Lanka.

In this region, Pakistan and Sri Lanka received a substantial amount of BRI loan on account of different projects. The China–Pakistan Economic Corridor (CPEC) is one of the flagship projects of BRI in South Asia. Initial estimates put the cost of the project at a staggering USD 62 billion. CPEC

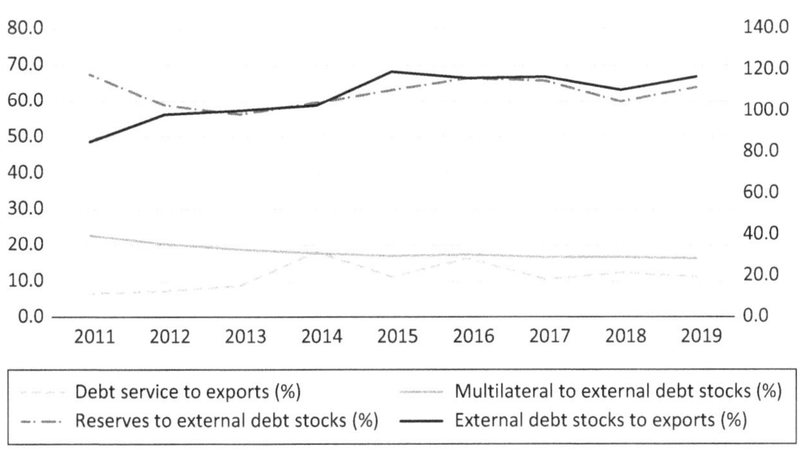

Figure 2.6 Trends in debt ratios of South Asia, excluding high-income countries (in per cent). External debt stocks to exports ratio is measured on the secondary axis. *Data source:* International Debt Statistics, 2021, World Bank.

also involves "expanding Gwadar port, and constructing energy pipelines, power plants, long highways and high-speed railways, fibre-optic cables and special economic zones" (Mobley, 2019).

In 2008, China provided a loan to Sri Lanka to build the Hambantota port in the southern part of the country. By 2016, Sri Lanka's debt to GDP ratio reached 79 per cent, and as a result the country was unable to repay the debt. A debt–equity swap was arranged, with China Merchants Port holding a 99-year lease of the port, 80 per cent stake in the project, and 15,000 acres of adjacent land to be developed as industrial zone for Chinese investors (Mobley, 2019).

This has been cited by the critics of China as an example of creating "debt and market traps to reshape international relations in its favour" (Chellaney, 2017).

The second view on Chinese lending brushes aside this "Debt Trap Diplomacy" thesis. Rather than Chinese finance, according to this view, local government mismanagement and existing macroeconomic imbalances are to be principally blamed in most of the cases (Brautigam & Rithmire 2021).

Reality lies somewhere between these two extreme positions. Government and private lenders of China made mistakes, for example, in Africa, some with catastrophic consequences. But the assertion that those were deliberate game plan has limited evidence, till now. However, being a relatively new international player in infrastructure lending, the Chinese government and private firms have to learn more, particularly about the political risks and the moment to pull out.

Europe and Central Asia is the region marked by one exceptional trend in external debt stocks to exports ratio since 2016. For consecutively two years after that, the ratio kept falling down before slightly increasing at 125.7 per cent in 2019. Debt service to exports neared 30 per cent mark in 2015, but subsequently it has been brought down to 22.4 per cent in 2019. Multilateral debt as a percentage to external debt stocks remained stable at around 5 per cent throughout the decade. But the real difference of this region from other debt-distressed regions lies in the fact that foreign exchange reserves kept on increasing since 2016 and stood at 44.5 per cent in 2019 (Figure 2.7).

Though overall external debt in this region is comparable with some other distressed regions, increasing foreign exchange reserve, decreasing external debt stocks, and debt service requirement indicate the relative comfort this region exercises in debt servicing. Whether high-income countries in this region will bail out distressed countries or not if there is a global sovereign debt crisis remains an open-ended conjectural question at the moment. However, some middle-income countries in this region may find it difficult to cope with such an eventuality.

Chinese footprint is also very much there in Europe, particularly in Western Balkans (including Croatia). The highest sovereign debt borrower

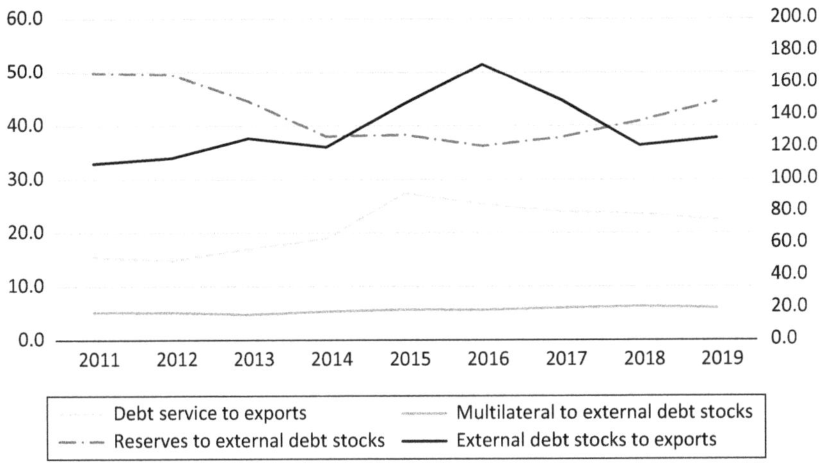

Figure 2.7 Trends in debt ratios of Europe and Central Asia, excluding high-income countries (in per cent). External debt stocks to exports ratio is measured on the secondary axis. *Data source:* International Debt Statistics, 2021, World Bank.

from China in this region is Montenegro. The country owes EUR 671 million to China till 2019, which is 22 per cent of its total external debt at EUR 3.1 billion. China is the second biggest lender and the single biggest bilateral lender to Montenegro. North Macedonia's Chinese debt amounts to EUR 714 million, which is around 14 per cent of total government debt in 2020 (Zweers et al., 2020).

Chinese debt constitutes around 13 per cent of Bosnia and Herzegovina's external sovereign debt. Additionally, Chinese non-government loans are also substantial in this country. Chinese share in Serbia's government debt is around 7.91 per cent. Albania is the only country in Western Balkans that reduced its indebtedness to China in the period between 2010 and 2019. Kosovo presumably has no Chinese debt as the country does not have an official relation with China (Zweers et al, 2020).

This is interesting because none of these countries in Western Balkans is eligible for the DSSI. All countries belong to the upper middle-income classification (by the World Bank). If a debt crisis emerges, these countries will expect relatively better access to international finance than some of their Asian or African counterparts. But that expectation may not tally with reality in future.

Low- and middle-income countries in the Middle East and North Africa are in the probable risk zone as far as debt accumulation is concerned. Reserves to external debt stocks dwindled to 83.5 per cent in 2016. The external debt stocks to exports ratio increased from 48.5 per cent in 2011 to 116 per cent in 2019. Though multilateral loans to external debt stocks remained steady at around 20 per cent, debt service requirements gradually inched upwards (Figure 2.8).

These are clear indications in the trends of debt ratios that the accumulation of debt in this region has reached the risky level. The pandemic will make these economies more vulnerable.

Like other regions, many countries in the Middle East and North Africa have been recipients of BRI loans. After the pandemic hit, countries like Iran, Egypt, and UAE requested debt waivers from China. China is apparently considering many such requests, but the Chinese government ruled out any possibility of total write-off (Chaziza, 2020).

Governments' gross debt to GDP ratios in most of the countries in this region increased in the last decade. Highly indebted countries include Sudan (over 200 per cent of GDP in 2019), Lebanon (over 170 per cent of GDP), Bahrain (over 100 per cent of GDP), Jordan, Egypt, Mauritania, and Tunisia (range between 70 per cent and 100 per cent of GDP). According to World Bank estimates, 11 countries in this region had been in unsustainable fiscal state in 2019, as their primary fiscal balances were unable to stabilise their debt to GDP ratios (Dabrowski & Bruegel, 2021).

Countries of Sub-Saharan Africa are at higher risk of defaults in the near future. Their external debt stocks to exports stood at 152.3 per cent in 2019. Reserves to external debt stocks plummeted to 27.8 per cent in 2019. Multilateral loans to exports hovered around 20 per cent, but debt service to exports went up to 14.3 per cent in 2019 from 3.8 per cent in 2011. This is one of the regions which needs substantial long-term debt support. In the

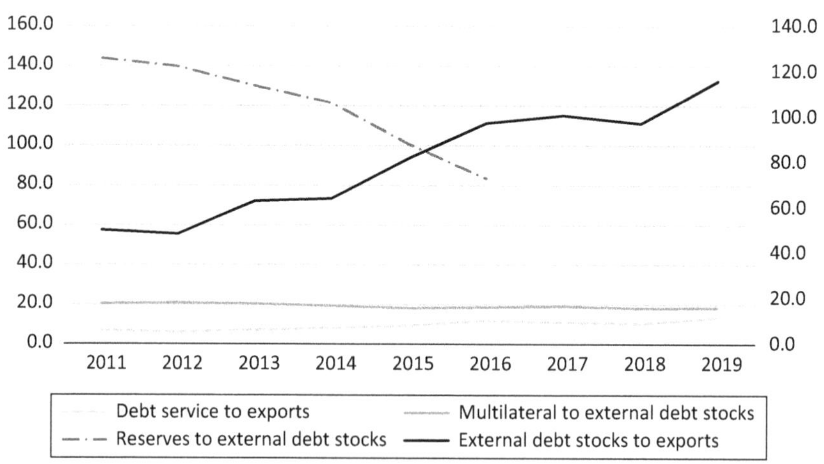

Figure 2.8 Trends in debt ratios of Middle East and North Africa, excluding high-income countries (in per cent). Based on available data. External debt stocks to exports ratio is measured on the secondary axis. *Data source:* International Debt Statistics, 2021, World Bank.

absence of any intervention, countries in this region are very likely to see quite a few defaults in the near future (Figure 2.9).

In the 1990s, the Western countries' investment and aid to Africa slowed down. This was after the Asian financial crisis in 1997 that gripped large parts of East Asia and South-East Asia. Western developed economies slowed down and probably started a rethinking on investments in developing and least developed regions. Amidst these, China emerged as the new financier, promising to offer rapid, flexible, and large "no strings attached" loans.[7] The BRI, initiated in 2013, further enhanced Chinese investments across the African continent. This time the focus has been on building infrastructures like roads, ports, bridges, and airports (Dynamic, 2021).

In 2018 China–Africa Cooperation Forum, China announced an additional USD 60 billion to be disbursed over three years as concessional loans, grants, and trade and development finance to Africa. By May 2020, the country has disbursed around USD 38.7 billion in Africa.[8] Even before the pandemic, the debt provided by China in the continent reached unsustainable level. Around 19 per cent of external debt repayment by different African governments went to China in 2018. Chinese loans accounted for more than one-fourth of total external loans in African countries with high debt distress. These countries included Kenya (27 per cent), Zimbabwe (25 per cent), Zambia (26 per cent), Cameroon (32 per cent), the Republic of Congo (45 per cent), and Djibouti (57 per cent) (Dynamic, 2021). As mentioned earlier, Zambia has already defaulted in 2020.

There have been calls by the multilateral financial organisations and some of the African states requesting China to consider waiver of some of

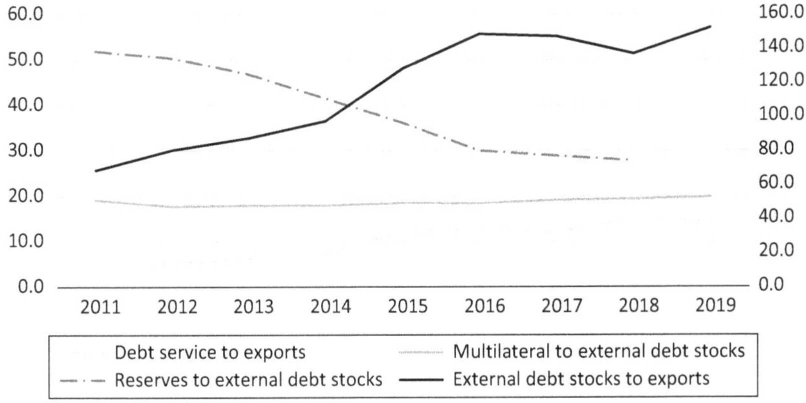

Figure 2.9 Trends in debt ratios of Sub-Saharan Africa, excluding high-income countries (in per cent). Based on available data, some data points are not available. External debt stocks to exports ratio is measured on the secondary axis. *Data source:* International Debt Statistics, 2021, World Bank.

these African debts. But in 2020, though China selectively cancelled some of the African debts and postponed a few others, the country has so far resisted the idea of blanket debt forgiveness in the continent. China is part of the G20 DSSI programme (Dynamic, 2021).

However, China has branded the call by the Western countries (particularly the United States) to boost the Chinese role in debt relief "politically driven", and has asserted that the country is fulfilling its role in the DSSI (Youming, 2021).

The next risky zone that may see more defaults in future is Latin America and the Caribbean region. Low- and middle-income countries here show an overall external debt stock to exports ratio at a whopping 164.2 per cent in 2019. This is the highest among all demographic regions. Debt service to exports went up to 26.9 per cent in 2019 from 15 per cent in 2011. Multilateral loan to external debt stocks remains below 10 per cent. Another alarming trend is in reserves to external debt stocks ratio, which fell down from 53.3 per cent in 2011 to 39.2 per cent in 2019 (Figure 2.10).

Except for three Caribbean and one Central American countries,[9] none in this region is considered to be eligible for the DSSI. That is the real predicament in this region.

Peru, Argentina and Mexico are the countries estimated to be the most severely hit in this region economically. Brazil, Chile and Colombia are also expected to go through a slow recovery process. Brazil and Colombia may have to start discontinuing their respective fiscal expansion programmes, if compliance with fiscal responsibility rules is maintained. Argentina is the country in serious trouble in this region. In 2019, GDP of Argentina fell

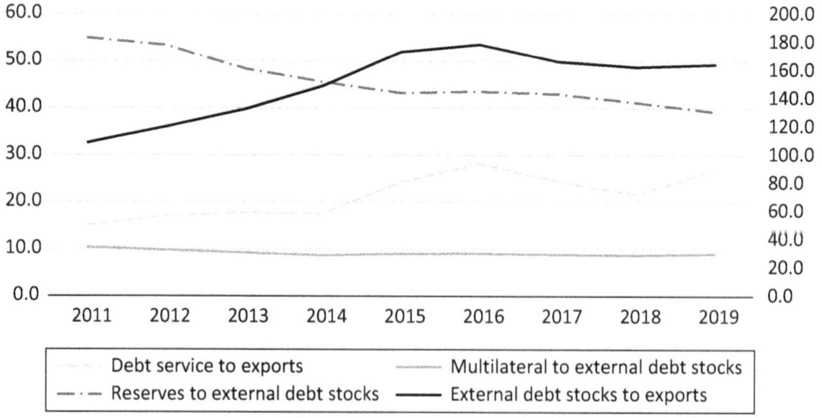

Figure 2.10 Trends in debt ratios of Latin America and Caribbean, excluding high-income countries (in per cent). External debt stocks to exports ratio is measured on the secondary axis. *Data source:* International Debt Statistics, 2021, World Bank.

by 2.1 per cent and inflation reached 54 per cent level. After the pandemic hit, Argentina completed its ninth sovereign debt restructuring with private creditors. The government of Argentina is in negotiations with the IMF for a new IMF-supported programme. Here it is also relevant to note that Brazil and Mexico are two countries in this region with access to a dollar swap line with the US Federal Reserve (Cottani, 2020).

So, overall this region is vulnerable. As mentioned earlier, Argentina, Ecuador, Belize, and Suriname (twice) from this region have already defaulted on sovereign debt in 2020. But unfortunately, none of these countries is eligible to participate in the DSSI. That aptly summarises the futility of international debt suspension efforts. IMF is very much present here, but given its history of imposing strict preconditions for any kind of financial help, the immediate future of Latin America and Caribbean countries looks quite bleak at the moment.

Conclusion

Across the world, there had been a rise in the accumulation of debt among low-income countries in the last decade. This accumulation had grown consistently. Some middle-income countries also accumulated debt in this period. For both these categories, there had been simultaneous drops in export performance and foreign exchange reserves. Aided by a general global slowdown, these economies have been in debt trouble for quite some time. Debt accumulation steadily increased even for high-income economies. The availability of fund with relatively lower interest rates in the post-2008 financial crisis world is one dominant reason behind this general trend.

Global growth did not pick up pace, as was expected, after the 2008 crisis. Slow growth induced deceleration in exports that resulted in downward pressure on foreign exchange reserves for many countries with unsustainable debt burden. If foreign exchange reserves go down, then debt servicing becomes difficult. In this situation, if external debt continues to rise unabated, it creates distress and subsequent defaults.

Now, if sovereign defaults happen in a handful of countries, then they can still be managed. However, if many countries across different regions of the world start defaulting, then the global economy will experience a squeeze in the availability of finance and that can lead to an acute sovereign debt crisis. Statistical data on debt accumulation across all regions point towards that possibility.

G20 countries, along with multilateral organisations, initiated a temporary debt support system last year. But the DSSI programme relies mainly on a temporary debt moratorium, which was later extended till the year-end of 2021. This moratorium, without any real effort to restructure existing debts, seems inadequate to address the current rising trend of debt accumulation.

Will current debt relief measures (both the DSSI and the CF) be adequate to deal with the problem? Very unlikely. The temporary nature of the DSSI has been the first hindrance towards any permanent resolution. Low-income economies will need more time to deal with debt accumulation, to begin with. A much lower average term to maturity of debt pushes these economies to a corner and renders them helpless in the short run.

Next is the issue of coverage and participation. The number of distressed economies due to unsustainable debt accumulation is clearly higher than the number of DSSI-eligible countries. Many of these distressed countries are reluctant to avail any debt relief measure like the DSSI. The principal reason is a fear of international credit rating downgrade. The longer these countries refuse to participate in any debt relief, the sharper will be the global debt distress in coming days. It has become a proverbial knife-edge problem for these economies. And this may prove to be counterproductive for the health of the global economy and the international financial system, if a global debt crisis emerges out of this.

Then comes the question of restructuring. A moratorium of few months or even a few years is not going to solve risky external debt accumulation all over the world. It has to be strongly supported by debt restructuring and selective waiver. Otherwise, it will be a mere postponement of the disaster.

To avert the possibility of a global sovereign debt crisis, therefore, a bigger relief programme is needed where debt restructuring and selective waiver will play an important role. Coverage of such a programme also has to be much wider and has to include all middle-income countries which are in distress.

Private creditors have to be brought into any such debt relief programme. Without bringing private creditors in the overall scheme of debt restructuring, any effort to resolve the impending debt crisis is likely to be futile.

Inherent contradiction within the big lender countries and institutions is a big hindrance in international debt resolution. Apart from the international multilateral financial institutions, the United States and the major economies in Europe (particularly Germany) and China are the current major suppliers of international credit. Ideally, all of them and the private creditors should have come under a common umbrella to deal with this global problem of unsustainable debt accumulation.

However, since 2018, both China and the United States are engaged in bitter trade war. This tussle over international trade is a manifestation of these countries' individual ambition of global supremacy. As a result, the ideal financial coalition to tackle global debt accumulation is unlikely to take any shape in reality. Open public bickerings against each other in recent times bear testimony to that.

In this situation, Bretton Woods institutions could have played a larger role in unifying the creditors under a common framework. But the IMF's intervention in some of the distressed regions, particularly in Latin

America, points towards a contrary situation. These institutions are still carrying their preconditional structural readjustment and reform-oriented baggage of the past. So, one unified platform of international creditors remains a utopia.

Debt relief also works the best when it is a supplementary measure to overall fiscal support. The countries that have undertaken direct fiscal intervention to deal with pandemic disruptions and resultant lockdowns and restrictions in the economy are going to benefit the most out of any debt relief measures. International cooperation in that area has become the need of the hour. However, given the inherent contradictions described before, there is little or no hope in that front as well.

The way things stand now, a coordinated framework of fiscal support with strong international debt relief measures remains absent in most of these debt-ridden countries. Defaults happened in 2020, and if no proactive international measure is taken to address this debt accumulation, the world economy may be heading towards a sovereign debt crisis. No half-measure like the DSSI is going to avert or mitigate that crisis.

Notes

1 Paris Club is an informal group of official creditors (https://clubdeparis.org/).
2 MEF, Italian Government. The Common Framework for debt treatment beyond the DSSI. Retrieved from https://www.mef.gov.it/en/G20-Italy/common-framework.html
3 For current fiscal year 2022, income classifications of the countries are done by the World Bank using the "World Bank Atlas method". Low-income economies are those with a GNI per capita of $1,045 or less in 2020, lower middle-income economies are with a GNI per capita between $1,046 and $4,095, upper middle-income economies are with a GNI per capita between $4,096 and $12,695, and high-income economies are those with a GNI per capita of $12,696 or more. (https://datahelpdesk.worldbank.org/knowledgebase/articles/906519-world-bank-country-and-lending-groups)
4 China finances BRI projects through key financial institutions, including China Development Bank, the Export–Import (Exim) Bank of China, four leading Chinese commercial banks, Asian Infrastructure Investment Bank (AIIB) that has its headquarter in Beijing, and the Silk Road Fund (Mobley, 2019).
5 Association of South-East Asian Nations (ASEAN).
6 South Asia category comprises Afghanistan, Bangladesh, Bhutan, India, Maldives, Nepal, Pakistan, and Sri Lanka (https://datahelpdesk.worldbank.org/knowledgebase/articles/906519-world-bank-country-and-lending-groups).
7 Loans from developed economies, more than often, came with preconditions of structural adjustment and allied reforms in the debtor economies. The loans and/or aids mostly used to be channelised through Bretton Woods institutions (World Bank and IMF).
8 Disbursal estimates are reported by China Africa Research Initiative (CARI) at Johns Hopkins University School of Advanced International Studies (SAIS).
9 Haiti, Honduras, St. Lucia, and St. Vincent and the Grenadines are the countries eligible for the DSSI from this region.

References

Brautigam, D., & Rithmire, M. (2021, February 6). The Chinese 'Debt Trap' is a Myth. *The Atlantic*. Retrieved from https://www.theatlantic.com/international/archive/2021/02/china-debt-trap-diplomacy/617953/.

Chaziza, Mordechai (2020). Coronavirus, China, and the Middle East. In Efraim Karsh (Ed.), *The COVID-19 Crisis: Impact and implications*. Begin-Sadat Center for Strategic Studies.

Chellaney, B. (2017, January 23). China's Debt-Trap Diplomacy. *Project Syndicate*. Retrieved from https://www.project-syndicate.org/commentary/china-one-belt-one-road-loans-debt-by-brahma-chellaney-2017-01.

Cottani, J. (2020). The Effects of Covid-19 on Latin America's Economy. Center for Strategic and International Studies (CSIS). Retrieved from https://www.csis.org/analysis/effects-covid-19-latin-americas-economy.

Dabrowski, M., & Dominguez-Jimenez, M. (2021, February). Economic Crisis in the Middle East and North Africa. *Policy Contribution*. Bruegel. Retrieved from https://www.bruegel.org/wp-content/uploads/2021/01/PC-02-2021-220121.pdf.

Dynamic, B. M. (2021, April). Chinese Loans to Africa: Trap or Treasure? In Jane Golley, Linda Jaivin, & Sharon Strange (Ed.), *The China Story Yearbook 2020: Crisis, April 2021*. ANU Press. Retrieved from http://press-files.anu.edu.au/downloads/press/n8254/pdf/08A_forum.pdf.

International Monetary Fund (IMF) (2021). Fiscal Monitor, April Issue. Retrieved from https://www.imf.org/en/Publications/FM/Issues/2021/03/29/fiscal-monitor-april-2021.

Jensen, L. (2021, March). Sovereign Debt Vulnerabilities in Developing Economies. Development Futures Series Working Papers. United Nations Development Programme (UNDP). Retrieved from https://www.undp.org/publications/sovereign-debt-vulnerabilities-developing-economies.

Mobley, T. (2019). The Belt and Road Initiative. *Strategic Studies Quarterly*, Vol. 13, No. 3. Retrieved from https://www.airuniversity.af.edu/Portals/10/SSQ/documents/Volume-13_Issue-3/Mobley.pdf.

Panigrahi, S. (2021). 6 Countries that Could Not Pay Their Sovereign Debt in 2020. Retrieved from https://medium.com/indextrader/5-countries-that-did-not-pay-their-sovereign-debt-in-2020-45146faa5cff.

Reuter (2021, January 28). Chad becomes First Country to Ask for Debt Overhaul under G20 Common Framework. Retrieved from https://www.reuters.com/article/us-chad-debt-idUSKBN29X0Q5.

Stiglitz, J., & Rashid, H. (2020). Averting Catastrophic Debt Crises in Developing Countries: Extraordinary Challenges Call for Extraordinary Measures. *Policy Insight No. 104*. Centre for Economic Policy Research (CEPR). Retrieved from https://cepr.org/sites/default/files/policy_insights/PolicyInsight104.pdf.

World Bank (2018, March 29). Belt and Road Initiative. Retrieved from https://www.worldbank.org/en/topic/regional-integration/brief/belt-and-road-initiative.

World Bank (2021, July 28). COVID 19: Debt Service Suspension Initiative. Retrieved from https://www.worldbank.org/en/topic/debt/brief/covid-19-debt-service-suspension-initiative.

World Bank (2021). International Debt Statistics. Retrieved on July 13 from https://datatopics.worldbank.org/debt/ids/.

Youming, W. (2021, July 7). Call for China to Boost Role in G20 Debt Relief Politically Driven. *Global Times*. Retrieved from https://www.globaltimes.cn/page/202107/1228097.shtml.

Zweers, W., Shopov, V., Van Der Putten, F. P., Petkova, M., & Lemstra, M. (2020). China's Approach to the Western Balkans. Clingendael Institute. Retrieved from https://www.clingendael.org/pub/2020/china-and-the-eu-in-the-western-balkans/1-chinas-approach-to-the-western-balkans/.

3 Global Liquidity and Emerging Market Economies

S. Krishnakumar

Introduction

The unprecedented coordination which occurred among countries and central banks across the world during the global financial crisis also set in motion the importance of policies towards regulation of cross-border capital flows in international policy circles. There has been no dearth of arguments, particularly from the post-Keynesian economists, about the importance of the same for long (Eatwell & Taylor, 2002). The IMF which had been in the forefront making a case for capital account convertibility also started critically viewing this issue of finance in the global economy in the aftermath of the crisis which has put the financial systems of a number of advanced economies also at risk (Arcand, Berkes and Panizza, 2012).

In this context, there was the report on global liquidity brought out by the Bank for International Settlements, clearly highlighting the various aspects of global liquidity and the vulnerabilities associated with the same (BIS, 2011). Popularly known as the Landau Report (after its main author), this Report brings out the *differentia specifica* of private liquidity from official liquidity. Amidst its many suggestions are the necessity of regulation of the financial system as an *ex ante* measure, policy intervention towards the prevention of the rise in excessive liquidity through a regulatory framework with macroprudential measures and focus on provision of central bank liquidity as *ex post* measure. But the Report itself expresses doubt about the purpose which foreign exchange reserves of individual countries would serve towards ensuring financial stability, given the negative externalities associated with the running down of the forex reserves. In fact, this period since the global financial crisis ratifies the concerns of the Report with many of the emerging market economies with large foreign exchange reserves being witness to their currencies going for a steep depreciation since 2010. While the prescriptions of the Report were widely welcomed in the context of the pressing need of regulation, it stopped short of making any argument with respect to controls on capital like the post-Keynesians have been arguing for long, nor did it make a strong case for the necessity of a proper reform of international monetary system through the expansion of

DOI: 10.4324/9781003343998-3

Special Drawing Rights (SDRs). And most importantly, it did not foresee the possibility of the other financial institutions like the institutional funds, pension and insurance funds and sovereign wealth funds emerging as major purveyors of global liquidity which could substantially influence asset prices and hence put financial stability to risk.

A cursory overview of the developments in the global economy would be in order here. It would be rather stating the obvious that the world of finance overshadows the real sector in the contemporary global economy. It is reflected in the large increase in the external assets and liabilities of countries over a period of time. Though there was short-term disruption of the two-way gross capital flows in the global economy during the global financial crisis, the external assets in the global economy has increased from $108.17 trillion (179% of world GDP) in 2008 to $170.04 trillion (203% of the world GDP) in 2019. But during the same phase, the total export of goods in the global economy has increased marginally from $16.22 trillion, i.e., 16% of the world GDP in 1995 to $18.75 trillion, i.e., 22.4% of the GDP in 2019.[1] While the share of the advanced economies in exports declined in the first two decades of the current century, that of the emerging and developing economies has increased from 21.8% to 31.7%. The lion's share of this increase is on account of the growing share of China and some of the East Asian economies. It is pertinent to note here that in the period since the global financial crisis, there has been a large increase in the share of external debt liabilities in the balance sheets of the developing economies. While the annual world GDP is $83.84 trillion and the annual value for exports in 2019 is at $18.75 trillion, the 2019 Ninth Triennial Survey on Foreign Exchange of the Bank for International Settlements reveals that the daily average turnover in the foreign exchange was at $6.6 trillion. This has witnessed a steep increase from its 2001 figures of $1.1 trillion (BIS, 2019). Even compared to the figures of the previous triennial of 2016, when it was $3.3 trillion, it has literally doubled, despite the sober performance of the real economy.

Global Liquidity: Official and Private

Before we proceed, it is essential to note the difference between private liquidity and official liquidity. The BIS Report brings out the differences between the same (BIS, 2011).The Report defines liquidity as the ease with which assets could be converted into liquid form. Due to the quick and sudden shifts which expose economies to "sudden stops", global liquidity continues to be a paradox of sorts (Chandrasekhar and Ghosh, 2008).

It is important here to bring out the difference between official liquidity and private liquidity. Official liquidity is the funding that is unconditionally available to settle claims through monetary authorities. Foreign exchange reserves at the central bank's discretion, the swap line arrangements with other central banks and the SDRs from the part of the IMF are all part of official liquidity. Still, the enjoyment of this liquidity is subjected to different conditions, and its access varies across countries. The unprecedented rise of the *ad hoc* central bank swap lines between friendly countries is a tactical shift detracting us from the more significant issue relating to the provision of international liquidity through the increase in the issuance of SDRs. Needless to say, the resources at the command of the IMF have barely increased, given the significant increase in external liabilities in the last three decades.[2]

In a world characterised by large-scale expansion of gross assets and liabilities of countries, cross-border liquidity is created by both private intermediaries and central banks. The fragility brought about by the creation of private liquidity can be contained by the *ex ante* steps in the regulatory field and *ex post* by the provision of liquidity by the central bankers, which serve as the lender of last resort. With low interest rates in all major central banks globally, the risk appetite plays an essential role in determining the amplitude and direction of the flow of private liquidity. Global private liquidity is created by the operations of banks, investment funds and other financial institutions. The extent of liquidity created would depend on the willingness of the counterparties to take on risks and extend credit. Sudden shifts in risk aversion, liquidity preference and private institutions' deleveraging play an essential role in determining the direction. And this is where the concepts devised by Keynes in his General Theory prove to be handy in making sense of the world of global liquidity.

The Global Financial Crisis and Unconventional Monetary Policies

Over the years, the global banking system has been witness to a shift from the "originate to hold" model to an "originate to distribute" model.[3] A good portion of the assets of the banking system have been financed on the basis of its wholesale (non-core) liabilities, rather than on the basis of the traditional retail deposits, exposing it to large risks. This also explains why there has been demand for regulation to assure that the banks maintain a particular optimal level of net stable funding ratio (NSFR).[4] The leverage ratios of the banks in the run-up to the global financial crisis were far too high and were not considered to be risky by the banks which were riding the high tide of the property bubble in the United States. Banks and financial institutions outside the United States could also partake in this boom through the purchase of the asset-backed securities (ABSs) and mortgage-backed securities (MBSs), the price of which collapsed in the course of the subprime crisis, forcing a number of European banks to sell off their assets. They were forced to do so because they could not renew and roll over their borrowings in the US wholesale dollar market. In fact, despite Europe having a reasonable current account in the run-up to the crisis, it was dragged into the crisis due to the maturity mismatch of the two-way capital flows on the financial account. The European banks could not renew their short-term dollar liabilities in the wholesale funding US money markets.

In the period after the crisis, not only were the European banks forced to deleverage, but also their role of intermediating dollar credit to different economies was now under shadow. The cross-border claims of reporting banks to BIS which increased from \$10.55 trillion (31.1% of the WGDP) in 2000 to \$32.91 trillion (56.5% of world GDP) in 2007 was thereafter witness to stagnation. It is pertinent to note that in terms of the share of the world GDP, the cross-border claims have not reclaimed their 2007 levels even in 2021 (Figure 3.1).

Given that the number of banks which report to the BIS has changed over time, this does not fully capture the phenomenon. The cross-border claim of banks located in the United Kingdom increased from \$2.04 to \$7.15 trillion between 2000Q1 and 2008Q1; it is at \$5.46 trillion even in 2021Q1. Though the cross-border claim of banks located in the United States has increased from \$877 billion in 2000Q1 to \$3.41 trillion in 2008Q1 and then gone for a decline, as of 2021, it has reached back to its 2008 levels. In fact, many of the European banks had gone through a process of deleveraging, and this phenomenon had played a pivotal role in increasing the intermediary international banking role played by many of the banks based in East Asia. In fact, there has been a distinct increase in the number of banks from Asia categorised as GSIBs.[5]

With the world engulfed in an unprecedented liquidity crisis in 2007–08, the major central banks of the world were forced to resort to large-scale purchase of assets. The reduction in short-term interest rates (like federal

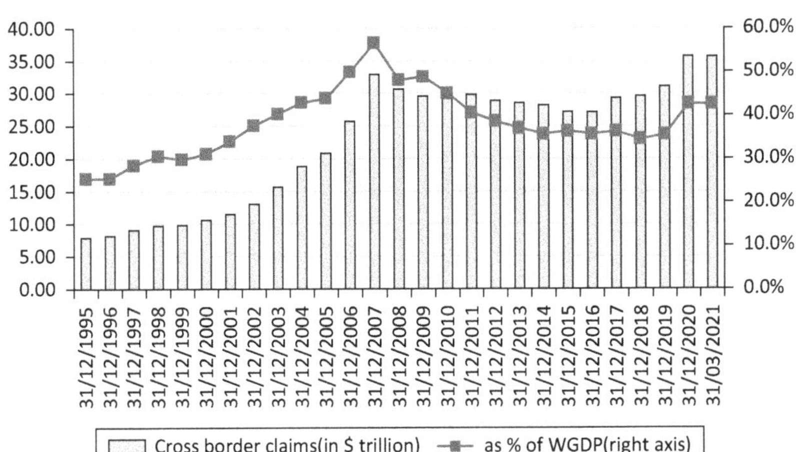

Figure 3.1 Cross-border claims of banks (\$ trillion). *Source:* BIS Locational Banking Statistics and WEO Database, Author's calculations.

funds rates) was found to be insufficient to facilitate recovery, and it had already reached near-zero levels, the central banks were forced to give forward guidance with respect to short-term interest rates. The purchase of assets by the central banks has resulted in the expansion of the balance sheets of all the major central banks. In the context of the COVID-19 crisis, there was yet another round of purchases done by the central banks pushing the world economy to lower rates of interest towards ensuring provision of liquidity. Recent data from the United States reveal that the assets of the Federal Reserve are at $8 trillion (i.e., almost 40% of the US GDP).[6] The central bank assets of the Bank of Japan have crossed 100% of the GDP of Japan. In fact, given the unprecedented situation during the global financial crisis, the central banks had resorted to large-scale purchases of private labelled assets too. The truth is that given the severity of the liquidity crunch during 2007 and the extraordinary circumstances arising from the epidemic, the central banks have been trying to play the role of market makers.

Dollar Credit Outside the United States to Non-financial Corporations

Large-scale asset purchases and low interest rates in the global economy have resulted in large capital flows to several emerging economies in *search for yield*. Given that low interest rates were something specific to Japan in the 1990s, this was largely referred to as "yen carry trade", i.e., borrowing in yen at low interest rates and investing in other currencies at higher rates. Given the low interest rates in the global economy in the current decade, it has become possible to borrow in any of the currencies of the advanced world (low interest rates) and invest in the rest of the world. This search of yield has resulted in a significant increase in global liquidity. Though the reduction in interest rates in the United States has been made to increase credit offtake within the United States, this has resulted in a faster pace of growth of dollar credit to non-financial corporations outside the United States. There has been a steep increase in this regard from $6.11 trillion, i.e., 42% of US GDP, in 2009 to $12.73 trillion, i.e., 61% of US GDP, in 2020 (Figure 3.2). This borrowing done by the non-financial corporations outside the United States in dollars through bank loans or bonds is considered an important indicator of global liquidity. Towards delivering credit to the non-financial corporations, the banks and other financial institutions outside the United States have to rely on short-term interbank or currency swap markets. And, therefore, too, any changes in monetary policy directives from Fed Reserve through its impact on the change in cost of dollar credit would push the global financial system to huge risks. This growing dollar credit outside United States had necessitated central bank cooperation with respect to the provision of dollar liquidity to meet the exigencies.

With the dollar crisis in March 2020, wherein the developing economies faced with the dearth of liquidity were forced to sell of Treasury securities,

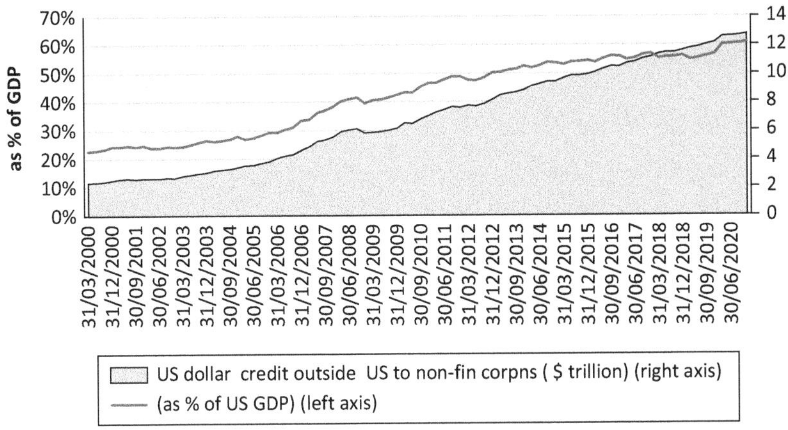

Figure 3.2 US dollar credit to non-financial sector outside the United States ($ trillion). *Source:* BIS Global Liquidity Indicators and WEO Database. Author's calculations.

and this was running against the usual practice of search for safe haven by economies during times of crisis, and thus posing a challenge to the dollar, the window of accessing dollar liquidity through borrowing against the Treasury holdings has been initiated from the part of the Federal Reserve to meet the rising demand for dollar liquidity.[7] It is only logical that in a world where there has been preponderance of dollar liabilities, such a line of liquidity would be required.

Global Liquidity and Rising Vulnerabilities of Emerging Market Economies

It is pertinent to note that the rising share of this dollar credit outside the United States is taken by the non-financial corporations based in emerging market economies. The dollar credit mobilised by the non-financial corporations based in EMDEs has witnessed a steep increase from $1.6 trillion in 2008 to $4 trillion in 2020 (Figure 3.3). This is almost one-third of the total dollar credit outside the United States. Many non-financial corporations based in EMDEs have been able to mobilise dollar credit at lower interest rates in international financial markets, thus sidestepping the high interest rates of their domestic banking systems. Given the stagnation in the real sector as well as declining investment ratios, the only factor driving this mobilisation of resources by the firms in these EMDEs has been the pure gains on the "carry trade" front (Bruno & Shin, 2017).

Borrowing in foreign currencies and investing in domestic assets also exposes the firms to risks associated with exchange rate appreciation of the

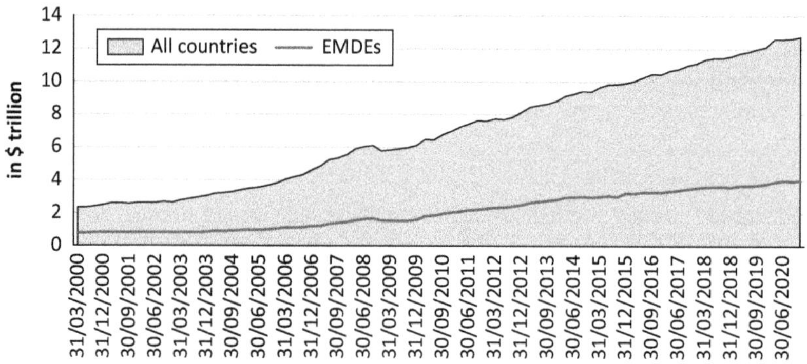

Figure 3.3 US dollar credit to non-financial corporations outside the United States ($ trillion). *Source:* BIS Global Liquidity Indicators. Accessed as on 27/7/2021.

dollar. To begin with, some of the firms invest in the non-tradable sector. They do not generate any export earnings based on which they service their debt. Given the risks of depreciation of the EME currencies, unless hedged, the foreign currency debt of corporates could cause financial stability risks (Chang & Velasco, 1999; Bruno & Shin, 2017). In the context of the taper-tantrum of 2013, when the Fed Reserve had suggested that it would go for a reduction in bond purchases into the medium term as growth picks up momentum, there was the quick trigger of capital outflows from the developing countries. The consequent depreciation of the currencies had resulted in serious balance sheet problems for the non-financial corporations in the developing world. The low rates of growth of many of the emerging economies have to be seen in the context of deleveraging necessitated by this event.

Drawing attention towards the increasing external exposure of non-financial corporations in emerging market economies like India, Turkey and Latin America, certain reports have drawn attention to its implications on their balance sheets in the eventuality of tightening monetary policies in advanced countries (CIEPR, 2015). The exogenous event of Swiss franc appreciation in 2015 had had a significantly deleterious effect on the balance sheets of the households of Baltics and Eastern Europe. A sizeable share of the loans of the banking system in these economies, not just to the non-financial corporations, but also to the households was denominated in foreign currencies (euros and Swiss francs) bearing lower interest rates. With the Swiss franc appreciation of 2015, the governments and central banks in Eastern Europe had to undertake emergent measures towards converting the foreign currency liabilities of households and firms to reduce the severity of macroeconomic consequences which would have followed (Krishnakumar, 2019).

While the firms borrow in a third country in a different currency and use the resources towards the purchase of assets in another country, given that the transaction does not figure in the balance of payments sheet of the country concerned, it does expose not just the firm but also the country to several other risks. These are cases where the triple coincidence of the country, currency and the place of borrowing do not occur (Avdjiev, McCauley, & Shin, 2016). It exposes the emerging market economy to a series of risks that, in some instances, do not show up in the external balance sheet of the country concerned. Given the favourable tide of liquidity, while the firms in EMDEs see the country's currency appreciating, they would excuse themselves of the costs of hedging against exchange rate risks, thus exposing them to risk when the exchange rate depreciates eventually at a later time. In their commentary on the state of the corporate debt of the emerging market economies, in the eve of the COVID-19 crisis, Avdjiev and others have drawn attention to the fickle nature of international credit, which is subjected to sudden stops (Avdjiev, McGuire, & Goetz, 2020).

Though cross-border flows of capital through loans and international debt securities have increased during the period even after the crisis, it was directed most to the regions of Developing Asia and the Pacific and Latin America and Caribbean. Since 2014, there has been a steep increase in cross-border flows to Developing Africa and the Middle East. Though there has been credit flows to the emerging Europe region, in terms of its GDP, there has been a decline over the period since the global financial crisis (Figure 3.4). The emerging Europe bloc which used to witness far larger

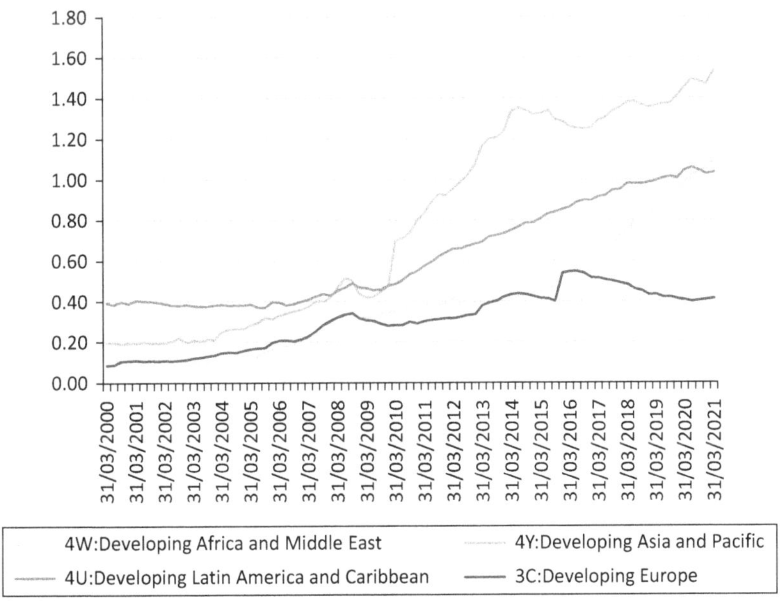

Figure 3.4 Cross-border credit in $ trillions (loans and debt securities to different developing country regions: 2000–20). *Source:* BIS Global Liquidity Indicators.

capital flows in terms of their respective GDP has been witness to retrenchment of capital flows after the surge following the great deleveraging of the European banks which happened in the aftermath of the crisis.

In the Landau Report on global liquidity too, it is mentioned that the "amplifier effects" on credit creation as a result of capital flows to different regions would differ. With its lax regulatory framework, emerging Europe was witness to large increase in credit creation in the run-up to the crisis. In the light of the macroeconomic problems confronted by the economies of Eastern Europe, in the wake of the deleveraging of Western European banks, the regulations have become tighter there in comparison to the different other regions. This again raises issues relating to capital tending to prefer destinations which would have liberal rules, and, underlies the importance of rules relating to financial regulation on cross-border flows being negotiated through multilateral consultations.

International Debt Securities

In the run-up to the global financial crisis, much of the capital flows were intermediated through the bank route. With the collapse of the dot-com bubble, the Fed Reserve went for a significant reduction in the interest rates. The low rates of interest further added to the froth in the housing market. To keep it ticking, there were different financial innovations engineered by the Wall Street bankers. Moreover, the world of banking in itself moved from that of "originate and hold" to "originate and distribute", with the considerable preponderance of non-core liabilities in the balance sheets of banks (Brooking Institution, 2012). The US money markets served as the source of financing the purchases of mortgage and asset-backed securities by several European banks. The inability to renew their short-term liabilities following the liquidity squeeze resulted in several European banks being forced to deleverage. It had a significant impact on these banks as purveyors of global liquidity.

With a banking crisis in the global economy, the corporations (both financial and non-financial) in the advanced countries took recourse to the international financial markets for resource mobilisation through the issuance of international debt securities. In this context, Shinn brought to light the fact that the banking glut has given way to the second wave of liquidity intermediated through the issuance of bonds and securities. In this case, too, as the interest rates in the advanced centres' increase, there would be a flight from these securities resulting in a steep rise in the yield from the same, with severe consequences on economic growth (Shin, 2013).

The period after 2010 has witnessed a massive upswing concerning the offshore issuance of international debt securities by emerging economies, which makes it occur to be the country's liability from where the issue has happened but ends up being part of liabilities of the consolidated balance sheet of the country. Concerning the international debt securities, we find a growing wedge between the nationality and the residence of the issuer. The mobilisation of resources through the route of international debt securities received a fillip in the early stage after the global financial crisis with many developed country corporates finding it possible to access market at lower interest rates than it was possible ever before, through the issuance of debt securities. This was understandable in the context of the banks going through a process of deleveraging as a result of the asset–liability mismatch through which they went through. Many of these corporations used these loans thus mobilised to pre-pay their loans which were taken in the past and not so much for investment. Further non-financial corporations with high ratings in the developing countries also resorted to this strategy of resource mobilisation.

With the capital flows occurring to the developing world driven by the search for yield, there has been a significant increase in mobilising funds in the international financial markets in their domestic currencies. There has been a large increase in the issuance of masala bonds (India) and the dim sum bonds (Chinese), though at a higher rate of interest compared to the hard currencies. But of the total outstanding stock of international debt securities, the share denominated in currencies other than the reserve currencies continue to be very trivial. Of the outstanding stock of the international debt securities issued by the emerging and developing economies of $4.43 trillion in 2020Q3, $291.7 billion (6.5%) alone is denominated in domestic currency. It is indeed revealing that of the total outstanding debt securities of China of $1225.3 billion in 2020Q3, only $107.2 billion (i.e., 8.75%) is denominated in renminbi, and in the Indian case, only $8.9 billion (i.e., 7.7%) of the total $114.3 billion is denominated in rupees.[8] In other words, notwithstanding the highly favourable environment wherein mobilisation of external resources has been easier for a subset of developing country corporates, the inability to borrow in the international financial markets in the local currencies, which was characterised as the "*original sin*" (Eichengreen, Hausmann, & Panizza, 2005), continues to hold for the emerging market economies in the international arena.

The share of the domestic debt owned by foreigners in the developing and emerging market economies makes it vulnerable to the changes in the international economic environment, particularly the advanced countries' monetary policies. In the emerging markets of Chile, Colombia, Poland, Mexico, Malaysia, South Africa and Indonesia, the share of the domestic debt held by foreigners is in the range of 20–40% (Arslanalp & Tsuda, 2014). An increase in interest rates in the international economy could result in the sale of the domestic bonds resulting in a rise in yield. For reasons whatsoever, if speculative expectations are set in motion about the possible depreciation of the currency, the foreign investors would abandon the securities to avoid larger capital losses. This would raise the yield of the bond and result in the future borrowing becoming costly. If sudden exit is possible, this could lead to steep depreciation of the currency. In case restrictions in the form of capital controls are not in place, it is not desirable for governments to allow foreign participation in the government debt markets, even when the same is denominated in local currency.

Other Financial Institutions as Purveyors of Liquidity

Ever since the beginning of the early 2000s, other financial institutions like hedge funds, pension funds, sovereign wealth funds and endowments have started playing an important role in the process of financial intermediation. Hedge funds like Black Rock, Vanguard, Pico and Fidelity, sovereign wealth funds like Abu Dhabi Investment Authority Fund, Norway's Global Pension Fund and General Insurance Corporation (GIC) and Temasek Holdings of Singapore, China Investment Corporation (CIC) and State Administration of Foreign Exchange (SAFE) of China, and a series of insurance and pension funds have been important players in the world of intermediation and had phenomenally large assets under their management. While the growth of hedge funds could be traced to the widening distributive disparities, and the rise of sovereign funds could be attributed to the fortunes made by the states due to the rise in the price of natural resources, the growing subscription for the insurance and pension funds is due to the retreat of the state from concerns related to the social security of their citizenry. Moreover, in the world of equity mobilisation, much more than through the primary market offers, there is a large preponderance of private equity players (Chandrasekhar, 2008).

The better regulatory framework of banking apart, the assets under management of these other financial institutions have been witness to a steep increase since the global financial crisis. As of 2019, the assets under management with other financial institutions like mutual funds, exchange-traded funds, insurance companies, pension funds, sovereign wealth funds and endowments at $135 trillion have exceeded those with the banks with $127 trillion (McKinsey And Co., 2018). The numbers are provocative indeed to force us to think as to whether this is again the game of regulatory arbitrage which is at work. Particularly so while it comes in the backdrop of the number of reports from either sides of the Atlantic that the various figures like capital requirements and the net stable funding ratio reveal that the risks in the banking sector were insignificant. With all its deficiencies, when the new regulatory regime could take credit for the same, would it not be appropriate to think of new means of surveillance and regulation of these sets of firms too?

Foreign Exchange Reserves

Other than a few economies in East Asia and the oil-rich economies, none have their treasure chest of foreign exchange reserves underwritten by the current account surpluses. Largely the surpluses in the financial account, and, in the past few years, the growing debt-creating liabilities have been adding to the foreign exchange reserves of the developing economies. It is pertinent here to note that while there has been a faster rate of growth for foreign exchange reserves of the emerging economies in the first decade of the century, that momentum could not be sustained due to multiple reasons like the commodity price slowdown as well as reduction in current account surpluses of the East Asian economies. With unfavourable debt servicing, many of the economies could not afford to continue with the process of accumulation of foreign exchange.

The meagre returns that could be earned from the Treasury securities of developed economies like the United States compared to those paid on the domestic bonds issued to sterilise the increase in associated supplies of domestic money supplies, the developing economies were incurring a severe fiscal cost. Rodrik refers to this phenomenon as the social cost of foreign exchange reserves, which reflects on the asymmetric nature of the international monetary system (Rodrik, 2006). In the Landau Report too, doubt is expressed about the feasibility of relying on foreign exchange reserves towards assuring stability. Running down own reserves to defend the exchange rates against the volatile fluctuations could be perceived as a weakness by the markets. The developing economies would not have incurred such charges had there been ample liquidity support from the International Monetary Fund.

Since the outbreak of the financial and banking crisis in 2007–08, there has been a steep rise in the addition to the foreign exchange reserves of the advanced economies. During the period from 2010 to 2021, while the forex reserves of the advanced countries increased from $3.4 trillion to $5.68 trillion, that of EMDEs increased from $6.2 trillion to $7.5 trillion (Figure 3.5). The forex reserves of EMDEs other than China have been hovering between $3.5 and $4 trillion during the period since 2010. It should be borne in mind that this category includes economies in East Asia and India, Russia and Brazil, which also hold a large chest of reserves, which implies that not for all of the EMDEs, the reserves have been increasing. The rise in the demand for reserve assets particularly by economies like Switzerland or Japan has never been a matter of concern. Whereas the accumulation of foreign exchange reserves done by the developing countries is driven by precautionary motive, the same is viewed as being pursued to increase the competitiveness of their exports.

But does the large size of the foreign exchange reserves of developing countries matter to begin with? A cursory glance through how the exchange rates of a set of 11 emerging economies changed ever since 2010 reveals that other than China, Thailand and Bangladesh, the rest were all witness to steep depreciation.[9]

Coming to the foreign exchange reserves of India, it has increased from $37.9 billion, i.e., 8% of the GDP, in 2000 to $549 billion, i.e., 21.2% of the GDP, in 2020, on account of the inflows on the financial account

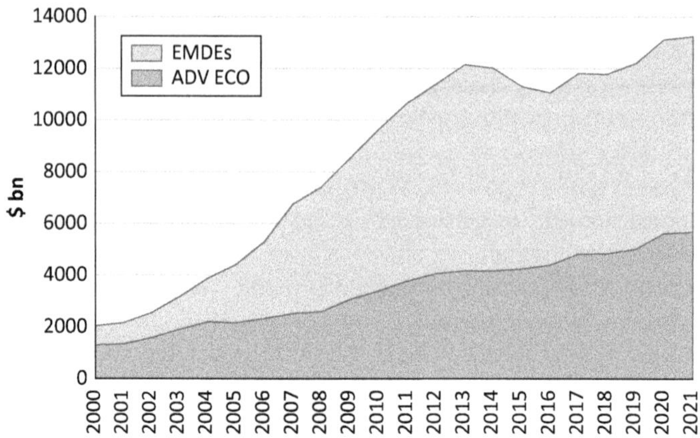

Figure 3.5 Total reserves (excluding gold) in $ billion. *Source:* International Financial Statistics, IMF.

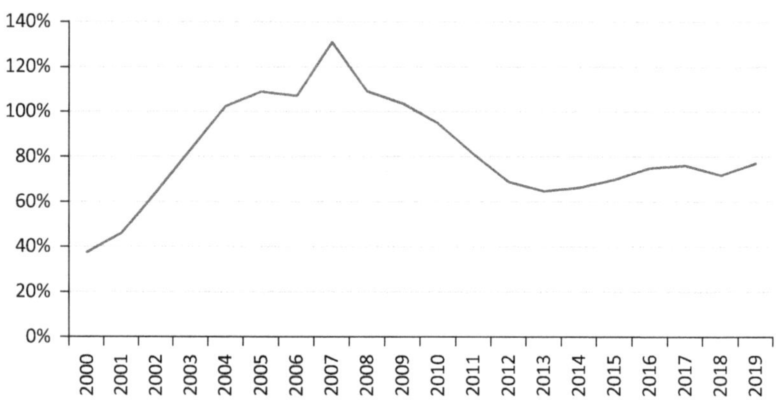

Figure 3.6 Foreign exchange reserves of India as a share of the external debt. *Source:* International Debt Statistics and WEO Database. Author's calculations.

having an increasing share of debt-creating inflows, riding the tide of the low interest rate in the global economy. This has been particularly so since the global financial crisis. However, the ratio of foreign exchange reserves as a share of the external debt has been on the decline. In 2008, while the foreign exchange reserves stood at 131% of the external debt, as of 2019, with far larger foreign exchange reserves, it covers only 77% of the external debt (Figure 3.6).[10] In other words, the smaller stock of foreign exchange reserves in 2008 could cover a larger share of the external debt compared to the larger pile of foreign exchange reserve we have today.

Indeed, the share of debt-creating inflows has been on the rise with respect to the external balance sheets of a number of developing countries. The composition of the stock of external liabilities of India clearly reveals the rising share of other investments, which includes most of the debt-incurring liabilities. It is pertinent to note here that as per the RBI data of June 2021, the short-term debt on residual maturity basis constituted 44.7% of the total external debt and stood at 41.6% of the foreign exchange reserves.[11] This reveals the extent of vulnerabilities to which even a country with a large stock of foreign exchange reserves is exposed to. Even when it comes to foreign direct investment, much of the same inflows are on account of the mergers and acquisitions, or of the inflows through the route of private equity or venture capital investors.

A perusal of the balance of payments data of India reveals that despite the COVID-19 pandemic, the net inflows in the capital account has been \$84.15 billion and \$63.37 billion in 2019–2020 and 2020–2021. The flow of funds in search for yield has resulted in an unprecedented blooming of tech unicorns in India. The recent issue of the India Private Equity Report reveals that the inflows to India through the private equity route through the sovereign wealth funds, pension and insurance funds have increased from \$14.8 billion in 2011 to \$62.2 billion in 2020, with the number of deals increasing from 531 to 1,106 (Figure 3.7). The steep increase in 2020 is partly explained by the stake sales done by Jio Platforms and Reliance Retail mobilising \$26.5 billion.[12]

Much of the private equity inflows have occurred in the field of consumer tech, i.e., fintech, edtech, food tech, verticalised e-commerce platforms and contract development and manufacturing organisations (CDMOs) in the pharmaceutical sector. As the India Private Equity Report as well as

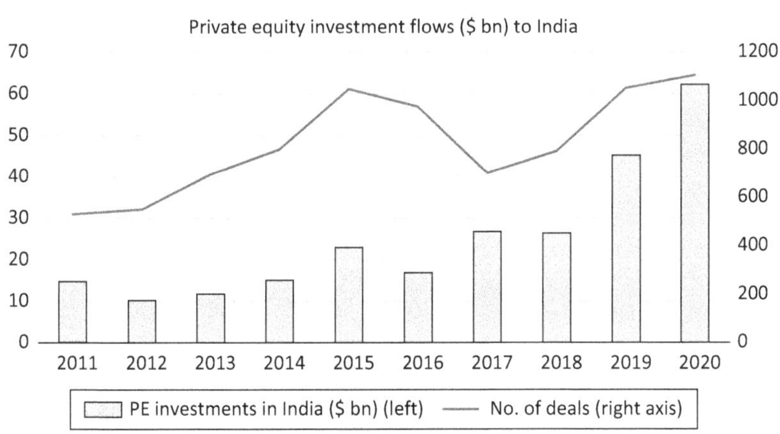

Figure 3.7 Private Equity Investment Flows (\$ billion) to India with the number of deals. *Source:* India Private Equity Report 2021, Bain and Co.

different reports in the press argue, the private equity inflow into these firms have benefited from the tightening of regulations in China in the field of fintech and edtech. In fact, returns to the private equity firms occur only when they nurture the firms and sell their stake in the same for a higher value. In the end, the large pool of investments in these sectors are matters of social concern on which public policy debates are still open-ended. Or, are we going to be tongue-tied with respect to policy matters in these fields even if it could lead to social benefit, given that the private equity and venture capital inflows are important indeed for the buoyancy of the market. Even then, would this momentum be sustained in the context of the reversal of the unconventional policies in the advanced economies? Won't the risks and vulnerabilities associated with economies which had ended up attracting large capital inflows be even higher?

Conclusion

The low interest rate induced asset price increases is reflected in the hike in the market indices in December 2021 from the lows of March 2020 with NASDAQ rising from 7334 to 15,6446 and BSE from 30,579, to 58,253. This is showing up froth in the property prices too. The BIS Report reveals that the global shelter prices have increased worldwide in real terms in 2021Q1 by 4.6% yoy and the prices of property has increased by 22.4% in real terms from their post-GFC levels.[13] As per the recent volumes of the Financial Stability Reports of the Federal Reserve, there has been a large increase in the leveraged buyout operations and a lot of froth in the market of cryptocurrencies. All of this is despite the greenshoots of recovery in the real sector being far from visible. This brings out clearly the disjuncture between the real economy and financial sector, reminiscent of the precept of Keynes of *enterprise turning out to be a bubble in the whirlpool of speculation*. At times, one fears as to whether the policymakers are again placing their hopes on a bubble-led recovery.

The merits of the Landau Report on global liquidity notwithstanding, the Report neither refers to Keynes nor is influenced by the conceptualisation of liquidity proposed by him. The recommendations of the Landau Report about the necessity of macroprudential policies in the light of asset price bubble apart, it seems that the policy centres seem to be thinking in terms of riding atop the bubble out of this recession. This chapter has tried to look at the issue of global liquidity in the period after the global financial crisis from the point of view of emerging economies.

The route of cross-border flows to developing countries is now dispersed between banking flows and international debt securities, with the latter emerging as an important route of resource mobilisation. In the emerging market universe, while the stock of claims on Emerging Asia and Latin America and Caribbean continues to be high and growing and there has been large flows to Emerging Africa and Middle East too, the flows to Emerging Europe has been a bit mellowed.

Given that there has been a steady increase in the dollar credit outside the United States to non-financial corporations, of which the emerging economies hold at least one-third, any reversal of the current monetary policies at the centre is sure to make the funding of dollar costly, proving to be consequential to the growth prospects of developing countries, exposing us to bouts of volatility. Developing country governments are tied down with no manoeuvrability possible on the monetary policy front; the dollar interest rate and the US monetary policy pursued are increasingly becoming too important to be ignored by any developing economy, irrespective of the exchange rate regime (Rey, 2015). Given the large increase in the dollar credit outside the United States, as the world braces towards the reversal of unconventional monetary policies, it is to be seen as to how the growing demand for dollar liquidity is going to be addressed.

Notes

1 These calculations by the author in this section are on the basis of the data of external assets and liabilities from the BOPS and International Investment Position, data of exports and imports from Direction of Trade Statistics and GDP figures from the World Economic Outlook Database, all extracted from the IMF Datawarehouse.

2 Nonetheless, as this work goes on print, there has been the largest ever allocation of $650 billion SDR allocation, but the issue of international liquidity among the developing economies continues to be pertinent for this assignment has been done in proportion to the quotas of the countries in the Fund. Even when it provides relief, it does not match up to the demand of the developing countries.

3 In other words, from a period where the banks used to create loans and hold them till maturity (originate and hold), it has moved to an era where the loans are created, securitized and sold off, thus getting them off from the balance sheets. There is no incentive for the banks now to exercise due diligence with respect to the quality of the loans. This contributed in a significant way to the making of the crisis.

4 NSFR (Net Stable Funding Ratio) requires banks to maintain a stable funding profile in comparison to their assets and off-balance sheet activities. Addressing concerns of financial stability in post-global financial crisis period, the Banking Committee on Banking Supervision (BCBS) has initiated this as a measure to restrict the mobilization of resources by banks through wholesale funding (BCBS, 2014).

5 Among the 30 banks in the G-SIB list published by the BIS, four are from China: Bank of China, China Construction Bank, Industrial and Commercial Bank of China and Agricultural Bank of China. These are other than the number of Japanese banks which figure in the list. https://www.fsb.org/wp-content/uploads/P111120.pdf

6 These calculations by the author are on the basis of the relevant data of central bank balance sheets of the United States and Japan from the database of the Federal Reserve Bank of St. Louis.

7 In March 2020, according to the Treasury International Capital, there was sale of $400 billion of Treasury securities. This was predominantly done by the foreign central banks who wanted dollar cash for emergent liquidity purposes. Sensing the consequences of the same on the cost of dollar liquidity, the Federal Reserve announced the FIMA Repo Facility which provided for borrowing against Treasuries. This was apart from the swap line facilities which have been otherwise provided by the Federal Reserve. For further details, see the small section on *A Retrospective on the March 2020 Turmoil in the Treasury and Mortgage-backed Securities Markets* (Federal Reserve Board, 2020).

8 The calculation is done on the basis of the nationality of the issuer data provided by the BIS Database which can be accessed at https://stats.bis.org/statx/srs/table/c3?c=4T

9 The economies in the list include the BRICS, the four main South Asian economies and East Asian economies of Thailand, Indonesia and Malaysia.

10 The author's calculations based on the Total Reserves minus Gold from International Financial Statistics of the IMF as well as the stock of external debt extracted from the World Bank (2021)

11 The short-term debt under residual maturity includes both the long term which is to mature within a year apart from the short-term debt of original maturity.

12 Though the major investors in the stake sale of Jio Platforms as well as in other ventures have been institutional funds based in Americas, there has been flow of funds from different SWFs based in the Middle East as well as the East Asian economies.

13 The figures quoted from the commentary in BIS website on BIS Residential Property Statistics 2021Q1, https://www.bis.org/statistics/pp_residential_2108.htm

References

Arcand, J. L., Berkes, E., & Panizza, U. (2012). *Too much Finance? Working Paper no 12*. Washington DC: International Monetary Fund.

Arslanalp, S., & Tsuda, T. (2014). *Tracking Global Demand for Emerging Market Sovereign Debt 2014/29*. Washington: IMF.

Avdjiev, S., McCauley, R., & Shin, H. S. (2016). Breaking free of the triple coincidence in international finance. *Economic Policy*, Vol 31, Issue 87, 409–51.

Avdjiev, S., McGuire, P., & Goetz, V. P. (2020). International dimensions of EME corporate debt. *BIS Quarterly*, June.

Bain and Co and IVCA. (2021). *India Private Equity Report*. Mumbai: Bain and Co.

BCBS. (2014). *Basle III: The Net Stable Funding Ratio*. October 2014. Basle: Bank for International Settlements.

BIS. (2011). *Global Liquidity—Concept, Measurement, and Policy Implications*. CGFS Papers 45. Basle: Committee on the Global Financial System.

BIS. (2019). *Triennial Central Bank Survey of Foreign Exchange and Over-the-Counter (OTC) Derivatives Markets in 2019*. Basle: BIS.

Brooking Institution. (2012). *Banks and Cross-Border Capital Flows*. Committee on International Economic Policy and Reform. Washington, DC: Brookings Institution.

Bruno, V., & Shin, H. S. (2017). Global dollar credit and carry trades: A firm-level analysis. *Review of Financial Studies*, Vol 30, Issue 3, 703–49.

Chandrasekhar, C. P. (2008). Global liquidity and financial flows to developing countries: new trends in emerging markets and their implications. *G-24 Discussion Papers 52*. New York and Geneva: UNCTAD.

Chandrasekhar, C. P., & Ghosh, J. (2008). *The Global Liquidity Paradox*. Retrieved from www.networkideas.org.

Chang, R., & Velasco, A. (1999). Liquidity crises in emerging markets: Theory and policy. *NBER Macroeconomics Annual*, Vol 14, 11–58.

CIEPR. (2015). *Corporate Debt in Emerging Economies: A Threat to Financial Stability?* September 2015. Washington, DC: Brookings.

Eatwell, J., & Taylor, L. (2002). *International Capital Markets: Systems in Transition*. Oxford: OUP.

Eichengreen, B., Hausmann, R., & Panizza, U. (2005). The mystery of original sin. In B. Eichengreen & R. Hausmann (Eds.), *Other People's Money: Debt Denomination and Financial Instability in Emerging-Market Economies* (pp. 233–65). Chicago, IL: University of Chicago Press.

Federal Reserve Board. (2020). *Financial Stability Report*. Washington, DC: Board of Governors of Federal Reserve Board.

Krishnakumar, S. (2019). *Capital Flows, Global Liquidity and Emerging Market Economies(1990–2015): Revisiting the Bretton Woods II Postulate*. Unpublished PhD thesis. New Delhi: Jawaharlal Nehru University.

McKinsey and Co. (2018, November). *Banks in the Changing World of Financial Intermediation*. Retrieved from https://www.mckinsey.com/industries/financial-services/our-insights/banks-in-the-changing-world-of-financial-intermediation.

Rey, H. (2015). Dilemma not trilemma: The global financial cycle and monetary policy independence. Discussion Papers. *CEPR Discussion Papers 10591*. London: C.E.P.R.

Rodrik, D. (2006). The social cost of foreign exchange reserves. *International Economic Journal*, Vol 20, Issue 3, 253–266.

Shin, H. S. (2013). The second phase of global liquidity and its impact on emerging economies. *Asian Economic Policy Conference*, Nov 3–5 2013, Federal Bank of San Francisco, pp. 215–224.

4 Our Preoccupation with Speculation and its Consequences for Commodity Derivatives Markets in India

Rose Mary K Abraham

Introduction

In India, commodity derivatives markets are stated to be speculative and dismissed outright on account of the dominant thinking that derivatives market is beneficial only if a fairly large volume of production is delivered on its platform (Kabra, 2007). Low participation of farmers/hedgers in the market is another reason. Apprehensions exist on its role in reducing price volatility or in controlling inflation/deflation. There is also a strong thinking that India is still a net importer of many commodities and there are many interventions in the spot markets and hence, in such commodities, no derivative trading can be promoted. The oligopolistic real sector players and cartels, who do not wish to lose their pricing powers in the wake of an exchange-traded commodity market that could beat down any unwarranted high price or peg up any unwarranted low price also contribute to the story of "speculation" in derivatives markets, thereby discrediting it. This chapter is an exploration into the historical roots of our preoccupation with such speculative concerns and it outlines the consequences of the same for the development of the market, particularly the agri derivatives segment. It also tries to give new dimensions to our understanding of speculative interest in the derivative market and tries to quantify the same.

Role of Commodity Derivatives Markets

Commodity derivatives markets are designed to cater to price discovery and price risk management or hedging. Price discovery essentially means finding the direction of price movement and an approximate level of prices in the spot market for a future date, assuming competitive markets and access to full information for participants. Price risk refers to the risk of economic loss from having an exposure to a commodity owing to volatility in its prices. Price risk occurs because production of many commodities is seasonal, whereas their consumption/further processing/export is spread throughout the year, requiring either storage or, as an alternative, some reasonable protection from price rise/fall when consumption/processing/export

DOI: 10.4324/9781003343998-4

becomes due. Derivative markets facilitate this price protection through contractual instruments like forwards, futures, options and swaps[1].

For instance, a futures contract protects the economic agent from the effect of price fluctuations, favourable or unfavourable, provided he is willing to be content with reasonable returns.[2] It facilitates hedging, or entering into a countervailing contract, through which those who have a bought (long) position (such as stockist) in the spot market will sell in the futures market and those who have a sold (short) position (e.g. farmers) would buy in the futures market. This ensures raw material supplies at pre-agreed prices to the processors/manufacturers and saves them the trouble and expense involved in accumulating inventories.

While helping to sell at a locked-in price on a future date, futures contract helps to prevent the post-harvest slump in agri-prices. Because, here the trader would be willing to buy up the surging market arrivals as he is able to reduce, though not eliminate, the risk associated with stock holding. Thus, futures market helps to reduce volatility in prices. However, it may not prevent inflation or deflation. Futures market is meant to move ahead of the spot market and send out signals regarding future price movements before the spot market reaches that price level (Figure 4.1). In fact, if it does not move ahead, then it means the futures market has failed. In a way, the market acts as a messenger or a forecast of forthcoming events. As noted in the Kolamkar Report (GoI, 2014), "when futures markets work well, they anticipate future prices efficiently. Through this, they shape the two key allocative decisions, of allocating farm land and allocating storage". Thus,

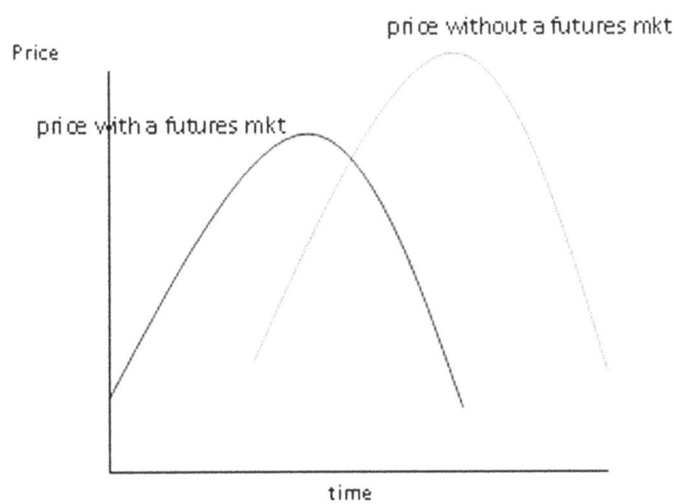

Figure 4.1 Price movements with and without futures markets *Source: Author's depiction*

futures price is a public good, which helps farmers/stockist make decisions on sowing or storage without actually participating in the market, though the real benefits are derived only when they are able to lock in their prices. The quality of the process of discovery of future prices depends on the depth and liquidity of the market, for which participation from speculative players is also crucial.

While it is most certainly possible that a hedger could lock his gains/income with or without some opportunity costs that may arise due to the contrary movements in spot prices vis-à-vis the hedged position, it is difficult to assess whether the presence of derivative trading has actually reduced volatility in spot markets. One way to look at it is by seeing the volatility before and after the introduction of derivative trading in a particular commodity. For a commodity like chana, for which trading is fairly stabilised at exchanges, the spot price volatility at Bikaner Mandi (which is also the delivery centre for NCDEX) with and without futures trading is assessed in Table 4.1 by calculating the spot price volatility during the ban period of the futures contract and for an equal period just before and after the ban period. It shows that price volatility was reasonably lower in the presence of futures trading. Another option is to compare the price volatility in a commodity having derivative trading (like chana or soyabean) with similar commodities where there is no derivative trading. As may be seen from Table 4.2, spot prices at major trading centres in respect of chana vis-à-vis tur and urad and Soyabean vs Groundnut indicate the beneficial impact of trading on volatility. Notwithstanding the near absence of cost-effective alternatives for price risk management and utility of the derivative markets to real sector players, historically, the market faced condemnation and vilification.

Historical Roots of the Allegation of Speculation

As observed by the Dantwala committee of 1967 (GoI, 1967), a good deal of confusion about the need and purpose of regulation of what is termed as "forward markets" has arisen mainly due to lack of precision in the definitions of the different types of contracts that are in vogue for the sale of commodities. While the law [Forward Contracts Regulation Act, 1952 (FCRA)] talked about "forwards" wherein contracts are mostly settled with 100% delivery of the underlying commodity especially if it is of non-transferrable nature, what was being regulated was "futures" trading, which involves standardised contracts, with at most, 2-3% of the volume traded getting settled with physical delivery of the underlying commodity. However, "futures contract" was not even defined under the said Act. Lack of physical delivery, or the usual process of settlement of futures contracts by paying in cash the difference between current spot price and contracted price, was perceived as speculation in those days, which is equally true of the present day.

The first notable instance of official accusation of speculation in commodity derivatives markets (after the establishment of organised exchanges

Table 4.1 Price volatility of chana during ban period vs period before and after the ban

Chana market: (Bikaner is the basis centre for chana at NCDEX)	*Formula used for calculating price volatility*	*Oct 2007–April 2008*	*Ban period: May–Nov 2008*	*Dec 2008–June 2009*	*August 2015–July 2016*	*Ban period: August 2016–July 2017*	*Aug 2017–July 2018*
Bikaner (Grain)	Avg of Max-Min/Min (% variation)	6.39	**6.56**	3.68	2.89	**5.99**	3.76
Entire Bikaner	Avg of Max-Min/Min (% variation)	6.10	7.00	3.68	3.20	3.90	3.87
Entire Bikaner	Standard Deviation of Modal Price	185.76	**124.74**	94.58	952.69	**1373.03**	804.49
Bikaner (Grain)	Standard Deviation of Modal price	366.39	**130.13**	94.58	1147.34	**533.95**	870.44

Source: Calculated from Agmarknet prices; Modal price is a calculated average price quoted by agmarknet factoring in government procurement

Table 4.2 Comparison of volatility in spot prices of goods traded on the exchange and otherwise

Year	*Pulses*			*Oilseeds*	
	Chana Delhi	*Urad Jalgaon*	*Tur Akola*	*Soybean Indore*	*Groundnut in Shell Bikaner*
2014	19.81%	31.63%	19.65%	19.18%	29.70%
2015	26.15%	41.94%	37.57%	17.88%	24.83%
2016	51.02%	52.27%	49.66%	15.69%	38.93%
2017	42.25%	45.16%	41.62%	12.08%	20.12%
2018	22.70%	59.75%	32.36%	17.11%	20.06%
2019	13.55%	40.23%	25.48%	14.17%	22.64%
2020	17.49%	26.08%	29.85%	18.32%	40.77%
2021	20.52%	21.82%	31.78%	26.34%	26.85%

Source: NCDEX

in 1875) appeared in the 1919 report of the Indian Cotton Committee chaired by J MacKenna (GoI, 1919), the then Agricultural Advisor to the Govt of India. In fact, their finding that speculation in the Bombay Cotton Markets was of "a degree which can only be regarded as highly undesirable"[3] was a pretext for cotton mill owners and cotton importing coloniser to receive cotton at lower prices by regulating futures trading, though it came at the cost of cotton growers (Abraham, 2020). The Committee stated that speculators who may or may not be in the cotton trade "could gamble in just paper contracts for the whole year without handling any actual cotton".

Since the legislators could not see any difference between gambling and forward trading, some of the provincial assemblies of pre-independent India chose to adopt gambling laws (Public Gambling Act, 1867) to control the "damage" caused by forward trading. For instance, in 1927, the government of the Central Provinces moved amendments to the Public Gambling Act, 1867 to make "satta gambling" an offence punishable under the Act with increased penalties. The Amendments made explicit reference to gaming

1 on the market price of cotton, opium or any other commodity or on the digits of the number used in stating such price, or
2 on the amount of variation in the market price of any such commodity or on the digits of the number used in stating the amount of such variation, or …

Resurrection of such laws were not without doubts on the efficacy of controlling forward trading through such laws, especially by giving vast powers to the police, who were prone to misuse such powers making "the evil of corruption greater than at present".[4] Informants crossed over to the other side, taking money from both the police and the gamblers, enabling the police to get conviction based on some small chits and amounts, while helping gamblers to shift their substantial sums to other venues.[5]

Speculation was also conceived to be antithetical to the concept of planning, which was the buzz word after independence. While debating the introduction of Forward Contracts Regulation Bill in the 1950s, some legislators like K P Tripathy of Tejpur and many others wondered what place could be given to "such sort of activity which is neither economic nor productive" in a planned economy. As stated by Manjuran of Travancore Cochin:

> "speculation is a wish expressed to conform the future to our present desires, and planning is our will to make the future conform to our present desires. Are we to give ourselves up to wishful thinking or are we to give ourselves up to wilful planning is the question in FCRA Bill."[6]

Some of the legislative members held the opinion that none of the producers or farmers was benefitting from the price rise, and "it was not by giving legal recognitions to such obnoxious trade but by banning them that peasants would be benefited".[7] For some, forward markets represented the capitalists' arena to exploit farmers by forcing them to enter into contracts for supplying crops to them long before the seeds are sown. The main concern then was about cornering of stocks by middlemen/traders for speculation. The Khusro committee of 1980 (GoI, 1980) was of the view that if gains to futures traders were accompanied by losses to producers, manufacturers, consumers and other social interests, it would not recommend resort to futures trading at all. This moralistic position against gambling and speculation and the concern for the hardships faced by the "poor innocent gamblers", who burnt their fingers, shaped the contours of regulation and state intervention in commodity markets in the years to come.

Consequences of Our Preoccupation with Speculation

For instance, the regulatory laws in this regard – The Bombay Forward Contracts Control Act, 1947 (BFCCA) and its successor FCRA – provided for the "regulation and *control* of forward trading and the *prohibition* of options" in goods. T T Krishnamachari, the Minister who introduced the Forward Contracts Regulation Bill of 1952, stated[8] that without some kind of regulation, "forward trading might degenerate into speculation, pure and simple". It was proposed to prohibit options altogether, since they were considered to be "an undesirable form of speculation"[9] with "demoralising effects on the market"[10] despite the fact that for farmers and hedgers, this could have been the simplest tool available to take price insurance. This ban on options continued for decades up till 2016 when the later regulator – Securities and Exchange Board of India (SEBI)[11] – permitted it. Further, only after the imposition of commodities transaction tax (CTT) in July 2013 that commodity derivatives transactions were accorded, technically, the "non-speculative" status by the Income Tax authorities.

Another consequence was that the first and former regulatory authority for commodity derivatives – Forward Markets Commission (FMC) – was kept as a mere advisory board/adjunct of the Government, rather than as an independent autonomous regulator, for the fear of it being taken over by the speculative interest groups/traders (Abraham, 2020). Even though many committees [(GoI, 1967), (GoI, 1980) and (GoI, 1994)] had recommended major amendments to FCRA to overhaul the system and make FMC a full-fledged regulator, no amendments had been carried out since 1960, save for the further tightening of the definition of a spot contract in 1971.[12] In 1998, 2006, 2008 and 2010, legislative attempts were made; however, the same could not be passed due to possible abetting of speculation in markets. For instance, the Parliamentary Standing Committee (Parliament, 2006) which examined the amendment Bill reiterated the concerns expressed in the introduction paragraph and suggested to not permit trading in agri commodities (para 1.31), and to not allow participation of pure speculators, hedge funds, banks and pension funds (para 1.34); or FPIs (para 2.19) and even questioned the necessity for derivative trading (para 1.28 & 1.30).

Delay in timely amendments in the regulatory law prevented the commodity derivatives markets from developing on the same footing as the equity derivatives markets, with wide-ranging participation from banks, mutual funds, FPIs and with a wide array of contracting structures like options. At the time of issue of the Ordinance in 2008, the Government had expressed the concern that any major crisis in this market for lack of proper regulatory empowerment may not only be a setback to further development of commodity futures trading, but would dissuade participants in the real sector from availing this price risk management instrument.

With no reform support for decades, India could not emerge as a price setter for any of the commodities traded here, despite being a major consumer or producer of many commodities globally. Chinese exchanges (Shanghai, Dalian, Zhengzhou and LME which is now owned by Hong Kong Exchanges and Clearing) account for 66% of the global contracts volume, 45% of the global notional turnover and 36% of the global open interest as at the end of December 2020.[13] Organised commodity trading started around 1991 in China as compared to being of 1952 vintage in India. To be a price setter in commodities, participation of foreign investors who import or export into the country becomes a *sine qua non*. India permitted foreign investors strictly as hedgers in 2018 with such conditions that not a single foreign investor trades in the market, while China opened up its local currency-based commodity trading to foreign traders in an attempt to challenge the US hegemony in commodity price setting. China offers income tax waivers for the first three years to foreign investors to incentivise hedging on their platforms. They also offer offshore trading arrangements at Hong

Kong.[14] State-owned entities also participate in their markets in addition to many retail investors. Further, in 1998, regulation of futures trading was transferred from the local governments to the China Security Regulation Commission (CSRC). Multiple listing of commodities in multiple varieties was avoided in favour of consolidation of liquidity into a few major contracts. The emergence of China proves that the most interventionist, communist regime could also run a vibrant commodity derivatives market [see Yang (2004), Yiping Huang (2013)].

On the other hand, for FMC, the level of prices was the concern rather than the quality of price discovery. Many felt that the FMC was arbitrarily suspending trading with sudden notices even when prices were within the stipulated ceilings, on the fearful expectation of prices soon crossing the limits. Regulation was reportedly aimed more at depressing the spot prices of commodities rather than increasing the hedging efficiency or hedging utility of the futures contracts. While introducing the FCRA Bill in the Rajya Sabha, the then Minister D P Karmarkar had said "the intention of this measure (FCRA) is to regulate, not to ban, all forward contracts". But this is exactly what FMC did on the job. Apparently, the FMC believed that the "question of prices was *not* one which could be determined merely by the forces of supply and demand, but had to be decided in the context of national income of the country and the requirements of planned development" (Pavaskar, 1985).

The 1967 Dantwala Committee (GoI, 1967) observed that the regulatory actions by the FMC by and large only served the purpose of reducing the volume of trading and open positions in forward markets. It did not check the rise in spot prices, if that was the intention. Often, the only visible impact of the restraint was to distort the relation between the spot and futures prices rendering the futures markets unsuitable for hedging. They could then be used only for speculation, the committee observed, as obviously only "hit and run" players can enter and exit on short notice. It can no doubt be argued that but for the restraints imposed, both futures and spot prices would have risen even more steeply. There is no easy way of proving or disproving this. According to the committee, all that can be said is that even when futures trading was completely banned, the spot market did not display any steadier price behaviour. This is true for the present-day scenario also. For instance, in 2016 when chana was banned by SEBI to contain rising prices (which was on account of production shortages), it did not prevent spot prices from rising further (Figure 4.2). The same scenario repeated during the precautionary ban imposed in Aug 2021 for chana.[15] Despite lack of evidence, additional commodities were banned from trading during Oct–Dec 2021 for around 1 year (Table 4.3).

To attempt to keep down prices in the futures market irrespective of their behaviour in the spot markets is to destroy the utility of the futures markets. The Dantwala committee emphasised that futures markets will fail to perform their legitimate function of providing an insurance against price

Figure 4.2 Movement of chana spot prices before and after the ban *Source: NCDEX*

fluctuations and thereby reducing the cost of marketing, if the powers of regulation are used to maintain futures prices at a level wholly out of line with prices in the spot market. The committee felt that the FMC's actions will command more respect and would be more effective, if it intervenes sparingly but decisively only when the situation palpably demands such an intervention. It was of the view that it is better to ban futures trading than to permit it in a crippled form. In fact, the committee focused on preventive action. According to the committee, all care should be taken before giving recognition to an exchange, but once it is given, it should be trusted to act with a sense of responsibility. It went to the extent of suggesting that if this view is not acceptable to the Government it would be better for everyone concerned not to recognise futures trading at all and spare all the trouble and expense of constituting a body like FMC to supervise it. In fact, as the government gears up for a new securities market law, it would help the cause of the market if a clause is introduced for parking the decision on suspensions to a professional body of experts like the monetary policy committee of RBI.

Thus, more than developing the markets, emphasis on speculation led to controlling the market mechanisms and price signals emanating from such mechanisms. Consequently, volumes reduced drastically in the derivative markets. Within a few years of the establishment of FMC, i.e. by mid-1960s, the derivative trading met with a near end, which remained in that limbo state up till the liberalisation of the commodity derivatives markets in 2003. However, suspensions came back with the next wave of inflationary spiral, during January–February 2007 and suspensions still continue as the prominent "signal" to prove government's commitment in fighting inflation, irrespective of its efficacy. As in the pre-independent days, even now consumers' interests are often given precedence over producers' interests.

Table 4.3 List of commodities suspended for trading since 2003

Commodities suspended from trading					
Sl no.	*Commodity*	*Date of suspension*	*Date of revocation*	*Duration of suspension*	*If revoked, could liquidity come back*
1.	Tur	23 Jan 2007	Never lifted	>14 years	-
2.	Urad	23 Jan 2007	Never lifted	>14 years	-
3.	Rice	27 Jan 2007	Never lifted	>14 years	-
4.	Wheat	27 Jan 2007	14 May 2009	27 months	No.
5.	Chana	7 May 2008	30 Nov 2008	6 months	Yes
6.	Soy Oil	7 May 2008	30 Nov 2008	6 months	Yes
7.	Rubber	7 May 2008	30 Nov 2008	6 months	Yes
8.	Potato	7 May 2008	30 Nov 2008	6 months	Yes
9.	Sugar	26 May 2009	30 Sept 2010	16 months	No
10.	Guar Gum	27 March 2012	10 May 2013	14 months	No
11.	Guar Seed	27 March 2012	10 May 2013	14 months	No
12.	Chana	28 July 2016	13 July 2017	12 months	No
13.	Castor seed (NCDEX specific)	28 Jan 2016	4 Jan 2017	12 months	No
14.	Pepper (NCDEX specific)	June 2013	June 2017	4 years	No
15.	Chana	16 Aug 2021	Continuing	Proposed for up till Dec 2022	-
16.	Mustard seeds and its derivatives (i.e. oil complex)	8 Oct 2021	Continuing	Proposed for up till Dec 2022	-
17.	Paddy (non-basmati) Wheat, Soya bean and its derivatives (its complex) Crude palm oil, Moong	20 Dec 2021	Continuing	Proposed for up till Dec 2022	-

Source: compiled from SEBI press releases and (GoI, 2014)

A list of commodities suspended for trading post 2003 is given in Table 4.3. The annual turnover of such commodities (Figure 4.3) shows that liquidity could never be regained to the same extent in most commodities, after suspension, especially if suspension lasted for more than 6 months. While the derivative market had started with agri commodities, over a period of time, the market shifted to non-agri commodities mostly

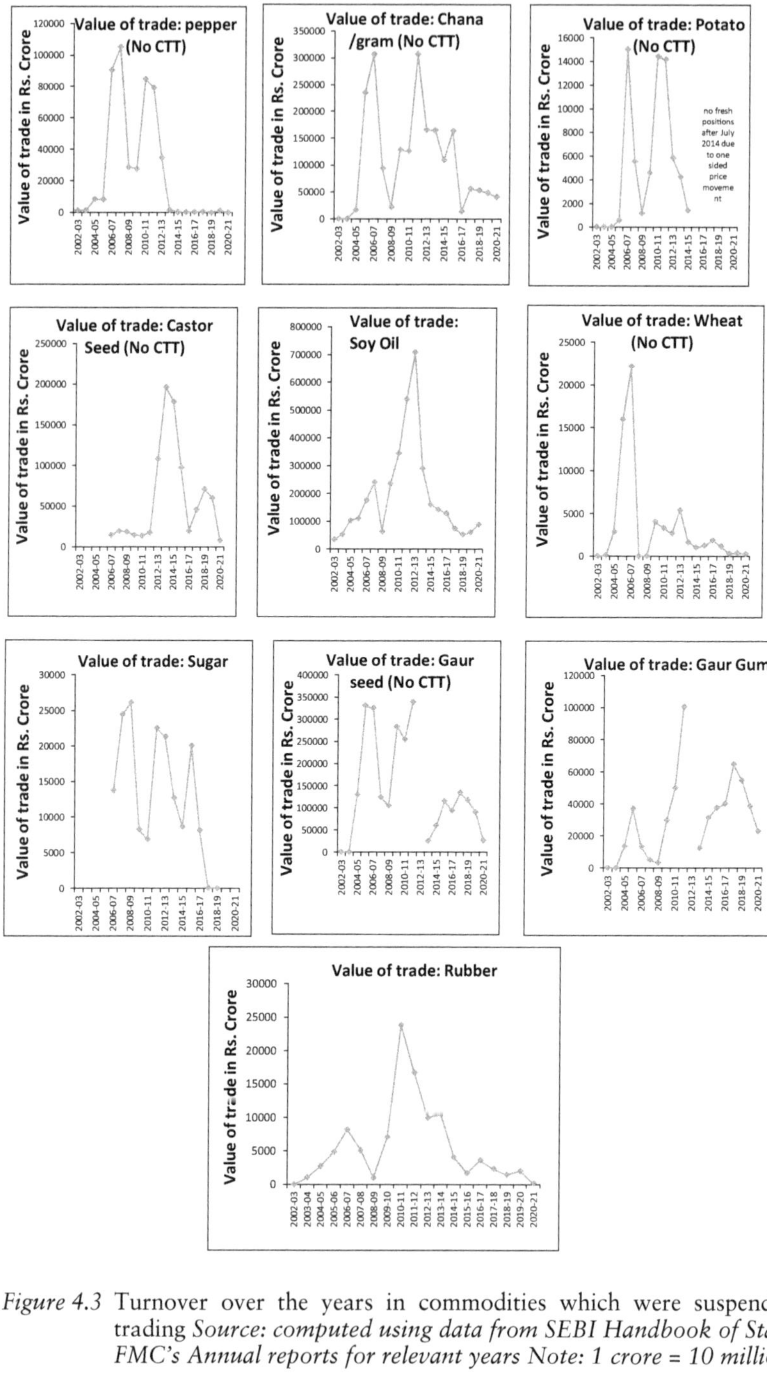

Figure 4.3 Turnover over the years in commodities which were suspended for trading *Source: computed using data from SEBI Handbook of Statistics, FMC's Annual reports for relevant years Note: 1 crore = 10 million*

on account of such interventions. In a steady decline, agri commodities' volume presently account for only 4.7% of the total turnover as compared to 52% in 2005-06 (see Table 4.4 & Figure 4.4). Further, over the years, there has been a shift from food-related products to industry-based agro-products. Alongside the decline in agri commodities, exchanges which specialised in agricultural derivatives, such as NCDEX, witnessed a decline in their market share despite most of their products being not subject to CTT (Figure 4.5).

Table 4.4 Share of various commodity groups in total derivatives turnover

Share of various commodity groups in total turnover			
	2005-06	*2011-12*	*2020-21*
Agri commodities	**52.0**	12.1	**4.66**
Precious metals	37.9	56.2	57.52
Base metals	**0.9**	16.0	**16.99**
Energy	9.1	15.7	20.31
Plastics	0.1	0.0	0.0
Total turnover in Rs. billion	20067.21	181261.04	92229.27

Source: Computed from SEBI Handbook of Statistics, Monthly Bulletin & FMC's Annual reports for relevant years

Note: To gauge the changing commodity spectrum, a snapshot of the various commodities traded in three important years – 2005-06 (the year when trading stabilises after recognition of national commodity exchanges), 2011-12 (the peak year of trading) and 2020-21 (the latest year of trading) – is taken.

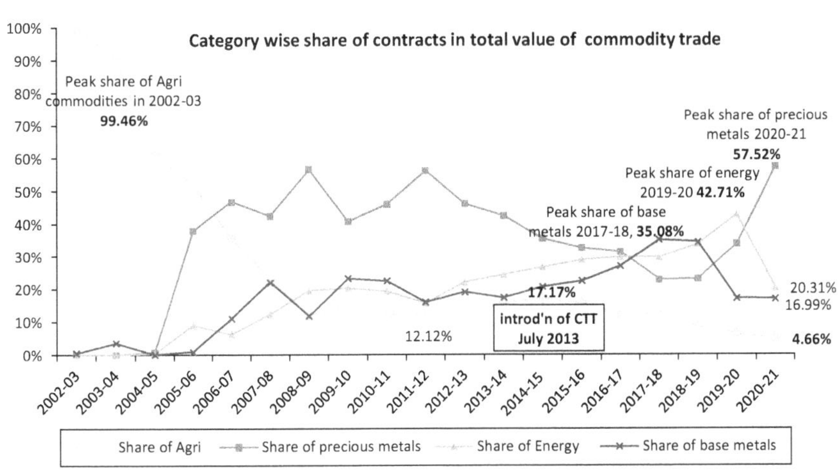

Figure 4.4 Category-wise share of commodity derivatives over the years *Source: computed using data from SEBI Handbook of Statistics, FMC's Annual reports for relevant years*

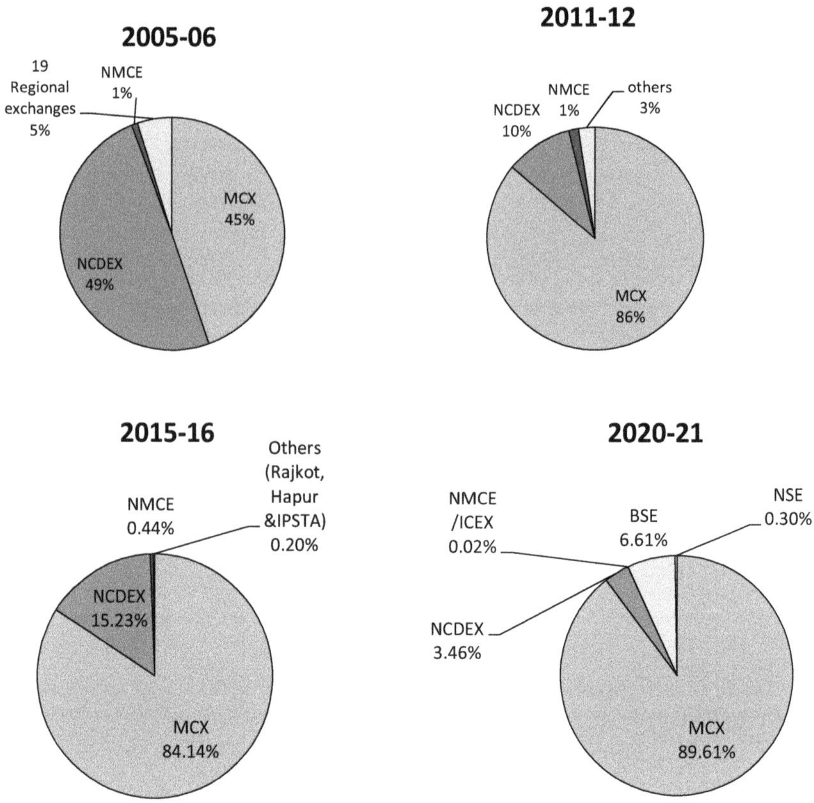

Figure 4.5 Exchange-wise share in commodity derivative turnover *Source: Computed from SEBI Monthly Bulletin & FMC's Annual reports for relevant years*

Frequent interventions, lack of depth and liquidity led to enhanced overseas hedging, even though the general perception in India is that commodity futures turnover is speculatively high. Recently mandated disclosures in the annual reports of top listed companies reveals that whatever hedging being done by the top 100 listed companies are mostly happening in foreign jurisdictions. Many apparently do not find the contract design suitable for hedging (choice of irrelevant grade or basis centre or higher/smaller lot size etc.) and domestic banks/institutions are not facilitating any custom-made forward contracts in India though such assistance has been done for overseas hedging since July 2012. A 2017 RBI report (RBI, 2017) showed that there has been a clear increase in the quantum of overseas hedging after 2013-14 (quantum of foreign exchange outflow on account of hedging is not provided) when the volumes were crashing in the domestic market on account of CTT imposition and payment scam at a spot exchange (NSEL).

The RBI report had recommended that those who hedge overseas should be encouraged to partly and progressively hedge their risks on the domestic exchanges. However, there is no policy nudge to this effect from the RBI in the March 2018 directions which came subsequent to this report, save for the ban on precious metals' hedging overseas. It is feared by many that easy overseas hedging may further prevent Indian exchanges from building liquidity in the market.

Assessing the Speculative Interest in the Market

What is the tolerable limit of speculation in commodity exchanges is a question that has eluded any clear answers. Section 43(5) of the Income Tax (IT) Act defines a "speculative" transaction as a transaction in which a contract for the purchase or sale of any commodity/stocks/shares is periodically or ultimately settled otherwise than by the actual delivery or transfer of the commodity or scrips. In a way, this is the only existing formal definition of a "speculative transaction" in India.[16] The consequence of being treated as "speculative" is that investors need to show income from such transactions separately in their tax returns [need to file a different type of IT return] and the same is taxed at the slab rate applicable for income as against concessional rates applicable for other similar transactions.[17] Further, speculative losses can be set off only against speculative gains and not against salary or capital gains from other segments. This complicates tax filing unnecessarily. Despite being non-delivery based, commodity derivatives have been accorded the "non-speculative" status similar to equity derivatives under IT Act since the imposition of CTT in 2013. Being exempted from CTT, agri commodity trading used to be treated as "speculative", till the Budget 2018-19 proposed otherwise. In fact, all transactions carried out in SEBI-recognised exchanges should be deemed as "non-speculative" whether delivery based or not, and whether transaction taxes are paid out or not (since they pay GST and stamp duty as well). In any case, this official definition of "speculative transaction" has no real significance for the academic studies.

Extent of Open Interest

A simple measure of speculative interest is given by the ratio or percentage of open interest to turnover. Open interest (also known as open contracts or open commitments) denotes the total number of futures contracts that are currently active or outstanding or remaining unsettled or not squared off. Open interest comes mostly from genuine players who intend to settle the contract with delivery or otherwise. Pure speculators generally do not keep any of their positions open beyond the day. The ratio of open interest to trading turnover is, therefore, a good measure of the extent of speculative activity in the market. Higher the ratio, lesser the hold of speculators in the market. It is seen from Figure 4.6 that the ratio of open interest to

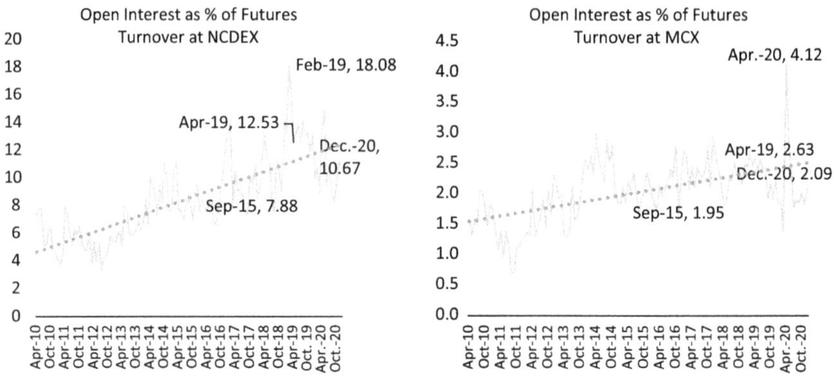

Figure 4.6 Percentage of open interest to turnover at NCDEX and MCX *Source: calculated from SEBI Handbook of Statistics; Open interest is taken as at the end of the month while turnover is for the entire month (The spike during March-April 2020 is due to the sharp fall in volumes traded on account of covid related lockdown)*

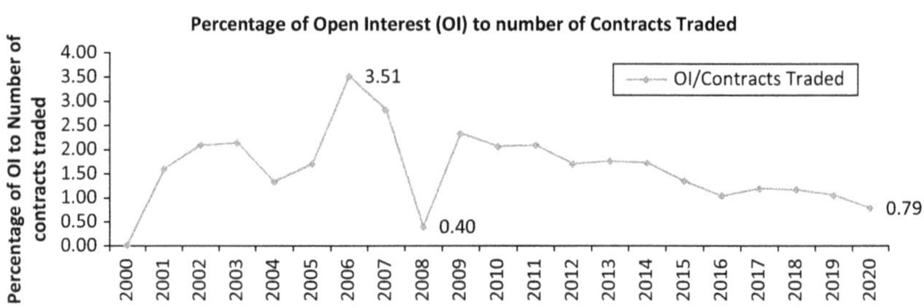

Figure 4.7 Speculative Interest in exchange traded segment across the globe *Source: Calculated from World Federation of Exchanges database. Open interest, as per WFE database, refers to the number of derivatives contracts (futures and options) outstanding or not settled on the last trading day of the year. Here open interest is taken as the ratio of total number of contracts traded*

turnover has improved in general, particularly since markets were brought under SEBI in September 2015. However, post 2019, the SEBI mandate to physically settle outstanding positions on expiry day seems to have led to a reduction in open interest in the market. This means that while physical delivery commitments may be driving out financial/speculative players, hedgers seem to have still not entered fully, resulting in an overall reduction in market volumes. Globally also, the ratio has been declining over the past decade as may be seen from Figure 4.7, and the Indian ratio appears to be higher than the global figures, particularly in the agri segment.

Participation of Hedgers

There is no correct estimation of hedger participation in the market. Commodity exchanges generally classify their trades as those reflecting proprietary trading and those based on client orders. Proprietary trading refers to trading done by trading members or brokers on their own account. While there is nothing that bars a value chain entity or an FPO/manufacturing corporate house from taking direct trading membership, such memberships are very few in number. The clients could be SMEs, farmers, processors and other such value chain participants or individuals. Many of them do not avail the hedge code which provides them with some exceptions from position limits, since it also brings along huge compliance burdens and periodic disclosures. Further, position limits in the non-agri segment are considered to be fairly large and sufficient and the need for a hedger code does not arise. For instance, in trading gold, 5 tonnes is the position limit. Hedge codes are availed mostly by essential/agri commodity traders for whom restrictions like stock limits and smaller position limits apply. The value of an exchange depends on the client and hedge orders it is able to generate. Between FY2011 and FY2021, client's share in the agri exchange NCDEX declined from around 63% to 57% (lowest being 50.5% in FY2016) while the hedgers increased from 0.4% to 1.4%.[18] This is a cause of concern as it indicates exit by value chain participants. Further, a better classification system for correctly identifying the pure speculative interests, hedger interest, specific industry/value chain participants etc. is required.

Another way of estimating hedger participation is through warehousing statistics. Around 1057 agri warehouses in the country had active registration with Warehousing and Development Regulatory Authority (WDRA), across public and private sectors, as on 31 March 2019. The total capacity of these 1057 warehouses is 7.909 million MT. This is quite small as compared to the total organised warehousing capacity in India, standing at 162.71 million MT in 2018-19.[19] Not all warehouses need to be registered with WDRA, but only those intending to issue negotiable warehouse receipts need to register.[20] Out of the total 1057 warehouses registered with WDRA, around 285 are accredited with commodity derivatives exchanges as delivery centres for agricultural commodities. The scope of WDRA registration is limited to agricultural and horticultural commodities at present. The total capacity of the exchange accredited warehouses is 0.957 million MT, with around 40% capacity utilisation rate. So roughly 27% of WDRA warehouses are exchange accredited with 12.1% of WDRA accredited capacity being potentially available for hedging-related deliveries. 99.2% of the electronic negotiable warehouse receipts (e-NWRs) issued (i.e. 76721 e-NWRs) are for exchange-based deliveries only, with limited alternate uses. This proves the power of derivative trading to galvanise reforms in the real sector, contrary to the belief of the Parliamentary committee that derivatives shall be introduced after real sectors mature with infrastructure.

One of the major reasons which kept real hedgers away from the market is the imposition of stock limits on agri/essential commodities under the Essential Commodities Act, 1955 which, when imposed, warrant immediate selling of stock held beyond the specified limit in the open market. The concept of stock limits is antithetical to long-term contractual commitments as buyers and sellers now cannot take or give delivery beyond the said limits, making participants defaulters at exchanges, liable for penalty. This limited hedger participation in the market and disproportionately affected agri derivatives. Only on 16 December 2019, stocks earmarked for delivery on exchanges got exempted from stock limits. However, it is still an executive order which can be withdrawn at any time and is not coded into the EC Act, to impart sufficient confidence to hedgers.[21]

Unlike in China, the major public sector commodity players like FCI or NAFED are absent from the Indian derivative market, even though they are entrusted with the function of price stabilisation. Government intervenes in the spot market through procurement operations at minimum support prices (MSP) by procurement agencies, who also share the mandate to provide stocks for public distribution, whether from MSP stocks or from open market procurement. In the process, these agencies are exposed to commodity price risk. Yet, there is no policy prescribed for mandatorily hedging these price risks, though, there is no legal restriction on their participation. Hedging is not a consistently adopted operation for commodity players in the public sector. Capacity constraints could be a reason, and without a policy push, it is difficult to see how their participation can improve. There are various ways in which Government entities can participate in the derivative market:

1. Doing part of their procurement operations by buying futures (say 25% of PDS requirements); or by writing put options contracts for buying at Minimum Support Price.
2. Intervening in the derivatives market to guide the market prices to the desired range (say MSP) just as central banks across the globe guide the exchange rate through interventions in the forward/swap segment.
3. Offloading or liquidating their procured stock, beyond buffer/reserve stocks, by selling futures or by writing call options to reduce losses from open market sale; such participation could enhance liquidity in far month contracts, while ensuring supply at consistent intervals, thereby reducing volatility. [In writing call options, the govt. agency receives some premium income, but exposes it to perceived losses as it may be forced to sell at a price lower than the ruling market price though it may be greater than procurement prices.]
4. Subsidising premium payments of farmers for put option purchases, through a direct benefit transfer, to give more flexibility to the farmer

to lock in at his desired level of prices rather than at MSP, while saving the government from actually doing the procurement or from maintaining extra warehouses; since premium payments are a fraction of the actual value of the commodity, it means government can expand the scope of price support to more farmers with the same expenditure. Alternatively, Government could limit its spot MSP operations to the small and marginal farmers while pushing the big farmers to hedging on the derivatives platform.

5 Offering interest subvention scheme for farmers, wherein banks are mandated to offer lower interest rates, subject to proof of hedging on the market: Hedging by farmers indeed protects the banks and it acts like an insurance for the loans they offer, affording them an option to reduce the interest chargeable on such loans without being dependent on the government for a subsidy. This could enhance liquidity in the far month contracts also.

Thus, if government is keen to control speculation, ideally, it should ask its procurement agencies to also participate in the derivative exchanges.

The Derivative to Cash Segment Ratio

Concerns are often expressed about the huge derivative turnover in India as compared to the cash/spot segment. As may be seen from Table 4.5, India clearly stands as an outlier when compared to other countries. However, there is no theoretical estimate on the most appropriate ratio of derivatives to spot.

In the commodity segment, generally, it is argued that if the derivative turnover is greater than the production or deliverable supply of the underlying commodity, then it is speculative in nature. However, this is like comparing the turnover in equity derivatives with total issued capital of the listed companies. The correct comparison could be to the quantum of domestic spot trade in these commodities as shown in Table 4.5. However, the exact quantum of domestic spot trade in commodities is not known in India.[22] For want of such information in the commodity space, one could make use of the concept of velocity of money, which essentially means number of times a unit of currency changes hands. Assuming that most of the commodity transactions could be with currency in hand or debit/credit card or cheque-based transactions, income velocity based on narrow money (which came in the range of 5–6 during FY 2011 to FY 2021) or currency with public (which ranged around 9–11)[23] should give us an indication of the potential turnover one could suitably have in the derivative segment, if only hedging-based transactions were to happen. The ratio of volume of trade (in metric tonnes) to production in respect of select agri commodities traded at NCDEX (Table 4.6) shows that only three commodities breached the value of 11.

Table 4.5 Equity derivative to spot ratios: a global comparison

Trading turnover in the calendar year 2020 in US $ million

Exchange	*Equity spot*	*Single stock options*	*Single stock futures*	*Stock index options*	*Stock index futures*	*Futures / equity spot ratio*	*Stock derivatives to equity spot ratio*
B3 – Brasil Bolsa Balcão Brazil	1390388	699884	1693	403216	12992454	**9.35**	**10.14**
NYSE/NASDQ/ICE futures/CME, USA	51100933	362895		31234752	136134984	**2.66**	**3.28**
Australian Securities Exchange	1305319	124084	3360	380621	2100243	**1.61**	**2.00**
Hong Kong Exchanges and Clearing	3145219	551546	6295	2425829	10004539	**3.18**	**4.13**
Japan Exchange Group Inc.	6337933				17136463	**2.70**	**2.70**
Korea Exchange	5221924		732324	50044301	6822667	**1.45**	**11.03**
National Stock Exchange of India Limited	1843440	2719053	2270043	61001669	1162849	**1.86**	**36.43**
Shanghai Stock Exchange/Shenzen Exchange/China Financial Futures Exchange	31580656			20921	13624884	**0.43**	**0.43**
Taiwan Stock Exchange/Taiwan Futures Exchange	1612257	840	242706	4317894	5300665	**3.44**	**6.12**
Borsa Istanbul, Turkey	871542	482	104381	640	177634	**0.32**	**0.32**
Deutsche Boerse AG, Germany	2211992	929810	368916	16702642	28439249	**13.02**	**20.99**
Euronext	2677807	289668	118048	1276447	3302778	**1.28**	**1.86**
Johannesburg Stock Exchange, South Africa	371157	7449	10800	40630	315585	**0.88**	**1.01**
World	140345236	15834977	5146168	170347276	244939027	**1.78**	**3.11**

Source: calculated using World Federation of Exchanges December 2020 Statistics

Notes: Related group entities are taken together since sometimes spot trading and derivatives trading happen on different platforms of the same exchange group; the turnover is represented through number of contracts traded

Table 4.6 Ratio of volume of trading in select agri commodities to annual production: 2010-2021

Ratio of volume of trading in agri commodities at NCDEX to its annual production over the years (in metric tonnes)

Commodity name	*2010-11*	*2011-12*	*2012-13*	*2013-14*	*2014-15*	*2015-16*	*2016-17*	*2017-18*	*2018-19*	*2019-20*	*2020-21*	*Average*
Barley	0.588	0.466	2.231	1.027	0.542	1.099	0.316	0.116	0.207	0.062	0.018	0.61
Castor seed	0.722	0.769	12.400	23.453	20.547	12.900	2.349	5.860	11.686	6.001	1.062	**8.89**
Chana	5.690	11.036	4.247	4.448	4.444	5.010	0.251	1.060	1.330	0.992	0.668	3.56
Chilli	0.871	0.971	1.445	0.910	0.036	0.025	0.000					0.61
Coriander	3.149	8.397	19.657	25.310	14.138	9.809	2.146	3.583	5.284	2.905	0.425	**8.62**
Cotton 29 mm				0.000	0.002	0.030	0.003					0.01
Cotton seed oil cake	2.624	2.727	5.333	3.606	1.807	2.426	1.693	1.667	2.432	1.790	1.149	2.48
Guar gum	12.599	10.185		0.731	2.403	5.720	10.676	15.707	15.668	11.775	7.902	**9.34**
Guar seed	52.502	31.869		1.086	3.755	10.908	13.705	20.557	20.412	11.565	3.943	**17.03**
Gur	0.669	0.376	0.451	0.376	0.158							0.41
Jeera	10.534	8.079	11.527	5.050	6.230	6.709	5.576	3.417	1.351	0.666	0.267	**5.40**
Kapas	0.182	0.267	0.435	0.407	0.273	0.354	0.302	0.216	0.153	0.069	0.011	0.24
Maize	0.069	0.087	0.351	0.195	0.089	0.045	0.057	0.009	0.007	0.002	0.001	0.08
Pepper	83.271	54.702	12.170	0.447				0.073	0.000	0.000	0.000	**18.83**
Potato	0.191	0.133	0.012	0.002								0.08
Mustard seed	3.852	7.635	5.568	3.044	2.353	3.657	2.346	1.305	1.059	0.729	0.767	2.94
Rubber	0.000	0.001	0.000									0.00
Refined soy oil	27.600	33.428	39.395	24.831	18.363	24.074	11.974	7.826	3.995	4.936	5.134	**18.32**
Soybean	3.589	4.034	4.228	4.117	2.570	3.354	1.673	2.155	1.315	1.415	0.937	2.67
Sugar	0.077	0.217	0.259	0.174	0.101	0.283	0.112	0.000	0.000	0.000	0.000	0.11
Turmeric	2.136	1.968	6.290	4.513	4.244	5.027	1.811	1.294	1.401	1.101	0.619	2.76
Wheat	0.031	0.024	0.040	0.011	0.008	0.009	0.011	0.007	0.002	0.002	0.000	0.01
Total	1.166	1.289	1.139	0.901	0.641	0.751	0.408	0.396	0.414	0.280	0.205	**0.69**

Note: The above list excludes illiquid agricultural commodities; Blank space indicates no trading in those years;
Source: NCDEX

Another complication in the system is that liquidity is extremely concentrated in the near month contracts. Even if one wants to enter into a contract for one year, it may not be possible for a person to get into such a contract as there is no counterparty willing to enter into such a contract in the market. Unless long-term players like FCI or NAFED enter the market, it is difficult to gain liquidity in the far month contracts. For an inventory manager keeping a commodity in the warehouse for a year, to remain protected, he needs to buy a futures contract every month and roll it over for the required period. This cash/future arbitrage involves one spot trade and 24 futures trades (12 months – sell/buy for each month). This essentially means a 1:24 turnover ratio. This could be the upper tolerance limit in this regard and no commodity has breached this level in the agri segment in India.

Extent of Physical Delivery

Extent of physical delivery is the most commonly perceived indicator for assessing speculation in the derivative markets. However, physical delivery is not the prime objective of derivative trading but only a requirement to keep the markets rooted to the spot market so that if futures price gets unduly rigged up, participants from spot market could threaten to enter and saddle them with deliveries. Thus, futures prices would converge with spot prices. 100% delivery is possible only in case of non-transferable forwards (which are customised OTC products) but not in futures which are standardised products. Futures markets exist mainly for financial hedge.[24] The seller may not have the commodity of the same standard to meet the delivery requirements of exchanges. However, since all grades and all varieties of the same commodity move more or less in tandem, financial hedging is possible through futures contracts and it is easier this way. Further, there could be an issue of crop failure after entering into the contract. The requirements of hedgers are also different (time period of exposure, underlying quality, location of produce etc.), while futures and options are standardised in respect of basic quality, specified delivery centres, expiry date etc. Exchange delivery (which involves assaying cost, transportation and warehousing cost) is costlier than the alternative of doing a financial hedge and then doing delivery in spot markets. In all such circumstances, financial hedge is a better option for such hedgers.

A table containing the ratio of volume of trading to total production (Table 4.6) in major commodities traded at NCDEX and their delivery as a percentage of the volume traded (Table 4.7) as well as total production in the country (Table 4.8) is given below. Of the 22 major contracts examined, the ratio of volume traded to total production is greater than 1 in around 12 cases (essentially implying volume traded is a multiple of production), which generally confirms the liquidity of the contracts. Raipuria Committee (GoI, 2001) had specified a target of 10 times the production. It can be seen that turnover as percentage of production is above 10 times only in select

Table 4.7 Delivery of commodities as a percentage of its volume of trading at NCDEX: 2010-2021

Delivery as a % of volume of trading in agri commodities at NCDEX over the years (in metric tonnes)

Commodity name	*2010-11*	*2011-12*	*2012-13*	*2013-14*	*2014-15*	*2015-16*	*2016-17*	*2017-18*	*2018-19*	*2019-20*	*2020-21*	*Average delivery %*
Barley	1.055	1.008	1.789	2.197	1.951	2.319	3.414	3.014	3.368	10.077	21.006	**4.65**
Castor seed	0.247	1.255	0.471	0.427	1.354	1.048	0.376	1.601	0.674	1.444	1.830	0.98
Chana	0.256	0.151	0.264	0.236	0.550	0.694	0.150	0.083	0.887	0.815	0.654	0.43
Chilli	0.705	0.890	0.739	0.770	0.971	5.904	0.000					1.43
Coriander	0.471	1.139	0.280	0.236	0.122	0.962	1.567	1.436	0.971	1.094	2.238	0.96
Cotton 29 mm					2.359	3.312	22.527					**9.40**
Cotton seed oil cake	0.277	0.410	0.545	0.568	0.568	0.620	0.954	0.922	0.577	0.505	0.618	0.60
Guar gum	0.221	0.318		0.316	0.376	0.272	0.374	0.294	0.334	0.304	0.199	0.30
Guar seed	0.067	0.146		0.162	0.161	0.088	0.133	0.181	0.193	0.304	0.859	0.23
Gur	0.000	0.000	0.000	0.000	0.000							0.00
Jeera	0.329	0.403	0.376	0.325	0.247	0.443	0.204	1.460	1.403	1.110	1.471	0.71
Kapas	0.000	0.000	0.000	0.000	0.000	0.000	0.000	0.000	0.000	0.000	0.000	0.00
Maize	0.780	1.409	0.645	0.608	2.666	4.735	1.831	5.873	6.895	28.977	24.800	**7.20**
Pepper	0.306	0.582	1.046	0.351				1.347	0.000	0.000	0.000	0.45
Potato	0.139	0.579	0.476	0.010								0.30
Mustard seed	0.618	0.530	0.449	0.473	0.411	0.413	0.305	0.466	0.898	0.734	0.857	0.56
Rubber	22.727	4.678	50.649									**26.02**
Refined soy oil	0.000	0.000	0.000	0.000	0.012	0.016	0.000	0.000	0.000	0.000	0.000	0.00
Soybean	0.041	0.149	0.189	0.140	0.286	0.148	0.573	0.723	0.760	0.404	0.875	0.39
Sugar	0.404	1.027	1.685	1.468	2.260	1.038	1.334	3.429	0.000	0.000	0.000	1.15
Turmeric	0.591	0.518	0.173	0.251	0.100	0.338	0.683	0.755	0.706	0.862	0.050	0.46
Wheat	0.862	2.362	0.752	2.729	1.997	8.081	3.728	5.088	6.665	27.163	0.000	**5.40**
Total	0.178	0.256	0.324	0.317	0.582	0.505	0.434	0.552	0.580	0.662	0.675	0.46

Note: The above list excludes illiquid agricultural commodities; Blank space indicates no trading in those years;
Source: NCDEX

Table 4.8 Delivery of commcdities as a percentage of production in the country: 2010-2021

Delivery as a percentage of productioa in agri commodities traded at NCDEX over the years (in metric tonnes)

Commodity name	*2010-11*	*2011-12*	*2012-13*	*2013-14*	*2014-15*	*2015-16*	*2016-17*	*2017-18*	*2018-19*	*2019-20*	*2020-21*	*Average delivery*
Barley	0.620	0.470	3.990	2.256	1.057	2.548	1.079	0.349	0.698	0.620	0.374	1.28
Castor seed	0.179	0.965	5.839	10.021	27.826	13.523	0.882	9.383	7.872	8.667	1.944	7.92
Chana	1.457	1.661	1.122	1.049	2.445	3.475	0.038	0.088	1.180	0.808	0.437	1.25
Chilli	0.614	0.865	1.068	0.700	0.035	0.149	0.000					0.49
Coriander	1.482	9.562	5.510	5.981	1.730	9.431	3.362	5.147	5.130	3.178	0.951	4.68
Cotton 29 mm					0.004	0.098	0.078					0.06
Cotton seed oil cake	0.728	1.117	2.906	2.049	1.026	1.503	1.615	1.537	1.404	0.905	0.710	1.41
Guar gum	2.782	3.234		0.231	0.903	1.553	3.992	4.614	5.237	3.580	1.572	2.77
Guar seed	3.522	4.663		0.176	0.603	0.962	1.828	3.723	3.941	3.512	3.389	2.63
Gur	0.000	0.000	0.000	0.000	0.000							0.00
Jeera	3.470	3.258	4.331	1.640	1.540	2.969	1.139	4.989	1.896	0.739	0.392	2.40
Kapas	0.000	0.000	0.000	0.000	0.000	0.000	0.000	0.000	0.000	0.000	0.000	0.00
Maize	0.054	0.123	0.227	0.119	0.237	0.213	0.105	0.051	0.048	0.069	0.014	0.11
Pepper	25.440	31.809	12.725	0.157				0.098	0.000	0.000	0.000	8.78
Potato	0.027	0.077	0.006	0.000								0.03
Mustard seed	2.382	4.045	2.500	1.439	0.967	1.510	0.716	0.609	0.951	0.535	0.657	1.48
Rubber	0.001	0.004	0.009									0.00
Refined soy oil	0.000	0.000	0.000	0.000	0.213	0.374	0.000	0.000	0.000	0.000	0.000	0.05
Soybean	0.147	0.601	0.800	0.575	0.735	0.498	0.959	1.558	1.000	0.572	0.820	0.75
Sugar	0.031	0.223	0.437	0.256	0.228	0.294	0.150	0.001	0.000	0.000	0.000	0.15
Turmeric	1.263	1.019	1.089	1.131	0.424	1.701	1.237	0.977	0.989	0.949	0.031	0.98
Wheat	0.026	0.056	0.030	0.030	0.015	0.069	0.039	0.036	0.011	0.046	0.000	0.03
Total	0.208	0.331	0.369	0.286	0.373	0.379	0.177	0.219	0.240	0.185	0.138	0.26

Note: The above list excludes illiquid agricultural commodities; Blank space indicates no trading in those years.
Source: NCDEX

agri commodities like guar seed, pepper and soy oil. On an average, volume traded is only 0.69% of the production and the ratio has been declining over the years.

In certain commodities like pepper (8.78%), castor seed (7.92%), coriander (4.68%), guar gum (2.77%), guar seed (2.63%) and jeera (2.40%), a reasonably good percentage of production, on an average, gets delivered through NCDEX alone. All highly liquid contracts like those for chana, castor seed, cotton cake, guar seed, refined soy oil, soyabean etc. record less than 1% of turnover as delivery. Delivery percentage is higher in illiquid contracts like wheat, rubber etc. Contracts which are dying down generally saw greater quantum getting settled with physical delivery (e.g. wheat and barley).

The actual delivery turns out to be low in contracts wherein either seller is given an option to deliver (e.g. soyabean) or in those contracts where both buyer and seller need to express intention for delivery.[25] While soyabean had sellers' option delivery logic, kapas, guar, net imported commodities like refined soy oil and crude palm oil (CPO) were intention matching contracts, resulting in fewer deliveries. It could also be the case that exchanges designed the contracts in such fashion considering the delivery challenges for them. In any case, except for kapas and CPO, SEBI has advised compulsory physical settlement for all agri contracts with effect from 1 April 2019. The deliveries as percentage of volume traded increased marginally from 0.58% in 2018-19 to 0.68% in 2020-21 consequent to this. However, deliveries as percentage of production had been steadily declining as the quantum of production had been increasing while agri volumes have been crashing steadily.

A high delivery rate is by no means an indicator of a successful contract. For instance, high delivery could result from the following factors:

a. Large one-sided price moves, with futures prices running way ahead of/below spot prices, could result in excessive delivery as squaring off could be impossible for many participants. In such instances, players will deliver on the exchanges even if it is a costly mode of delivery. Such one-sided steady price movements could happen during periods of extreme shortage, or during an abundant liquidity situation when surplus from old crop is followed by huge supplies in the new crop.
b. When participants feel that circumstances demand a counterparty guaranteed trade, exchanges become a preferable mode of delivery.
c. In certain cases, excess deliveries could also be a consequence of an attempted squeeze by one or more players in the spot segment. This could happen in relatively smaller crops with limited geographic spread as with pepper, where a few buyers have access to funds to buy a significant portion of the crop. At times, regulatory orders may force entities to close out their positions. For instance, castor contracts in 2014-15 were suspended on account of manipulation by a few connected major

players in spot market who also played in the futures. Closure of these contracts has resulted in around 28% of the production of that year getting delivered on the exchange (Table 4.8).

d. At times, delivery may increase due to regulatory arbitrage between spot and derivatives segments. In case of pepper, once a heavily traded commodity, which involves around 25-30% of production getting delivered through the exchange (Table 4.8), the contract specification at NCDEX, where it was traded, did not specify the permissible level/absence of mineral oil[26] and hence, traders preferred to deliver it through the exchange. In July 2013, the contracts were suspended, and the new contracts re-launched later in 2017 with SEBI's permission to make it mandatory to have compliance with FSSAI standards. However, liquidity could not be regained.

In short, the amount of settlement in terms of actual physical delivery is not the benchmark to judge the futures markets.

Conclusion

The above discussion shows that the development of the commodity market was hindered by concerns of low delivery and speculation which led to frequent interventions like suspension of contracts or imposition of stock limits. This led to a structural shift in the market in favour of non-agri commodities and processed agri products. As regards the perception issues outlined in the introduction paragraph, we have seen from the discussion above that most contracts traded in India have either very low liquidity or bare minimum turnover as compared to production. Physical delivery in contracts should not be considered as a firm indicator of a successful contract as it is required mostly in illiquid contracts or cornered contracts. What is important is not delivery per se, but "threat of delivery" (wherein higher futures prices could induce sellers to come and deliver on an exchange platform). Judging a market based on the extent of deliveries leaves us, thus, in a low-level equilibrium trap. For those who insist on getting the commodity, SEBI may need to re-launch the 100% delivery-based non-transferable specific delivery contracts on the exchange platform.

The thinking that commodities with frequent government interventions in spot markets should not be selected[27] for launching derivatives trading has no place as long as the government protection or MSP coverage remains limited to select localities and to a marginal set of producers. Derivative contracts are needed in case of commodities which witness high fluctuations in prices due to any of the factors such as shortage/surplus of production, crop failure, variation in rainfall, sudden import/export flux etc., including any government intervention. They are needed in case of commodities which are consumed in a substantial way so that trading interest remains firm and is able to attract many buyers and sellers. This is needed for commodities which witness "cobweb cycles" in their production and prices (wherein, high prices in one year induce farmers to produce more in the next year but only to see a fall in prices that year due to supply glut in the market. This leads to production shortage and high prices next year unless enough stock has been stored and timely supplied in the market next year by the government. The cycle of high/low production and low/high prices continues and may either explode beyond control or dissipate over time if farmers learn to react using other channels such as by participating in futures markets). Cobweb cycles occur most commonly in agriculture, because the decision of what to produce in the coming year is often based on the prices of the previous year, rather than the expected price during harvest time. Derivatives market is the only way to get out of this cobweb cycle, enabling the farmer to lock in his price at the sowing time itself, provided the farmers are able to change crops based on price signals at sowing time. As regards the perception that small farmers do not benefit from the derivative markets, they can collectively participate as Farmer Producer Organisations (FPOs) which increases their negotiating powers and confidence. Over 100 FPOs, representing 2.3 lakh farmers, have already participated at NCDEX.

It may be an inadvertent error to wait for hedgers to come in first and then start the trading. Speculation (buying without full funds or selling without stocks) also plays a very useful function in the market and makes hedging possible by providing much needed breadth and liquidity to the contracts. In the absence of such speculation no hedging would be possible, and in the absence of hedging, normal marketing would become too risky – in fact speculative. As mentioned by the Khusro Committee, in the absence of futures trading, speculation will become a very large part of the ready/spot activity, even of genuine traders and manufacturers;[28] and the consumer price will be higher and the producer price will be lower, both to the detriment of consumers and producers. In the absence of a futures market, there can be a serious and threatening form of hoarding of physical commodities on rising commodity prices. Once the option of locking-in one's prices comes in, the tendencies to unnecessarily hoard the commodities ought to come down. Further, if stocks are tightly held and prices are unduly rigged up, only the bear speculator on the futures market can bring about a change in the psychology of expectations.

Speculation is not something which happens only on the exchange platform. Those who do not lock-in their prices at the time of taking exposure to a commodity could be viewed as taking a speculative position on the future price movements. Some of these large players who have held excessive stocks (over and above the reserve stocks) without hedging whether through exchanges or directly from the physical market through some OTC contract have run into heavy losses[29] or even gone bankrupt. This should also be viewed as an unproductive use of capital for speculative purposes, especially when these entities are using public capital (including equity and bank debt). Going forward, participation by Government agencies and other financial institutions could be encouraged in India to enhance liquidity so that tendencies for overseas hedging are contained. The market could be made more meaningful for hedgers by suitably designing contracts and exempting exchange-based traders and clients from stock limits. A suitably designed spot trading platform which facilitates trading in e-NWR could integrate the spot and derivatives under a same regulator, circumventing the challenges posed by Constitutional provisions and state's APMC laws.

For those firms which keep substantial inventory of commodities, hedging should be like a systematic investment plan (SIP) in a mutual fund. They should not try to time the market for entering into a contract, but should systematically lock into the hedge contract in a rule-bound manner, within say seven days of taking exposure to the commodity.[30] Commodity price risk can thus be covered with better risk management, governance, disclosure and regulatory mandates. Further, SEBI also needs to quantify the speculative interest in the market by looking at the order level data, time period of holding on to a position and linking the above to the return enjoyed by each of such players[31] and his role in trend setting and trend reversals etc. Essentially, a position profiling of the clients participating in the market is essential in today's context before judging them as playing a stabilising or the destabilising role in the market. As mentioned in the Habibulla Committee Report (Habibullah, 2003), *it is manipulation, and not speculation, which is detrimental to the functioning of the market.*

Notes

1 In respect of standardised contracts like futures or options, we are assuming that futures price and spot prices do converge. The difference between the two – basis risk – may exist if the available standardised futures contract does not exactly match the produced variety.
2 Options facilitate its buyer to gain from upside price movements, while protecting from the downside risk.
3 Para 250–252 of the report.
4 Source: Comments of L R Tairsee while processing the amendments to the Bombay Prevention of Gambling Act in 1936.
5 Source: Observation of M W R G Smith, Police commissioner who was specially invited to attend the legislative assembly debate on 19 February 1936.
6 Source: Discussion on Forward Contracts (Regulation) Bill on 2 December 1952, accessed from Parliamentary Debates Part Vol II 24 Nov–22 Dec 1952, page720.
7 Comment by V. P Nayar (Communist – Travancore – Cochin) as quoted in *Forward Contracts Bill Under Fire: Parliament Listens to Very Widely Divergent Views,* Times of India, 22 November 1952, pg. 5
8 Source: Lok Sabha Debate on 11 August 1952 during the discussion of FCRA Bill: Parliamentary Debates Vol IV, Part II, 30 July to 12 August, p: 6133-34
9 Source: Statement of Objects and Reasons of FCRA Bill 1952
10 Source: Comment of the Expert Committee (Shroff Committee)
11 W.e.f. September 2015, FCRA was repealed and the regulatory functions of FMC were handed over to SEBI.

12 Which essentially made a contract with netting or cash settlements or which dispensed with physical delivery by any mode as a forward/derivative contract.
13 Source: compiled from the annual data of World Federation of Exchanges.
14 Source: *What to expect from China's futures market opening up*, Bloomberg, 4 July 2018; *China is working to change global commodities trading – to its own benefit*, CNBC 6 June 2018.
15 When the ban was put in place, price of chana was even below MSP. As of April 2022, prices still hover around MSP with a further increase of around Rs. 100-–150. Similarly, mustard prices remained at the elevated level for another two more months since the ban.
16 The Securities Contracts Regulation Act 1956 uses the word "undesirable speculation" without attempting to define it.
17 Hence, if the investor is in the 30% income slab category, he pays tax at the rate of 30% as against say 10% (or 15%) long-term (or short term) capital gains as applicable for delivery-based share trading.
18 Source: SEBI Handbook of Statistics and Bulletin April 2021.
19 Source: as per the WDRA Annual Report 2018-19, across public and private sectors, including cooperatives. The warehouses of central agencies like FCI, HAFED, NAFED etc. are still not WDRA accredited warehouses.
20 The structuring is similar to the FCRA system which allowed a host of exchanges to exist for trading in free commodities whereas exchanges need to be recognized and regulated by FMC only if they intend to trade in select notified commodities.
21 In September 2020, many commodities were taken out of the list of essential commodities and the trigger point for imposition of stock limits in terms of price rise was codified into the Act. However, the Act was part of the farm laws amendments, which triggered the farmers' protest and was withdrawn w.e.f. 29 November 2021.
22 A potential source of information for taxable commodities could be the GSTN database. However, this is not available in the public domain.
23 Source: RBI Handbook of Statistics Table No. 229
24 Implies hedging without giving/taking physical delivery, but by paying the difference between contracted price and current ruling price for the offset contract; The gain in futures market is equivalent to the loss in spot market, and vice versa (without adjusting for transaction charges). This method of settlement can avoid cornering /squeezes etc.
25 Even though regulators had permitted futures only as physically settled contracts, the following three types of delivery logics were adopted depending on how outstanding open positions at the expiry of the contract were to be settled: (a) compulsorily by physical delivery (known as Compulsory Delivery); (b) by physical delivery at the option of the seller, else by cash settlement (called as Sellers Option), e.g. Kapas and soyabean; (c) by physical delivery only if both buyer and seller agree to settle by delivery, else the contract is cash settled (Both Option / Intention Matching), e.g. non-agri commodities.
26 Sources: *FSSAI claims 65% of NCDEX black pepper tested is adulterated* Economic Times, 4 July 2013; *NCDEX seek nod to clean adulterated pepper stock,* Business Standard, 20 August 2013; *NCDEX to reintroduce pepper futures trade* Financial Express, 22 July 2017
27 In fact, Raipuria committee of 2001 (GoI, 2001) had recommended to keep only a small negative list of commodities while opening the rest of the commodities for derivatives trading.
28 Page 14 of (GoI, 1980).
29 For instance, FCI's annual food subsidy runs to around Rs. 1.2 trillion. Further, as per the Financial Stability Report of RBI (June 2019), a one standard

deviation (SD) shock would increase NPAs in the mining sector by 26%, food processing by 24%, petroleum by 34%, metals by 46%, jewellery by 27% and power by 37%. A 2 SD shock to the metal segment will lead to a decline of 23 basis points (bps) in system-level capital to risk-weighted assets ratio (CRAR) of banks, whereas power sector exposure will lead to around 21 bps decline in system-level CRAR under a similar shock. Further, such a shock to the metals and power sectors would make one scheduled commercial bank (SCB) (apart from the two SCBs whose CRAR is already below 9 per cent without any shock) going below the mandated 9 per cent CRAR. As noted by Dantwala committee (1967), only by entering into a hedge contract can a person free himself of the speculative incidence in his ready business dealings. In a way hedging is counter-speculation.

30 This would also help such firms from later facing vigilance enquiries on why they entered into a contract at a particular price.

31 Whether the return is for his risk-bearing role (for buying when the prices were crashing to selling when the prices are high) as propounded by Keynes' normal backwardation theory (Keynes J. M., 1930), or for his forecasting ability to correctly predict the changes in prices as propounded by Hicks-Houthakker forecasting theory [(Hicks, 1946) (Houthakker, 1957)] or for his market maker function for providing liquidity in the market.

References

Abraham, R. M. (2020, March–June). Evolution of Regulatory Policy in Commodity Derivatives Markets in India. *Social Scientist*, *48*(3–6), 103–116.

GoI. (1919). *Report of the Indian Cotton Committee.* Calcutta: Superintendent of Government Printing, India.

GoI. (1967). *Report of the Forward Markets Review Committee (Chairman: M L Dantwala).* New Delhi: Directorate of Commercial Publicity, Ministry of Commerce, Government of India.

GoI. (1980). *Report of the Committee on Forward Markets (Chairman: A M Khusro).* New Delhi: Ministry of Civil Supplies, Government of India.

GoI. (1994). *Report of the Committee on Forward Markets (Chairman: K N Kabra).* New Delhi: Ministry of Civil Supplies, Government of India.

GoI. (2001). *Report of the Group on Forward and Futures Market.* Dr. Kalyan Raipuria (Chairman). New Delhi: Ministry of Agriculture, Government of India.

GoI. (2014). *Report of the Committee to Suggest Steps for Fulfilling the Objectives of Price-Discovery and Risk Management of Commodity Derivatives Market (Chairman: D S Kolamkar).* New Delhi: Department of Economic Affairs, Ministry of Finance, Government of India.

Habibullah, W. (2003). *Report of the Inter-Ministerial Task Force on Convergence of Securities and Commodity Derivative Markets.* New Delhi: Ministry of Consumer Affairs, Government of India.

Hicks, J. R. (1946). *Value and Capital.* Oxford: Clarendon Press.

Houthakker, H. S. (1957). Can Speculators Forecast Prices. *The Review of Economics and Statistics*, *39*(2), 143–151.

Kabra, K. N. (2007). Commodity Futures in India. *Economic and Political Weekly (Money, Banking and Finance)*, *42*(13), 1163–1170.

Keynes, J. M. (1930). *A Treatise on Money (Chapter XXIX).* London: Macmillan.

Parliament. (2006). *17th Report of the Standing Committee on Food, Consumer Affairs and Public Distribution on Forward Contracts (Regulation) Amendment Bill, 2006*. New Delhi: Lok Sabha Secretariat.

Pavaskar, M. (1985). *Saga of the Cotton Exchange*. Bombay: Bombay Popular Prakashan published for East India Cotton Association Ltd.

RBI. (2017). *Report of the Working Group to Review of the Guidelines for Hedging of Commodity Price Risk by Residents in Overseas Markets*. Mumbai: Reserve Bank of India.

Yang, D. L. (2004, April). Futures Markets in the People's Republic of China: Development and Prospective. *American Journal of Chinese Studies*, *11*(1), 25–35.

Yiping Huang, X. W. (2013). Financial Reform in China Progress and Challenges. In H. P. Yung Chul Park (Ed.), *How Finance Is Shaping the Economies of China, Japan, and Korea* (pp. 44–142). New York: Columbia University Press.

5 Rural Credit and Growth in Indian Agriculture[1]

Akanksha Pratik Sonker

Introduction

India embraced the macroeconomic stabilisation programme in the nineties that included a package of deflationary policies that limited the expansion of bank credit, curtailed government expenditure, laid emphasis on fiscal consolidation and restricted budget deficits as a proportion of the GDP (Patnaik, 2003). The paradigmatic shift involving the transformation of state intervention, limiting state support to agriculture and the curtailment of public expenditure, placed constraints on public policy. The fiscal conservatism stance of the government was further reinforced by the implementation of the Fiscal Responsibility and Budget Management Act (FRBM) in 2003-04 that legally bound the State to restrict spending to limit its fiscal deficit. This has resulted in a sharp decline in public expenditure accruing to agriculture and the rural areas in the form of phased removal of input subsidies, public investment on research and extension services, irrigation and drainage, rural infrastructure and rural employment programmes (Patnaik, 2003; Chandrasekhar, 2017).

Thus, the neo-liberal regime that incentivises private investment through tax concessions and abjures deficit-financed public expenditure (as it views this intervention as inflationary and potentially disruptive of markets) has weakened pro-active fiscal policy through the instruments of taxation and public expenditure (Chandrasekhar, 2009). Instead, the loss of tax and debt-financed public expenditure as a principal stimulus to growth was substituted by debt-financed private investment through the provision of credit. This was aided by the surge in commercial lending owing to the infusion of liquidity in the form of large capital inflows.

It is against this background that the policies initiated for agriculture need to be viewed. Agriculture remains one of the sectors that has lost its growth momentum in the post-reform period. Due to the adherence to fiscal conservatism, the government is reticent to undertake the necessary public investment in rural development and agriculture to restore its viability and enhance the productivity of Indian agriculture. Instead, to drive rural growth, the government decided to take recourse to the credit-led growth strategy through the expansion of rural credit.

DOI: 10.4324/9781003343998-5

Thus, it is in this regard that this chapter seeks to critically evaluate the strategy of credit-financed growth in the rural countryside and the agricultural sector by examining the data on commercial banks that are the major purveyors of agricultural credit. The second section examines the changing contours of the banking sector in the post-reform era with centrality to rural credit. The third section reviews the progress in rural banking over the three decades of neo-liberal reforms. The fourth section makes an assessment of the sectoral composition and growth of the credit disbursed by the commercial banks. The fifth section evaluates the trend, composition and the direction of flow of agricultural credit especially after the credit surge in 2003-04.The sixth section evaluates the role played by credit in serving the objectives of driving growth in the agricultural sector. The seventh section analyses the impact of credit on agricultural growth and its ramifications for the rural economy. The eighth section discusses the limitations of the strategy of growth envisioned by the credit-financed consumption and investment. The final section makes concluding remarks.

Developments in the Banking Sector in the Post-Reform Era

Notwithstanding the achievements of the "social-development banking" phase in expanding the outreach of institutional credit, redressing the inequities in its distribution, supporting inclusive growth and rural transformation, the neo-liberal reforms introduced in the nineties (based on the recommendations of the Narasimham Committee) changed the nature of rural banking in the country.

The neo-liberal policies sought a retreat of the State in credit provision as it saw its role as inimical to the growth of financial institutions and restrictive of their "functional autonomy". The reforms sought to impose homogeneous legislation and regulatory frameworks across countries in the form of prudential and supervisory norms on rural financial institutions that were by design established to serve objectives of socio-economic growth and cater to a specific targeted clientele of the weak and marginalised sections. As a result, these reforms led to a transformation in the character of these institutions that have metamorphosed into entities seeking commercial viability over their mandated goals of contributing to socio-economic growth and development.

The reforms sought to dismantle the directed credit programmes, deregulate interest rates, increase competitiveness in the banking sector by permitting the entry of private and corporate entities in the form of small finance banks, payment banks etc., broaden the permissible ambit of activities undertaken by the banks and implement homogeneous regulations like prudential norms involving income recognition, asset classification and provisioning.

Initially, the reforms also proved to be a major setback to the achievements of the social banking era and witnessed a decline in the number of small loan accounts, closure and merger of rural bank branches and a contraction of credit to the weaker and disadvantaged sections of the society and crucial sectors like agriculture. This severely curtailed the flow of institutional credit to the rural areas, led to widening regional and sectoral disparities in credit provision that accentuated income and wealth inequalities and saw the strengthening of the informal sector especially the moneylenders in the rural credit market (Ramchandran and Swaminathan, 2005; Shetty, 2005; Chavan and Ramakumar, 2007).

But the post-liberalisation phase has not been homogeneous. The period after 2004 which coincided with the enactment of the Fiscal Responsibility and Budget Management Act that curtailed the use of public expenditure as a stimulus saw credit as an instrument for stimulating growth in the rural economy. As a result, this period saw greater infusions of rural institutional credit, and renewed efforts were made at bringing the marginalised sections back into the ambit of the formal banking structure. This period sought the doubling of credit to agriculture (2004-05) and adopted "financial inclusion" as a policy directive in 2005. This was facilitated by the introduction of "no frills accounts" (Basic Savings Bank Deposit Accounts (BSBDA)) with a savings product, and facilities for overdraft and remittances. The period after 2004 also saw a shift away from the traditional brick and mortar banking structure to a greater reliance on alternate models like Banking Correspondents (BCs)/ Banking Facilitators (BFs), Self-Help Group-Bank Linkage programs (SHG/ BLP), micro-finance institutions etc. and entry of private and corporate entities through setting up of payments banks and small finance banks.

However, there was a paradigmatic shift in the approach towards financial inclusion from the one pursued during the social and developmental banking phase of 1969-90. While earlier, financial inclusion entailed "the elevation of the entitlements of previously disadvantaged groups to formal credit" at concessional rates despite weakening of conventional bank indicators (like low returns), today it is viewed as a "business opportunity" for banks to bring the unbanked population into their fold without compromising on commercial considerations dictated by the free market (Wiggins and Rajendran, 1987 as cited in Chavan, 2007).

Progress of Rural Banking

The population per branch, which is an important indicator of the spread and penetration of the banking sector, declined from 64,000 in 1969 to about 14,000 in 1991 owing to the phenomenal expansion of the banking network during the social banking phase. But this trend was reversed in the post-reform era owing to the rationalisation of bank branches in pursuit of commercial viability that resulted in the population per branch to increase to around 15,000 in 1996-97 and further to 16,000 by 2002-03. This was reversed with the implementation of the bank authorisation policy[2] in

2005 and the financial inclusion policy due to which the population per branch has declined consistently from 16,000 in 2006 to 8,943 in 2019-20. However, the corresponding figures for the rural population per branch (rural population per rural/semi-urban branch) are not very impressive. The rural population per branch increased steadily from 13,428 in 1990-91 to 17,901 in 2005-06, and although it declined thereafter to 9,763 in 2019-20, it was still higher than the corresponding figures for the urban/metropolitan areas that stood at 7,540 (Chart 5.1).

During the social banking phase, the network of rural branches had expanded from 1,443 in 1969 to 34,791 in 1990 accounting for 58.2% of the total bank branches. Chavan (2005) notes that between 1975 and 1990, the growth of rural bank branches (at an annual growth rate of 17.5%), widely outpaced the growth in the other centres. However, that rate turned negative over the nineties. The rural bank branches continued to increase slowly till 1995 which coincided with the last branch expansion programme (1990-95) of the RBI that was subsequently discontinued (Shetty, 2005). In addition to this, changes in the branch licensing policy permitted banks to relocate offices or convert them into satellite offices (Shetty, 2005). The large-scale rationalisation of bank branches

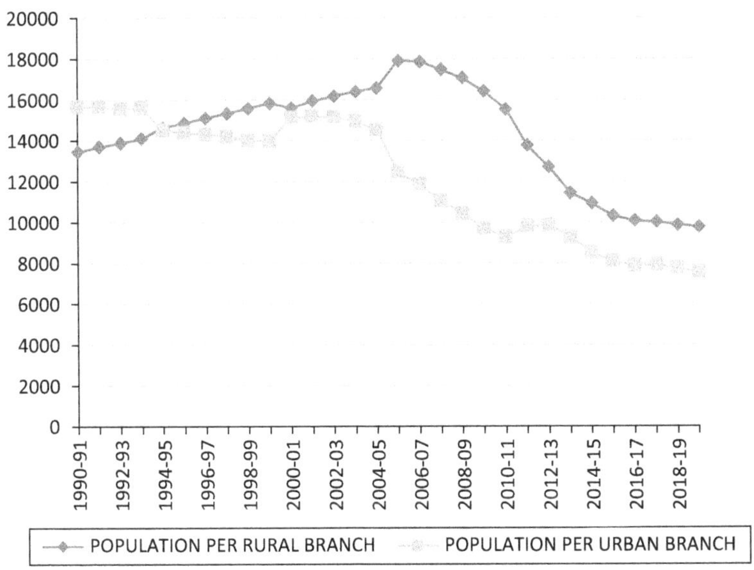

Chart 5.1 Population per Branch of Scheduled Commercial Banks Source: Estimated from various issues of Handbook of Statistics on the Indian Economy, RBI and Agricultural Statistics at a Glance, GOI. Note: The figures for rural (urban) population are arrived at by applying the corresponding proportion of rural (urban) population from the respective Census data as published in the Agricultural Statistics at a Glance.

through closure and mergers of unviable rural branches that followed led to a decline in the number of rural bank branches to 28,146 in 2006. This in turn adversely affected the rural credit delivery mechanism that was built and strengthened during the social banking phase and which was instrumental in reducing the role of the informal sector. After 2006, although the absolute number of rural bank branches began to increase again (owing to the branch authorisation policy and the adoption of financial inclusion policy) to reach a total of 52,358 in 2020, their share in total bank branches continued to decline to 34.9% in 2020 (Table 5.1). The reason for this decline is the reliance of commercial banks on other modes of credit delivery like Banking Correspondents instead of physical branches. However, because of inherent trust and viability issues[3], despite the massive recruitment of banking correspondents under the financial inclusion plans, the volume of transactions and the bank accounts opened by the Banking Correspondents remain grossly inadequate in terms of their number.

Rural Deposits

Despite the decline in rural branches, the share of rural deposit accounts in the total deposit accounts of the commercial banks has continued to hover around 30%. This occurred even when the share of deposits mobilised in the rural areas continued to decline from 15.5% in 1991 to 9.2% in 2011 (Table 5.1). The relatively stable share of the rural branches in the number of deposit accounts could be the result of the "no-frill" bank accounts opened as part of the financial inclusion drive (2005) and other policy directives that mandated that wage payments under NREGA and other government schemes, pension payments and cash transfers of subsidies should be routed through bank accounts. However, these initiatives failed to raise enough resources through these deposits as most of these accounts remained dormant. The Annual Report of RBI (2012) revealed that of the 103 million "no frills" accounts that were opened by March 2012, three-fourths were lying dormant. Between 2012 and 2020, the share of rural deposits both in terms of number of deposit accounts and amount outstanding has risen. While some of this rise can be attributed to the Pradhan Mantri Jan Dhan Yojana[4] (2014), the rest is an outcome of an influx due to demonetisation (2016).

Rural Credit

But the more disturbing trend relates to the distribution of credit to these areas. The share of rural borrowal accounts in total accounts of the commercial banks has fallen drastically from 53% in 1991 to 28.7% in 2018 before recovering marginally to 29.1% in 2020 (Table 5.1). The share of credit flowing to the rural sector has also dwindled from 24.4% in 1991 to only 9.1% in 2020 (Table 5.1). Thus, while the urban/metropolitan centres

Table 5.1 Progress in Rural Banking (No. of Accounts in Thousands, Amt. in Rs Billion)

Year	*No. of Branches*		*Credit*				*Deposits*				*Credit-Deposit Ratio*	
	Rural Branches	*As% of Total*	*No. of Rural Accounts*	*As % of Total*	*Rural*	*As % of Total*	*No. of Rural Accounts*	*As % of Total*	*Rural*	*As % of Total*	*Rural*	*All India*
1969	1,443	17.6			1.2	3.3			3.1	6.3	37.6	71.9
1975	7,112	35.5			6.1	6			11.7	8.5	51.9	73.5
1980	16,111	46.9			26.4	10.7			46.4	12.6	56.9	66.9
1985	29,408	54.6	16,233	48.3	69.8	14	57,514	26.6	104.1	13.4	63.9	61.9
1990	34,791	58.2	24,801	52.7	254.7	24.4	1,02,113	30.6	262.3	15.3	97.1	66
1995	33,004	52.9	29,407	50.6	335.3	15.9	1,09,944	28.2	518.2	13.7	64.7	59.8
2000	32,734	50.0	25,080	46.1	594.3	12.9	1,25,852	30.5	1205.4	14.7	49.3	56.7
2005	32,082	46.9	29,357	38.1	1604.8	13.9	1,41,908	30.4	2131.0	12.2	75.3	72.4
2008	30,762	40.5	33,546	31.4	3231.3	13.4	1,68,034	28.9	3034.2	9.3	106.5	59.5
2010	30,083	35.4	37,074	31.2	3851.5	11.5	2,24,155	30.5	4203.4	9.2	91.6	75.6
2015	45,157	35.7	52,777	36.6	6553.6	9.5	4,93,970	34.3	9156.8	10.3	71.6	78.4
2018	50,777	35.8	66,579	28.7	9028.8	9.1	6,42,225	33.6	12097.9	10.6	69.3	76.7
2020	52,358	34.9	79,366	29.1	9581.4	9.1	7,04,881	34.1	15054.5	10.9	63.6	76.5

Source: RBI, Basic Statistical Returns of Scheduled Commercial Banks in India and Handbook of Statistics on the Indian Economy (Various Issues)

corner about 80% of the credit, the rural areas receive less than a tenth of the total bank credit.

The rural-urban divide is more distinctly visible in the per capita credit accruing to the rural and the urban areas as shown in Chart 5.2. Chart 5.2 shows that there is a stark divergence in the per capita credit accruing to the urban/metropolitan centres and their rural countryside which is more pronounced after 2004-05.

Between 2004-05 and 2010-11, the credit per capita in the urban areas grew at CAGR of 20% per annum as opposed to only 14% per annum in the rural areas. This also suggests that the credit boom in 2003-04 disproportionately benefitted the urban areas. As a result, the ratio of credit per capita of the rural areas to that of the urban areas that stood at 21.2% in 1990-91 slumped to a nadir of 10.1% in 2010-11 and then stagnated at about 12.8% till 2019-20.

A similar trend was observed in the declining credit-deposit ratio. During the social-development banking phase, the RBI had mandated that banks must maintain the rural credit-deposit ratio at over 60%, in order to use these resources for rural development and to prevent credit migration to the urban/metropolitan centres. As a result, the rural credit-deposit ratio touched 97.1% in 1990. However, the dwindling of credit to the rural areas with the initiation of reforms led to a decline in this ratio to 63% in 1994 (Table 5.1). A brief recovery in 1995 owing to the initiation of the Special

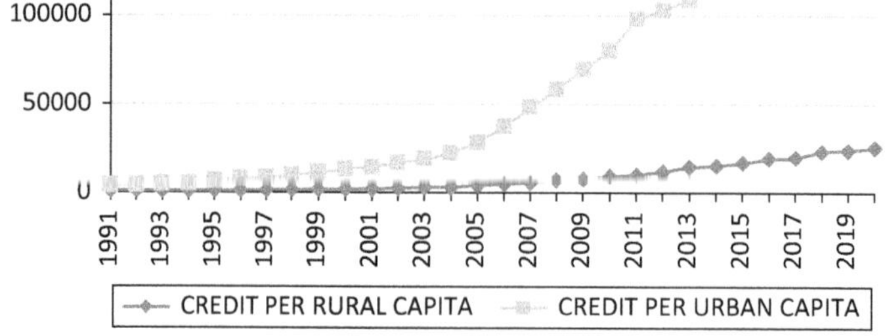

Chart 5.2 Credit per Capita Source: Estimated from various issues of Handbook of Statistics on the Indian Economy, RBI and Agricultural Statistics at a Glance, GOI. Note: Credit per rural capita refers to the credit disbursed through rural and semi-urban branches per rural population while the same for the urban areas is the credit disbursed by the urban and metropolitan per the urban population.

Agricultural Credit Program was followed by a continuous decline in the rural credit-deposit ratio to 49% in 2001. However, the credit-deposit ratio saw a marked improvement thereafter and peaked to 106.5% in 2008. This was largely owing to the impact of the Doubling of the Agricultural Credit Programme (2004), enhanced credit disbursement through Gram Swarozgar Yojana, the one-time settlement scheme (2004), interest subvention scheme (2006-07) and the Agricultural Debt Waiver and Debt Relief Scheme (ADWDR) (2008-09) that channelised credit to the rural areas. However, this euphoria was also short-lived as the period after 2010 saw a drastic decline in the credit-deposit ratio of the rural areas from 92% in 2010 to 63.6% in 2020 which was significantly lower than the credit-deposit ratio of the metropolitan centres (89.1%) and the national average of 76.5% (Table 5.1). The rise in the credit-deposit ratio in the metropolitan areas reflects a diversion of credit away from the rural areas to these centres as the credit advanced to these regions widely outpaced the deposits mobilised in these areas.

In sum, these trends reflect the retrogression in rural banking as the share of the rural areas in deposits and advances and bank branches of the commercial banks has declined substantially below the levels attained at the time of the commencement of the neo-liberal reforms. It indicates that the historical concentration of credit in the urban centres that was reversed during the social banking phase has only been perpetuated further over the three decades of the neo-liberal regime, which has effectively slowed the flow of resources to the rural countryside. It also points to the tendency that the commercial banks have used their rural branches for syphoning off resources from the rural countryside instead of channelising the same for promoting rural development and agricultural growth.

Composition of Bank Credit

The composition and distribution of bank credit has historically favoured the needs of the urban and metropolitan centres, but one of the key achievements of bank nationalisation and the social banking phase was to redirect credit to the erstwhile neglected sectors of the economy like agriculture and rural development, backward and under-developed regions and the vulnerable sections of the population.

However, as the country ushered in the nineties with the implementation of the New Economic Policy, the improvement of financial indicators of credit institutions and augmenting commercial viability took precedence over the attainment of socio-economic goals of equitable growth and development which altered the character and orientation of bank credit that has become more urban centric as represented in Chart 5.3.

The credit portfolio of the commercial banks was heavily dominated by loans to industry (43.3%) and trade (14%) which accounted for close

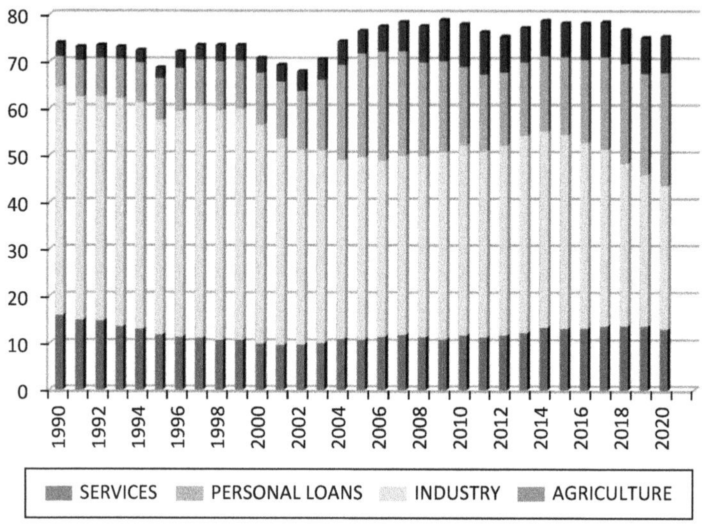

Chart 5.3 Sectoral Distribution of Bank Credit of Scheduled Commercial Banks
Source: RBI, Basic Statistical Returns of Scheduled Commercial Banks in India (Various Issues). Note: The figures do not sum up to 100% due to the exclusion of sectors like trade, finance, transport services and other sectors.

to 60% of the total credit advanced between 1991 and 2003 (Chart 5.3). Agriculture, on the other hand, saw its share in total credit decline from 15.1% in 1991 to 9.6% within a decade of "reforms". This was accompanied by a concomitant increase in the share of personal loans that grew upto 12.6% from 6.4% during the same period.

The period after 2004 is noteworthy in many ways. This period coincided with the intensification of fiscal conservatism post the adoption of the Fiscal Responsibility and Budget Management (FRBM) Act in 2003-04 that necessitated the dependence on credit rather than public expenditure as the principal instrument for spurring growth and development in the rural countryside. At the same time, this period was characterised by a credit boom due to the liquidity surge triggered in part by large capital inflows in the country. As a result, this phase saw renewed efforts to revive the rural economy by augmenting rural credit through the implementation of programmes like the Doubling of Agricultural Credit Programme (2004), revival of the rural credit cooperatives (2006), interest subvention scheme (2006-07), Agricultural Debt Waiver and Debt Relief Scheme (2008-09) and adoption of financial inclusion as a policy measure (2005). All these measures were aimed at shifting the sectoral composition of credit in favour of the rural countryside.

However, a cursory glance at the composition and the rate of growth of credit in various sectors belied such promises. The rapid expansion in credit during this phase was accompanied by a significant change in the sectoral composition of credit. One of the disturbing outcomes of the credit boom was the rise in the share of personal loans to about a quarter of the total loans during this period that came by displacing loans advanced to industry and agriculture (Chart 5.3). The share of industrial loans in total credit advances declined from 41% to 37% while that of agriculture stagnated at around 10–11% which indicates that the credit boom disproportionately favoured retail lending (category of personal loans advanced for purposes like consumer durables, housing, etc.) instead of the commodity producing sectors. Chart 5.4 shows that between 2003-04 and 2006-07, the aggregate credit of the commercial banks grew at an average annual rate of 26.8%, agricultural credit grew at 32%, industrial loans at 24.8% while retail (personal) loans grew at 40%. In fact, despite a fractional increase in the share of agricultural loans, their share remained subordinate to that of personal loans in the portfolios of the banks which not only reflects their misplaced priorities but also their bias towards their urban clientele. Another disquieting tendency witnessed during this period was the growing exposure of the commercial banks to the sensitive sectors (capital markets, real estate). The loans to the sensitive sectors as a proportion of total gross advances of the commercial banks that stood around 3.3% in 2003-04 shot upto 21% in 2007-08 and then moderated to about 17% in 2011-12 following the global financial crisis of 2008-09 (Appendix Chart 5(A)).

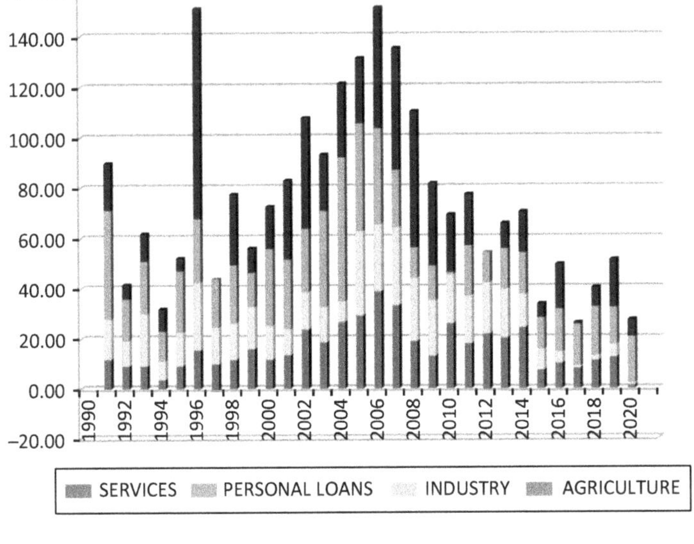

Chart 5.4 Growth in Credit by Commercial Banks in Principal Sectors Source: RBI, Basic Statistical Returns of Scheduled Commercial Banks in India (Various Issues).

The global financial crisis derailed this credit-led strategy of growth as the average annual rate of growth of credit slowed down substantially after 2008-09 from a peak of 31.4% in 2006-07 to a meagre 6.3% in 2019-20 (Chart 5.4). A part of the decline was also attributed to the banks being saddled by the rising non-performing assets[5] and the adverse impact of demonetisation[6]. But even this slowdown in credit growth conceals a disquieting tendency. This is because while the rate of growth of credit advances has turned negative for industry and decelerated sharply for agriculture, retail lending continues to consolidate both its growth and share in the loan portfolio[7] of banks and accounts for about a quarter of the total advances of the commercial banks in 2020 (Chandrasekhar and Ghosh, 2017). At the same time, the share of bank loans to the sensitive sectors also increased from about 17.4% in 2011-12 to 24.5% in 2020-21 (Appendix Chart 5(A)).

Another perplexing outcome of the interest rate de-regulation as part of financial liberalisation is that the interest rate structure had turned regressive for the rural sector. In 1990, over 85% of agricultural loans were disbursed at interest rates below 14% per annum but the situation was reversed drastically by 1995 when about 90% of agricultural credit was advanced at interest rates higher than 14% per annum. The interest rates continued to reign high for agriculture till the early 2000s when over 75% of the farm loans were charged an interest rate ranging between 12 and 17% per annum while retail loans were priced at much lower interest rates of 7% per annum. The rise in the cost of institutional credit adversely affected investment in agriculture by eroding net margins. This tendency was sought to be partially rectified by the introduction of the interest subvention scheme (2006-07) that provided short-term farm loans at an interest rate of 7% per annum, but this did not extend to the medium- or long-term loans.

Even the credit disbursed by the rural branches lacked a rural character as the share of credit accruing to agriculture showed a secular decline from 40% in 1990-91 to 32% by 2002-03 and after a transient increase during 2004-2008 settled at 32% (Appendix Table A5.3). This suggests that even the rural branches of the commercial banks refrained from agricultural lending and over two-thirds of their credit advances went into non-agricultural sectors like industry and personal loans compelling the rural population to depend on non-institutional sources of lending for meeting their agricultural credit requirements. Although this began to change after 2008 as agricultural loans slowly accounted for over half of the total credit advanced by rural branches, the overall prospects of expansion of rural and agricultural credit remained unpromising due to the dwindling share of rural branches and the credit advanced by them. As a result of which agricultural loans constituted only about 13% of the total loans of the commercial banks in 2019-20.

Thus, it is this tendency that paints a picture of the transformation of credit that accompanied financial liberalisation and the credit boom that has implications for the credit-growth linkage that the government claimed to further. Moreover, the increase in demand created due to such credit-financed consumption and housing expenditure leaked out to the urban areas without providing any stimulus to growth and development in the rural areas. Thus, there is an urgent need for policy intervention to redirect credit from retail lending to the productive sectors like agriculture and rural development.

Agricultural Credit

The direct outcome of a contraction of rural credit was a decline in credit to the agricultural sector in the nineties. To compound the problem further, the squeeze on resources earmarked for agriculture began as early as 1992-93 when the RBI withdrew its contribution to National Rural Credit (Long Term Operations) (NRC (LTO)) fund of NABARD which is utilised for providing assistance to rural credit institutions to finance agriculture and rural development projects through refinance at concessional rates and the subsequent shortfall in resources were to be raised through market borrowings (Mujumdar, 1999; Satish, 2007).This coupled with a dilution and re-defining of the priority sector, imposition of prudential norms and capital adequacy norms (that not only made banks wary of agricultural lending but also reduced their resource base), taxing the proceeds of NABARD and the cooperative banks, permitting the diversification of the regional rural banks and cooperative banks into non-target avenues and withdrawing state support for rural cooperatives all led to a drastic decline in agricultural credit (Mujumdar, 1999; Satish, 2007).

But after 2003-04, fiscal conservatism was gaining momentum with the enactment of the Fiscal Responsibility and Budget Management Act, and hence the government's retraction from public expenditure was sought to be substituted by private investment facilitated by a surge in credit flow. Thus, the government's initiatives during this period focused on augmenting credit flow to the rural areas in the form of Doubling of Agricultural Credit Programme[8] (2004), revival of the rural credit cooperatives (2006), interest subvention scheme (2006-07)and Agricultural Debt Waiver and Debt Relief Scheme (2008-09).The neglect of agriculture was also sought to be reversed which has resulted in a phenomenal increase in credit advances to agriculture, often exceeding annual targets (Chart 5.5).

But despite the remarkable increase in the flow of credit to agriculture, the rural hinterland is engulfed in a severe agrarian crisis and intensified rural discontent as reflected in farmer suicides, distress migration and farmer protests. This section seeks to examine the flow and distribution of agricultural credit.

Trends in Agricultural Credit

The credit intensity of agriculture is measured as the ratio of institutional agricultural credit to agricultural GDP. It serves as an indicator of the productivity of institutional credit or the extent to which institutional credit

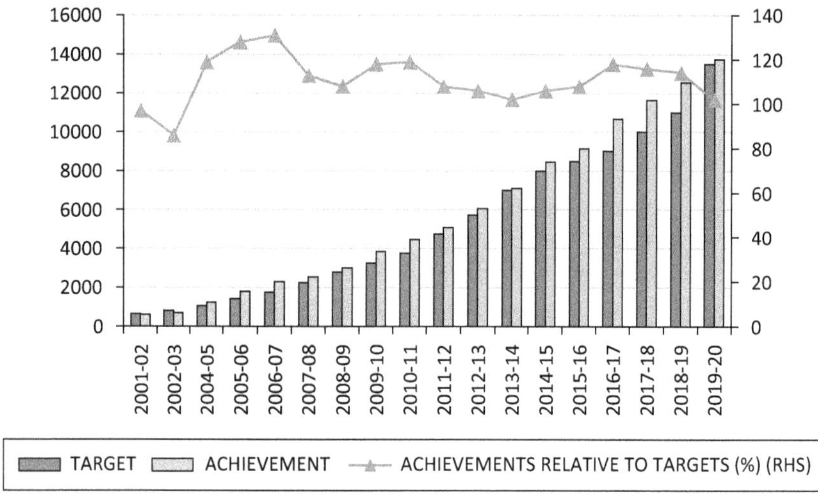

Chart 5.5 Targets and Achievements of Agricultural Credit Source: RBI, Annual Report and GOI, Economic Survey (Various Issues).

fulfils the credit needs of the agricultural sector. Chart 5.6 shows that the credit intensity of agriculture stood at 6.2% in 1991-92 and remained low through the nineties due to the contraction of credit to agriculture. The ratio began to improve after 1996-97 and gathered momentum after 2004 to rise consistently from 22.2% in 2004-05, peaked at 42.3% in 2016-17 (due to a host of policy measures discussed earlier) and then declined marginally to 41% in 2019-20. However, this indicator is misleading as an increase in this ratio (especially after 2011-12) has occurred due to a slowdown in agricultural production or agricultural GDP as opposed to a faster growth in agricultural credit.

Hence, a better index would be to examine the relative share of agriculture in total credit. From the discussion in the previous section, it is clear that the share of agriculture in total credit had shown a secular decline from about 15% in 1990 to 9.6% by 2001, increased marginally to 11.3% during the period coinciding with the credit boom (2003-04 to 2007-08) and then stagnated at about 13% for the period during 2010-11 to 2019-20.

The second indicator used is the total credit to GDP ratio as shown in Chart 5.7. While the total credit to GDP ratio in 1990-91 stood at 21.2%, the agricultural credit to GDP ratio stood at only 3.2%. But while the former stagnated at around 21% throughout the nineties, the latter declined to 2.3% in 1999-2000 (Chart 5.7). Even when the total credit to GDP ratio recovered after 1997-98, the agricultural credit to GDP ratio continued to remain sluggish till 2002-03. After the credit boom in 2004, the credit to GDP ratio shot up from 36% in 2004 to 56% in 2013-14 while the

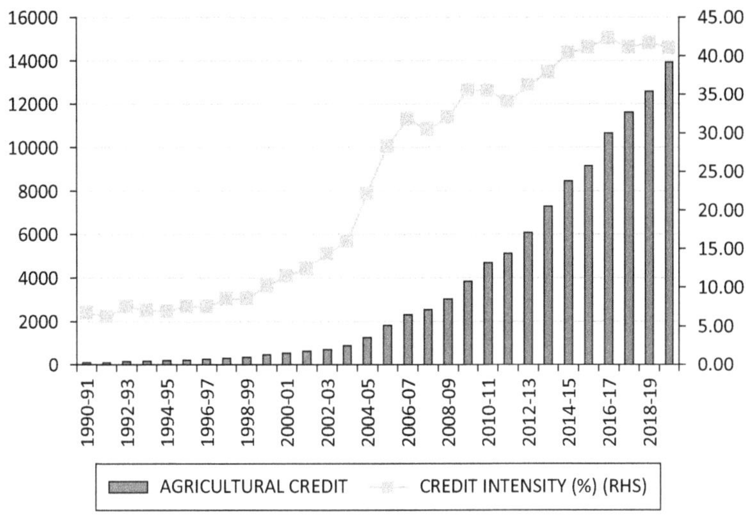

Chart 5.6 Credit Intensity of Agriculture Source: Estimated from various issues of Annual Report, NABARD and Handbook of Statistics on the Indian Economy, RBI.

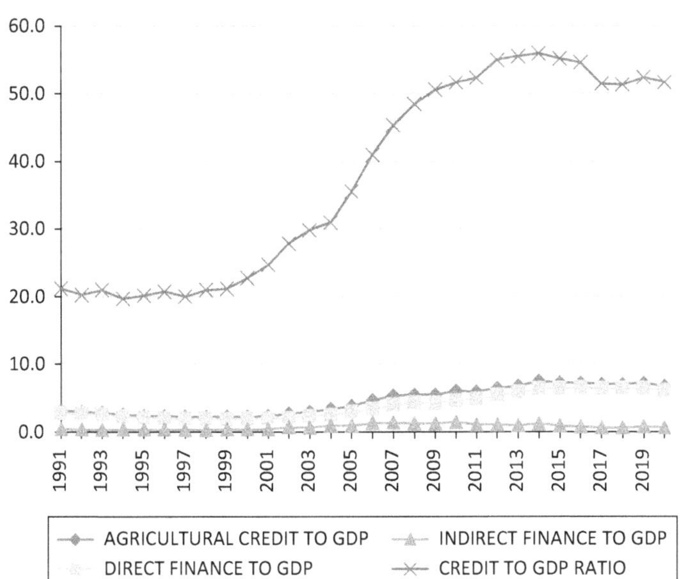

Chart 5.7 Credit to GDP Ratio Source: Estimated from various issues of Basic Statistical Returns of Scheduled Commercial Banks in India and Handbook of Statistics on Indian Economy 2020-21, RBI.

agricultural credit to GDP ratio grew only modestly from 3.8% to 7.5% during the same period. This shows that despite the massive increase in credit provision, the agricultural sector was not a major beneficiary of this boom. However, both these ratios declined thereafter to 51.7% and 6.7% respectively in 2019-20.

Growth and Composition of Agricultural Credit

The credit advanced by the commercial banks decelerated sharply in the immediate aftermath of the neo-liberal reforms especially with the imposition of provisioning and capital adequacy norms that made banks extremely risk averse and curtailed lending to offset losses arising out of such lending (ERF, 2018). As a result, the credit-deposit ratio of the commercial banks declined from 60.6% in 1990-91 to 51.7% in 1998-99. Between 1990-91 and 2000-01, when the real aggregate credit (at constant 2004-05 prices) of the commercial banks was growing at 7.4% per annum, real agricultural credit grew at only 2.7% per annum as opposed to an annual growth rate of 6.5% in the eighties. Agricultural borrowal accounts constituted 44% of the total bank accounts of the scheduled commercial banks in India in 1991; however, their share had declined to 32% by 2004 due to an absolute decline in the number of accounts from 27.74 million in 1992 to 19.84 million in 1999 (Appendix Table 5.1). Consequent to this, even the share of agricultural credit in total credit advances declined from 15.9% in 1990 to 9.6% in 2001.

But due to the policy transition in 2004 seeking to fuel rural and agricultural development through the provision of credit (instead of public expenditure), this declining trend was arrested due to the aforementioned policy measures. The overall credit-deposit ratio of the commercial banks also rose from 53.5% in 2001-02, to 62.6% in 2004-05 and further to 79.1 % in 2012-13. As a result, there was a phenomenal growth in credit to the agricultural sector at the average rate of 17.3% per annum between 2001 and 2011 and about 23.1% per annum during 2003-04 to 2007-08 with a sharp increase in the number of agricultural borrowal loans from 19.8 million in 2001 to 46.6 million in 2011.

However, in the period thereafter there has been a significant deceleration in credit growth with the aggregate credit-deposit ratio of the commercial banks declining from 79.1% in 2012-13 to 73.7% in 2019-20. Even the real growth of agricultural credit (at constant prices) was reduced to only 7.3% per annum during 2011-12 to 2019-20. While the absolute number of agricultural borrowal accounts have grown to 113.4 million in 2020, their share in total loan accounts of the commercial banks declined from about 51.2% in 2015 to 41.6% in 2020 and even the share of credit advanced to agriculture remained low at 13% in 2020 (Table 5.1 and Appendix Table 5.1).

While this may appear as a significant improvement relative to the steep decline in the nineties, there are certain features[9] of this growth in agricultural credit that warrant further investigation in terms of its composition and distribution (Chavan and Ramakumar, 2014).

First is the increasing urbanisation of agricultural credit (Ramakumar, 2013). In 1996, over two-thirds of the agricultural accounts constituting around 52% of the total agricultural credit were held by the rural branches while the urban/metropolitan branches accounted for only 6% of the total agricultural loan accounts and 20% of the total agricultural credit advanced (Table 5.2). This began to change gradually after 2004 with the share of agricultural accounts held by rural branches declining to 48% of the total agricultural accounts and accounting for only 38.2% of total credit in 2019-20. This was accompanied by a corresponding rise in the share of the urban and metropolitan branches in advancing credit to agriculture (Chavan and Ramakumar, 2014). The share of agricultural accounts held by urban/metropolitan branches increased from 5.3% in 2004 to 14% in 2009 and to 16.9% in 2018 while their share in total agricultural credit increased from 19% in 1996, peaked to 37.6% in 2006 and remained at 25.5% in 2020 (Table 5.2).

Infact, the urban and metropolitan branches accounted for about 65% of the share of total indirect advances to agriculture in 2020. It is this urban-centric distribution of credit to agriculture that is usually capital intensive in nature and benefits the large corporations and business firms involved in agricultural production (like input dealers, food and agro-based processing companies, agri-clinics and agri-business centres) over the small and marginal farmers based in the rural countryside (Chavan and Ramakumar, 2014).

This tendency follows from the second feature of agricultural credit which is an increase in the proportion of indirect finance (Chavan and Ramakumar,

Table 5.2 Distribution of Agricultural Borrowal Accounts (in Per Cent)

Year	*Rural Branches*		*Urban/Metropolitan Branches*	
	No. of Accounts	*Amt. Outstanding*	*No. of Accounts*	*Amt. Outstanding*
1996	64.6	51.7	6.1	19
2001	63.4	48.3	6	22.4
2004	64.7	40.9	5.3	33.9
2006	59.8	37.1	7.5	37.6
2009	54.9	38.7	14.0	33.4
2010	57.6	38.5	9.1	33.7
2014	53.9	38	11.1	28.6
2018	47.5	37.9	16.9	26.4
2020	48.0	38.2	16.3	25.5

Source: Estimated from the various issues of RBI, Basic Statistical Returns of Scheduled Commercial Banks in India

2014). While earlier, the definition of agricultural credit entailed advances to the direct cultivators of land, in the post-reform era, this was widened to include indirect advances that accrue to intermediary agencies or entities facilitating agricultural production like agribusiness firms and input dealers (Chavan and Ramakumar, 2007, 2014). Hence, till the mid-nineties, the number of accounts for indirect finance to agriculture accounted for only a miniscule share (less than 1.5%) in the total agricultural borrowal accounts. However, their share in total agricultural accounts has increased from 1.3% in 1996 to 6.2% in 2014, declined briefly to 4.5% in 2018 before rising again to 6.8% in 2020 (Appendix Table 5.1).

Similarly, the share of direct advances in total agricultural credit by the scheduled commercial banks stood at 86% in 1991 while indirect advances accounted for a relatively small share (14%) (Chart 5.8). However, even the share of direct advances in total agricultural credit has been on a decline from 88% in 1993 to 72.1% in 2006 while the share of indirect advances to agriculture increased from 16.1% in 2001 to 28% in 2006 and stood at over 20% in 2011. It is only after 2011 that this trend was reversed as the share of direct finance to agriculture was restored to 91.4% in 2017 and has remained around that level in the subsequent years.

However, this increase in the proportion of direct advances in total advances was also achieved due to the re-defining of direct agricultural credit in 2007 and 2012 while the definition of agricultural lending itself was modified to include farm credit, agricultural infrastructure and ancillary activities in 2015. Besides loans to individual farmers, non-financial intermediaries

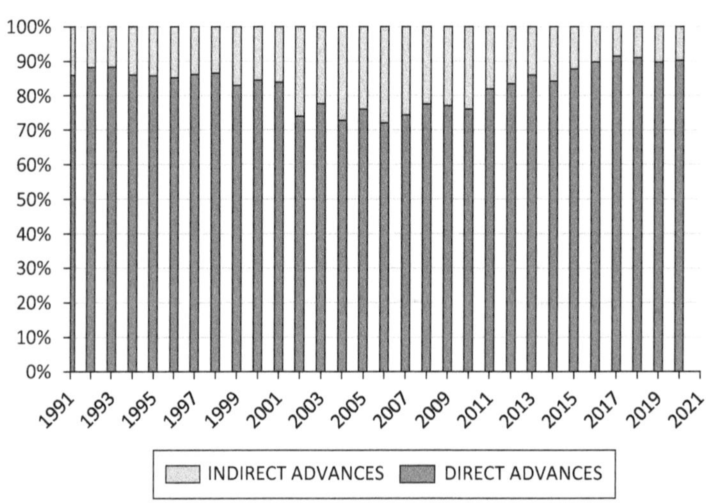

Chart 5.8 Composition of Commercial Banks' Advances to Agriculture Source: RBI, Basic Statistical Returns of Scheduled Commercial Banks in India (Various Issues).

and self-help groups (SHG)/Joint Liability Groups (JLG), the scope of direct finance to agriculture (after the recommendations of the Internal Working Group chaired by C.S. Murthy) was expanded to include loans to corporate farmers, farmers' producer organisations, partnerships firms and companies of individual farmers engaged in agriculture and allied activities with credit limit upto Rs10 million[10] in 2007 (RBI, 2019). The revised RBI guidelines of October 17, 2012 restored the advances to corporates and partnerships as direct credit and also doubled the limit of these advances from Rs 10 million to Rs 20 million[11](NABARD, 2014). The inclusion of corporate borrowings (upto Rs 20 million) in the direct finance category also points to a shift of agricultural lending in favour of larger borrowers.

Thus, the distribution of agricultural credit according to loan size provides interesting insights into the glaring inequalities in its distribution that have occurred over time (Table 5.3).

At the commencement of the neo-liberal reforms, agricultural borrowal loans below the credit limit of Rs 25,000 accounted for 97.1% of the total agricultural loan accounts and accounted for over half of the credit advanced to this sector. However, their share in total agricultural accounts had declined to 93% in 1998 and their share in agricultural credit had declined to 46.2%.

After the revision of the credit limit of small borrowal accounts to Rs 0.2 million in 1998, the share of agricultural credit advanced to small borrowal accounts has progressively declined from over 70% in 1998 to 41.5% in 2020 while the large borrowers (with loan size above Rs 0.2 million) that constitute 14.5% of the total agricultural loan accounts cornered around 60% of the total agricultural credit (Table 5.3).

Table 5.3 Distribution of Agricultural Credit According to Loan Size (in Per Cent)

Year	*Less thanRs25,000*		*Rs25,000 toRs0.2 Million*		*AboveRs0.2 Million*	
	No. of Accounts	*Amt. Outstanding*	*No. of Accounts*	*Amt. Outstanding*	*No. of Accounts*	*Amt. Outstanding*
1991	97.1	55.2	2.7	25.7	0.1	19.2
1995	96.1	52.0	3.7	26.0	0.2	21.9
1998	93.3	46.2	6.1	26.8	0.6	27.1
2000	85.4	35.2	13.6	32.4	1.0	32.4
2005	66.6	17.8	30.3	34.1	3.1	48.2
2010	40.0	6.4	52.8	35.5	7.2	58.1
2015	19.6	2.6	66.5	40	13.9	57.4
2018	17.5	2.0	67.0	37.5	15.5	60.5
2020	15	1.8	70.5	39.7	14.5	58.5

Source: Estimated from various issues of Basic Statistical Returns of Scheduled Commercial Banks in India, RBI

However, even within the large borrower category (loans above Rs 0.2 million) there is a concentration of credit with the share of borrowers of loan sizes exceeding Rs 10 million in total credit increasing significantly after 2004 (Chavan and Ramakumar, 2014). Till 1995, only 9.1% of the total agricultural credit and 2.8% of direct advances accrued to borrowers with the credit limit of over Rs 10 million. This began to change in the 2000s as the share of credit advanced to this category of borrowers increased from 14% in 2000 to 26.2% in 2004 peaked to 30.2% in 2007 and remained around 27% till 2011 before declining to 15% by 2018-19 (Chart 5.9).

The fourth feature pertains to the composition of agricultural credit (Chavan and Ramakumar, 2014). The direct agricultural advances can be decomposed further into short term and longterm depending on the duration for which they are advanced. Short-term loans are crop loans or loans taken by cultivators for financing seasonal agricultural operations. Long-term loans are taken for investments in land reclamation, minor irrigation and for purchasing farm equipment and machinery.

Chart 5.10 shows that the share of long-term credit has declined from 41% in 1990-91 to 29% in 2000-01 and after briefly rising to 35% in 2006-07 slumped to 19% in 2013-14. The reason for this decline is the deteriorating condition and slow decimation of the long-term cooperatives, cheaper rates of refinance available for short-term loans as opposed to long-term credit and the Interest Subvention Scheme (2006-07) (that permits the provision of short-term loans at a lower interest rate of 7% per annum) that has distorted the structure of credit provision to the disadvantage of long-term requirements. This tendency is largely because banks perceived short-term credit as low credit risk requiring lower monitoring costs and supervision and hence proved to be a better asset-liability management as compared to long-term credit that locks up funds for longer periods, requires higher transaction costs and poses a greater risk (Balakrishnan et.al, 2008). However, the provision of long-term credit is essential as it helps in capital formation, and hence, a decline in their share would adversely impact agricultural growth. Nevertheless, after 2013-14, the share of long-term credit has recovered from 19% in 2013-14 to 40.8% in 2019-20 after the constitution of Long-Term Rural Credit Fund (LTRCF) in 2014-15 that sought to extend long-term refinance facilities to the rural financial institutions.

Distribution of Credit

The neo-liberal reforms have not only transformed the nature of credit but have also altered its pattern of distribution among rural borrowers. The following sections seek to examine the distribution of credit to small and marginal farmers and rural borrowal accounts.

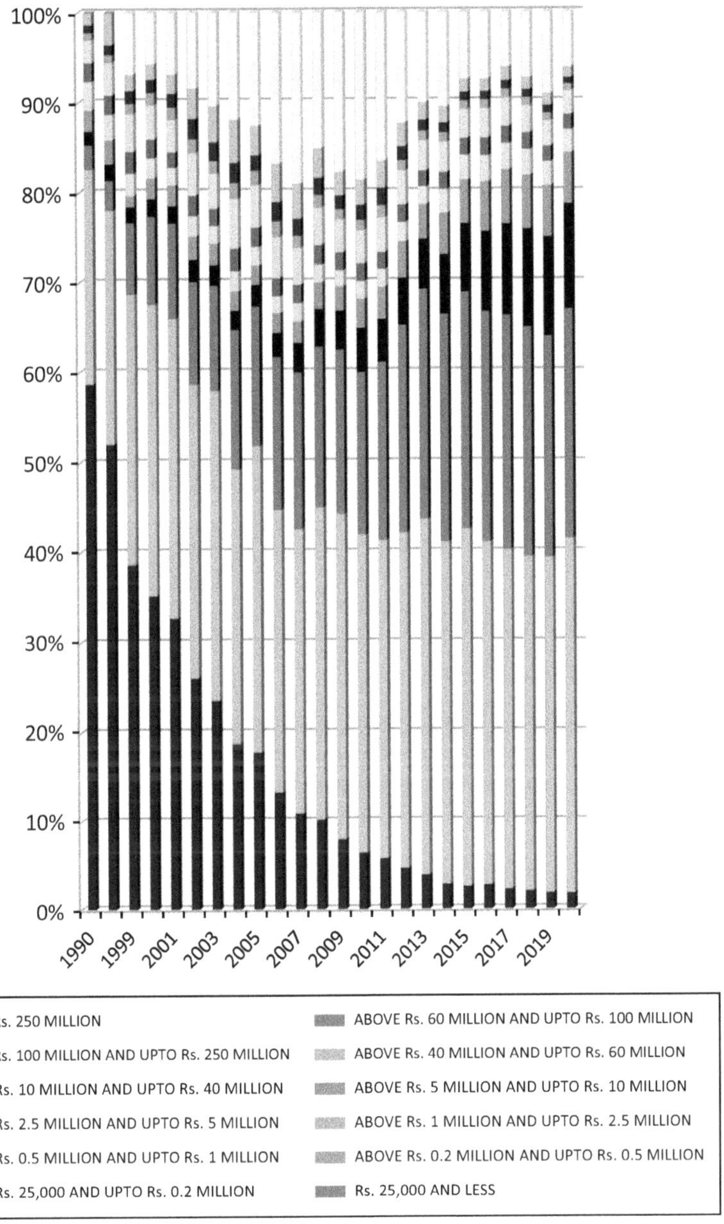

Chart 5.9 Composition of Credit According to Loan Size Source: RBI, Basic Statistical Returns of Scheduled Commercial Banks in India (Various Issues).

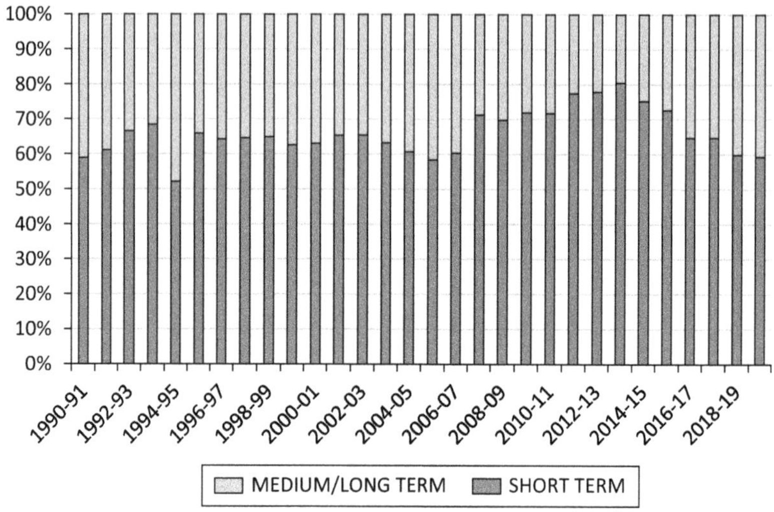

Chart 5.10 Composition of Direct Institutional Credit for Agriculture Source: NABARD, Annual Report and GOI, Pocket Book of Agricultural Statistics (Various Issues).

Small and Marginal Farmers

Due to the failure to implement land reforms, the distribution of land remains extremely skewed in the country, and hence due to the interlinked land, labour, credit, input and commodity markets, only a small segment of farmers have a control over credit and other resources.

The share of small and marginal farmers in total operational holdings has increased from 80% in 1990-91 to 85% in 2011-12 and they account for 47% of the operated area and contribute more than half of the output of agriculture and allied activities (RBI, 2019). But despite this, the small and marginal farmers accounted for less than half the share in total agricultural credit advanced by the commercial banks for as long as 2003-04.The share of the small and marginal farmers in total agricultural advances that had increased from 41.5% in 1980-81 to 54.5% in 1990-91 declined steadily through the 1990s to 48.6% in 1999-00 (Table 5.4). Even with the introduction of Doubling of Agricultural Credit Programme and the one-time settlement scheme to provide debt relief to small and marginal farmers in 2004, the share of small and marginal farmers in total credit and the accounts held increased only briefly to 52% for a year. While the larger farmers continued to consolidate their share in total agricultural credit between 2003-04 and 2007-08. It is only with the introduction of the Agricultural Debt Waiver and Debt Relief Scheme (2008-09) that cleared the past debt of the farmers and made them eligible to access institutional credit that the share of small and marginal farmers in total credit and agricultural accounts increased to

Table 5.4 Distribution of Agricultural Credit According to Size of Land Holdings (Accounts in Thousands, Amt. in Rs Billion)

Year	*Up to2.5 Acres*				*Above2.5 Acresto5 Acres*				*Above5 Acres*				*Total*	
	No. of Accounts	*% in Total*	*Amt.*	*% in Total*	*No. of Accounts*	*% in Total*	*Amt.*	*% in Total*	*No. of Accounts*	*% in Total*	*Amt.*	*% in Total*	*No. of Accounts*	*Amt.*
1980-81	1,587	51.7	2.5	25	693	22.6	1.7	16.6	790	25.7	5.9	58.6	3,070	10.1
1985-86	1,950	46.8	6.2	28	1232	29.5	5.9	26.3	988	23.7	10.4	46.2	4,170	22.4
1987-88	2,236	47.4	8.2	28	1442	30.6	7.6	25.8	1038	22.0	13.6	46.2	4,716	29.5
1990-91	1,960	48.1	11.8	30.2	1,219	29.9	9.5	24.3	899	22.0	17.8	45.5	4,078	39.2
1995-96	2,024	37.4	20.0	26.1	1,689	31.2	19.5	25.5	1,703	31.4	37.0	48.4	5,416	76.6
2000-01	2,382	40.8	37.4	25.8	1,860	31.8	36.4	25.1	1,599	27.4	71.4	49.2	5,841	145.
2005-06	5,004	40.5	168.2	25.1	3,670	29.7	176.2	26.2	3,670	29.7	326.8	48.7	12,344	671.
2006-07	5,963	41.6	232.5	24.7	4,008	27.9	215.9	22.9	4,379	30.5	493.4	52.4	14,350	942
2007-08	6,605	41.3	253.5	26.2	4,463	27.9	232.2	24.0	4,932	30.8	481.4	49.8	16,000	967
2008-09	8,544	38.8	342.7	24.4	6,641	30.2	332.8	23.7	6,811	31.0	727.5	51.9	21,996	1,403
2009-10	8,127	37.5	426.3	26.6	7,175	33.1	443.3	27.7	6,385	29.4	730.6	45.7	21,687	1,600
2010-11	9,253	37.0	460.2	24.4	9,690	38.8	574.4	30.4	6,044	24.2	854.6	45.2	24,987	1,889
2011-12	13,735	45.0	897.1	33.0	10,021	32.8	829.2	30.5	6,782	22.2	990.4	36.5	30,538	2,717

Source: RBI, Handbook of Statistics on Indian Economy (2016-17)
Note: Data after 2011-12 is unavailable due to revised reporting system effective from April 1, 2013.

63.5% and 77.8% in 2011-12 (Table 5.4). However, despite this improvement, their share in total agricultural credit remains considerably low relative to their share in total land holdings.

As per the NSSO's All India Debt and Investment Survey (AIDIS) data, the share of borrowings of cultivator households from non-institutional sources had increased from 30.6% in 1991 to 38.9% in 2002 and further to 41.6% in 2012. Thus, with the commercial banks accounting for over 75% of the total formal agricultural credit, their role in directing credit to the small and marginal farmers becomes crucial in facilitating their access to credit at reasonable rates.

Rural Small Borrowal Accounts

Small borrowal accounts are those accounts whose credit limits fall below a specific limit. This limit which was earlier fixed at Rs 10,000 in 1972 was raised to Rs 25,000 in 1984 and further to Rs 0.2 million in 1998. These accounts are usually held by small and marginal farmers, rural artisans and other borrowers from the informal sector.

The rural small borrowal accounts constituted for over 53% of the total small borrowal accounts in the country in 1996 and accounted for 43% of the total credit accruing to the small accounts loans (Table 5.5). However, their share in terms of both the number of accounts and in total credit advanced has come down to 32.9% and 36% respectively in 2010 which is indicative of the neglect of agriculture and the rural population by the commercial banks. However, after a transitory increase in their share between 2011 and 2016, their share has declined marginally to 32% and 38% respectively in 2020.

Implications on Agriculture

The change in the nature of agricultural credit has important implications on the agricultural sector. Agricultural credit supports growth in this sector through the provision of short-term loans for procuring farm inputs and adopting better farm techniques as well as through advancing term loans for undertaking farm investments to augment agricultural growth and productivity (Mohan, 2004; Chavan, 2013).This section examines the extent to which credit has achieved these objectives.

Provision of Inputs

With the initiation of the Green Revolution and in the post-reform period, there has been an increase in the quantum of purchased inputs and a subsequent demand for credit especially with the dismantling of the input subsidies and a shift to commercial agriculture with diversification into high valued production (like horticulture) that requires highly monetised inputs and large capital investment to be ploughed into the fields. Thus, two important indicators of the increase in institutional credit are the ratio of total

Table 5.5 Small Borrowal Loans (Accounts in Thousands, Amount in Rs Billion)

Year	*Rural Small Borrowal Loans*		*Total Small Borrowal Loans*		*Share of Rural Small Borrowal Loans in Total Small Borrowal Loans*	
	No. of Accounts	*Amt. Outstanding*	*No. of Accounts*	*Amt. Outstanding*	*No. of Accounts*	*Amt. Outstanding*
1996	27,525	157	51,905	363	53	43.2
2001	22,193	360	50,456	1,063	44	33.9
2005	28,295	691	71,106	1,999	39.8	34.6
2010	33,729	1,300	1,02,632	3,607	32.9	36
2016	46,330	2,592	1,24,944	6,207	37.1	41.8
2017	44,630	2,588	1,30,267	6,586	34.3	39.3
2020	66,850	3,509	2,09,622	9,238	31.9	38

Source: Estimated from various issues of Basic Statistical Returns of Scheduled Commercial Banks in India, RBI

institutional credit to the gross value of output and the ratio of short-term agricultural credit to the value of inputs (Mohan, 2004, NABARD, 2014).

The ratio of total institutional credit to gross value of output increased gradually from 5% in 1991-92 to 7.7% in 1999-00 and then marked a significant increase from 8.7% in 2000-01 to 16.5% in 2004-05 and further to 28.2% in 2010-11. This ratio then declined briefly till 2013-14 and increased marginally to 34.3% in 2018-19 (Table 5.6).

The ratio of short-term agricultural credit to the value of inputs that remained below 19% throughout the nineties grew from 21.4% in 2000-01, to 38.5% in 2004-05 and further to 91.4% in 2010-11(Table 5.6). But after 2011-12, the volume of short-term credit outpaced the value of inputs due to which this ratio shot upto 112.6% in 2017-18 from about 98.6% in 2011-12 before declining to 106.1% in the following year. However, even this indicator is misleading as it portrays an incorrect picture of a sharp rise in short-term credit. Table 5.7 shows that the period 2011-12 to 2018-19 was characterised by a sharp deceleration in the growth of crop loans accompanied by a decline in the growth of consumption of critical farm inputs.

Between 1990 and 2003-04, when the real short-term credit (at constant 2004-05 prices) grew at an annual average rate of 10.3%, the growth of consumption of fertilisers and seeds remained low and was negative for the pesticides. This changed dramatically over the next period when the crop loans grew at 21.9% per annum leading to a spectacular growth in the use of other inputs. However, in the subsequent period, the growth in short-term credit slowed down considerably and even fell below the growth recorded in the first period. This (among other factors) led to a sharp decline in the growth of consumption of farm inputs. This indicates the strong relation between the availability of credit and the consumption of inputs.

Financing Private Sector Capital Formation in Agriculture

While public investment is instrumental in driving growth in agriculture through public capital formation, with the fiscal consolidation measures restricting public expenditure, the decline in public capital formation was sought to be compensated by encouraging investments by the private sector. Private investment by farmers is required for land reclamation, minor irrigation, purchasing agricultural machinery etc. Hence, the provision of institutional long-term credit is an important means for undertaking private capital formation in agriculture. The flow of term credit to agriculture was adversely affected in the nineties which also reflected in the extent to which institutional credit facilitated the growth of private capital formation in agriculture.

Table 5.9 shows that after a few fluctuations, the proportion of private capital formation financed by institutional credit declined from 79.2% in 1994-95 to 35.1% in 2001-02. This ratio improved consistently during the

Table 5.6 Institutional Credit for Agriculture and Allied Sectors (in Rs Billion)

Year	*Value of Output*	*Value of Inputs*	*Agricultural GDP*	*Short-term Credit*	*Total Credit*	*Short-term Credit as % of Value of Inputs*	*Total Agricultural Credit as % of*	
							Value of Output	*Agricultural GDP*
1990-91	2,144	576	1,544	66	112	11.5	5.2	7.3
1991-92	2,482	676	1,803	77	125	11.3	5.0	6.9
1995-96	3,946	1,036	2,937	145	220	14.0	5.6	7.5
1997-98	4,915	1,204	3,747	206	320	17.1	6.5	8.5
1999-00	5,995	1,527	4,553	290	463	19.0	7.7	10.2
2000-01	6,060	1,554	4,606	333	528	21.4	8.7	11.5
2004-05	7,581	1,977	5,654	761	1,253	38.5	16.5	22.2
2008-09	12,139	2,909	9,432	2,105	3,019	72.3	24.9	32.0
2009-10	13,887	3,275	10,835	2,767	3,845	84.5	27.7	35.5
2010-11	16,632	3,673	13,197	3,356	4,683	91.4	28.2	35.5
Year	*Value of Output*	*Value of Inputs*	*Agricultural GVA*	*Short-term Credit*	*Total Agricultural Credit*	*Short-term Credit as % of Value of Inputs*	*Total Agricultural Credit as % of*	
							Value of Output	*AgriGVA*
2011-12	19,081	4,017	15,018	3,962	5,110	98.6	26.8	34.0
2014-15	26,825	5,839	20,936	6,354	8,453	108.8	31.5	40.4
2017-18	34,962	6,688	28,298	7,532	11,626	112.6	33.3	41.1
2018-19	36,684	7,092	30,163	7,522	12,568	106.1	34.3	41.7

Source: Estimated from RBI (2020).Handbook of Statistics on Indian Economy and various issues of Annual Report, NABARD and National Accounts Statistics, MOSPI, GOI

Note: The data on the value of output and value of inputs of agriculture and allied sectors are taken from MOSPI's National Accounts Statistics based on the series with Base: 2011-12 and the back dated series of the same.

Table 5.7 Annual Growth in Real Credit and the Use of Inputs (in Per Cent)

Period	*Annual Growth Rates*			
	Short-Term Credit	*Fertilisers*	*Pesticides*	*Seeds*
1990-91 TO 2003-04	10.3	2.44	-4.38	5.8
2004-05 TO 2010-11	21.9	7.66	5.04	14.9
2011-12 TO 2018-19*	5.2	-0.70	1.58	3

SOURCE: Estimated from various issues of Economic Survey, GOI and Handbook of Statistics on Indian Economy, RBI
Note: The figures on real credit are arrived at by deflating the data on short-term credit using the GDP deflator 2004-05=100 upto the period 2010-11 and GDP deflator 2011-12=100 for the latter period.
*The data on the growth of farm inputs is for the period 2011-12 to 2017-18

Table 5.8 Average Annual Growth in Real Term Credit and Private Investment (in Per Cent)

Period	*Term Credit*	*Private Investment*
1990-91 TO 2003-04	11.6	5.5
2004-05 TO 2010-11	17.3	11.3
2011-12 TO 2017-18	19.7	0.8

SOURCE: Data for term credit taken from NABARD, Annual Report and Data for Private Capital Formation taken from GOI (2020a). Agricultural Statistics at a Glance 2020 and NABARD (2014). Agricultural Credit in India: Trends, Regional Spreads and Database Issues.

period coinciding with the credit surge rising steadily from 58.8% in 2003-04 to 82.2% in 2004-05 and peaked to 120.5% in 2006-07.Thereafter, it declined to 47.8% in 2013-14 indicating that at most 47.8% of the total private capital formation was actually financed by institutional credit.

Although this ratio again showed an improvement after 2014-15 to rise to 153.7% in 2018-19, there is a distinct difference in its revival from the one witnessed during 2003-04 to 2007-08. This is because the increase in this ratio after 2014-15 was largely due to a decline in private investment as opposed to an increase in credit (Table 5.8). Between 2004-05 and 2010-11, the real average annual growth rate of private investment was 11.3% and that of term loans was 17.3%. But in the subsequent period, the average annual rate of growth in real private investment (at constant 2011-12 prices) declined sharply to just 0.81% while agricultural credit continued to grow at 19.7% per annum (due to the setting up of the Long-Term Rural Credit Fund (LTRCF) in 2014-15), thereby inflating the ratio.

This indicates that despite the increase in credit, private investment in agriculture has declined drastically or that the credit policy has proved to be unsuccessful in reviving investment, capital formation and agricultural growth. This also reiterates that the mere expansion of credit in the absence

Table 5.9 Financing of Private Capital Formation by Institutional Term Credit (in Rs Billion)

Year	*Private Sector Capital Formation*	*Term Credit*	*Term Credit as % of Private Capital Formation*
Base: 2004-05			
1991-92	108	49	45.2
1992-93	156	51	32.6
1994-95	136	108	79.2
1995-96	149	75	50.3
1999-00	481	173	36.0
2001-02	613	215	35.1
2003-04	545	320	58.8
2004-05	599	492	82.2
2005-06	692	751	108.6
2006-07	755	909	120.5
2009-10	1,615	1,079	66.8
2010-11	1,958	1,327	67.8
Base: 2011-12			
2011-12	2,382	1,149	48.2
2012-13	2,337	1,339	57.3
2013-14	2,900	1,386	47.8
2014-15	2,845	2,099	73.8
2015-16	2,424	2,502	103.2
2016-17	2,815	3,763	133.7
2017-18	2,958	4,094	138.4
2018-19	3,282	5,046	153.7

Source: Data for term credit taken from various issues of NABARD, Annual Report; Data for Private Capital Formation taken from various issues of GOI, Agricultural Statistics at a Glance and NABARD (2014). Agricultural Credit in India: Trends, Regional Spreads and Database Issues.

of other facilitating factors like public investment (that ensures the viability of private investment) fails to enhance private investment in agriculture.

Impact of Credit on Agricultural Growth

Many empirical studies have analysed the impact of agricultural credit on growth in this sector to establish that its impact is limited as growth in agriculture is determined by other factors like public investment, remunerative prices for output, access to subsidised inputs etc. Binswanger and Khandker (1992) observed that rural finance has a much smaller impact on employment and output than in the non-farm sector and that the impact of credit on agricultural output is limited to influencing the use of inputs and encouraging private investment. Narayanan (2016) examined state-level panel data to conclude that only input use (like fertilisers) was highly sensitive to the availability of institutional credit but not agricultural GDP suggesting that credit may only be an enabling input. Another study by Subbarao (2012) showed that the agricultural output elasticity of institutional credit was statistically significant and positive and a percentage increase in institutional credit led to a 0.22% increase in agricultural GDP with a year's lag.

In order to analyse the impact of agricultural credit on agricultural GDP, we track the co-movements of the year-on-year nominal growth of agricultural GDP and agricultural credit as shown in Chart 5.11.

It is observed that for a greater period under analysis, the two series do not move in unison and grow at widely divergent rates over different periods as shown in Table 5.10.

During the eighties, as real agricultural credit grew at an annual rate of 6.5% per annum, it (amongst other factors) aided growth in the agricultural sector at the rate of 4.3% per annum. With the shift to the neo-liberal reforms, while aggregate bank credit continued to grow at 8.7% per annum, the pace of real agricultural credit declined to 6.1% that led to a slowing of growth of agriculture. However, over the period 2004-05 and 2010-11, while real agricultural credit expanded sharply at 16.6% per annum or about 2.5 times the rate of growth witnessed in the eighties, the real rate of

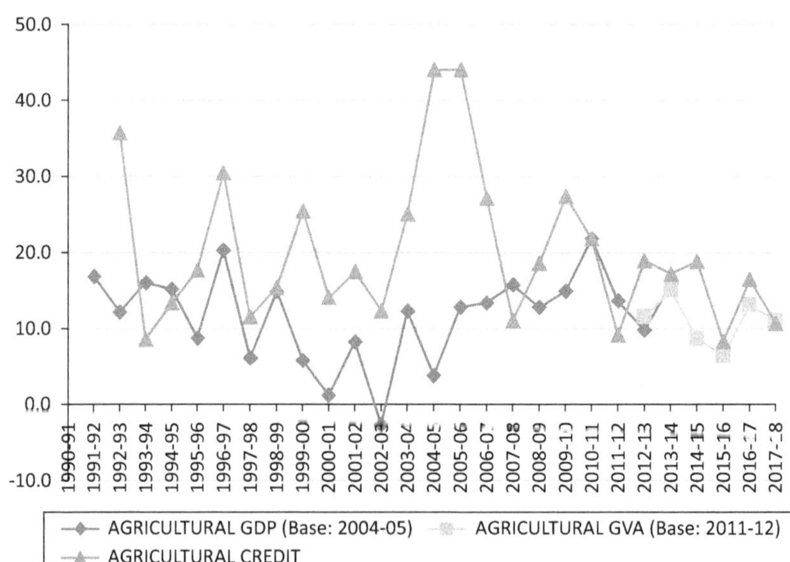

Chart 5.11 Annual Growth of Agricultural Credit and Agricultural GDP (in Nominal Terms) Source: Estimated from various issues of Annual Report, NABARD and Handbook of Statistics on the Indian Economy, RBI.

Table 5.10 Growth of Agricultural Credit and Other Rural Indicators (in Per Cent per Annum)

Period	*Total Bank Credit*	*Agricultural Credit*	*Agricultural GDP*	*Growth in Agricultural Productivity*	*Growth in Rural Employment Usual Status (UPSS)*
1980-81 TO 1990-91	6.8	6.5	4.3	3.2	1.8*
1990-91 TO 2003-04	8.7	6.1	2.7	2.9	1.5**
2004-05 TO 2010-11	15.7	16.6	4.1	3.3	-0.29
2011-12 TO 2017-18	5.8	8.6	2.8	3.0	-1.02

Source: Estimated from various issues of Basic Statistical Returns of Scheduled Commercial Banks in India, RBI; Agricultural Statistics at a Glance 2020, GOI; National Account Statistics 2020, MOSPI and Employment and Unemployment Surveys, NSSO.
Note: The figures on real agricultural GDP are arrived at by deflating the data on credit by the GDP deflator.
*The growth in rural employment for the first period is for the period 1983-84 to 1993-94.
**The growth in rural employment corresponds to the period 1993-94 to 2004-05.
Agricultural productivity is defined as the gross value of output of agriculture and allied sectors (at constant 2011-12 prices) per net sown area.
The periodisation is based on major policy shifts.

agricultural growth increased to only 4.1% per annum which was fractionally lower than the rate of agricultural growth achieved in the eighties.

A similar trend is observed in terms of growth in agricultural productivity (gross value of output in agriculture and allied sectors per net sown area). The growth in agricultural productivity achieved during the period 2004-05 to 2010-11 was almost comparable to the growth rates achieved during the eighties despite the massive growth in credit.

In a similar vein, against a respectable growth of 1.8% per annum in rural employment recorded during the eighties, the post-reform period, especially the period characterised by the credit surge, failed to generate rural employment which turned negative throughout the period after 2004-05. This indicates that credit (along with public investment) served as an important driver of growth during the Green Revolution period; however, it failed to augment a commensurate increase in agricultural growth or rural employment due to the transformation of the composition, nature and distribution of credit as well as the reduced facilitating role of public investment in driving growth. Thereafter, the growth of aggregate credit was reduced to a third and that of agricultural credit almost halved due to factors like growing non-performing assets (NPAs) and demonetisation which also led to depressed growth of agriculture and other indicators.

We next examine the extent to which agricultural credit promotes growth in agricultural productivity using Spearman's Correlation Coefficient and a test of significance. For this we rank 17 major states (in a decreasing order) according to credit per hectare of gross cropped area and agricultural productivity defined as net state domestic product in agriculture per net sown area (Appendix Table 5.2) over three periods. It was observed that the correlation coefficient between agricultural productivity and agricultural credit showed a low value varying between 0.13 during 1990-91 to 2003-04, 0.36 during 2004-05 to 2010-11 and 0.44 during 2011-12 to 2015-16. However, none of these values were significant at the 5% level of significance. This occurs because of the skewed distribution of credit which is disproportionately appropriated by the southern states like Tamil Nadu, Kerala, Andhra Pradesh, Telangana and Karnataka due to better banking infrastructure while states that have relatively higher agricultural productivity like West Bengal, Punjab, Himachal Pradesh and Jammu and Kashmir do not have the requisite access to agricultural credit. Thereby, indicating a low or a weak relation between agricultural credit and agricultural growth and hence suggesting that there are other important factors like public investment, remunerative prices etc. that drive agricultural growth.

Beyond correlation, we next examine the role of credit and the relative effectiveness with respect to public expenditure in furthering agricultural growth by raising agricultural productivity. For the analysis, we undertake state-wise panel data regression for 17 major states for the period 1993-94 and 2015-16.

Thus, the following equation is used for estimating the model using panel data:

$LnLLp_{it}=f(Lnpubexp_{it}, lnagricredit_{it}, lnrain_{it}, lnagrigsdp_{it})$
lnLLP= Land productivity (Net State Domestic Product in agriculture and allied sectors per hectare of net sown area)
Pub exp= Public expenditure in agriculture and allied sectors and irrigation and allied sectors per gross cropped area
Agricredit=Agricultural credit per hectare of gross cropped area
Ln rain=Rainfall in mm
Lnagrigsdp=Agricultural gross state domestic product is used as a control variable

While there are other factors that affect agricultural productivity like fertilisers, extension of irrigation, cropping intensity etc., these variables were excluded from the regression as they were highly correlated with public expenditure and credit.

All the variables in the regression were taken in their logarithmic form. The results of the fixed effects model regression (determined using the Hausman Test) are presented in Table 5.11.

The results show that both agricultural credit (per hectare of gross cropped area) and public expenditure (per hectare of gross cropped area) are significant determinants of agricultural productivity but public expenditure per gross cropped area has a relatively greater impact with a lag period of a year while credit has an indirect affect on productivity by providing access to better farm inputs and enabling private investment. This warrants that

Table 5.11 Determinants of Agricultural Productivity

Variables	*Agricultural Productivity LnLLP*
Ln.agricultural credit	0.0266***
	(0.0160)
L1.Lnpublicexpenditure	0.0377***
	(0.026)
Ln.agriculturalgsdp	0.9148***
	(0.038)
Lnrain	0.0283*
	(0.0266)
Constant	-0.0823***
	(0.284)
R^2	0.9
Observations	374
No. of Years	22

Note: *** 1% level of significance * 10% level of significance.
The figures in the parentheses represent robust standard error.

credit alone cannot spur agricultural growth and needs to be complemented by public expenditure not just to raise agricultural productivity and augment rural infrastructure like roads, irrigation projects (which will not be undertaken by the private entities due to the lumpy investment and long gestation period) but also to encourage private investment, expand the absorptive capacity of credit and render private investment economically feasible.

Limitations of the Credit-Led Growth Strategy

The credit-led strategy suffers from several limitations.

- One of the major short-coming of this strategy is that a sizeable share of the country's rural population (especially the farming community) falls outside the purview of institutional credit and depends on the informal sector (like moneylenders, input dealers) for meeting its credit requirements. As per the NSSO's All India Debt and Investment Surveys, the share of non-institutional sources in the outstanding debt of cultivators increased from 33.7% in 1991 to 38.9% in 2002 and further to 41.7% in 2012 while the same for the rural households has increased from 36% to 42.9% and to 44% during the same period. Thus, unless the government prioritises financial inclusion of the weaker sections; this growth strategy would only aggravate income and regional inequalities.
- Also, there are limits to the growth envisioned through this strategy as the expansion of credit can spur both investments and growth in a supply-constrained economy, but in an economy faced with sluggish demand, unutilised capacity and unemployment, credit-financed investment and consumption ceases to act as the principal source of stimulus to growth. Besides, there are limits to the extent of easing borrowing requirements, reduction of interest rates, pumping liquidity into the system etc. which again constrains the scope of accelerating growth in the economy (Chandrasekhar, 2009).
- The rural financial institutions responsible for spurring growth are saddled with growing over-dues and non-performing assets that constrains the expansion of credit and could thereby jeopardise the growth process.
- There exists an inherent fragility associated with this growth strategy especially through credit infusion or large capital inflows as it could be disrupted by exogenous factors that may be unrelated to the country's performance.

Conclusion

Thus, the structural adjustment and the stabilisation measures constrained the scope of State's action though the fiscal policy and accorded overriding importance to the credit or the monetary policy to drive growth in agriculture and the rural economy. However, the promise of growth through the expansion of rural credit has largely belied the rural countryside.

The shrinking presence of commercial banks in the rural areas is evident in the declining share of deposits and advances, falling credit-deposit ratio and the narrowing spread of rural bank branches. Even during the credit surge, the benefits of the credit expansion largely eluded the productive sectors like agriculture and industries and have instead accrued to the retail sectors or the sensitive sectors that induce fragility in the banking system. Even the distribution of agricultural credit has been skewed in favour of large borrowers, mainly the corporate and business groups engaged in agriculture-related activities, and has largely bypassed the small and marginal farmers who constitute the major segment of the farming community, the small borrowers and those engaged in the informal sector. This tendency is engendered in the rise in the proportion of indirect finance of agricultural credit, urbanisation of credit with a concentration among large borrowers (Chavan and Ramakumar, 2007). And finally, after a brief spell of euphoric growth, the sharp deceleration in credit (owing to the growing non-performing assets) has threatened to derail the credit-led growth process.

The study concludes that the transformation of the nature, composition and distribution of rural credit in the post-reform era is such that it fails to serve its intended purpose of spurring growth and development in the agricultural sector and the rural economy. Also, the growth envisioned through this approach is not only inherently unsustainable and volatile (culminating either in a crisis or warranting State bail-outs) but also deeply inequalising in nature, less suited for generating employment and output and incapable of addressing social deprivation (Chandrasekhar, 2016a).And thus, the role of the monetary lever in promoting agricultural growth can at best be supplementary to public investment and definitely not a substitute. It is imperative to ensure that the expansion of credit is matched by enhanced outlays for public expenditure to restore the viability of crop production. Hence, unless the declining viability of agriculture is addressed through requisite public investment, this credit-led growth strategy could turn into an unmitigated disaster by pushing the farming community into debt and destitution.

Notes

1 The chapter is based on the author's PhD research work being carried out at the Center for Economic Studies and Planning, Jawaharlal Nehru University, New Delhi.

2 The policy linked the expansion of bank branches in the metropolitan areas to the number of branches opened in the unbanked areas. Under this policy, banks were permitted to open a branch in the metropolitan centre for every additional branch opened by them in the rural, semi-urban and urban centres, given that the branches opened in the metropolitan centres do not exceed the total number of bank branches proposed to be opened in the rural, semi-urban and urban centres.

3 The use of the "agency model" or the Banking Correspondent/Banking Facilitator is fraught with risks like credit risk, operational risk, legal and liquidity risk and even a risk of reputation for the banks. This model also limits the facilities available to the customer to only cash deposits/withdrawals instead of a range of financial services (RBI, 2009).
4 Of the 328 million accounts (as of September 2018) opened under the Pradhan Mantri Jan Dhan Yojana, 59.1% were opened in the rural and semi-urban areas; however, the average balance in these accounts has reduced over time (RBI, 2019).
5 The gross non-performing assets as a proportion of total gross advances of the commercial banks increased from 3.1% in 2011-12, to 4.3% in 2014-15 and further to 11.2% in 2017-18 (RBI, 2020).
6 On November 8, 2016, the Indian Government declared that the currency notes of denomination of Rs 500 and Rs 1000 would no longer be treated as legal tender, in effect resulting in a de-recognition of 86% of the value of the Indian currency. The public was permitted to deposit or exchange (upto Rs 4500/2000) the old notes till the deadline of December 30, 2016. This disrupted normal banking operations as banks were saddled with growing deposits that required banks to pay interest rates to the depositors while the banks could not increase lending at the same pace because of limits on cash withdrawals nor invest these deposits as these would likely be withdrawn when the withdrawal limits would be relaxed. This in turn slowed credit growth (Chandrasekhar, 2016b).
7 Between 2011-12 and 2019-20, while the share of agricultural loans in total advances of the commercial banks stagnated at about 12-13%, that of industry declined from 42% to 31% with a corresponding increase in the share of retail/personal loans from 16% to 24%.
8 This scheme also comprised of a host of measures like debt restructuring programme, a one-time settlement scheme, debt waivers and write-offs and other relief measures for both small and marginal farmers as well as farmers indebted to informal lenders (NABARD, 2014).
9 The features of the revival of credit in the 2000s are discussed in Chavan and Ramakumar (2007, 2014). This section builds on their findings by extending the period of analysis further upto the 2019-20.
10 The RBI had earlier contemplated shifting these corporate lending to agriculture to the indirect finance category to redress the inequities arising in the distribution of credit to agriculture in its July 2012 guidelines; however, it retracted on its statement soon thereafter as these lendings were included again under the direct finance category after October 17, 2012 (NABARD, 2014).
11 For credit advances above Rs 20 million, the amount exceeding Rs 20 million were allowed to be treated as indirect advances to agriculture.

References

Balakrishnan, P., Golait, R., &Kumar, P. (2008). *Agricultural Growth in India since 1991*. Development Research Group Study No. 27, Department of Economic Analysis and Research, RBI, Mumbai.

Binswanger, H., &Khandekar, S. (1992). The Impact of Formal Finance on the Rural Economy of India. *Journal of Development Studies*, Vol. 32, No. 2, pp. 234–262.

Chandrasekhar, C.P. (2009). The Monetary Lever. *Macroscan*. Retrieved from https://frontline.thehindu.com/columns/article30185861.ece.

Chandrasekhar, C.P. (2016a). Financial Development and Growth under Capitalism. In N. Nawn, et al. (eds), *Economic Challenges for the Contemporary World*. Sage Publications, New Delhi.

Chandrasekhar, C.P. (2016b). An Overburdened Instrument. *Macroscan*. Retrieved from http://www.macroscan.org/cur/sep16/pdf/Overburdened_Instrument.pdf.

Chandrasekhar, C.P. (2017). The Roots of the Agrarian Distress in India. *Macroscan*. Retrieved from https://www.macroscan.org/cur/jun17/pdf/Agrarian_Distress.pdf.

Chandrasekhar, C.P.,& Ghosh, J. (2017). Growth in the Time of a Credit Squeeze. *Macroscan*. Retrieved from https://www.macroscan.org/fet/aug17/pdf/Credit_Squeeze.pdf.

Chandrasekhar, C.P., Ghosh, J., &Patnaik, P. (2017). *Demonetisation Decoded: A Critique of India's Currency Experiment*. Routledge India, Taylor and Francis Group, London and New York.

Chavan, P. (2005). How Inclusive are Banks under Financial Liberalisation?*Economic and Political Weekly*, Vol. 40, No. 43, pp. 4647–4649.

Chavan, P. (2007). Access to Bank Credit: Implications on Dalit Rural Households. *Economic and Political Weekly*, Vol. 42, No. 31, pp. 3219–3225.

Chavan, P. (2013). Credit and Capital Formation in Agriculture: A Growing Disconnect. *Social Scientist*, Vol. 41, No. 9/10. pp. 59–67.

Chavan, P.,&Ramakumar, R. (2007). Revival of Credit in the 2000s: An Explanation. *Economic and Political Weekly*, Vol. 42, No. 52, pp. 57–63.

Chavan, P.,&Ramakumar, R. (2014). Bank Credit to Agriculture in India in the 2000s: Dissecting the Revival. *Review of Agrarian Studies*, Vol. 4, No. 1. Retrieved from http://www.ras.org.in/bank_credit_to_agriculture_in_india_in_the_2000s.

ERF. (2018). *Indian Banking: Current Challenges and Alternatives for the Future*. Report for AIBOC. ERF, New Delhi.

GOI. (2020a). *Agricultural Statistics at a Glance*. Ministry of Agriculture and Farmers' Welfare, GOI, New Delhi.

GOI. (2020b). *Pocket Book of Agricultural Statistics 2020*. Ministry of Agriculture and Farmers Welfare. Department of Agriculture, Cooperation & Farmers' Welfare. Directorate of Economics and Statistics, New Delhi.

GOI. (2020c). *National Accounts Statistics*. Ministry of Statistics and Programme Implementation, New Delhi.

GOI. *Economic Survey*. Various Issues. Ministry of Finance, New Delhi.

Mohan, R. (2004). Agricultural Credit in India: Status, Issues and Future Agenda. Lecture delivered (February 5, 2004) at the *17th National Conference of Agricultural Marketing*, Indian Society of Agricultural Marketing, Hyderabad.

Mujumdar, N.A. (1999). Reviving Rural Credit. *Economic and Political Weekly*, Vol. 34, No. 25, pp. 1577–1579.

NABARD. (2014). Agricultural Credit in India: Trends, Regional Spreads and Database Issues. *Occasional Paper59*. NABARD, Mumbai.

NABARD. *Annual Report*. Various Issues. NABARD, Mumbai.

Narayanan, S. (2016). The Productivity of Agricultural Credit in India. *Occasional Paper No. 61*. NABARD, Mumbai.

NSSO. *All India Debt and Investment Surveys*. Various Issues. Ministry of Statistics and Programme Implementation, GOI, New Delhi.

NSSO. *Employment and Unemployment Surveys*. Various Issues. Ministry of Statistics and Programme Implementation, GOI.

Patnaik, U. (2003). Global Capitalism, Deflation and Agrarian Crisis in Developing Countries. *Social Policy and Development Programme Paper No. 15*. United Nations Research Institute for Social Development. Geneva.

Ramachandran, V.K. & Swaminathan, M. (2005). *Financial Liberalisation and Rural Credit in India.(Agrarian Studies).*Tulika Books, New Delhi.
Ramakumar, R. (2013). Bank Credit to Agriculture in India: Trends in the 1990s and 2000s. *The Marxist*, Vol. XXIX, No. 3. Retrieved from https://cpim.org/sites/default/files/marxist/201303-ramkumar.pdf.
RBI. (2009). *Report of the Working Group to Review the Business Correspondent Model.* Chaired by P. Vijaya Bhaskar. Mumbai.
RBI. (2019). *Report of the Internal Working Group to Review Agricultural Credit* (Chaired by M.K. Jain), Mumbai.
RBI. *Annual Report.* Various Issues. RBI, Mumbai.
RBI. *Basic Statistical Returns of Scheduled Commercial Banks in India.* Various Issues. RBI, Mumbai.
RBI. *Handbook of Statistics on Indian Economy.* Various Issues. RBI, Mumbai.
RBI. *Handbook of Statistics on Indian States.* Various Issues. RBI, Mumbai.
RBI. *Report on Trend and Progress of Banking in India.* Various Issues. RBI, Mumbai.
Satish, P. (2007). Agricultural Credit in the Post-Reform Era: A Target of Systematic Policy Coarctation. *Economic and Political Weekly*, Vol. 42, No. 26, pp. 2567–2575.
Shetty, S.L. (2005). Regional, Sectoral and Functional Distribution of Bank Credit. In V.K.Ramachandran and M.Swaminathan (eds), *Financial Liberalisation and Rural Credit in India (Agrarian Studies).* Tulika Books, New Delhi.
Subba Rao, D. (2012). *Agricultural Credit – Accomplishments and Challenges.* Speech delivered (July 12, 2012) at NABARD's 30th Anniversary Celebration in Mumbai. RBI.
Wiggins, S. and Rajendran, S. (1987). *Banking in Southern Tamil Nadu: Performance and Management.* Final Research Report No 3, The University of Reading, U.K.

Appendix

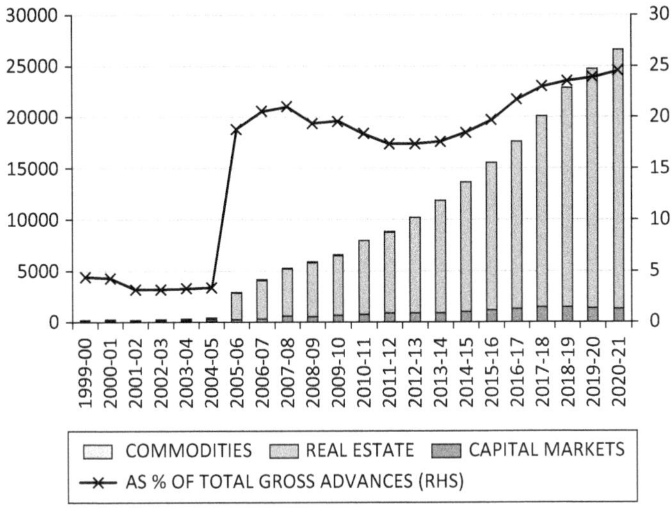

Chart 5(A) Lending to Sensitive Sectors by Commercial Banks (in Rs Billion) Source: RBI, Report on Trend and Progress of Banking in India (Various Issues)

Table 5A.1 Composition of Agricultural Borrowal Loans of the Scheduled Commercial Banks (No. of Accounts in Millions, Amt in Rs Million)

Year	*Agriculture*				*Direct Credit*				*Indirect Credit*			
	No. of Accounts	*% in Total*	*Amt.*	*% in Total*	*No. of Accounts*	*% in Total*	*Amt. Outstanding*	*% in Total*	*No. of Accounts*	*% in Total*	*Amt. Outstanding*	*% in Total*
Mar-90	24.5	45.5	166261	15.9	24.1	98.2	144353	86.8	0.4	1.8	21908	13.2
Mar-95	24.8	42.7	249480	11.8	24.4	98.5	214205	85.9	0.4	1.5	35275	14.1
Mar-01	19.8	37.9	517304	9.6	19.6	98.6	434203	83.9	0.3	1.4	83101	16.1
Mar-05	26.7	34.6	1243849	10.8	26	97.6	946354	76.1	0.6	2.4	297495	23.9
Mar-07	33.2	38.9	2301911	15.2	32.5	97.8	1714968	74.5	0.7	2.2	586943	25.5
Mar-10	42.8	36	3902983	11.7	41	95.9	2968496	76.1	1.8	4.1	934487	23.9
Mar-15	73.9	51.2	9042717	13.1	70.1	94.9	7926911	87.7	3.8	5.1	1115806	12.3
Mar-18	90.9	46.1	11992610	13.7	86.8	95.5	10910400	91	4.1	4.5	1082210	9
Mar-20	113.4	41.6	13679700	13.0	105.6	93.2	12346350	90.3	7.7	6.8	1333350	9.7

Source: RBI, Basic Statistical Returns of Scheduled Commercial Banks in India (Various Issues)

Table 5A.2 State-Wise Ranking of States Based on Agricultural Credit and Agricultural Productivity

States	*Ranks of Agricultural Credit per Gross Cropped Area*			*Ranks in Agricultural Productivity*		
	1990-91 TO 2003-04	*2004-05 TO 2010-11*	*2011-12 TO 2015-16*	*1990-91 TO 2003-04*	*2004-05 TO 2010-11*	*2011-12 TO 2015-16*
Haryana	6	6	6	6	4	4
Himachal Pradesh	9	7	7	3	3	5
Jammu and Kashmir	13	13	10	5	6	6
Punjab	5	4	4	2	2	2
Rajasthan	14	15	15	17	17	17
Gujarat	7	8	13	13	12	12
Maharashtra	8	9	11	15	15	15
Karnataka	4	5	5	11	16	16
Kerala	2	2	2	4	5	8
Tamil Nadu	1	1	1	8	7	3
Uttar Pradesh +Uttarakhand	10	10	8	9	11	11
Madhya Pradesh + Chhattisgarh	15	16	16	12	14	14
Andhra Pradesh+ Telangana	3	3	3	16	9	7
Bihar +Jharkhand	11	12	9	10	10	9
West Bengal	12	11	14	1	1	1
Odisha	16	14	12	14	13	13
Assam	17	17	17	7	8	10

Source: RBI, Handbook of Statistics on Indian States (Various Issues)

Table 5A.3 Composition of Bank Credit Disbursed by Rural Branches of the Commercial Banks (in Per Cent)

Year	*Agriculture*	*Of Which:*		*Industry*	*Personal Loans*	*Total*	*Of Which:*	
		Direct Finance	*Indirect Finance*				*Artisans and Village Industries*	*Other Small-Scale Industries*
1995	39.2	35.1	3.1	27.2	9.7	100	2	6.7
1996	38.6	35.9	2.6	27.5	9.1	100	2	6.6
1997	39.9	37.4	2.5	24.5	10.7	100	2.2	5.5
1998	37.6	35.3	2.3	25.9	11	100	2	5.1
1999	36.5	34.4	2.1	27.3	10.6	100	2.1	5.5
2000	37.4	35.5	1.9	24.9	12.5	100	1.7	4.8
2001	36.2	34.5	1.7	25.1	13.5	100	1.3	4.1
2002	32.7	30.2	2.5	23.6	13	100	1.7	3
2003	32.3	30.3	2	24.2	14.6	100	1.5	3.1
2004	35.9	33.1	2.7	19.9	19.9	100	1.5	3
2005	33.3	31.2	2.1	26.5	19.5	100	1.2	2.5
2006	32.2	30	2.2	26.8	20.6	100	1	2.6
2007	36.1	33.8	2.3	23	19.3	100	1.1	2.5
2008	32.5	30.6	2	29.2	17.9	100		
2009	38.7	36.5	2.3	24.9	16.3	100		
2010	39	35.2	3.8	23.7	16.7	100		
2011	44.5	41.6	2.9	15.9	18.8	100		
2012	48.3	44.7	3.6	11.2	15.8	100		
2013	50.8	47.4	3.3	11.2	15.4	100		
2014	56.5	53.2	3.3	7.6	15.7	100		
2015	56.8	54	2.8	7.8	15.9	100		
2016	56.4	54.2	2.2	7.7	16.2	100		
2017	56.9	54.9	1.9	7.2	17.1	100		
2018	54.3	51.9	2.4	9.5	18.6	100		

Source: RBI, Basic Statistical Returns of Scheduled Commercial Banks in India (Various Issues)

6 Decline of DFIs in India during Post-Financial Liberalisation

Santosh Kumar

Introduction

The Minister of Finance, Government of India, made the announcement in the budget proposal of the year 2020-21 for setting up a Development Financial Institution (DFI) with the government's support of Rs. 200 billion to infuse financial assistance in building up infrastructure across India. The need of financial resources for a mammoth infrastructural programme in India has been estimated to be to the extent of Rs. 111 trillion in time to come for the projects in the pipeline. However, the proposed DFI is expected to develop a Rs. 5 trillion lending portfolio in the next five years. Such initiative is based on the Reserve Bank of India's "Discussion Paper on Wholesale and Long-term Finance Bank" which was brought out by the RBI in 2017. This discussion paper is rooted in the Report of the Committee on Financial Sector Reforms under the chairmanship of Raghuram G. Rajan way back in 2008. The Raghuram Rajan Committee emphasised on setting up specialised banks to take up long-term financing of the corporate sector and refinancing to the lenders to the Micro, Small, and Medium Enterprises (MSMEs) sector. Such emphasis on specialised banks for industrial and infrastructural progress in India is based on the existing literature and experience which have given special emphasis to finance in the industrial and economic progress of countries across the world. However, such a U-turn on the horizon of the Indian financial system during the period of financialisation raises doubts about the initiative of setting up afresh DFI after having decimated the chain of national- and regional-level DFIs in India.

Irrespective of the time and space, the role of finance in the process of economic development has been an important concern for economists with very divergent perspectives, including Keynes (1936), Schumpeter (1934), Gerschenkron (1962), Morishima (1994), Gurley and Shaw (1955), Cameron (1953), Minsky (1986), and King and Levine (1993). They all have recognised the positive role of finance in accelerating the economic progress of a country. Looking at the relationship between finance and industrial development in a capitalist economy, Schumpeter (1934) observes that the services provided by financial intermediaries such as mobilisation of

DOI: 10.4324/9781003343998-6

savings, evaluation of projects, management of risk, monitoring of managers and facilitation of transactions in economic activities are essential for technological innovation and economic development.[1] In the bank-based financial structure, the Development Financial Institutions (DFIs), which are also called Development Banks, are characterised differently if compared with commercial banks with respect to their role in financing industrial development. A DFI is a specialised financial institution that plays multiple roles to promote and nurture enterprises. It is often more than just a financial institution, being a source of non-financial assistance to industries. It makes available long- and medium-term finance to existing as well as new industries. It simultaneously ensures the success of these industries by providing them managerial, entrepreneurial and technical assistance. DFIs' financial assistance is very often characterised by subsidised lending to trigger industrial activities, especially in the backward regions or social welfare–oriented industries. Given the fact that many Western countries established the specialised financial institutions with a character of DFIs to catch up faster industrialisation process, India also ventured to establish many national- and regional-level DFIs since the independence to chart out the industrialisation path with heavily state intervention in the real and financial segments of the economy (Chandrasekhar, 2011). The late 1980s had witnessed around 52 state- and national-level DFIs to promote regionally balanced and planned industrialisation in India. However, the start of financial liberalisation as a corollary of economic liberalisation led to the dilution of DFIs, as mentioned at the beginning of this section. The greater space to the international finance based on market principles allowed the withdrawal of concessional finance and favourable regulatory provisions available to DFIs. The decline of DFIs in India witnessed the rise of commercial banks, stock markets, mutual funds, and non-institutional sources, which motivated industrialisation only in commercially viable industries and regions even though such financialisation is potentially a threat to the country's financial stability. This chapter attempts to address the episode of rise and fall of development financing in the modern economic history of India with particular reference to industrial funding. By addressing this issue, the chapter also highlights the changing role of the state from an agent of storing equality as was envisaged in the Constitution of India to an agent of speculative finance to widen the economic distance between rich and poor. The following section of the chapter illustrates the role of DFIs in industrialisation based on the catching-up theory of industrialisation. The third section describes the rising trend of DFIs in the overall bank-based financial system till the start of financial liberalisation in India. The fourth section attempts to highlight different dimensions of the trend of DFIs' financing which highlight the decline of DFIs in India during the post-financial liberalisation period. The fifth section attempts to highlight the determinants of the decline of DFIs' role in the Indian financial system with specific emphasis on the state's role in favour of global finance. The state's nature during the finance era has been highlighted to understand the emerging economic paradigm, which in itself brings the state to margin in the overall decision-making. The sixth section concludes with policy implications and recent developments in India's development banking.

Role of DFIs in Industrialisation

Catching up with the stage of economic development of the developed world, the industrialisation is considered as one of the foremost requirements. Industrialisation leads to not only better economic growth but also to hosts of external and internal economies of scale which encourage the scope of industrial activities. The expansion of industry has a direct favourable implication for employment opportunities outside the realm of the agriculture sector for the surplus labour force accommodated in the agriculture sector even with zero labour productivity. The expansion of employment opportunities outside the agriculture sector also has positive implications for per capita income. Further, beyond a point, even agricultural growth becomes dependent upon the availability of certain manufactured inputs such as machines, chemical fertilisers and pesticides, cold storage, etc. Kaldor (1966, 1967) provided strong grounds to support industrialisation to accelerate economic growth.[2] Kaldor's first law states that the faster the growth rate of manufacturing in an economy, the quicker will be the growth of its GDP. Instead of simply being a correlation between two variables, Kaldor regarded the relationship as fundamentally a causal one, the causation running from the growth of manufacturing production to the growth of GDP in normal circumstances. However, keeping in mind the parameters of economic development, which is defined much broader than the economic growth, the industrialisation has to be such that it tends to reduce the regional disparities, tends to reduce the dependence on foreign countries by encouraging import substitution, and tends to promote industries which play as positive externalities for agriculture sector by creating demand for inputs by industries as well as producing inputs which raises the productivity of agriculture sector.

Sustained industrial development requires the state's intervention in the allocation of investment and for stimulating effective demand in the economy.[3] There are two ways to guide the portion of assets for the appropriate pattern of industrialisation. Firstly, the state can undertake the investment itself, financing it with tax collection and other sources of deficit financing; and secondly, the state can use the financial system to finance private or public investment with the help of a range of mechanisms such as directed credit, differential interest rates, specialised financial institutions and regulatory measures.[4] The latter option points to the role of finance and the financial system in industrial development, emphasising industries in the private sector. Any industrial unit requires undertaking two types of expenditures: long-term and short-term. The long-term spending is necessary for the creation or acquisition of fixed assets such as land, building and machinery, while the short-term expenditure is required for maintaining a regular supply of raw materials, financing inventories and ensuring payment to workers. To meet the long- and short-term expenditures, the industrial unit requires long- and short-term finance, respectively. The short- and long-term finance are interchangeable to some extent, e.g. by rolling over short-term loans, but this cannot happen beyond a point, particularly when industrial units are installed newly. Since new industrial investments require long gestation periods to go into commercial production and earn profits, the long-term financing of new industrial investments is quite risky as the long run is associated with a greater degree of economic uncertainty. However, risk is there in short-term funding as well but not to the extent of long-term financing.

The association of a greater degree of risk with long-term lending becomes a kind of obstacle in the path of industrial development. Simultaneously, the lack of technology, infrastructure, entrepreneurship and a well-established capital market in developing countries hinders new industrial investments. If these industrial investments are carried out in backward regions, the entrepreneurs face further more significant risks. Given these features of industrial investments, DFIs are considered an essential source of financial and non-financial assistance for new investors in large-, medium- and small-scale industries. Allocation of financial resources along with provision of other important inputs by DFIs may break the vicious circle of economic backwardness and provide the basis for additional investments (Singh 1974). DFIs are also sources of assistance in foreign currency to facilitate the import of foreign technology for entrepreneurs who cannot access them independently. For these reasons, DFIs can promote the economic development of underdeveloped countries by promoting entrepreneurship, creating investment opportunities, channelling savings into available productive investments, strengthening decision-making ability among new or existing entrepreneurs, improving accessibility to technology and know-how, and supporting vertically integrated industrial structures. Some analysts such as Cameron (1953), Gerschenkron (1962), Diamond (1957), and Basu (1965) have emphasised the role of DFIs or their prototypes as financial institutions particularly suited to further industrial and economic development.

The initial prototype of DFI was the Crédit Mobilier of France, which was chartered by a decree of the president of the Republic (Louis-Napoleon Bonaparte) on 18th November 1852 (Cameron 1953). The Crédit Mobilier promoted, financed and developed a number of industrial undertakings in France and other European countries. This institution functioned as a financial institution which would sell the shares of the undertakings it promoted when they were ripe for the market and therefore obtained the means for financing new enterprises. Its chief interest also lay in the promotion of public utility undertakings which by their very nature could not be expected to show immediate returns. It promoted a large number of railways in France and abroad as well. The role of the Crédit Mobilier in the economic development of Europe was considerable, and perhaps the most important of all its contributions to economic development was the idea of developing the spirit of enterprise, which was implicit in its conception. Gerschenkron (1962) says, "it was the great eruptive effect of the Prereires that profoundly influenced the history of Continental banking in Europe from the second half of the past (19th) century onward."[5] While inspired by the French experience with the Crédit Mobilier, Germany used the joint-stock banks to fulfil the objectives of development banking. The period after 1848 witnessed establishment of many joint-stock banks such as the Bank für Handel und Industrie (Darmstadt) in 1853, the Discontogesellschaft (Berlin) and the Berliner Handelsgesellschaft in 1856, the Deutsche Bank (Berlin) and the Commerz- und Disconto-Bank (Hamburg) in 1870, the Dresdner Bank in 1872, and the National bank für Deutschland (Berlin) in 1881 (Neuberger and Stokes 1974). Though there were well over a hundred banks of these types, the banks mentioned above constituted the core of development banking in Germany before World War I. These banks, also called the Kreditbanken, played a crucial role in promoting heavy industries in Germany. These banks were very closely associated with the industrial units in terms of financing their long- and short-term capital requirements. They were also closely involved in the day-to-day decision-making of the firms.

The Japanese government sponsored the establishment of the Industrial Bank of Japan (IBJ) in 1902 on the lines of the Crédit Mobilier of France. It had three purposes: to provide long-term loans to modern industries, promote the inflow of foreign portfolio capital while avoiding foreign control of domestic industries, and develop a market for corporate and local government bonds by creating appropriate institutional arrangements. It subscribed to the debentures of companies and granted loans to industrial concerns on the security of real estates, land and factory premises and to small industrialists on their personal securities. It is notable that the bank's participation in equity finance was subject to the approval of the Ministry of Finance. The duration of loans was restricted to five years, but in some cases, it extended loans for 15 years, for example, in the shipping industry (Basu 1965). Another specialised bank that came into existence was the Hypothec Bank of Japan, which was meant primarily for long-term financing to different types of industries, including agriculture. It was the most successful bank, which had by 1914 its issues of debentures and loans constituted more than half the total for all specialised banks (Cameron, Patrick and Tilly, 1967). Such specialised banks were born out of Matsukata's financial design, which tried to shape the Japanese financial system to suit progressive industrialisation. Brazil also witnessed the constitution of widely discussed the Banco Nacional de Desenvolvimento Economico e Social (BNDES) in 1952, which was a milestone in the economic history of Brazil.[6] It made a crucial contribution to the development of electricity, railways, roads and various infrastructural facilities. It provided long- and short-term loans to various industrial projects that were intended to make the Brazilian economy independent in terms of capital goods and technology. It operated as per the economic targets of the Brazilian government. Maia, Mondi, and Roberts (2005) observed that BNDES has effectively identified the country's industrial development goals and accordingly has initiated financing options for industries.

Rise of DFIs in India during Pre-financial Liberalisation Period

After India got independence on 15th August 1947, the National Government's basic economic and social goals were given definitive shape in the Constitution adopted in 1950. A distinguishing feature of the economic policy in independent India was planning with socialist goals. The planning strategy was shaped by mainly three factors: firstly, the experience with the Great Depression of the interwar period, which destroyed any faith in the virtues of the free market; secondly, Keynesianism, a product of the Great Depression; and thirdly, the starkly contrasting performance of the Soviet Union vis-à-vis other Western countries during the period of depression. The planning strategy also considered India's experience with *laissez-faire* policies during the colonial period and the deprivation that resulted under the colonial regime. Overall planning was seen as essential for throwing off the yoke of foreign domination in the economic realm and raising the living standard of the masses, i.e. for realising the promises of free India.

The architect of the planning strategy P.C. Mahalanobis stressed the presence of heavy and capital goods industries because such emphasis was seen as essential for self-reliant development. He also emphasised promoting cottage industries, which have high output–capital ratios to address any consumption goods shortage. Given the above-mentioned socio-economic objectives of the country and the strategy of planning, an appropriate financial system was required. The Shroff Committee (1954) highlighted the understanding of the Planning Commission about reorientation of the attitude and functioning of the financial institutions in India in the following words:

> The proper discharge of its functions by the banking system will necessitate its operation more and more in the light of priorities for development indicated in the Plan and less and less in terms of returns on capital. The banking system – and the whole mechanism of finance including insurance, the stock exchanges and other institutions concerned with investments – will thus have to be fitted increasingly into the scheme of development visualised for the economy as a whole; for, it is only thus that the process of mobilising saving and utilising them to the best advantage becomes socially purposive.[7]

The commercial banks were not involved in lending to meet the long-term requirements of industries. They confined themselves mainly to providing working capital which too was constrained by the low-level deposits. As on 30th June 1953, 34 per cent of total advances by commercial banks went to the industry while 48.7 per cent went to commerce and financial activities (Panandikar 1975). Any increase in advances by commercial banks to industries required either diversion of resources from other types of assets, such as investment in government securities, or advances to commerce, etc., or a substantial increase in deposits. Under such circumstances, the Government of India initiated the establishment of a series of DFIs in India to cater the long- and medium-term financial requirements of industries in India. DFIs were expected to strengthen different segments of industries by providing them non-financial complementary assistance as well. Such non-financial assistance was needed as new entrepreneurs lacked technical and managerial skills due to the underdevelopment of the Indian industrial sector.

With the establishment of the Industrial Finance Corporation of India (IFCI) on 1st July 1948 under the IFCI Act, 1948, development banking had arrived on the horizon of the Indian economy. The preamble of the IFCI Act, 1948, stated: "The IFCI is created to make medium and long-term credits more readily available to industrial concerns in India, particularly in circumstances where normal banking accommodation is inappropriate or recourse to capital issue method is impracticable."[8] After establishing the IFCI, the State Financial Corporation Act, 1951, was passed by the Indian parliament under which the state governments could establish the State Financial Corporations (SFCs) to cater the financial needs of medium- and small-scale industries (Govt. of India, 1951). This Act led to the establishment of 18 SFCs across the country. In 1955, the Industrial Credit and Investment Corporation of India (ICICI) was established on the recommendation of the International Bank of Reconstruction and Development-cum-American Investment Mission. In fact, the way the ICICI was established primarily to finance the private sector industries indicates the emergence of financial platforms assisted by the United States and the American interventionist role in India's organised financial system. In the 1960s, the state governments set up State Industrial Development Corporations (SIDCs) to promote the improvement and development of industries in their respective regions. It was felt that in relation to the investment needs likely to arise for industrial development in future, "the totality of contribution of these institutions appeared to be insufficient both in magnitude and in range of financing."[9] This led to a significant breakthrough in development banking in India by establishing the Industrial Development Bank of India (IDBI) in July 1964. The setting up of Industrial Reconstruction Corporation of India (IRCI) in 1971 and the Small Industrial Development Bank of India (SIDBI) in 1989 was with more specific objectives of development banking as the IRCI was to assist the sick industries and the SIDBI was meant to assist small-scale industries. By 1989, India had witnessed around 60 DFIs, including EXIM Bank, National Bank for Agriculture and Rural Development

(NABARD), Khadi Development Corporation, Power Finance Corporation, and Rural Electrification Corporation.

The rising role of DFIs in the financing of industries appears from the fact that average annual assistance sanctioned and disbursed increased from Rs. 27.1 million and 19.3 million, respectively, during the pre-plan period (1948–51) to Rs. 9,502.2 million and 6,180.5 million, respectively, during the Fifth Five-Year Plan (1974–79). This continued further, and the average annual assistance sanctioned and disbursed further rose to Rs. 186,048.5 million and Rs. 130,560.5 million during the two annual plans of 1990–92 (see Table 6.1). The growth of development banking in India is also clearly visible from the fact that financial assistance by DFIs increased continuously, as shown in Figure 6.1. The rising of development banking can also be observed from the fact that financial assistance disbursed by DFIs as a percentage of Gross Capital Formation (GCF) in the private sector increased from 4.51 per cent during the First Five-Year Plan to 41.67 per cent during the Fifth Five-Year Plan (see Table 6.2). This share further increased to 59.32 per cent during the Seventh Five-Year Plan. The majority of the assistance went primarily to the private sector, which garnered close to 80 per cent of the cumulative financial assistance sanctioned by DFIs up to 1992 (see Figure 6.2). Such a model of financial assistance by DFIs was based on the state's aid to private capital based on nationalistic capitalism, which visualised domestic capitalism as a better replacement to the hegemony of

Table 6.1 Trends of Plan-wise Financial Assistance Sanctioned and Disbursed by Development Banks between 1948 and 1979 (Rs. million)

Period	*Sanctioned*	*Disbursed*
Pre-Plan (1948–51)	81.3 (27.1)	57.9 (19.3)
First Plan (1951–56)	339.3 (68.0)	144.6 (29.0)
Second Plan (1956–61)	1,210. (242.0)	764.0 (153.0)
Third Plan (1961–66)	5,591.0 (1,118.0)	3624.0 (725.0)
Three Annual Plans (1966–69)	4,209.0 (1,403.0)	3,885.0 (1,295.0)
Fourth Plan (1969–74)	15,475.0 (3,094.1)	10,079.4 (2,015.9)
Fifth Plan (1974–79)	47,511.4 (9,502.2)	30,902.4 (6,180.5)
Annual Plan (1979–80)	1,9035.0	12,623.0
Sixth Plan (1980–85)	195,383.0 (39,076.7)	141,421.0 (28,284.2)
Seventh Plan (1985–90)	492,276.0 (98,455.2)	340,314.0 (68,062.8)
Two Annual Plans (1990–92)	372,097.0 (186,048.5)	261,121.0 (130,560.5)

Notes: (i) Figures in parentheses are annual averages.
(ii) Institutions covered are IFCI (1948 onwards), SFCs (1953 onwards), ICICI (1955 onwards), Refinance Corporation of India (RCI) (from 1958 to 1963), LIC and SIDCs (1961–62 onwards), IDBI and UTI (1964 onwards), and IRCI/IRBI (1970–71 onwards).

Sources: (i) Figures for Pre-Plan and First, Second and Third Five-Years Plans from Kaushal K. Arora (1992), *Development Banking in India*, Atlantic Publishers & Distributers, (ii). For remaining plans, calculated from the various issues of *Operational Statistics*, IDBI.

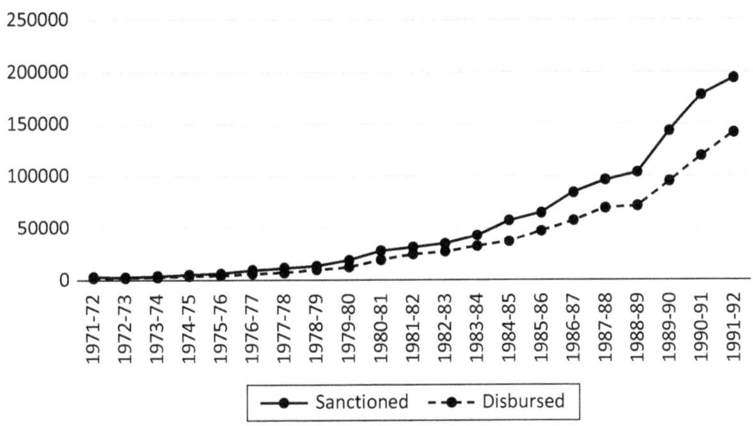

Figure 6.1 Financial assistance sanctioned and disbursed by development banks (Rs. million). *Source:* Report on Development Banking in India (various issues), IDBI.

Table 6.2 Plan-wise Trends of Financial Assistance as Percentage of Gross Capital Formation in Private Sector between 1950 and 1992

Plan period	*Share of financial assistance (%)*
First Plan (1951–56)	4.51
Second Plan (1956–61)	6.28
Third Plan (1961–66)	14.07
Three Annual Plans (1966–69)	18.06
Fourth Plan (1969–74)	24.86
Fifth Plan (1974–79)	41.67
Annual Plan (1979–80)	59.11
Sixth Plan (1980–85)	45.95
Seventh Plan (1985–90)	59.32
Two Annual Plans (1990–92)	57.61

Sources: Figures for First, Second and Third Five-Year Plans from Kaushal K. Arora (1992), *Development Banking in India*, Atlantic Publishers & Distributers. (ii) For remaining plans, calculated from the various issues of *Operational Statistics*, IDBI and *Report on Development Banking in India*, IDBI.

foreign capital (Patnaik, 1972). The rise of financial assistance by DFIs was conditional, keeping in mind the balanced regional industrialisation in which the subsidised finance by DFIs was available mainly for setting up industries in the backward regions and also for setting up new industries. Such phenomenal rise of financial assistance to industries must have affected the pattern of industrialisation that emerged since independence (Mahalanobis Committee, 1964, Hazari Committee, 1967, Dutt Committee, 1969a).

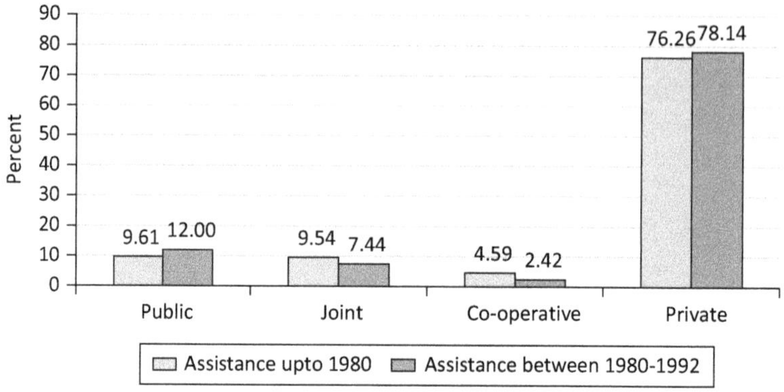

Figure 6.2 Sector-wise share in cumulative financial assistance sanctioned by development banks up to 1991–92 (%). *Source*: Report on development banking in India (various issues), IDBI.

Such rise of financial assistance by DFIs has been accompanied by the non-financial assistance by the DFIs to new and existing entrepreneurs. Such non-financial assistance was routed through the technical consultancy organisations (TCOs), which were set up by DFIs, mainly IDBI, IFCI and ICICI. There were in total 18 TCOs at all-India level. Their main functions were primarily to conduct a survey for industrial potentialities in different regions, prepare project profiles and feasibility studies, identify potential entrepreneurs and provide them with technical and managerial assistance, carry out techno-economic appraisals and put up projects on a turnkey basis where necessary (see Table 6.3).

Declining Trend of Development Banking during Financial Liberalisation

There was a gradual shift in the nature of the financial sector after the start of financial liberalisation based on the recommendations of the Narasimham Committees (1991 and 1998). The financial liberalisation was an essential step to make the economic liberalisation strategy successful. The policy package of Bretton Woods Institutions in the form of Structural Adjustment and Macroeconomic Stabilization was made conditional upon the Indian economy to overcome the momentary BOP crisis in 1990. The new superstructure of the financial system was visualised to be the impetus of the rising share of the private sector in the country's economic activities, though the existing DFIs assisted primarily the private sector. However, the new order ensured that their lending to the private sector in the backward region and socially crucial industries were discarded for industries that had better economic returns. In an attempt to

Table 6.3 Operations of TCOs between 1980–81 and 1991–92

S. No.	Type of service	From inception (1972) to 1980–81	1981–82	1982–83	1983–84	1984–85	1985–86	1986–87	1987–88	1988–89	1989–90	1990–91	1991–92
1.	Feasibility/pre-investment studies/ project profiles/reports	4,529	1,902*	1,069	991	1,019	1,537	2,158	2,426	3,147	3,431	2,769	3,485
2.	Project appraisals	860	NA	124	338	356	867	113	26	44	37	28	56
3.	Survey/studies (industrial potential surveys, area developmental surveys, and others)	301		13	107	261	225	125	198	144	228	262	81
4.	Modernisation/rehabilitation diagnostic studies			4	91	115	121	150	271	209	247	175	348
5.	Functional industrial complexes/ turnkey assignments	–		6	–	7	31	12	9	9	12	19	11
6.	Other assignments				26	–	288	188	152	151	173	227	242
	Total	**5,690**	**1,902**	**1,216**	**1,553**	**1,758**	**3,069**	**2,746**	**3,082**	**3,704**	**4,128**	**3,480**	**4,223**
7.	Entrepreneurship Development Programmes (EDPs)												
	(a) Programmes conducted			119	67	80	116	100	156	216	191	173	248
	(b) Entrepreneurs trained	NA	NA	3,698	1,851	1,851	3,080	2,625	4,030	4,267	4,815	4,442	7,197
8.	Entrepreneurship awareness camps/Gramodaya EDPs/ Skill Upgradation programs/ MEGSA/ SEEUY			–	–	–	–	–	6	57	15	22	47

Source: Report on Development Banking in India (various issues), IDBI.

create a competitive financial system, the argument of a level playing field was advanced. Special treatment to the DFIs by the Government of India was removed under the pressure of controlling the fiscal deficit, thereby triggering the state to withdraw the subsidies available to DFIs (more discussion on such contours of financial liberalisation has been taken up in the later section of the chapter). In the light of new financial order, we witnessed the fall of development banking in India, which is clearly reflected in Figure 6.3, which is shown as DFIs' financial assistance sanctioned and disbursed as a percentage of the Gross Domestic Capital Formation (GDCF). The rising trend of financial assistance stopped by 1993–94. It dramatically declined during the post-2000 period. Now it is a minuscule proportion of GDCF. Even in the overall setting of the banking system, there is a dramatic fall of DFIs' assets compared to commercial banks after the financial liberalisation (see Figure 6.4). The same was not true before the financial liberalisation. During the pre-financial liberalisation period, the size of assets of DFIs increased vis-à-vis commercial banks; and this highlights that the banking system was more towards creating long-term capital formation with lesser possibility of assets–liabilities mismatch as DFIs have more long-term liabilities as compared to commercial banks. It is to be mentioned here that most of the banking crisis originates based on short-term liabilities and long-term assets. Figure 6.3 may suggest that the decline of DFIs was visible since 2000–01, but the analysis of financial assistance reveals that the nature of DFIs' financial assistance was altered much before that, since the start of the policy package of Structural Adjustment Program and Macroeconomic Stabilization. To understand this decline of DFIs in India, we may analyse the nature of financial assistance of the DFIs.

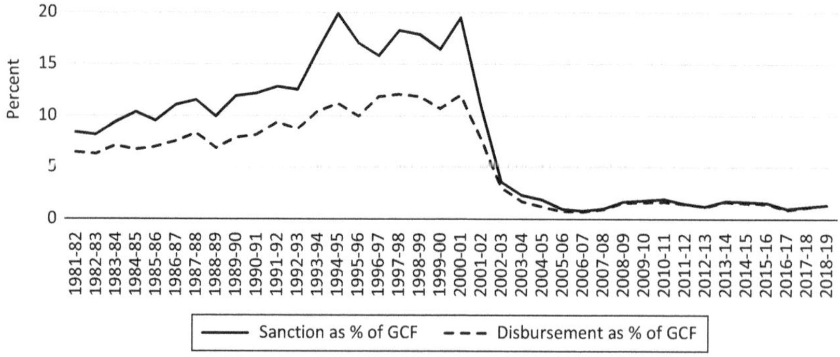

Figure 6.3 Financial assistance sanctioned and disbursed by DFIs (% of GCF). *Source:* Author's calculation based on the data from the *Handbook of Statistics on Indian Economy* (Real Time as on 12th July 2021), RBI.

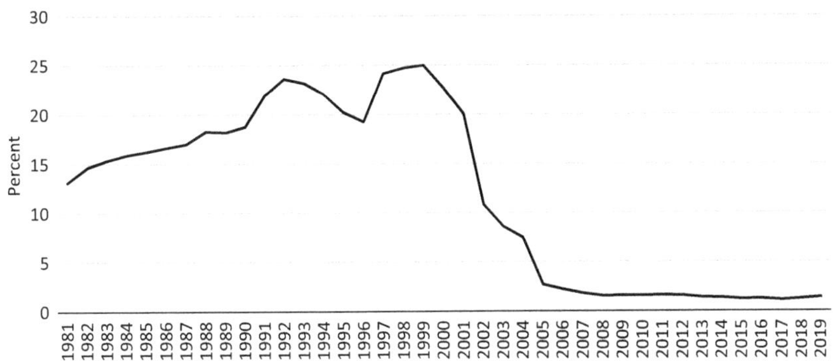

Figure 6.4 Assets of DFIs as percentage of commercial banks' assets. *Source:* Author's calculation based on the data from *Handbook of Statistics on Indian Economy* (Real Time as on 12th July 2021), RBI.

Since the data on financial assistance clearly reflects the fall of DFIs' financial assistance, whatever the financial assistance by DFIs was recorded during the period of financial liberalisation also highlights the dictates of financialisation on the nature of financial assistance by the DFIs against the notion of development banking in India. There are three dimensions of the financial assistance, highlighting the DFIs' developmental role, which were discarded and ultimately the DFIs became non-existent in the Indian economy. These three dimensions of financial assistance by DFIs are (i) purpose-wise financial assistance, (ii) state-wise financial assistance, and (iii) industry-wise financial assistance.

The analysis of three dimensions of financial assistance by DFIs has been confined only up to 2003–04 primarily for two reasons: firstly, the two largest DFIs – ICICI and IDBI – were converted into commercial banks in 2002 and 2005, respectively; and secondly, the publication of data on financial assistance on such dimensions for public consumption was discontinued due to the discontinuation of the Report on Development Banking, which used to be published by the IDBI. However, the analysis of financial assistance on the above three main dimensions would highlight how the development banking ended during the period of financialisation:

i. **Changes in the pattern of purpose-wise financial assistance:** The DFIs were primarily constituted to finance industrial development with the provision of long-term loans where in some cases the duration of loan was 15–20 years. Raising the level of investment was an essential objective of the Mahalanobis strategy of industrialisation in India.[10] The availability of data on purpose-wise classification of financial assistance by DFIs suggests that the pre-liberalisation financial assistance was mainly to create production capacity in the economy, which was done through financing for new investments as well as expansion and diversification of industries. Financing for new investments was meant to create new sets of entrepreneurs, and the DFIs played an essential role in that. Financing for new investments and new entrepreneurs was a risky venture as compared to financing for the expansion of the existing industries and existing entrepreneurs. The provision of long-term finance by the DFIs was an instrument to promote industrialisation in India. A study of DFIs by Kumar (2013) highlights that the share of new investments in cumulative financial assistance sanctioned by DFIs for the period 1992–93 to 2003–04 witnessed a steep decline by almost 15 per cent compared to the share of new investments from 1980–81 to 1991–92. The percentage of assistance for diversification and expansion witnessed a marginal decline by around 2 per cent, which is to say that DFIs continued to assist the existing firms with long-term financial assistance. There was also a dramatic decline in the share of assistance for modernisation and rehabilitation of industries during the financial liberalisation period. Such a pattern of decline of DFIs' financial assistance highlights the withdrawal of DFIs from their developmental objective. Modernisation and rehabilitation were also an essential aspect of industrial revival, and DFIs were supposed to take care of assisted industries. However, they preferred to stay away from such commitment and therefore they withdrew the financial assistance from the sick industries. The sickness of industries has been an outcome of the business cycle and the growing competition during the globalisation period. But the DFIs' changing pattern of financing under the market principles affected their traditional role. The share of financial assistance advanced in the form of working capital witnessed a dramatic rise during the financial liberalisation period. It increased from 7.58 per cent during 1980–81 to 1991–92 to 39.04 per cent during 1992–93 to 2003–04 (Kumar, 2013). It highlights a significant departure of DFIs from its traditional role of financing capital formation to funding the working capital requirements of industries. In some way, the DFIs ventured into the domain of the commercial banks, where the latter are recognised as a primary source of financing working capital. Such a trend of financing patterns of DFIs was shaped under the financial sector reforms adopted in India since 1991.

ii. **Changes in the pattern of state-wise financial assistance:** The provision of financial assistance to backward areas was a significant feature of the DFIs' lending policy, which gained traction after identifying the backward regions by the Pande Working Group (1969b) and Wanchoo Working Group (1969c). The share of backward regions in the total financial assistance sanctioned by the DFIs increased from 21.67 per cent in 1980–81 to almost 40.40 per cent in 1990–91, which indicates that after the identification of backward regions, their share increased

(Kumar, 2013). It was an indicator of DFIs' concerns for regionally balanced industrialisation. However, the share of backward areas in total financial assistance by the DFIs witnessed a decline after 1992 and it went down dramatically since 1997. The data on state-wise financial assistance by DFIs also suggest the decline of the share of industrially backward states in total financial assistance by DFIs. The gain was made by the industrially developed states during the financial liberalisation. The highest gain was observed for Maharashtra's share in cumulative financial aid sanctioned by DFIs. It gained from 18.52 per cent during 1980–81 to 1991–92 to 26.03 per cent during 1992–93 to 2003–04. It was followed by Gujarat, which witnessed a rise in its share from 12.27 per cent during 1980–81 and 1991–92 to 14.06 per cent during 1992–93 to 2003–04. But most of the industrially underdeveloped states witnessed a decline in their share in the cumulative financial assistance by DFIs during the financial liberalisation period (see Figure 6.5). The period of financial liberalisation also witnessed concentration of financial assistance by DFIs in the hands of only few states highlighting the rising inequality in financial assistance by DFIs. and this is clearly being reflected in Figure 6.6, which measures the degree of concentration using the Herfindahl-Hirschman Index (HHI).[11] Based on the principle of either finance cause growth or growth attracts the finance; in the era of market-based financial system, the trend of financial assistance by the DFIs highlights that market did not favour the backward states; and the DFIs which were established to strengthen the backward regions actually retreated from their assigned goal of regionally balanced industrial development in India.

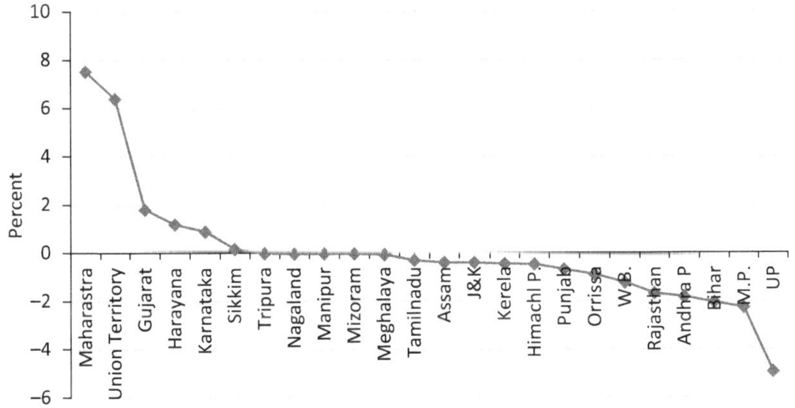

Figure 6.5 Difference of state-wise share in cumulative assistance sanctioned between pre- and post-financial liberalisation periods. *Source:* Calculated from the data given in *Report on Development Banking in India* (various issues), IDBI.

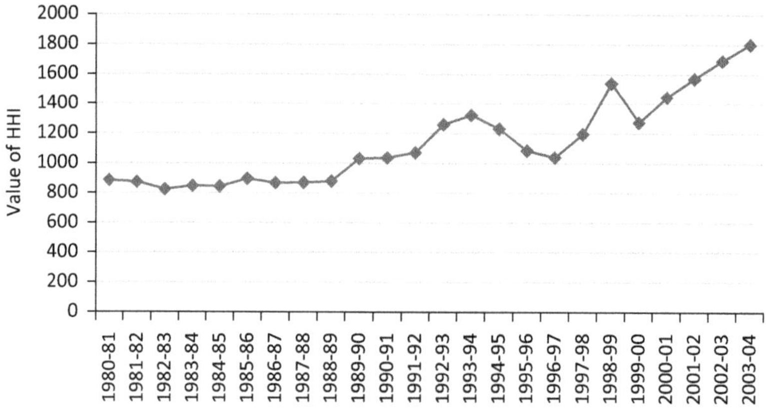

Figure 6.6 HHI for state-wise share in financial assistance sanctioned. *Source:* Calculated from the data given in the Report on Development Banking in India (various issues), IDBI.

iii. **Changes in the pattern of Industry-wise financial assistance:** Various industrial policy statements, which were grounded in the Industrial Policy Resolution 1956, stressed a regionally more dispersed industrialisation. They emphasised the importance of industries related to agriculture, consisting of those that drew inputs from agriculture and those that produced inputs such as fertilisers or technical appliances for the agricultural sector.[12] Traditional industries such as food products, textiles, paper products and rubber products, which were important from the point of view of generating employment, catering the needs of local consumers, and having direct connection to the agriculture sector, recorded a substantial decline in financial assistance provided by the DFIs during the period of financial liberalisation. They together shared 21.52 per cent of cumulative assistance sanctioned by the DFIs during the period between 1980–81 and 1991–92, but this share declined to close to 11.72 per cent during the period between 1992–93 and 2003–04 (Kumar, 2013). Such a fall in share was the result of the negative average annual growth rates of absolute value of financial assistance to these industries from the DFIs during 1992–93 to 2003–04. Other industries such as fertilisers, chemicals, cement, metal products, machinery, electronic and electrical products, and transport equipment also witnessed a significant decline in their shares in financial assistance provided by the DFIs during financial liberalisation. The industries that gained the financial assistance provided by the DFIs during the period between 1992–93 and 2003–04 are mainly electricity generation, the service sector, and other industries, including infrastructure.

Contours of Financial Liberalisation and Decline of DFIs

Observations in the above section clearly highlight the decline of DFIs in India. Such decline can be attributed to the financial liberalisation as it aimed to reduce the state's role in the financial sector, allowed proliferation of financial instruments and financial institutions for market profit, and emphasised the opening up of the domestic financial sector to the global market. The Narasimham Committees (1991 and 1998), under the chairmanship of M. Narasimham, laid down the road map of financial sector reforms in India. The first Narasimham Committee (1991) highlighted the importance of the DFIs. It held that they had by and large been able to fulfil the objectives for which they were set up. In particular, the Committee noted that these institutions had been largely successful in accelerating the growth of industrial development by providing much-needed financial support on fairly liberal terms and at stable rates of interest for setting up new projects, expansion of existing projects and modernisation of projects by induction of new technologies.[13] However, it felt that they needed to be more competitive, more efficient and more profitable and therefore it recommended specific points on the lines of market principles. The second Narasimham Committee under the chairmanship of M. Narasimham, which was exclusively on banking sector reforms, submitted its report in April 1998. It was slated to initiate the second generation of reforms in the financial sector as a sequel to the recommendations of the first Narasimham Committee. The recommendations by both the committees concerning DFIs are mentioned below briefly:

a. Withdrawal of the concessional funds, which were available from the RBI and central and states governments to the national- and state-level DFIs.
b. Allowing the commercial banks to provide term-lending to increase the competition in the banking sector, even though that has a potential problem in terms of assets–liabilities mismatch.
c. Progressive deregulation of interest rates so that market-related rates based on actual risk perception are allowed to be discovered and an element of price competition introduced concerning lending by the DFIs vis-à-vis commercial banks.
d. Withdrawal of IDBI's promotional and refinancing role to SFCs, SIDBI and SIDCs.
e. Phasing out of the existing privileged and concessional access to resources for the DFIs through the Statutory Liquidity Ratio (SLR) mechanism and making DFIs dependent on the capital market through borrowing at market-related rates to meet their requirements.
f. Discouraging the representation of DFIs on the boards of firms in the corporate sector that have been heavily dependent on the DFIs for debt.

g. Conversion of DFIs into commercial banks, with the stipulation that if a DFI does not acquire banking license within a stipulated time, it should be categorised as a Non-Banking Financial Company (NBFC).
h. Subjecting the converted DFI into a commercial bank to the statutory reserve requirements such as CRR and SLR regarding its liabilities to bring it on par with the provisions relating to commercial banks.
i. Allowing mergers of DFIs with commercial banks.
j. Implementation of Basel norms (1997) and "core principles" for effective supervision of the banking sector.

Such recommendations created an atmosphere where the idea of development banking became shaky and untenable in India. In the light of above-mentioned recommendations, there were withdrawals of secured and subsidised financial resources available to DFIs from the government, including RBI. The available data for the period 1980–2004 shows that the average annual share of government and RBI in total liabilities of all India DFIs declined from 23.5 per cent during 1980–92 to 6.4 per cent during 1993–2004 (Kumar, 2013). The existing DFIs such as IFCI, which is now categorised as Non-Banking Financial Company (NBFC), have witnessed zero share of government and RBI in its total liabilities since 2017 till date.[14] Other existing DFI – SIDBI too has witnessed fall in the share of government sources from 4.69 per cent of its total liabilities in 2004 to 1.38 per cent in 2019. Similarly, the state-level DFIs, which were the primary source of term financing for industries at the regional level, also witnessed the drying up of their finance from the concessional sources. The SFCs witnessed a fall in share of borrowing from RBI and governments in their total financial resources raised annually from 4.3 per cent during 1980–81 to 1991–92 to 1.3 per cent during 1992–93 to 2003–04. Similar was the trend for SIDCs as well. Apart from this, IDBI, which was an assured source of financial resources for the SFCs and SIDCs, also reduced its financial assistance to SFCs and SIDCs substantially. The data available about the liabilities and assets of the SFCs even after 2004 suggests that the share of concessional sources has not increased in the liabilities of the SFCs and they have been left to market sources for mobilisation of financial resources. The share of RBI, IDBI, SIDBI and governments in the total liabilities of SFCs was 44.27 per cent in 1983, which declined to 12.38 per cent in 1993, which further fell to 28.65 per cent in 2003 and 8.66 per cent in 2019.[15] RBI's special provision of the LTO (NIC) Fund that was the source of assured financial resources of DFIs was discontinued since 1992. Figure 6.7 highlights the steep decline of the assured source of industrial finance for long- and short-term to DFIs. This highlights that the RBI's direct involvement with development was being replaced by its only inflation targeting objective during the period of financialisation.

Such decline of the government's financial resources to the DFIs became the cause of the financial assistance pattern by the DFIs that we observe

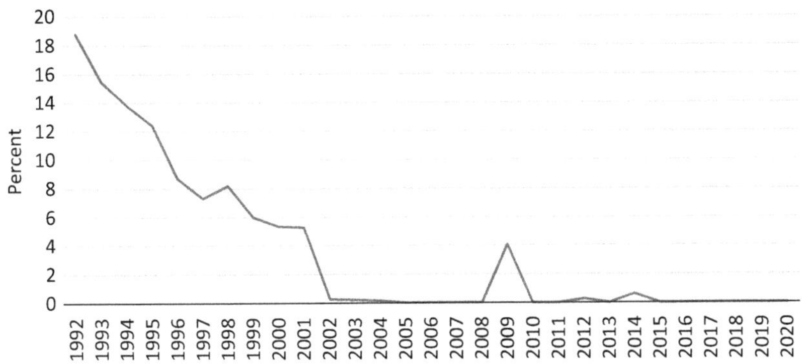

Figure 6.7 RBI's financial assistance to DFIs as percentage of RBI's total assets. *Source:* Calculated from the data given in *Handbook of Statistics on Indian Economy – 2020*, RBI.

above during the period of financial liberalisation. Concerning the drying up of financial resources for projects in backward areas, the Standing Committee on Finance of the 13th Lok Sabha (lower house of legislation) quoted the opinions of various executive officers from different all-India DFIs in its report on "Financial Institutions – Objectives, Performance, and Future Prospects." The Managing Director, ICICI Ltd., stated on 18th September 2000 before the Committee: "In the past we had a subsidy built-in which allowed us to raise money at cheaper cost. So we could fund projects in particular (backward) areas. Today, we have been forced to approach the market."[16] This statement by the ICICI's official reflects the general perspective that concessional funds are essential for development banking. A note submitted to the Standing Committee by the IDBI also expressed similar views about the decline of IDBI's financial assistance to the backward areas. As per the Report, more than 40 per cent of total financial assistance by the IDBI was going to backward areas during the 1980s, but that declined to close to 35 per cent as per available data on the share of backward areas in the total financial assistance sanctioned by the IDBI for the period 1994–1997.[17]

The decline in resources of industrial finance to DFIs from assured sources also witnessed emergence of other sources of industrial finance to Indian industries during the financial liberalisation era. These sources are domestic as well as foreign. Domestic sources consist of primarily commercial banks, new issues market, commercial papers, NBFCs and insurance companies. Foreign sources consist of primarily External Commercial Borrowings (ECBs), ADRs/GDRs, and Foreign Direct Investments (FDI). Commercial banks have coexisted with DFIs since independence complementing each other as part of the dominant bank-based system in India

(Chandrasekhar, 2011). Financial liberalisation was considered as a mechanism to deepen the financial market by giving prominence to stock market and external financial resources that was expected to widen the choices for the corporate sector for financial resources and also help them maintain healthy debt–equity ratio (Murali, 1999). The Security and Exchange Board of India (SEBI) became a statutory body in 1992 to regulate the raising of funds through New Issue Market (NIM) and it launched various reforms to instil faith in individual investors, institutions and the corporate sector in the operation of the stock market. Given the facts that the Narasimham Committees recommended commercial banks to enter into the sphere of term financing to industries and strengthening of the capital market to provide additional long-term financial resources, the Indian financial sector witnessed to become an important source of financing for firms (see Figure 6.8). Based on liabilities structure of some important industries over the period from 1988 to 2004, it was found that the share of term-borrowings from commercial banks witnessed sufficient rise, highlighting the engagement of commercial banks in the term financing, which was previously in the realm of term-lending institutions (Kumar, 2013). The post-2004 trend of scheduled commercial banks' lending has continued raising the share of term-lending in the total non-food credit of scheduled commercial banks (Figure 6.9). However, such a trend of rising long-term liabilities is being accompanied by widening assets–liabilities gap, which have implications for

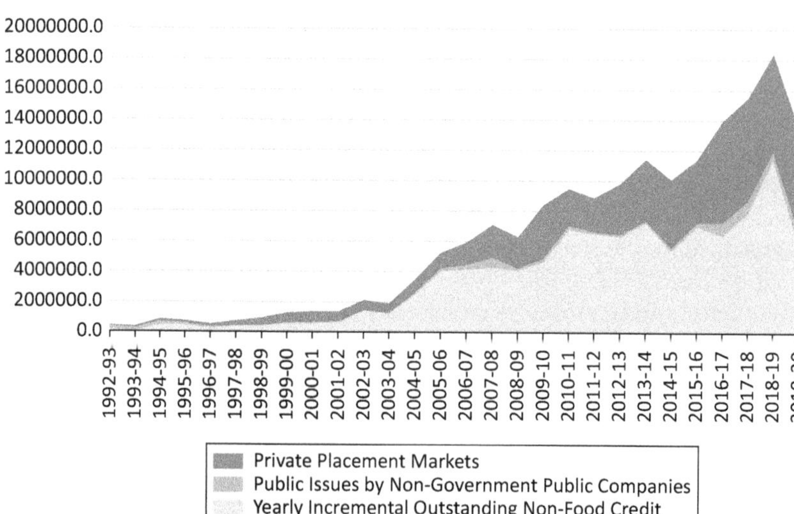

Figure 6.8 Domestic financial resources for Indian industries (Rs. million). *Source:* Calculated from various issues of *Handbook of Statistics on Indian Economy*, RBI

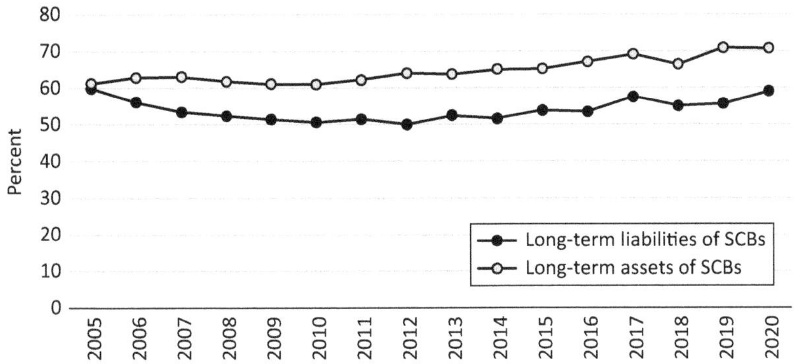

Figure 6.9 Long-term liabilities and assets of SCBs as percentage of their total liabilities and assets. *Source:* Calculated from various issues of *Handbook of Statistics on Indian Economy*, RBI

instability of the banking system during prolonged economic recession. The rise of long-term liabilities of scheduled commercial banks (SCBs) has been accompanied by the rise of non-food credit as share of GDP_{MP} of India. The average share of yearly incremental non-food credit of SCBs as percentage of GDP_{MP} was 2.68 per cent during 1992–93 to 1998–99, that further increased to 5.51 per cent during 1999–2000 to 2005–06 and subsequently to 8.12 per cent during 2006–07 to 2013–14 highlighting unprecedented credit boom in the Indian economy followed by slowdown in credit take-off during the post-2014 period due to some unprecedented and undesirable interventions in the Indian economy.

The stock market also contributed to raising the industrial finance for the Indian corporate sector, partially reducing the need of the DFIs for long-term finance, especially large firms. However, the Indian experience has been characterised by the dominancy of private placement routes of raising funds by the corporate sector in India and not the public issues which ensures the larger participation of investors. Dominant trend of private placements for raising the industrial finance through the Indian stock market implies the narrow base for participating firms. Table 6.4 shows that the share of public issues by the non-government financial companies as a percentage of GDP has declined from an average of 1.44 per cent per annum during 1992–93 to 1998–99 to 0.31 per cent per annum during 2014–15 to 2019–20. However, the share of private placement has increased from an average of 1.32 per cent per annum during 1992–93 to 1998–99 to 3.59 per cent per annum during 2014–15 to 2019–20. The composition of domestic financial resources highlight that even after almost 30 years of financial liberalisation, the Indian economy is a bank-based financial system. The limitation of Asset is limited in benefiting the Indian industries of different scale and from different regions. Figure 6.10 shows that the stock market has mainly benefitted

Table 6.4 Average Values of Different Sources as Percentage of GDP_{MP}

Period	*Yearly incremental outstanding Non-food credit*	*Public Issues by non-government public companies*	*Private placement markets*
1992–93 to 1998–99	2.68	1.44	1.32
1999–2000 to 2005–06	5.51	0.29	2.79
2006–07 to 2013–14	8.12	0.50	3.73
2014–15 to 2019–20	4.83	0.31	3.59

Source: Calculated from various issues of *Handbook of Statistics on Indian Economy*, RBI.

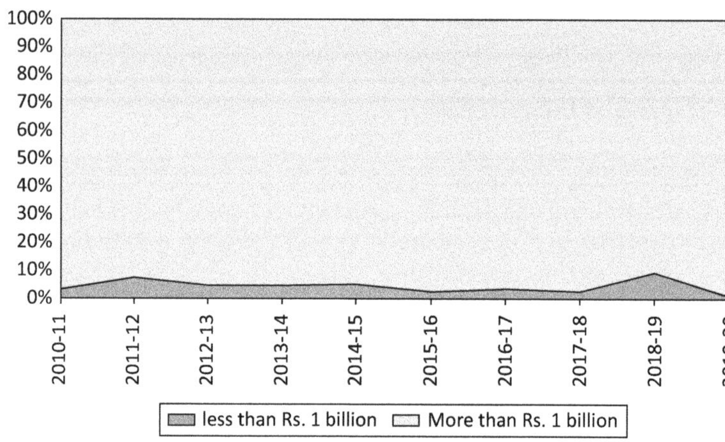

Figure 6.10 Size-wise distribution of resource mobilisation (equity issues). *Source:* Author's calculation based on data from *Handbook of Statistics*, 2020, SEBI.

the large-scale industries, while the small- and medium-scale industries have gained the least from the launch of the capital market. The data available for 2010–11 to 2019–20 suggests that of the funds raised through equity routes, 95 per cent has gone to the large-scale firms, which have launched issues for more than Rs. 10 million. Also the benefits of the stock market have accrued to industries from the developed regions leaving the industries from undeveloped regions either deprived of industrial finance or dependent upon the finance from traditional sources of industrial finance such as banks (see Figure 6.11).

Amongst the foreign financial resources which mattered the most for industrial investments are ADRs/GDRs and ECBs. Foreign direct investments (FDIs) too serve a purpose for raising the production capacity in the economy provided it goes to add to the existing production capacity. However, FDIs are meant to increase the foreign ownership of Indian companies and

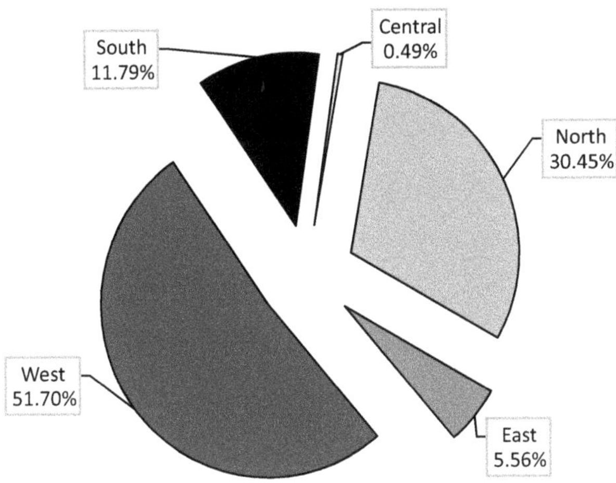

Figure 6.11 Region-wise average share of distribution of resource mobilisation (equity issues) for 2010–20. *Source:* Author's calculation based on data from *Handbook of Statistics, 2020*, SEBI.

therefore not meant to serve as the source of financial resources for domestic entrepreneurs at par with DFIs. ECBs have been the foreign financial resources for domestic firms and it has shown a positive trend, but after 2007–08 it has witnessed decline. The dominant foreign flows have been in the form of FDIs (see Figure 6.12). ADRs/GDRs too which created hope for the Indian companies during the financial liberalisation have lately disappointed the domestic businesses for their hope for raising foreign financial resources. If we compare the domestic and foreign financial resources for domestic commercial sector, we witness that in spite of almost 30 years of economic reforms, the Indian economy has primarily been dependent upon the domestic financial sources, which highlights that the financial liberalisation as a part of economic globalisation strategy has disappointed economists on the front of stable foreign capital flows to modernise the Indian industries and strengthen stable economic progress with economic development objective. Figure 6.13 highlights that the share of foreign resources in total financial flows to the domestic commercial sector was 30.09 per cent in 2007–08 and that has declined to 15.81 per cent in 2017–18. There was a sudden spike in the share of foreign financial resources in the form of FDIs to 37.59 per cent in 2019–20, in the backdrop of falling domestic credit boom due to economic slowdown which set in since the adoption of demonetisation and subsequent implementation of the Goods and Services Tax.

The decline of concessional financial resources to the all-India DFIs and the growing role of commercial banks in long-term lending during the financial liberalisation period accompanied by other sources of industrial finance

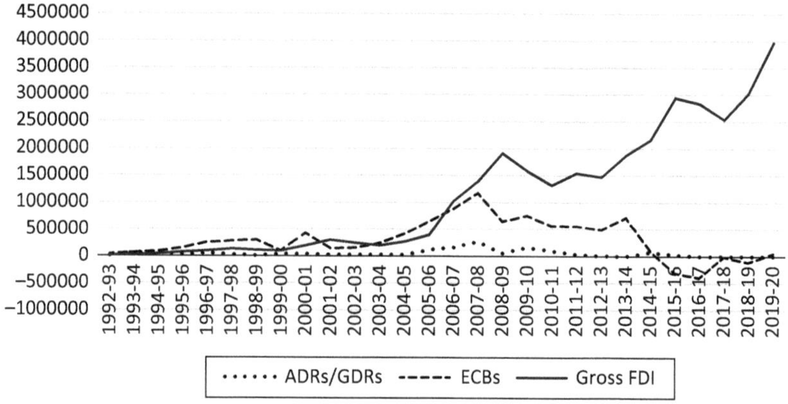

Figure 6.12 Foreign financial resources for Indian corporate sector (Rs. million). *Source:* Calculated from various issues of *Handbook of Statistics on Indian Economy*, RBI

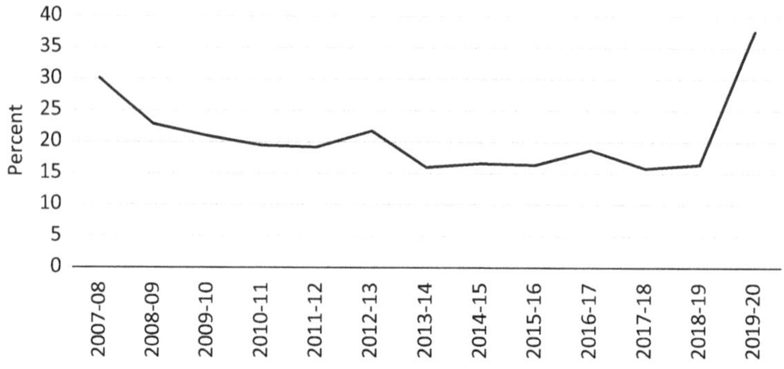

Figure 6.13 Share of foreign financial resources as percentage of total financial flows to commercial sector. *Source:* Calculated from various issues of *Handbook of Statistics on Indian Economy*, RBI.

subjected the DFIs to severe competition in which they were expected to lose as they did not have a large network of branches to mobilise the funds. The effects of such growing competition and withdrawal of concessional financial resources was visible in the evidence on the cost of borrowing from the DFIs compared to the commercial banks. The borrowing from the DFIs involved no cost advantage as lending rates of the DFIs were the same or sometimes even higher than the lending rates of commercial banks after 1995–96 (Kumar, 2013). Further, to follow the recommendations of the Narasimham Committees, the ICICI was reverse merged effectively in 2002 with the ICIC bank to create the largest private commercial bank in India. Following this merger, the IDBI was converted into a Deemed Banking Company on a stand-alone basis in 2004, and finally it was merged effectively with IDBI bank in 2005. The conversion of the two most important DFIs in India into commercial banks brought in some way an end to state-sponsored DFIs for industrial financing. The failure of proposed merger of the IFCI with Punjab National Bank in 2004 due to the opposition of certain political parties and Coordination Committee of the IFCI Officers' and Employees' Association led to conversion of the oldest DFI in India into Systematically Important Non-Deposit taking Non-Banking Financial Company (NBFC-ND-SI) in 2007 and it is still continuing as NBFC-ND-SI in India.

Conclusion

This study with the specific case of DFIs in India points out the decline of development banking in India during the financial liberalisation period. The rise of DFIs' financial assistance meant for raising the investment in the private sector primarily during the era which was characterised by *dirigisme*. The analysis clearly shows that DFIs directed their financial assistance as was desired by the state for mainly capital formation. Industrial development in the backward region was also an important concern for the state, which was fulfilled by DFIs as they were incentivised by concessional financial resources by the state to carry on such financing. Generation of new entrepreneurship and sustainability of business in the backward region was also a concern for DFIs, which was observed in the form of growing non-financial assistance by TCOs during the period before financial liberalisation. However, the start of financial liberalisation, which was part of the Macroeconomic Stabilisation and Structural Adjustment Programs sponsored by international financial institutions, created disincentives to the functioning of DFIs with the withdrawal of state's subsidies and regulatory supports to such DFIs. The withdrawal of subsidised finance to DFIs was also accompanied by the emergence of other domestic and foreign sources of industrial finance. Financial liberalisation promoted the interest of global finance by promoting institutions and markets which were driven by speculative financial objectives, and this required the state to withdraw subsidised finance and control over the functioning of financial intermediaries as per the logic of the McKinnon–Shaw hypothesis of financial liberalisation (McKinnon 1973, Shaw 1973). This led to the ultimate demise of DFIs in India and created skewed deficiencies of the availability of finance at the regional level. The developed regions witnessed better sources of financial resources, while the backward regions witnessed the decline of the same from not only the DFIs during the financial liberalisation period but also from the new sources of financial resources meant for financing the industrial capital formation. The new financial structure that has emerged caters the needs of large-scale industries and also those that are located in the developed regions. In spite of 30 years of financial liberalisation, the over-reliance on commercial banks highlights the fact that neither stock market nor the foreign sources of finance have emerged as the dominant source of financing for industrialisation as was expected by the policymakers in favour of financial liberalisation. Also, given the liabilities structure of commercial banks in India, it is not viable for banks to afford the rising mismatch of assets and liabilities. The decline of DFIs in India highlights the nature of the state that has undergone change under the influence of global finance, which derives its greater dividends from an economic structure that is acquiescent to the external forces at the cost of internal economic strength.

Notes

1 For details of Schumpeterian notion on finance and economic development, see Robert G. King and Ross Levine (1993) 'Finance and Growth: Schumpeter Might be Right', *The Quarterly Journal of Economics*, Vol. 108, No. 3, August, pp. 717-736.
2 Nicholas Kaldor (1966), *Causes of the Slow Rate of Economic Growth of the United Kingdom,* Cambridge University Press, Cambridge, and also Nicholas Kaldor (1967), *Strategic Factors in Economic Development,* New York State School of Industrial and Labour Relations, Cornell University, Ithaca, NY. The former one discusses about the developed countries, while the latter one discusses about the developing countries.
3 It was observed in the case of European countries that real output was exceeding the effective demand in the early industrialisation phase and this had created problems of realization of profits. See Celso Furtado (1971), *Development and Underdevelopment,* University of California Press, USA.
4 State can also use tax policies and regulations to promote industrial development such as policies related to Special Economic Zones.
5 Alexander Gerschenkron (1962), *Economic Backwardness in Historical Perspective: A Book of Essay,* The Belknap Press of Harvard University Press, Cambridge p. 13.
6 Initially, it was named The National Bank for the Economic Development without the "Social" term which was added only in the 1980s.
7 Quoted from the Shroff Committee Report (1954), *The Shroff Committee Report on Finance for the Private Sector*, Government of India, April, p. 42.
8 IFCI (1988), *Industrial Finance Corporation of India: Growth and Development*, Viva Photolithographers, New Delhi, p. 19.
9 'The IDBI – Purposes, Setup and Policies', quoted in *the Report of the Industrial Licensing Policy Inquiry Committee*, Government of India (1969), p.47.
10 Named after statistician P.C. Mahalanobis, who was architect of the Second Five-Year Plan of India, where the major emphasis was on development of heavy industries for higher long-term growth with an objective of independent economic development of India.
11 HHI is an index, which is used to measure the degree of monopolisation of market share. Usually the value of HHI above 1,000 is considered to have elements of monopoly in the share.
12 The interdependence of agriculture and industry is reflected from the fact that in 1980–81, the weight of agro-based industries was 33.68% followed by

metal-based industries and chemical-based industries whose shares were 21.93% and 12.86%, respectively (*Report on Currency and Finance – 1980-81*, RBI, p. 41).

13 'Narasimham Committee Report on the Financial System (1991)', Chapter – VIII, reproduced in Raj Kapila and Uma Kapila (eds.) (1995), *Recent Developments in Indian Economy Part-V: Banking and Financial Sector Reforms,* Academic Foundation, Delhi, pp. 218-288.

14 Calculated on the basis of data available in the *Handbook of Statistics on Indian Economy*, RBI, 2020.

15 Calculated on the basis of data available in the *Handbook of Statistics on Indian Economy*, RBI, 2020.

16 Point No. 1.23, *Financial Institutions: Objectives, Performance, and Future Prospects,* Standing Committee on Finance, 13th Lok Sabha, Ministry of Finance, Delhi, 2000.

17 *Ibid.,* Point No. 1.24.

References

Arora, Kaushal K. (1992). *Development Banking in India.* Atlantic Publishers and Distributers, New Delhi.

Basu, S.K. (1965). *Theory and Practice of Development Banking: A Study in the Asian Context.* Asia Publishing House, New Delhi.

Cameron, Rondo E. (1953). The Credit Mobilier and the Economic Development of Europe. *The Journal of Political Economy*, Vol. 61, No. 6, December, pp. 461–488.

Cameron, Rondo E., Olga Crisp, H.T. Patrick & Richard Tilly (1967). *Banking in Early Stages of Industrialisation: A Study in Comparative Economic History.* Oxford University Press, New York.

Chandrasekhar, C.P. (2011). Development Banks: Their Role and Importance in Development. Available at http://www.networkideas.org/alt/apr2011/development_banks.pdf.

Diamond, William (1957). *Development Banks.* Johns Hopkins Press, Baltimore.

Furtado, Celso (1971). *Development and Underdevelopment.* University of California Press, California, USA.

Gerschenkron, Alexander (1962). *Economic Backwardness in Historical Perspective: A Book of Essay.* The Belknap Press of Harvard University Press, Cambridge.

Govt. of India (1951). *The State Financial Corporations Act, 1951.* Ministry of Finance, New Delhi.

——— (1964). *The Report of Committee on Distribution of Income and Levels of Living (Mahalanobis Committee, 1964)*, Planning Commission, New Delhi.

——— (1967). *The Report on Industrial Planning and Licensing Policy (Hazari Committee).* Planning Commission, New Delhi.

——— (1969a). *The Report of the Industrial Licensing Policy Inquiry Committee (Dutt Committee)*, Ministry of Industrial Development, New Delhi.

——— (1969b). *Report of the (Pande) Working Group on Identification of Backward Areas*, Planning Commission, New Delhi.

——— (1969c). *Report of the (Wanchoo) Working Group on Fiscal and Financial Incentives for Starting Industries in Backward Areas*, Planning Commission, New Delhi.

——— (1991). *The Narasimham Committee Report on the Financial System (1991)*, reproduced in Uma Kapila and Raj Kapila (eds.) *Recent Development in Indian Economy Part-V, Banking and Financial Sector Reforms, 1995*. Academic Foundation, Delhi, pp. 218–288.
——— (1998). *Second Narasimham Committee Report on Banking Sector Reforms*. Ministry of Finance, New Delhi.
——— (2000). *Report on Financial Institutions – Objectives, Performance and Future Prospects*. The Standing Committee on Finance, 13th Lok Sabha, Ministry of Finance, New Delhi.
Gurley, J.G. & E.S. Shaw (1955). Financial Aspects of Economic Development. *The American Economic Review*, Vol. 45, No. 4, pp. 515–538.
IDBI (Annual). *Report on the Development Banking in India*. IDBI, Mumbai.
——— (Annual). *Operational Statistics of IDBI*. IDBI, Mumbai.
Kaldor, Nicholas (1966). *Causes of the Slow Rate of Economic Growth of the United Kingdom*. Cambridge University Press, Cambridge.
——— (1967). *Strategic Factors in Economic Development, New York State School of Industrial and Labour Relations*. Cornell University, Ithaca, NY.
Kapila, Raj & Uma Kapila (1995). *Recent Development in Indian Economy: Banking and Financial Sector Reforms, Part-V*. Academic Foundation, New Delhi.
Keynes, John Maynard (1936). *The General Theory of Employment, Interest and Money*. The Macmillan Press, London.
King, Robert G. & Ross Levine (1993). Schumpeter Might Be Right. *The Quarterly Journal of Economics*, Vol. 108, No. 3, August, pp. 717–736.
Kumar, Santosh (2013). *Decline of Development Banking in India during Financial Liberalization (1992–2004): Determinants and Implications*, Unpublished Thesis. Jawaharlal Nehru University, New Delhi.
Maia, Jorge, Lumkile Mondi & Simon Roberts (2005). Industrial Development and Industrial Finance in Brazil and South Africa: A Comparative Assessment. Annual Forum 2005 on Trade and Uneven Development: Opportunities and Challenges, United Nations University-World Institute for Development and Research, Helsinki. https://www.tips.org.za/research-archive/annual-forum-papers/2005/item/728-industrial-development-and-industrial-finance-in-brazil-and-south-africa-comparative-assessment.
Minsky, Hyman P. (1986). *Stabilizing an Unstable Economy*. Yale University Press, New Haven, CT.
McKinnon, Ronald I. (1973). *Money & Capital in Economic Development*. The Brooking Institutions Press, Washington, DC.
Morishima, M. (1994). *Capital and Credit: A New Formulation of General Equilibrium Theory*. Cambridge University Press, Cambridge.
Murali, K. (1999). *Disintermediation' and Private Corporate Financing: An Analysis of the New Issue (Primary) Market in India*, Unpublished Ph.D. Thesis. Jawaharlal Nehru University, New Delhi.
Panandikar, S.G. (1975). *Banking in India*. Orient Longman, Bombay.
Patnaik, Prabhat (1972). Imperialism and the Growth of Indian Capitalism. In Roger Owen and Bob Sutcliff (eds.), *Studies in Theory of Imperialism*. Longman, London.
RBI (Annual). *Handbook of Statistics on Indian Economy*. RBI, Mumbai.
——— (1954). *The Shroff Committee Report on Finance for the Private Sector*. RBI, Mumbai, April.

——— (1964). *Report of Working Group on State Financial Corporations*. RBI, Mumbai.
Schumpeter, Joseph (1934). *The Theory of Economic Development*. Harvard University Press, Cambridge.
Shaw, E.S. (1973). *Financial Deepening in Economic Development*. Oxford University Press, New York.
Singh, P.N. (1974). *Role of Development Banks in a Planned Economy*. Vikas Publishing House, Delhi.

7 Impact of India's Bilateral Investment Treaties on FDI Quality

A Firm-Level Analysis

Amrita Goldar

Introduction

Literature by and large remains contentious on whether or not Bilateral Investment Treaties (or BITs) have had a positive impact on foreign direct investment (FDI) flows. There have been significant variations in experience depending on the countries, regions and sectors in question. However, even to the extent that BITs have indeed led to increased FDI flows, there remains this question about the quality of FDI flowing in. In other words, an investigation is required if, in addition to providing an investment source to the economy, the incoming FDI generated positive externalities for the economy as well. This issue of quality of FDI stems from what is traditionally thought of as a 'good FDI', i.e. what is the FDI expected to do that would increase the welfare of the host economy.

Literature expounds the many ways in which FDI is thought to benefit the host. Foreign affiliates or multinational enterprises (MNEs) bring in new technologies, in both disembodied and embodied forms, skills, marketing expertise and latest management practices from their parents into host countries. Knowledge resources spillover to domestic companies through various channels. Domestic firms tend to improve their technologies to meet increased competitive challenges thrown up by the entry of foreign affiliates and also learn from the demonstration of new technologies by them. (Pradhan, 2006).[1] On the flip side, it should be noted that the above positive impacts on the economy conform to a best-case scenario. In many cases, FDI inflows have not led to the benefits outlined above. This may be because FDI flows are not uniform in character and could vary greatly depending upon the FDI home country, the host country's resources, etc. Thus, even though theory outlines the possible benefits of FDI inflows, the actual benefits that accrue or would accrue to a developing country may differ case-to-case and need to be studied. Recent trends of developing countries entering into an increasing number of BITs with important investor countries are further adding to the complexity of the situation. In this light, it becomes particularly important to examine if

DOI: 10.4324/9781003343998-7

the quality of FDI is changing in developing countries like India and if it is being influenced by their entering into BITs that provides legal security against appropriation of any sort.

UNCTAD (2016) defines a BITs as "an agreement between two countries regarding promotion and protection of investments made by investors from respective countries in each other's territory". These BITs provide enforceable rules to protect foreign investment and reduce the risk faced by investors. Following the rules, the risk of violations/expropriations by the host country is substantially reduced and thus, the expected returns to investment increased substantially. This, in turn, provides incentives for investors from the FDI source country to invest even more in the host developing country.

While various papers constituting the existing literature have talked about the impact of 'good' FDI on specific characteristics of firms mentioned above such as export orientation, technology spillover, etc., none of these papers have gone into the question of whether the existence of agreements such as BITs has led to an improvement in the quality of FDI flow from a particular source country. The analysis presented in this chapter thus seeks to fill a very important gap in the existing body of knowledge.

In this chapter, an attempt would be made to examine the impact of BIT on certain performance indicators of manufacturing firms in India, focusing on the impact of foreign investment and how that impact is influenced by investment treaties. Using information from different firm-level databases, the impact of BITs on FDI quality would be looked at from four vantage points of firm performance – export intensity, wage share in sales (to capture the employment generation impact), local materials usage (needed for spillover impacts) and technology orientation. In each case, the marginal impact of foreign ownership and BIT signing would be analysed using a panel data analysis framework. For analysing the role of BITs, an interaction term for the foreign firms would be created which would look at whether or not the principal foreign entity investing in a particular firm belonged to a country with whom India has signed a BIT.

The chapter is organised as follows: the second section explores the different sides of the quality of FDI issue and the ways that they affect the development and growth of host countries. This section forms the basis for all subsequent sections wherein the idea of FDI being heterogeneous in its impact is delved into deeper using econometric techniques. The third section presents data collection techniques and provides an overview of the methodology employed where both models and parameters selected are discussed in detail. The fourth section provides the analysis results for four separate model runs. Conclusions are presented in the fifth section.

Quality of FDI: A Theoretical Background

There are several perspectives on the concept of the quality of FDI and the ways they affect the development and growth of host countries. Following are some of the important perspectives most often emphasised in the theoretical and empirical literature:

Sectoral Perspective on the Quality of FDI

It is said that "FDI into manufacturing sector and particularly into technology intensive industries constitutes higher quality FDI than the FDI flowing into extractive or natural resource-based sectors" (Pradhan, 2006). Due to their weak base in high-technology intensive sectors, for developing countries there is an attractive possibility of FDI coming in and establishing vertical inter-firm linkages, generating technology and knowledge spillovers within the host economy (Kumar, 2002). The potential is lower for labour-intensive industries where developing countries already have a well-developed production base. In these sectors, FDI tends to crowd out domestic enterprises due to their technological and other intangible assets superiority (Pradhan, 2006).

Localisation of Production Perspective on the Quality of FDI

For host countries' development, it is crucial that FDI not only comes into technology intensive sectors, but also that a large part of their production activities takes place locally. Localisation of production in an FDI project includes both its vertical integration in the host country and its intensity of use of local raw materials and intermediates. Kumar (2002) and Pradhan (2006) argue that "the extent of knowledge transfers and its diffusion in the host country is proportional to the degree of vertical integration (measured as the proportion of value-added in sales), which in turn captures the extent of localization of production".

Technological Perspective on the Quality of FDI

All technological activities done by foreign subsidiaries in the host country are an important aspect of the quality of FDI. This is the reason for many host countries including India for including technology transfer requirements for the entry of foreign firms. In some cases, only FDI projects showing a commitment to undertaking local research and development (R&D) activities are ones permitted. It should however be kept in mind that the knowledge spillovers work only when foreign affiliates bring new technologies and skills to the host country and are engaged in sizeable knowledge creation activities (Pradhan, 2006).

Market-Orientation Perspective on the Quality of FDI

Depending upon the markets that they seek to target, an FDI project can be classified as domestic market seeking or export oriented. While domestic market-seeking FDI is primarily inclined to serve the domestic market, the prime focus of export-oriented FDI is on regional or global export markets (Pradhan, 2006; Pradhan, Das and Paul, 2006). In this classification, export-oriented FDI is generally considered to be higher quality FDI than domestic market-seeking FDI. This is because the export-oriented FDI has greater potential to generate strong links with local economy compared to domestic market-oriented FDI given its motivation to exploit the locational advantages offered by the host country like low-cost labour, raw materials, components and parts, among other elements, for export activities. (Pradhan, 2006)[2]

Since the latter group of FDI is being motivated to serve the domestic market, they can erode the market share of domestic firms because of their superior asset bundles. On the contrary, export-oriented FDI may encourage downstream domestic investment by increasing demands for intermediate goods, and since they primarily focus on the external market, they are less likely to adversely affect their domestic counterparts (Pradhan, 2006).

Firm-Level Data and FDI Quality

For analysing the effect of BIT on the quality of FDI, it is important to look at firm-level data. To carry out such an analysis, data from the ProwessIQ Company database have been used to build a panel data set of 5,069 Indian firms over the time period 1990-2014. The database was used to collect data on firm-level parameters such as sales, profitability, research and development expenditure, raw materials, energy consumed, etc. While ProwessIQ typically has data for 15,186 manufacturing firms over the aforementioned data period, companies with data for less than 10 years were eliminated from the data set as part of the analysis.

The variable of crucial importance in the entire dataset relates to the data on foreign ownership. ProwessIQ provides information on company-wise foreign ownership patterns. Using this data, firms were characterised as foreign or domestic based on the percentage of foreign ownership (i.e. 10% of total equity or above). Once a firm was identified as being foreign, the nationality of the principal foreign investor was determined. The identification of the source country has been done with the help of Capitaline company database as well as the Money Control website (www.moneycontrol.com), which helped in determining the ownership and nationality of the FDI source. Based on this data, a BIT variable was created that mapped out if and when a BIT was signed by this investor country and India. Data for Indian BITs signed was sourced from UNCTAD's International Investment Agreements database.

Of the 5,069 firms used in the analysis, about 410 were identified as foreign. Of these 410 firms, information on source country FDI ownership was available for 278 firms. The small set of foreign firms is explained by the lack of data on the nationality of principal foreign equity holders as well as its sporadic availability (data less than 10 years). These 410 firms represent various manufacturing sectors of the economy. Some of the major sectors that they belong to are: pharmaceuticals (37), transport equipment (33), chemical products (56), general purpose machinery (23), iron and steel (20), special purpose machinery (20), mineral products (18), plastics (16), etc.

Model Used

Since the database constructed is in the form of longitudinal data, panel data methods have been used to analyse the impact of BIT on various facets of FDI quality. The model used can be written as:

$$y_{it} = \mu_t + \beta x_{it} + \gamma z_i + \alpha_i + \varepsilon_{it}$$

In other words, the various facets of FDI quality such as export orientation, technology intensity, etc. would be regressed against independent explanatory variables *x* that vary across time (such as size, profitability, etc.) as well as variables *x* whose values stay the same such as incorporation year, foreign dummy, etc. α_i and ε_{it} are both error terms. ε_{it} is different for each firm at each point in time. α_i only varies across firms but not across time.

It is further assumed that α_i is uncorrelated with the *x* because no time-invariant variables are omitted, or because the variables that are omitted are not correlated with the variables that are in the model. Thus, a random effects model is used to provide estimates of both the βs and the γs, i.e. coefficients for both sets of explanatory variables.

It may be pointed here that the explanatory variable *x* includes a dummy variable for foreign firms based on equity holding of foreign promoters where foreign firms' cut-off has been taken to be 10 per cent equity ownership. It also includes an interaction term (foreign new) between the foreign firm dummy variable and the BIT dummy that takes into account when the BIT signed with a particular firm becomes operational.

It needs mentioning here that for two of the models, relating to namely – export intensity and technology orientation, a panel tobit model was also run. This was done because for most firms the dependent variable value was zero. The tobit model assumes that the observed data, or y_{it}, represents possibly censored version of y^*_{it}. As they are left censored, this would mean that: $y = y^*$ if $y^* > 0$ and $y = 0$ if $y^* \le 0$. Thus, the model becomes

$$y^*_{it} = \mu_t + \beta x_{it} + \gamma z_i + \alpha_i + \varepsilon_{it} \text{ where } y = y^* \text{ if } y^* > 0 \text{ and } y = 0 \text{ if } y^* \le 0$$

Model Particulars

To study the impact of BIT on FDI quality, four different facets of firm performance are looked at. The following model examines the BIT impact on firm-level export intensity, technology orientation, wage share and local content utilisation. The various explanatory variables used in the analysis are outlined in Table 7.1.

It is noteworthy that since the following is a micro-econometric analysis using firm-level data, it is assumed that the BIT variable is exogenous. The Treatment Effects model was run in the larger macroeconomic case earlier because of the endogeneity issue and the direction of causality between FDI and BIT. At the smaller firm level, however, there is no such risk of endogeneity and firms can be assumed to have no significant influence on BIT signing. It is thus appropriate to use panel data methods for the collated database of firm particulars over time.

Note that wage share has been taken as the variable for understanding the FDI impact on employment creation. While data on employment in firms exists in ProwessIQ, it is reported by very few firms. The number of observations drops drastically when employment was used in any of the models. Additionally, while checking for observed selection bias, it was found that only the very large firms report their employment figures. Using employment would thus have skewed the modelling results.

Mentionable also is the difference between the Foreign_new and Foreign_firm dummies. Foreign_new turns one in whichever year a firm has greater than 10 per cent foreign equity ownership, and remains the same thereafter. Foreign_firm dummy converts to one for all years (1990-2014) if the firm had 10 per cent or higher FDI in any of the analysis years. Foreign firm dummy is therefore time invariant.

Earlier Studies

A number of recent studies exist that look at the effect of FDI on the performance of firms. Ghosh and Sinha Roy (2013) look at the impact of FDI on export performance. They find that ownership along with import of technology, in-house R&D, import of raw materials, and marketing, advertising and distribution costs are the major determining factors of firm-level exports. An older paper written by Kumar and Siddharthan (1993) found the presence of an inverted U-shaped relationship between firm size and export behaviour in Indian industries. They further found that a firm's technological activity favourably influences its export behaviour only in medium and low technology industries. MNE affiliates in general do not exhibit significantly different export behaviour from other firms and tend to focus instead on the domestic markets. Similar results were also found by Pradhan and Abraham (2005) in their analysis. They note that while local market-oriented FDI may crowd out domestic firms and investments, export-oriented FDI can stimulate investment by generating demands for intermediate goods. They further found that export behaviour of foreign affiliates is strongly correlated with their intensity to import raw material. They thus suggest that a liberal policy with respect to imports would encourage foreign firms to export further. Joseph and Reddy (2010) hypothesise

Table 7.1 Variables Use in the Firm-Level Analysis

	Variables	*Construction*	*Explanation*
1.	Size	Log(sales)	Denotes the size of the firm
2.	Lkratio	Employee cost/net assets	Labour-capital ratio
3.	Xint	Exports/sales	Export intensity
4.	Kint	Net assets/sales	Capital intensity
5.	Wage share	Compensation to employees/sales	Labour Intensity
6.	Empl	Log(employees number)	Number of employees in the firm
7.	Tech_intensity	(Research expenditure+ technology royalties paid +forex expenditure on technology)/total expenditure	Technology orientation
8.	Reer	Real effective exchange rate	Denotes exchange rates movements
9.	Power	Power consumption/ expenditure	Energy consumption intensity
10.	Pat_L1	Profits after tax/sales	Profitability of the firm last year
11.	Local_mat	(Raw material consumption – imported raw material)/total raw material	Local content in production
12.	Age of the firm	Current Year – Incorporation year	Denotes how old the firm is
13.	Selling_cost_intensity	Selling costs/total expenditure	Selling costs incurred
14.	Capimp	Import of capital goods /f_sales	Denotes how much of technology is imported from outside
15.	Foreign_new	Dummy=1 if fdi share>10% equity Dummy=0, otherwise	Denotes whether the firm if significantly controlled by foreign entities
16.	Foreign_firm	Dummy=1 if in any year fdi share>10% equity Dummy=0, otherwise	Denotes whether the firm if significantly controlled by foreign entities
17.	Bitint	Interaction term (BIT multiplied by foreign firm dummy, i.e. for_dum)	Denotes whether India has signed a BIT with the significant foreign entity

that the presence of foreign firms improves the competitiveness and export orientation of domestically owned firms in developing countries through "horizontal spillovers" and "backward spillovers".

In a later paper, Ghosh and Sinha Roy (2014) analyse the impact of FDI on technology acquisition and labour demand. They find that foreign ownership did not have a significant role in determining firm-level labour demand. Also, that new technology acquisition by foreign firms is not labour displacing in the short run for major sectors. The issue of FDI and its role in determining wage and employment has been looked at by previous papers written by Pradhan et. al. (2004) and Banga (2005). While the former paper finds that foreign firms do not have an adverse effect on employment, Banga (2005) finds that higher FDI in an industry leads to higher wages and no effect on employment.

Petkova (2013) in her paper looks at the effect of FDI on firm productivity and growth. She finds there is a positive relationship between foreign ownership and output, fixed assets and wage growth. She however does not find a significant relationship between FDI and enhanced productivity. A later paper by Goldar and Sharma (2015) however found a positive effect of FDI on firm productivity and medium-term profitability. But they did not find any significant impact of FDI on export performance like the papers mentioned above.

Analysis Results

For each of the facets of FDI quality, the results are as follows:

Export Intensity

Several international studies have highlighted the positive impact of MNEs on the export capacity of domestic firms. In the Indian case, however, results are still not supportive of this conjecture. It is often stated that export activity involves costs associated with the establishment of distribution networks, transport infrastructures or knowledge of consumers' tastes in foreign markets, which MNEs are more able to afford. By following the export processes of foreign firms (through imitation or, in specific circumstances, through collaboration), domestic firms may reduce the entry costs into the foreign market. The gains obtained in this way may have favourable repercussions on the productive efficiency of domestic firms as well.

Table 7.2 shows the results for export intensity analysis of firms. The results show that there is a strong significant relationship between size and export intensity, i.e. larger firms generally export more. Earlier studies such as Kumar and Siddharthan (1994), Aggarwal (2002) and Kumar and Pradhan (2003) have all found firm size as an important determinant of export intensity of firms.

Table 7.2 Impact of FDI and BIT on Export Intensity (Tobit Model)

Export Intensity (Xint)	*All Firms*			
	Model 1	*Model 2*	*Model 3*	*Model 4*
Lkratio	-.0084565**	-0.0088152**	-0.0092375**	-0.0096417**
	(.0029881)	(0.0029868)	(0.0029847)	(0.0029885)
Size	.0138191**	0.0137039**	0.0141956**	0.0141838**
	(.0013307)	(0.0013302)	(0.0013234)	(0.0012754)
Age	-.0001901	-0.0002662	-0.0001344	0.0000334
	(.0001764)	(0.000175)	(0.0001712)	(0.0001762)
local_mat	-.1477446**	-0.1475656**	-0.1480717**	
	(.0054443)	(0.0054457)	(0.0054443)	
Capimp	.0780526**	0.0792406**	0.080578**	0.138248**
	(.0123913)	(0.0123937)	(0.0123875)	(0.011636)
Pat_L1	.0002953	0.0004765	0.0001901	
	(.0043886)	(0.00439)	(0.0043893)	
Reer	.0002033**	0.0001998**		0.0002499**
	(.0000571)	(0.0000571)		(0.0000445)
tech_intensity	.0873334	0.0864732	0.0926665	0.1179951
	(.0783307)	(0.0783648)	(0.0783464)	(0.0783119)
Selling_cost intensity	.7325802**	0.727693**	0.7306726**	0.7482849**
	(.0333907)	(0.0333676)	(0.0333614)	(0.0334341)
for_new	-.0148031**			-0.0137131**
	(.0037857)			(0.0038943)
For_firm		-0.0420962**	-0.043382**	
		(0.0143479)	(0.0143837)	
Bitint	-.0058479	-0.0124501**	-0.011308*	0.0022591
	(.0061507)	(0.0057795)	(0.0057705)	(0.0060906)
_cons	.183585	0.1921865**	0.2058624**	0.0519463**
	(.0108672)	(0.0110448)	(0.0103402)	(0.0086095)
Observations	24,116	24,116	24,116	25,058

Note: the figures in brackets represent standard errors

Also, firms that are more capital intensive in nature, as reflected by lower labour-capital ratios, were more likely to export. Firms with high-technology orientation are also expected to export more. A strong relationship between capital goods imports and export orientation was also seen.

Exchange rate movements (i.e. depreciation) were seen to have a positive impact on exports. Also, results show that companies that use more local content have a lesser likelihood of exporting. It could be that these firms using local inputs cater to domestic rather than international demand. Newer firms were found to be more export oriented than older firms as shown by the negative relationship. But the coefficient was not found to be significant. A positive significant relation was noticed between export intensity and selling and distribution costs as well.

It is interesting to note that foreign firms have a significantly lesser likelihood of exporting. In the four iterations of the model below, both foreign_new and foreign_firm dummies were applied. In all variations, the dummy for foreign firms showed a significant negative relationship. It would thus seem that most foreign firms operating in India for the study period were more geared towards catering to the Indian domestic market rather than exporting internationally. However, the BIT interaction term, i.e. foreign firms that are under the protection of BITs signed with India, was not found to be significant in the two variants. Even in the iterations where it was found to be significant, the coefficient had a negative sign which would imply that BITs had an additional impact on reducing export intensity. In other words, the existence of a BIT is not seen to add any impetus to the already existing propensity to export of firms. If anything, they were found to have a negative impact on exports.

Employee Cost Share

One possible avenue for spillover could be domestic firms hiring workers who, having previously worked for an MNE, have knowledge and experience of the technology and are able to apply this in the domestic firm (Crespo and Fontoura, 2007). Bergman (2006) in her paper states that labour turnover is a spillover mechanism that may benefit the local industry, since circulation of the labour force enables some original knowledge to be transferred between the foreign and domestic firms. It is however very hard to map the effect of this sort of intra-industry migration of workers. Using existing firm-level databases, an alternate facet of employee welfare following enhanced FDI flows is looked at. The variable examined in this case is the marginal impact of foreign firms and BIT on enhancing wages and/or employment in the specific firm which received FDI. Table 7.3 shows the results for panel regression runs on all firms using employee compensation shares as the dependent variable.

It is noteworthy that the wage share variable includes elements of both employment as well as wages/salaries. There are certain variables that have a direct link with higher salary levels of employees such as embodied skills, etc. associated with capital-intensive industries that show up as a positive significant relationship. There are others that have a bearing on the number of people employed such as the age of the firm and the size. All results need to be interpreted keeping these two points in mind.

For the analysis, the results show that smaller firms are more likely to have higher wage shares as a proportion of output. Older firms (with earlier incorporation years) have higher wage share as well.

It is interesting that there is a positive and significant relationship between wage share and both technology orientation (more R&D investment, etc.) as well as power consumption. Higher technology orientation signifies greater complexities in the production process. These firms might be using more skilled labour and thus the wage shares might be high due to the higher salary typically given. A similar study done by OECD and ILO (2008) on impact of FDI on wages and working conditions found that the

Table 7.3 Impact of FDI and BIT on Employee Cost Shares

Wageshare (Employee Cost Share)	*All Firms*			
	Model 1	*Model 2*	*Model 3*	*Model 4*
Size	-0.0015551**		-0.0027264**	
	(0.0002909)		(0.0002972)	
Age				0.0009891**
				(0.0000396)
Kint	0.0081911**			0.0084323**
	(0.0002338)			(0.000229)
local_mat	0.005882**	0.0071427**	0.0047372**	0.012593**
	(0.0017213)	(0.0017537)	(0.0017698)	(0.0016935)
Capimp	0.01131**	0.0284109**	0.0231297**	0.0233599**
	(0.0038198)	(0.003878)	(0.003913)	(0.0037513)
Pat_L1	-0.0344592**	-0.0383091**	-0.0372876**	-0.0347048**
	(0.0013682)	(0.001403)	(0.0014046)	(0.0013459)
tech	0.1643123**	0.1594938**	0.1788398**	0.1018079**
	(0.0241488)	(0.0247884)	(0.0248298)	(0.0238149)
Xint	0.0084322**	0.0065324**	0.0089908**	0.0015069
	(0.002068)	(0.0021138)	(0.0021266)	(0.0020373)
Selling	-0.1142317**	-0.118107**	-0.1195012**	-0.104524**
	(0.0105941)	(0.0109138)	(0.0108936)	(0.0104565)
Power	0.2582689**	0.2763307**	0.2731094**	0.244085**
	(0.0107415)	(0.0110539)	(0.011038)	(0.0106083)
for_new	0.0085018**	0.0068754**	0.0085833**	0.0014988
	(0.0011423)	(0.0011621)	(0.0011747)	(0.0011383)
Bitint	0.0008654	0.00000674	0.0019556	-0.0068437**
	(0.0018901)	(0.0019357)	(0.0019435)	(0.0018712)
_cons	0.0736324**	0.0641086**	0.0861991**	0.0289539**
	(0.0028806)	(0.0016891)	(0.0029393)	(0.0020666)
Observations	24,004	23,974	24,006	23,974

Note: the figures in brackets represent standard errors

positive wage effect spreads across not just the workers directly employed by MNEs, but workers working in domestic firms participating in the supply chains established by MNEs.

Capital imports were also seen to have a positive influence on all firms. This can be because firms that are more capital import based employ better-skilled workers which translate into higher wage rates. The positive relationship between capital intensity and wage shares can also be explained using the same logic.

For wage share, both the foreign dummy terms showed a significantly positive relationship in most versions of the model. This means that foreign firms are more likely to have higher wage shares. However, foreign firms hailing from home countries that have signed BITs with India were not more likely to have higher wage shares. This is reflected by the insignificance of the BIT dummy's coefficient.

Local Material Usage

An important channel for positive spillovers is the links that domestic firms establish in local markets as suppliers to MNEs (backward linkages) or customers of intermediate inputs produced by them (forward linkages). Crespo and Fontoura (2007) state that with increasing returns to scale, the presence of MNEs may benefit domestic suppliers if it increases the demand for local inputs. In their attempts to assure a certain level of quality, MNEs may also benefit domestic suppliers in several other ways: providing technical support for the improvement of the quality of goods, or for the introduction of innovations (e.g. through personnel training), providing support for the creation of productive infrastructure and for the acquisition of raw materials, as well as providing organisational and management support (Crespo and Fontoura, 2007). The possible increase in the efficiency of domestic firms brought about by the competition among them to become MNE suppliers should also be considered. Regarding the channel of forward linkages, the most evident link is observed in the MNEs' supply of higher quality inputs possibly at a lower price to domestic producers of end-user consumer goods.

Since local content usage is an important first step to effectuate the abovementioned backward and forward linkages, the following model looks at the impact of FDI as well as other explanatory variables on local content usage of both domestic and foreign firms. The results are presented in Table 7.4.

The results show that both export orientation and size are negatively related with local content usage. Firms that are export intensive and/or larger in size use higher levels of imported materials. Newer firms are however seen to use lesser local inputs in their production processes. Firms that are more labour intensive (reflected by the lkratio) and have lesser technology orientation also show significantly higher usage of local materials. This is also reflected by the significantly negative association of capital imports with local content usage. A stronger currency is also associated with higher locally available material utilisation.

The strong positive association between power consumption and local content was both surprising and puzzling. Based on literature, there should be a strong correlation between capital intensity, technology orientation and power consumption. However, the results show that while the relation with local content utilisation is negative for both technology and capital intensity, it is positive for power consumption.

As regards the foreign variables, foreign firms are seen to be using lower levels of local inputs in all iterations. However, they were significant in only two of the models. Interestingly, in all model iterations, the signing of BITs shows up having a significantly negative impact on the usage of local products in the production process. The gains from BIT signing through spillover effects thus seem to be very limited for Indian firms according to this result.

Table 7.4 FDI and BIT Impact on Local Content Usage

Local Content Usage (local_mat)	*All Firms*			
	Model 1	*Model 2*	*Model 3*	*Model 4*
Lkratio	0.0044985		0.0032823	
	(0.0033993)		(0.003719)	
Size	-0.0270659**		-0.025322**	-0.0250764**
	(0.0011152)		(0.00115)	(0.0011465)
Age		-0.0031791**		
		(0.0001665)		
Xint			-0.2006552**	-0.2014518**
			(0.0081235)	(0.0081227)
Compen		0.1523793**		0.0932973**
		(0.0224738)		(0.0273017)
Kint	-0.0025947**	-0.0020088**	-0.0025186**	-0.0033369**
	(0.0004905)	(0.0004939)	(0.0009332)	(0.0009572)
Capimp	-0.10075**	-0.0783537**	-0.1090195**	-0.1104707**
	(0.0136305)	(0.013595)	(0.0152072)	(0.0151974)
Pat_L1	0.0035005	-0.00065	-0.0056003	-0.0023416
	(0.004193)	(0.0042504)	(0.0054506)	(0.0055298)
Reer	-0.0002761**	-0.0002892**		
	(0.0000611)	(0.0000638)		
tech	-0.2073442**	-0.2582377**	-0.1590973*	-0.1755448*
	(0.0912743)	(0.0916188)	(0.0962045)	(0.0962735)
Selling	0.0591369	0.049607	0.2178166**	0.2278884**
	(0.0391147)	(0.0393582)	(0.0421805)	(0.042279)
Power	0.2591991**	0.307188**	0.3350565**	0.3107131**
	(0.0366207)	(0.0371235)	(0.042729)	(0.0433048)
for_new	-0.0055662	-0.0045391	-0.0148175**	-0.0153903**
	(0.0044125)	(0.0044695)	(0.0045556)	(0.0045539)
Bitint	-0.0609252**	-0.0602107**	-0.0633932**	-0.0634189**
	(0.0073302)	(0.0073798)	(0.0075171)	(0.0075151)
_cons	1.012713**	0.8925114**	0.9987125**	0.9918081**
	(0.0087585)	(0.0066236)	(0.0092236)	(0.0094554)
Observations	28,414	28,414	24,004	24,004

Note: the figures in brackets represent standard errors

Technology Orientation

MNEs are usually found to be Research and Development (R&D) and capital intensive, hence a potential source of intra-industry spillover is the transfer of production and process technology from MNEs to the domestic companies. The foreign firms make the domestic players aware of the existence of the technology; and the presence of MNEs and resulting competition are likely to speed up the domestic firms' technology absorption (Bergman, 2006). Technology and productivity gaps between the foreign and local firms may stimulate spillover effects. If a technology gap exists, some differences in productivity and innovations between foreign-owned and domestic firms should be expected. If the local firm is less productive than the foreign firm, there is a scope for it to catch up, by imitating the technology of foreign leaders. It is thus important to see whether there is an increase in technology orientation of a firm following increases in foreign investment in the Indian case. Table 7.5 shows the results of technology orientation of firms regressed against various explanatory variables.

The results for technology and size show that larger size firms tend to have greater technology orientation as reflected by investment in R&D, etc. A positive relationship between technology orientation, capital imports and imported inputs required in the production process (reflected by low local material usage) was also seen. There was a significant positive relationship between previous year's profitability of firms and their investments in R&D. It seems that the possibility of internal funding through profits spurs investments made in accessing/developing new technologies.

As expected, there is a significant impact of foreign firms in determining technology orientation. This was witnessed for models using both for_new

Table 7.5 FDI and BIT Impact on Technology Orientation of Firms

Technology Orientation (Tech)	*All Firms*			
	Model 1	*Model 2*	*Model 3*	*Model 4*
Lkratio	-0.0000132 (0.0002388)		-0.00000785 (0.0002385)	
Size	0.0008727** (0.0000902)	0.0011611** (0.000093)	0.0008966** (0.0000898)	0.0011785** (0.0000928)
Age	0.00000911 (0.0000106)	-0.0000302** (0.0000109)	0.0000122 (0.0000105)	-0.0000272** (0.0000108)
Xint	-0.0002481 (0.0004915)	-0.0003614 (0.0004888)	-0.0001861 (0.0004908)	-0.0002941 (0.0004882)
local_mat	-0.002195** (0.000446)	-0.0023121** (0.0004445)	-0.0021834** (0.0004455)	-0.0023015** (0.0004441)
Compen		0.0192393** (0.0017209)		0.0192989** (0.0017705)
Kint				-0.0000237 (0.0000606)
Capimp	0.0069254** (0.0010424)	0.0064628** (0.0010399)	0.0068082** (0.0010421)	0.0063989** (0.0010446)
Pat_L1	0.0017081** (0.0003655)	0.0023477** (0.0003692)	0.0017035** (0.0003653)	0.0023363** (0.0003692)
Selling	0.0338366** (0.0026631)	0.0353211** (0.0026549)	0.0338826** (0.0026586)	0.0353107** (0.0026505)
for_new	0.00117** (0.000318)	0.0010709** (0.0003173)		
for_firm			0.0041887** (0.0006701)	0.0039405** (0.0006598)
Bitint	0.0008908* (0.0004991)	0.0009033* (0.0004975)	0.0009317** (0.0004735)	0.0009076* (0.0004722)
_cons	-0.0002107 (0.0007411)	-0.002691** (0.0007672)	-0.0010128 (0.0007451)	-0.0034054** (0.0007718)
Observations	24,116	24,118	24,116	24,116

Note: the figures in brackets represent standard errors

and for_firm as the explanatory variables. An additional fillip to technology orientation is given post the signing of BIT as well. This can be read off from the significant positive coefficient for the BIT interaction dummy.

Conclusion

This paper tried to explore the impact of BITs on the quality of FDI flows to India. The issue of quality of FDI was tackled through looking at the four dimensions of 'good' FDI generally discussed in the literature. This included improvements in firm export intensity, technological orientation, local content utilisation and wage shares.

Using information from different firm-level databases, the role of foreign (with more than 10% equity held by foreign entities) and BITs on these four FDI quality metrics was analysed using fixed effects and Tobit panel data models. The results showed that foreign firms had a significant role in determining some of the FDI quality outcomes. The role of BITs was measured through the creation of an interaction term for the foreign firms, which looked at whether or not the principal foreign entity invested in a particular firm belonged to a country with whom India has signed a BIT.

The results for the BIT interaction term showed that BITs have had a positive influence on two of the four FDI quality metrics. BITs were shown to have a negative influence on both export orientation and local content requirement. It thus seems that post-BIT, countries import a higher share of components (capital and intermediate inputs) and seek to largely serve the domestic market. The coefficient for BITs' impact on local content requirement was found to be significantly negative in all model iterations. A positive impact for BITs showed up in the models for employee cost shares and technology orientation. The positive coefficient for employee costs was found to be insignificant in all iterations. A strong impact of BITs on technology orientation of the firm was however noticed.

The data therefore seems to indicate that while positive BIT effects have been felt by firms, the potential for spillover effects seems to be low. Both local content requirement and employment impacts that are the vehicles of larger diffusion of beneficial effects of FDI have not been significantly influenced or even positively influenced by BITs. The technology orientation aspect however seems to be a positive fall-out of the heightened security for FDI following a BIT.

Notes

1 Pradhan (2006) Quality of Foreign Direct Investment, Knowledge Spillovers and Host Country Productivity: A Framework of Analysis, ISID Working Paper 2006/11, Delhi.

2 Note however there need not be any gains made with respect to forex earnings with FDI firms set up. There might be the case that rather than being net forex earning, such FDI turns forex spending as FDI firms tend to spend more on technical fees, royalties, imported raw materials, etc.

References

Aggarwal, A. (2002), Liberalisation, Multinational Enterprises and Export Performances: Evidence from Indian Manufacturing, *Journal of Development Studies*, 3, 119–137.

Banga, R. (2005), Impact of Liberalisation on Wages and Employment in Indian Manufacturing Industries, *ICRIER Working Paper No. 153*, Indian Council for Research on International Economic Relations, New Delhi.

Bergman, A. (2006), FDI and Spillover Effects in the Indian Pharmaceutical Industry, *RIS Discussion Paper No. 113*, New Delhi.

Cameron, C. A., and Trivedi, P. K. (2005), *Microeconometrics: Methods and Applications*, Cambridge University Press, New York.

Crespo, N., and Fontoura, M. P. (2007), Determinant Factors of FDI Spillovers – What Do We Really Know?, *World Development*, 35(3), 410–425.

DIPP (2017), *FDI Statistics, SIA Newsletter, Various Years*, Secretariat for Industrial Assistance, Department of Industrial Policy and Promotion.

Ghosh, M., and Roy, S. S. (2013), FDI, Firm Heterogeneity and Exports: An Examination of Evidence in India, *Working Paper No. 05-13*, Centre for Advanced Studies, Jadavpur University, Kolkata.

Ghosh, M., and Roy, S. S. (2014), FDI, Technological Choices and Spillovers in an Emerging Market Economy: A Study of the Indian Manufacturing Industries, *FREIT Working Paper No. 651*, Forum for Research in Empirical International Trade, San Rafael.

Goldar, B., and Sharma, A. K. (2015), Foreign Investment in Indian Industrial Firms and Its Impact on Firm Performance, *Journal of Industrial Statistics*, 4(1), 1–18.

Guzman, A. T. (1998), Why LDCs Sign Treaties that Hurt Them: Explaining the Popularity of Bilateral Investment Treaties, *Virginia Journal of International Law*, 38, 639–688.

Joseph, T. J., and Reddy, V. N. (2010), FDI Spillovers and Export Performance of Indian Manufacturing Firms after Liberalisation, *Economic& Political Weekly*, 44(52), 97–105.

Kumar, N. (2002), *Globalization and the Quality of Foreign Direct Investment*, Oxford University Press, New Delhi.

Kumar, N. (2013), Foreign Direct and Portfolio Investment Flows and Development: A Perspective on Indian Experience, in Uma Kapila (ed.), *Indian Economy Since Independence* (new revised 24th edition), Academic Foundation, New Delhi, 713–734.

Kumar, N., and Pradhan, J. P. (2003), Economic Reforms, WTO and Indian Drugs and Pharmaceuticals Industry: Implications of Emerging Trends, *CMDR Monograph Series*, No. 42, The Centre for Multidisciplinary Development Research, Dharwad.

Kumar, N., and Siddharthan, N. S. (1994), Technology, Firm Size and Export Behaviour in Developing Countries: The Case of Indian Enterprises, *Journal of Development Studies*, 31(2), 289–309.

Neumayer, E., and Spess, L. (2005), Do Bilateral Investment Treaties Increase Foreign Direct Investment to Developing Countries?, *World Development*, 33(10), 1567–1585.

OECD and ILO (2008), The Impact of Foreign Direct Investment on Wages and Working Conditions, *OECD-ILO Conference on Corporate Social Responsibility*, 23–24 June 2008, OECD Conference Centre, Paris.

Petkova, N. (2013), The Real Effects of Foreign Investment: Productivity and Growth, *Discussion Paper*, Department of Finance, University of Oregon, available at http://www4.ncsu.edu/~njtraum/seminar/Petkova_ForeignInvestment.pdf.
Pradhan, J. P. (2006), Quality of Foreign Direct Investment, Knowledge Spillovers and Host Country Productivity: A Framework of Analysis, *ISID Working Paper 2006/11*, Delhi.
Pradhan, J. P., and Abraham, V. (2005), Attracting Export-Oriented FDI: Can India Win the Race?, *Working Paper No. 156*, Gujarat Institute of Development Research, Ahmedabad.
Pradhan, J. P., Abraham, V., and Sahoo, M. K. (2004), Foreign Direct Investment and Labour: The Case of Indian Manufacturing, *Labour and Development*, 10(1), 58–79.
Pradhan, J. P., Das, K., and Paul, M. (2006), Export-Orientation of Foreign Manufacturing Affiliates in India, Factors, Tendencies, Implications, *ISID, Working Paper No.: 2006/8*, New Delhi.
Ranjan, P. (2014), India and Bilateral Investment Treaties—A Changing Landscape, *ICSID Review*, 29(2), 419–450.
Rao, K. S. C., Dhar, B., Ranganathan, K. V. K., Choudhury, R. N., and Negi, V. (2014), FDI into India's Manufacturing Sector via M&As: Trends and Composition, *ISID Working Paper No. 161*, New Delhi.
Roodman, D. (2009), How to do Xtabond2: An Introduction to Difference and System GMM in Stata, *Stata Journal*, 9(1), 86–136.
Rubin, D. B. (1986), Statistical Matching Using File Concatenation with Adjusted Weights and Multiple Imputations, *Journal of Business and Economic Statistics*, 4, 87–94.
UNCTAD (2000), *International Investment Agreements: Flexibility for Development*, UNCTAD Series on Issues in International Investment Agreements, New York and Geneva.
UNCTAD (2006), *Investment Provisions in Economic Integration Agreements*, United Nations, New York and Geneva.
UNCTAD (2015), *Bilateral FDI Database*, United Nations Conference on Trade and Development, Geneva.
UNCTAD (2016), *International Investment Agreements Navigator, Investment Policy Hub, United Nations Conference on Trade and Development (UNCTAD)*, Geneva, available at https://investmentpolicy.unctad.org/international-investment-agreements
Vandevelde, K. (2000), The Economics of Bilateral Investment Treaties, *Harvard International Law Journal*, 41(2), 469–502.

8 India's Tariff Jumping FDI: A Case of Overseas Investment Flows under ASEAN-India FTA

Murali Kallummal and Somdutta Banerjee

Introduction

India's commitments in regional trade deals were limited before it exhausted its efforts under multilateral trade deals like the WTO. The effort increased as the success at multilateralism was looking slower than the efforts in the direction of regional initiatives. A number of economists like Bagawati and others have had an enormous impact on the trade policy formulation of India as they provide a strong rationale for free trade and the removal of trade barriers. Trade agreements need actually to reflect domestic economic structures. Domestic compulsions and international technological development should shape the provisions to trade liberalisation, and there is a need for special treatment of deficit sectors.

The old understanding proposed by the mercantile economist like Ricardo, 'the law of comparative advantage' in today's age, has become redundant as the world has undergone enormous change. Over the last couple of decades, economists have modified trade theories by accounting for factors of production such as capital, labour, technology, the growth of supply chains and even the recent transformation seen in the areas like digital space. There is a growing recognition that the free trade agreements (FTAs) are the second-best liberalisation effort. It led to a surge in such deals, with growing popularity worldwide and numbers touching 568 RTAs in 2021. India and ASEAN economies have been under the free trade agreement since 2010. Southeast Asian economies have been associated almost exclusively with the initiatives since the late 1980s with the Association of South-East Asian Nations (ASEAN). By 1992, ASEAN had agreed on an ASEAN Free Trade Area (AFTA) to capture the synergies arising from the international production networks created in the region by foreign investors, by a scheduled stage-wise increase in market access in each other's economies. ASEAN-10 countries are similar in development status and a hub of the production network (Francis and Kallummal, 2006). Therefore, we have taken up the AIFTA for a detailed analysis. Having a considerably long association in cultural and economic links with Southeast Asia, India is expected to gain from the ASEAN-Indian free trade agreement (AIFTA).

DOI: 10.4324/9781003343998-8

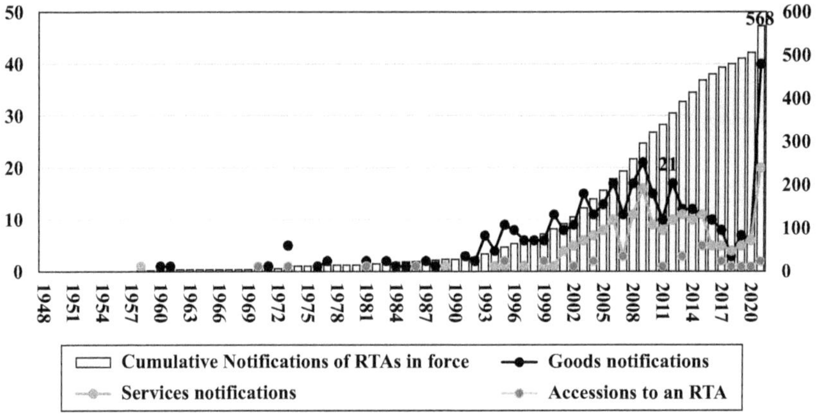

Figure 8.1 Total Notification of RTAs/FTAs: 1948 to 2021 (Numbers) Source: WTO, RTA database.

Therefore, the policymakers had visualised the region's proximity to the world as one significant way of creating a global network.

For an FTA-led economic growth and development in the Indian case, the AIFTA will have to bring many gains in multiple areas, expand agricultural processing, rationalise and expand manufacturing sectors, and a few services sectors. On the other hand, for small export-oriented economies like Vietnam, Cambodia, Thailand and Malaysia, market access in India has become critical (Kallummal, 2021). That is the benefit they are looking for in regional cooperation. It gets translated into their market access expectations out of FTA deals. The AIFTA was notified under the WTO in GATT Article 24 and Article 5 of the General Agreement on Trade in Services (GATS), an exemption from the most favoured nation (MFN) rule. India's goods sector liberalisation began with a trade agreement with a limited scope like the APTA. Concerning Indo-Sri Lanka FTA, bilateral trade showed a significant surge immediately after implementing the ISLFTA. India's share in Sri Lanka's exports and imports increased by around two percentage points. It is also observed that Sri Lanka is becoming increasingly more dependent on India for its imports. Concerning FTA with Korean Comprehensive Economic Partnership Agreement (CEPA). In two years of its implementation, it was observed that India's export growth to Korea had been significantly lower than its global exports. From India's perspective, Korea's salience in the trade basket has not improved since the implementation of CEPA.

Overall, the CEPA (India-Korea FTA) does not appear to have significantly impacted the bilateral trade. Within two years of AIFTA's implementation, India became a more important trading partner of ASEAN.

However, from India's perspective, ASEAN's salience in India's trade basket has not improved after implementing AIFTA. An analysis of India's trade with ASEAN shows that India has become a supplier of raw materials to ASEAN in the post-FTA period (Francis and Kallummal, 2013; Francis and Kallummal, 2009). However, the FTA has not enhanced India's access to raw materials and intermediate products from ASEAN.

With the stalemate at the WTO (Doha Round), India continued with its look east policy. Additional efforts were taken by India to expand its preferential trade agreements like the EHAs with Thailand to India-ASEAN FTAs. These initiatives included comprehensive trade deals with Japan and Korea, the latest being with Malaysia and ASEAN (services), these also included an investment chapter. The underlying expectation was to deepen regional integration through the channel of investment. In the case of ASEAN, the necessity of this was recognised since the beginning (in 2003). Indian service providers, thus, have an opportunity to cater to the growing demand for services in ASEAN and, in turn, contribute more to economic income and the development of a broader regional perspective (Takkar & Nataraj, 2014). Sastra and Prasopchoke (2007), using a gravity model and Computed General Equilibrium (CGE) model, examined the trade potential and the economic impact of bilateral free trade agreements between the ASEAN member countries and the seven FTA partners. Their study observed China, the USA, Japan and India as strategic FTA partners of ASEAN. Veeramani and Saini (2011) carried out a quantitative assessment of the impact of AIFTA on selected plantation commodities, i.e. coffee, tea and pepper. A partial equilibrium modelling approach was used to simulate the likely increase in imports of the plantation commodities by India under the proposed tariff reduction schedules of the India-ASEAN FTA. The result suggested that AIFTA would significantly increase such imports by India, driven mainly by trade creation rather than trade diversion. Doung et al. (2020) examined the relationship between FTAs and inward FDI in Vietnam using panel data for Vietnam's 17 leading foreign investors during 1997–2016 and 23 investors for the sub-period 2005–2016. The sub-period shows that FTAs also significantly affect inward FDI through interactions with the real exchange rate, human capital and factor endowments.

Li et al. (2017) observe that ACFTA has a significant and positive effect on FDI flows.[1] Several studies (Sudsawasd, & Mongsawad, 2007; Vogiatzoglou, 2007; Kepaptsoglou, Karlaftis & Tsamboulas, D, 2010; Bengoa, Sanchez-Robles & Shachmurove, 2020; Kox & Rojas-Romagosa, 2020; Wahyuningsih, 2021) perform the gravity model in this context. The impact of FTA has a contradictory effect on trade in terms of creation and diversion. Baier and Bergstrand (2007), Kahouli and Maktouf (2013) and Plummer & Cheong (2009) do not provide clear evidence of the positive effects of these agreements to create or divert trade. For example, Endoh (1999) and García, Pabsdorf and Herrera (2013) noted that the FTA in Latin America exposed trade creation or trade diversion with Japan. Nevertheless,

Fukao, Okubo and Stern (2003) have provided evidence of trade diversion due to NAFTA. Caves (1996), Blonigen (2005) explore the determinants of FDI. In the similar note Chakrabarti (2001) finds that most determinants of cross-country FDI are statistically fragile.

This chapter will find the investment linkage with the tariff liberalisation in the goods market under the AIFTA. Section I analyses the overall trends in FDI flows to India and ASEAN as a group and individually. It attempts to establish that ASEAN has been active in terms of FDI flows, attracting foreign capital in all forms even before AIFTA. It also provides a peek into the goods market liberalisation under AIFTA, which began in 2010 and yearly reduction at mutually agreed rates. It then suggested the potential zero duty market access under the Agreement and scope for Investment flows. Section II traces India's OFDI flows to ASEAN as a region, providing a comparison of the global flows; this is done to delineate the impact of FTA with ASEAN from the overall global OFDI flows. Individual ASEAN countries are analysed, and differences are highlighted to better understand the trade policy differences based on the country's characteristics. We have analysed the differences in terms of three types of instruments, namely the equity, debt and bank guarantee, to assess the level of confidence and the firm's involvement in the ASEAN market. An OLS model is applied in this study in order to identify the impact of the FTA on India's OFDI. However, a similar analysis for ASEAN's investment flows to India cannot be done as the data and information on such investments is not readily available, and it is one of the limitations. Finally, the last section provides a summary and conclusion.

Investment Sentiments in ASEAN and India

The overall investment sentiment in ASEAN and India is an essential first step. Therefore, an analysis of the total FDI flows is undertaken under two heads to understand the causal links between tariff liberalisation and the expanded market potentials. Firstly, we look at the long-term trend in FDI flows to capture the overall sentiment existing in Southeast Asia and India. Then, investment conditions in these two economies/groups are analysed concerning FDI inflows, outflows and net flows (Figure 8.2).

There is evidence that both the economies had attracted FDI investments from 1970 to 2016, even though the Asian crises badly hit many Southeast Asian economies during 1998–2000 (Dhar and Kallummal, 2002). For the entire region of ASEAN and India's FDI inflows increased to USD 206.28 billion in 2019 from a low of USD 26 billion in 2000, at an exponential growth rate of almost 15 per cent (see Figure 8.4). While the total outflows in terms of values are much lower, the total AIFTA outflow increased from USD 9.5 billion in 2000 to USD 68.14 billion in 2019, with a growth of 14.7 per cent. Therefore, the outflows show a growth rate of 0.7 percentage

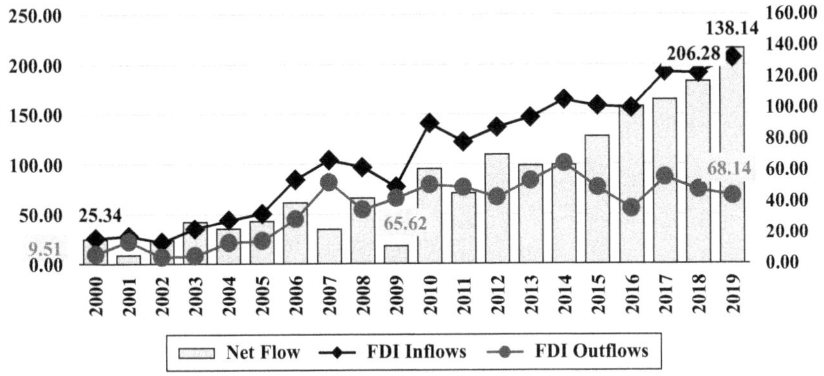

Figure 8.2 ASEAN–India FTA's Inflows and Outflows of FDI: 2000 to 2019 (USD bn.) Source: UNCTAD FDI Statistics

points higher than the inflows. Investment inflows spiked by USD 56 billion in 2010 immediately after ASEAN–India FTA was signed in 2009. Both economies recorded less impressive inflows in 2016, with negative flows of USD 25 billion. Nevertheless, the positive net FDI flow showed the two markets did provide considerable opportunities for the global investors. A simple comparison in the shares of the AIFTA region suggests modest FDI inflows; the FDI inflows increased by 3.3 per cent and 0.7 per cent in comparison to FDI outflows to 7.9 and 2.6 per cent for the period 2000 to 2019.

Continuing with the long-term analysis of the FDI inflows and outflows between ASEAN and India across five decades, it is seen that average FDI inflows had a steady pace and is hovering around the value of 5.4 per cent. Whereas, in the case of the FDI outflows, it increased from a low level of 0.2 per cent in 1970 to a high level of 5.4 per cent for the period 2010 to 2019, suggesting a very high decadal growth rate (see figure 8.3). Both India and ASEAN economies showed a surge in FDI outflows over the five decades, particularly true for the last decade.

However, figure 8.4 suggests the growth rate in investment flows is higher for India when compared with ASEAN countries as a block. India's FDI inflows marked a growth rate of 14.9 per cent compared to its FDI outflows, a staggering 18.1 per cent from 1997 to 2019.

On the other hand, ASEAN as a group showed lower growth in both inflows and outflows. ASEAN's FDI inflows registered a growth rate of 11 per cent, while outflows reported an increase of 10 per cent. It indicates that the ASEAN market has matured from (1990 to 2000) in terms of FDI inflows compared to the 1970–1980s. As a result, investment activities were much more robust (Kallummal et al., 2018). The combined FDI flows of ASEAN and India suggest increased FDI inflows from USD 26 billion to 146 billion. In comparison, the FDI outflows rose only from USD 10 billion

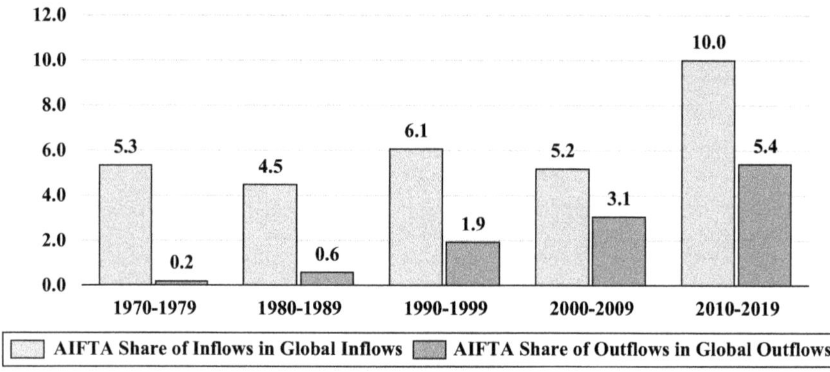

Figure 8.3 Decadal FDI Investment Flows of AIFTA Share to Global Flows: 1970 to 2019 Source: UNCTAD FDI Statistics

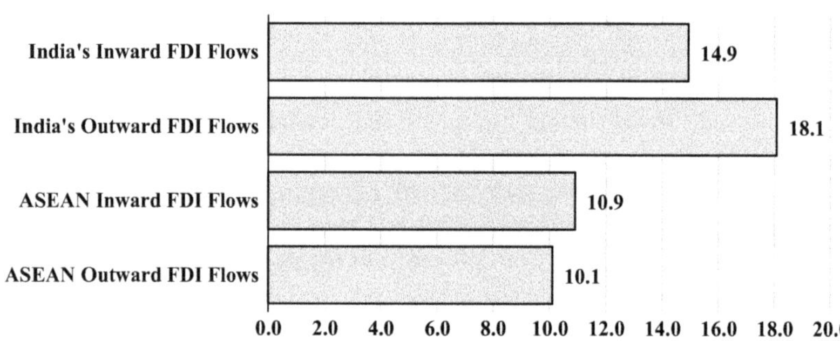

Figure 8.4 The Growth Rate of FDI Flows of AIFTA Partners 1997 to 2019 Source: UNCTAD FDI Statistics

to USD 41 billion. Implying an increase of six times in inflows compared to four times in outward flows (see Table 8.1).

Market Access for Goods Sector by India

Table 8.2 lists India's comparative tariff liberalisation undertaken under its seven dominant FTAs. She provided the highest market access to goods from SAFTA (LDCs were offered a significant share up to 99% with only 25 products in the exclusion list). Market access conceded by India under the ISFTA is up to 91%, AIFTA 90% and followed by other FTAs.

Table 8.3 indicates the liberalisation of India's goods sector at the national tariff lines. It also suggested a similar extent, with only 0.9 percentages being the difference at 89.3 per cents. AIFTA also showed similar levels

Table 8.1 Investments Activities of ASEAN and Indian Economies: 2000 to 2019

AIFTA FDI Activity	*2000*	*2005*	*2010*	*2015*	*2019*
Inward Flow (USD bn.)	25.3	50.4	140.4	158.3	206.3
Outward Flow (USD bn.)	9.5	23.0	79.3	76.5	68.1
Net Inflows (USD bn.)	**15.8**	**27.2**	**61.1**	**81.7**	**138.1**

Source: UNCTAD FDI Statistics

Table 8.2 India's Trade in Goods and FTAs (Updated in 2020)

S.No.	*FTA Acronym*	*Member Countries*		*Market Access in Tariff Lines (HS Six Digits)*	*FTAs/ PTAs*[(1)]
		No of Countries	*Names*		
1	AIFTA	11	Brunei, Cambodia*, India, Indonesia, Laos*, Malaysia, Myanmar*, The Philippines, Singapore, Thailand and Vietnam*	90.2%	FTA & EIA
2	SAFTA	8	Afghanistan*, Bangladesh*, Bhutan, India, Maldives, Nepal*, Pakistan and Sri Lanka	Ap. 96% [($)]	FTA
3	ISLFTA	2	India and Sri Lanka	Ap. 91%	FTA
5	IMCECA	2	India and Malaysia	Ap. 84%	FTA and EIA
6	JICEPA	2	India and Japan	Ap. 86%	
7	IKCEPA	2	India and Republic of South Korea	Ap. 84%	FTA

Note: Partial Scope Agreement (PSA)/Preferential Trade Agreement (PTA); Free Trade Agreement (FTA) and Economic Integration Agreement (EIA); Ap. = approximately; * = LDCs; ($) = only for LDCs in SAFTA; % = India had two separate tariff concession schedules as Singapore is a zero duty country. None of the renegotiation changes has been addressed here.
Source: Kallummal Murali, (2021) 'Import Surge of Agricultural Products under the FTAs: Protection of Substitutable Products to Address Livelihoods Concerns'. Paper presented in a conference at CDS, memo.

in merchandised sectors, like the agricultural and non-Agricultural sectors were liberalised.

Establishing a predictable regime across 11 partners of AIFTA with 81 per cent is based on predictable market access under AIFTA. The highest liberalisation in Singapore (99.8%), Cambodia (98.2%) followed by Lao PDR with 97.3%, and the lowest in Vietnam with 81 per cent of the 10,711 national tariff lines (see Table 8.4).

The AIFTA agreement considers it fit for preferential access only those products that undergo a value addition of 35% along with a change in tariff

Table 8.3 India Tariff Schedules – CLMV and the Philippines

Category	*CLMV (NTLs)*	*% – CLMV*	*The Philippines (NTLs)*	*The Philippines – %*
Exclusion List (EL)	1,297	10.7	1,297	10.7
Normal Track – 1 (NT-1 – 2013)	7,776	63.9	7,775	63.9
Normal Track – 2 (NT-2 – 2018)	1,252	10.3	1,252	10.3
Special Product (SP)	40	0.3	40	0.3
Sensitive Track (ST)	1,805	14.8	1,805	14.8
Market Access for ASEAN Economies	10,873	89.3	10,872	89.3
Total TLs	12,170	12,171	12,169	12,169

Note: CLMV = Cambodia, Lao, Myanmar and VietNam, the LDC group.
Source: Calculation based on India's Tariff concession schedules under the AIFTA.

sub-heading (CTSH) – only goods that undergo a substantial value addition are qualified for the same. AIFTA ignores the Rules of Origin (ROO) requirement under the Comprehensive Economic Partnership Agreement (CEPT) in the ASEAN Free Trade Area, which qualifies cumulative value addition and qualifies all aspects like local trade and manufacturing across the ASEAN members and facilitates economic integration with regional integration and international allies.[2] It may put ASEAN countries in an advantageous position over and above Indian firms. The direct impact of AIFTA is seen in the deepening of liberalisation in the goods sector across 2013 and 2018, leading to more than 35% value addition and CTSH. In the automobiles and electronics sectors, the FTA-led liberalisation in India has not deepened and integrated the sectors with the regional supply chains – as these sectors appear to have been incorporated before the AIFTA (Banga and Das, 2012). However, some preliminary signs can be seen in three industries: textiles, construction equipment and manufactured metal products. It is getting integrated with the implementation of AIFTA and CEPA with Korea. Suppose there are FDI inflows that are channelled through international capital flows, an essential source of economic growth in the economy of any country. In that case, the results will supplement the domestic resources such as capital, technology and knowledge improvement and managerial skills and productivity growth, particularly from the perspective of a developing country (Harrison, 1994; Mun et al., 2008; Nguyen, 2020a).

In particular, the attraction of FDI inflows also plays a crucial role in the technology transfer process (Wang, 1990; Tybout, 2000; Nguyen, 2018). This process is a significant channel to access new technologies for domestic firms (Du et al., 2012; Chaudhry et al., 2013). Therefore, the local firms in host countries get the opportunity to enhance productivity and production efficiency and join the global value chain. Precisely, inward FDI flows can accelerate exports (Aitken et al., 1997; Nguyen, 2020b; Francis 2019). In

Table 8.4 India's Market Access in Goods Sector in ASEAN-10 Countries (2010)

Tariff Category (%)	*Brunei*	*Cambodia*	*Indonesia*	*Malaysia*	*Myanmar*	*The Philippines*	*Singapore**	*Thailand*	*Lao PDR*	*VietNam*
EL	13.0	2.0	7.2	8.6	18.0	13.7	--	12.6	2.8	19.1
HSL	0.0	0.2	6.4	1.0	--	4.7	--	0.3	--	5.8
1. HSL-A	--	*0.2*	--	*0.0*	--	--	--	*0.3*	--	0.4
2. HSL-B	--	--	--	*0.3*	--	--	--	--	--	1.1
3. HSL-C	--	--	*6.3*	*0.7*	--	*4.7*	--	--	--	4.2
NT-1	69.0	80.1	41.9	65.4	60.0	56.3	--	66.7	68.8	59.5
NT-2	11.0	4.0	4.7	12.1	8.0	18.0	--	8.9	8.7	8.6
ST	7.0	13.7	39.9	12.9	14.0	7.2	7.0	11.5	19.8	6.9
Market Access (% of TLs)	87.0	98.2	92.8	91.4	82.0	86.2	99.7	87.4	97.3	80.9
Total National Tariff Lines	10,689	8,182	8,738	10,396	9,776	8,186	10,813	8,300	8,300	10,711

Note: HSL = highly sensitive list, EL = exclusion lines, ST = sensitive tariff lines, ?NT = normal tracks 1 & 2, * = Singapore's NTLs from WITS Comtrade.
Source: Calculation based on AIFTA Tariff Schedule of ASEAN countries.

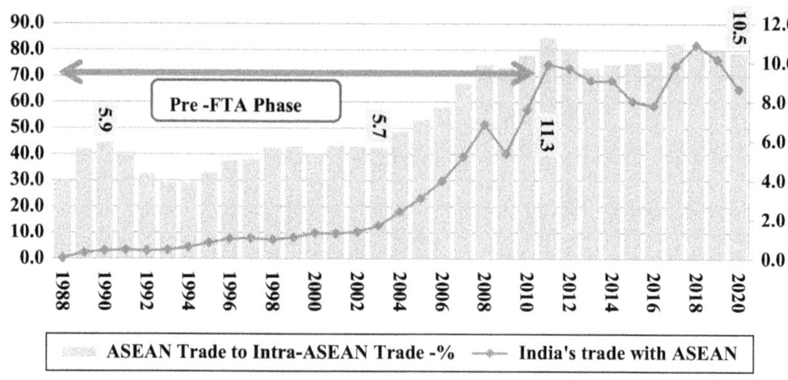

Figure 8.5 India and ASEAN Goods Trade 1988 to 2020 (USD bn.) Source: WITS Comtrade.

this regard, Helpman et al., 2004 pointed out that only productive firms choose to serve in the foreign markets via FDI while less effective firms self-select domestically oriented markets. A comparison of the total AIFTA goods trade suggested a share fall of 18.1 percentage points, as seen from Figure 8.5.

Indian Investment Analysis of Outward Direct Investments

This section will analyse India's financial commitments in ASEAN markets and the firm-wise commitments across the world. Using the descriptive analysis, we have identified the various markers like the firms' characters like the financial instruments used, ownership types, sectors and the entity type to undertake the analysis. Finally, we have also used the OLS regression to establish the findings. OECD identified that trade and investment are increasingly recognised as mutually reinforcing channels for cross-border activities. FDI generally occurs in tandem with greater international trade integration, reflecting increasing vertical integration and establishing transnational distribution networks. However, the ability of FDI to contribute to developing export capabilities depends on context. Export processing zones may be a tool for closer integration into world trade, but they come at a cost. (OECD, 2002).

AIFTA and the Outward Direct Investment Scenarios

Based on the general understanding, the aggregated analysis of FDI inflows (Francis, 2010) and outflows in Section II shows that India has been an active country among the ASEAN and India grouping. Therefore, the outward flows of Investment by Indian firms are taken up for analysis in this sub-section. This chapter aims to find the link between the goods liberalisation under the AIFTA and the corresponding investment flow. The creation of either regional value chains (RVC) or global value chains (GVC) requires a detailed analysis of bilateral investment activities (inflows and outflows) for both India and ASEAN separately. Investment flows for individual firms between trading partners have been analysed based on gains or no-gains scenarios and preferential concessions offered under FTAs. The results of this exercise would indicate any realigned investment activity that would display changes in market access due to the AIFTA.

As reported by RBI, India's outward foreign direct investment (OFDI) was USD 6 billion, catapulting to USD 41 billion in 2010, the highest ever recorded. However, there was a secular decrease in OFDIs only to increase in 2014 to USD 38 billion, as seen in Figure 8.6a. After this, India's OFDIs only decreased, and it was USD 22 billion in 2020. Along with a decrease in global OFDI flows, the share of the Indian OFDI to ASEAN showed reversed trends. The OFDI share to ASEAN increased from 14% to 31% in 2010, after which it remained in the range of 21% to 27%.

India's outward FDI flows were at their highest level in 2010 with USD 12.5 billion, after which it fell to USD 4.5 billion in 2020. Figure 8.6b and 8.6c analyses three components of financial commitments under the OFDI flows, equity, loans and guarantees issued. All of them showed similar trends

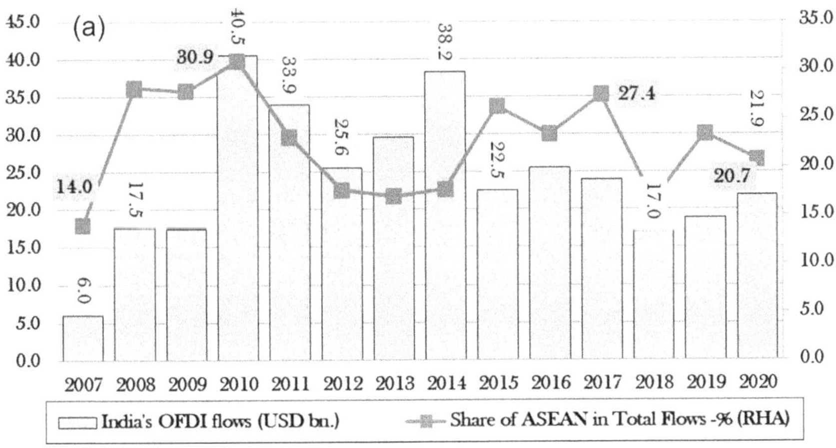

Figure 8.6 OFDI Flows of India (World, ASEAN and Share) Source: Compilation of OFDI data by RBI.

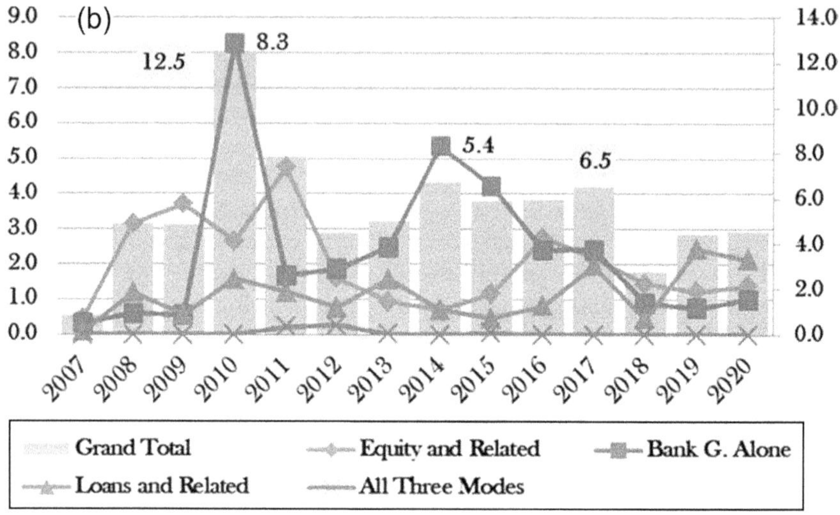

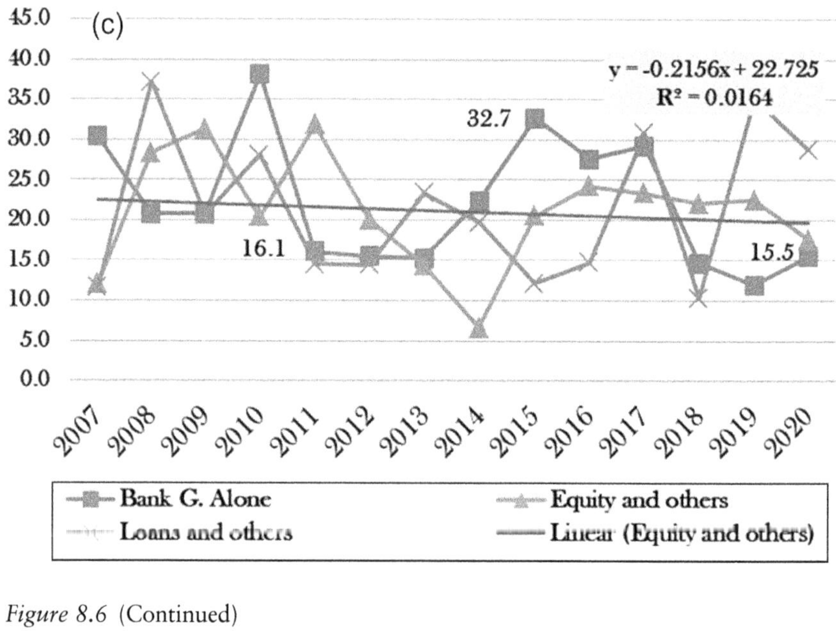

Figure 8.6 (Continued)

between 2007 and 2017. Detailed analysis reveals that in share terms, the equity portion of OFDI decreased simultaneously. On the other hand, the percentage of both loans and guarantees issued increased in proportion to total OFDI flows from India. Thus, a marginal increase in Indian firms and banks OFDI's flows in the ASEAN markets is suggested by both increased share of loans and the guarantees issued. However, the decreasing equity investments need to be further assessed by considering individual firms' investment patterns. Overall, the trends suggested a depressed investment level in the post-FTA period, which is also evident from the profiling of OFDI in Table 8.5 to World and ASEAN.

The OFDI flows alone suggest a growing investment interest for Indian firms in the ASEAN markets. Bifurcated analysis of the post-FTA into two equal phases suggested a decreasing interest in the second phase by USD 5.6 billion. For the same period, 2007 to 2020, into the pre-FTA period (2007-2010) and the post-FTA period (2011-2020). The yearly average OFDI investment numbers have increased to 1,177 in the post-FTA period than 530 in the pre-FTA period. In comparison, the annual average OFDI

Table 8.5 Firm-Wise Indian OFDI Flows to World and ASEAN's (Avg. and USD)

OFDI Flows	*ASEAN to World*					*India's OFDI (USD billion and Nos.)*
	All Modes	*Loan and Related*	*Equity and Related*	*Bank Guarantee Issued*	*Average (%)*	
Pre-FTA (2007–2010) – Bn.	0.0	34.5	25.1	27.8	29.1	23.14
Avg. Annual (Nos.)	***1***	***129***	***374***	***19***	***124***	***2,121***
I – Post-FTA (2011–2015) -Bn.	55.0	20.7	20.0	17.0	28.2	29.96
Post-FTA (2016–2020) – Bn.	1.3	20.8	22.2	25.5	17.5	24.3
Avg. Annual (Nos.)	***2***	***325***	***759***	***88***	***313***	***11,771***
India to ASEAN and World						
India's OFDI to ASEAN (USD Bn.)	**0.6**	**15.9**	**28.1**	**32.8**	**22.39**	**77.4**
India's OFDI to ASEAN (No.)	**11**	**3,768**	**9,099**	**950**	**3,457**	**13,891**
Avg. ASEAN (USD Bn.)	**0.1**	**0.00**	**0.00**	**0.03**	**0.01**	**0.01**
India's OFDI to World (USD Bn.)	**2.5**	**139.6**	**125.9**	**70.6**	**84.6**	**338.6**
India's OFDI to World (No.)	**43**	**4,092**	**42,523**	**19,293**	**16,488**	**66,201**
Avg. World (USD Bn.)	**0.1**	**0.03**	**0.00**	**0.00**	**0.01**	**0.01**

Source: Calculation based on a compilation of RBI data on OFDI.

flows marginally decreased to USD 5,422.4 million in the post-FTA period compared to USD 5,785.4 million in the pre-FTA period.

Table 8.6 analyses seven different flows to ASEAN in the pre- and post-FTA phases – equity, loans and guarantee issued for the World and ASEAN markets. Table 8.6 compares pre-FTA and post-FTA shares of India's OFDI flows to ASEAN markets under the three categories (equity, loan and guarantee issue). Overall the yearly trends showed consistent with the segregated assessment. The loan and related instruments increased from 14.8% to 23%. On the other hand, the equity dropped to 33.4% in the post-FTA period from 42.1% in the pre-FTA period. The bank guarantee issued showed an almost steady level of 42.1% in pre-FTA to 42.5% in the post-FTA period.

It reveals that amongst ASEAN OFDI flows in the post-FTA phase, 'equity & related', 'loans & related' and 'bank guarantee alone' did not perform as the post-FTA phase; all three flows have shown a fall in India's OFDI flows to the world. Thus, the OFDI flows from India to ASEAN did not show any positive change in the post-FTA phase – in compositional terms across the five categories except for 'All Three Modes'. At the same time, the 'all three modes' did show a significant increase in compositional shares in comparison to the World and the ASEAN countries suggested a rise of 42 percentage points. Therefore, it is evident that India's firms are more confident to lend to their WOS and JV partners in the post-FTA phase than in the pre-FTA phase.

Sectoral Pattern in India's OFDI Flows

The following sub-section analyses the sectoral composition of India's OFDI flows to ASEAN-10 countries – it is divided into pre-FTA (2007 to 2010) and post-FTA (2011 to 2020) periods. In addition, the table also provides a detailed analysis in terms of firm-level investments and values.

The OFDI flows by India to ASEAN in the pre-FTA is 2,121 assets with a value of USD 23,143 million and 11,889 investments with a value of USD 54,224 in the post-FTA phase decomposed into nine sectoral compositions. The AIFTA propelled Indian firms to diversify investments into previously lesser focused sectors like 'Financial Insurance, Real Estate & Business Services', 'Agriculture, hunting, fishing, forestry & mining' and 'Transport, storage & communication services' with increases observed in the number of investments and investment values. FTAs should have enabled the manufacturing sector. Almost 90% of market access liberalisation has been completed by 2018, when measured in number and values showed 28% and 32% respective outward flows. A detailed analysis of member countries and their sectors is done to understand the dynamics of AIFTA and its impact on investment flows. A simple reading suggested Singapore be the dominant destination of India's OFDIs. In the post-FTA, in number and values terms, the external flows showed a reduction of 15.2% and 22%, respectively. Table 8.7 showed an increase in OFDI flows across five sectors: Financial

Table 8.6 Instrument-Wise OFDI Flows to World and ASEAN's: 2007 to 2020

Firms and Instruments – OFDI	*OFDI Flows (In USD Mn.)*			*Comparison of Pre–Post-FTA (% Share)*			*Differential Impact of AIFTA Col. 6 (Pre–Post)*
	World	*ASEAN*	*% Share to the World*	*Composition% in OFDI in World*	*Composition% in OFDI in ASEAN*	*Percentage point (World vs ASEAN)*	
1	*2*	*3*	*4 =(3/2-%)*	*5 = (% of 2)*	*6 = (% of 3)*	*7= (5-6)*	*8 = (Diff. of Col 4)*
Pre-FTA (2007 to 2010)							
Equity and Related	39,707.6	9,971.2	25.1	48.8	43.1	-5.7	
Bank G. Alone	28,259.8	9,743.0	34.5	34.7	42.1	7.4	
Loans and Related	12,333.8	3,426.8	27.8	15.1	14.8	-0.3	
No Investments	0.0	0.0	0.0	0.0	0.0	-0.0	
All Three Modes	1,138.2	2.3	0.2	1.4	0.0	-1.4	
Post-FTA (2011 to 2020)							
Equity and Related	86,154.9	18,119.8	21.0	33.5	33.4	-0.1	-4.1
Bank G. Alone	1,11,352.4	23,060.0	20.7	43.3	42.5	-0.8	-13.8
Loans and Related	58,315.4	12,494.1	21.4	22.7	23.0	0.4	-6.4
No Investments	0.0	0.0	0.0	0.0	0.0	0.0	0.0
All Three Modes	1,318.5	550.4	41.7	0.5	1.0	0.5	41.5
India's Total OFDI (USD Mn.)	**3,38,580.6**	**77,367.6**					

Note: Equity and Related = Equity Alone, Equity and Loan and Equity and Bank Guarantee; Loans and Related = Loans Alone, Loans and Equity and Loan and Bank Guarantee; and All Three modes = Loans, Equity and Bank Guarantee issued.
Source: Calculation based on a compilation of RBI data on OFDI.

Table 8.7 Sectoral Composition of India's OFDI Flows Under the AIFTA

Sector	*Pre-FTA (2007–2010)*		*Pre-FTA Avg. (Investments)*	*Post-FTA (2011–2020)*		*Post-FTA Avg. (Investments)*	*Average Change in the Post-FTAs*
	Financial Commitments in USD Million)	*No. of Firms*		*Financial Commitments USD Million)*	*No. of Firms*		
India's OFDI Flows to ASEAN Markets							
Agriculture, Hunt., Fishing, Forestry and Mining	1,480	136	11	10,978	1,212	9	-2
Community, Social and Personal Services	153	84	2	1,029	560	2	0
Construction	223	127	2	1,615	488	3	2
Electricity, Gas and Water	166	20	8	653	125	5	-3
Financial Ins., Real Estate and Business Services	2,943	663	4	13,784	3,524	4	-1
Manufacturing	6,513	680	10	8,269	2,626	3	-6
Miscellaneous	134	35	4	473	108	4	1
Transport, Storage and Communication Services	10,798	116	93	10,086	905	11	-82
Wholesale, Retail Trade, Restaurants and Hotels	733	260	3	7,338	2,341	3	0
India's OFDI Flows to ASEAN	**23,143**	**2,121**	**11**	**54,224**	**11,889**	**5**	**-6**
India's OFDI Flows to World Markets							
Agriculture, Hunt., Fishing, Forestry and Mining	3,131	597	5	33,410	4,251	8	3
Community, Social and Personal Services	1,748	614	3	6,938	3,071	2	-1
Construction	2,594	617	4	16,691	2,867	6	2
Electricity, Gas and Water	1,060	113	9	3,780	907	4	-5

Financial Ins., Real Estate and Business Services	13,896	3,677	4	54,553	14,219	4	0
Manufacturing	32,987	3,961	8	71,396	15,783	5	-4
Miscellaneous	1,325	290	5	1,069	379	3	-2
Transport, Storage and Communication Services	18,294	368	50	38,076	2,756	14	-36
Wholesale, Retail Trade, Restaurants and Hotels	6,405	1,357	5	31,227	10,874	3	-2
India's OFDI Flows to World	**81,439**	**11,594**	7	**257,141**	**55,107**	5	-2

Source: Calculation based on a compilation of RBI data on OFDI.

Insurance, Real Estate & Business Services, Agriculture, Hunting, Fishing, Forestry & Mining, Transport, Storage & Communication Services, Manufacturing and Wholesale, Retail Trade Restaurants & Hotels with 93% share of total OFDI flows in value and 89% of the number of firms. However, across all the sectors and ASEAN 10 countries, average investments showed a fall with increased intensity and spread across countries.

Across all ASEAN countries, India's FDI flows increased in value and number, except for the Philippines. Table 8.8 shows India's OFDI flows to ten ASEAN economies. Based on the pre-FTA and post-FTA trends of the ten ASEAN economies, based on the growth rate in investment flows and the composition shares criteria, the ten countries have been divided into four groups; see column 10 of Table 8.8. Economies that registered a high growth rate in the post-FTA phase in investments and suggested more significant compositional change (See table 8.9) between the two periods were listed as 'promising destinations' where both values were above the average values and those listed as 'new destination' where no investments were recorded the pre-FTA period.

AIFTA suggested many Indian firms seeking mainly Singapore as its destination for all channels and modes, followed by five promising destinations were Malaysia, Indonesia, Myanmar, Vietnam and the Philippines. These five accounted for only 6% of the post-FTAs OFDI flows. Two economies like Cambodia and Brunei Darussalam are new destinations. Thailand and Lao PDR is the third group called the 'laggards'; it should be noted that India and Thailand had signed EHA in 2003. Among the ASEAN economies, only Singapore belonged to the last category of 'stable destination'. Singapore

Table 8.8 India's OFDI Flows (in USD million)

ASEAN-10	*2007*	*2010*	*2015*	*2018*	*2019*	*2020*	*2007–20*	*Four Groups*
1	*2*	*3*	*4*	*6*	*7*	*8*	*9*	*10*
SINGAPORE	740	12,072	5,277	2,518	4,177	4,279	72,822	SD
MALAYSIA	6	76	453	51	14	76	1,517	PD
INDONESIA	1	258	102	82	23	10	1,212	PD
MYANMAR	28	45	2	65	103	103	511	PD
THAILAND	11	7	21	24	24	12	503	LG
VIETNAM	30	20	22	38	57	39	456	PD
THE PHILIPPINES	17	42	25	18	23	4	310	PD
CAMBODIA			1	2	1	0	19	ND
LAOS		2	1	0			15	LG
BRUNEI							2	ND
India's Total OFDI flows	**833**	**12,521**	**5,904**	**2,798**	**4,424**	**4,524**	**77,368**	--

Note: SD = Stable Destination, PD = Promising Destination, LG = Laggards and ND = New Destination.

Source: Calculation based on a compilation of RBI data on OFDI.

Table 8.9 India's Average OFDI Investments in ASEAN 10 Economies

ASEAN Economies	*Pre-FTA – 2007 to 2010*		*Avg. Firm-Wise Investments*	*Post-FTA – 2011 to 2020*		*Avg. Firm-Wise Investments*
	USD Mn.	*No. of OFDI*		*USD Mn.*	*No. of OFDI*	
SINGAPORE	22,040	1,535	14	50,782	9,086	6
INDONESIA	208	116	2	1,310	473	3
VIETNAM	354	162	2	858	597	1
BRUNEI	135	37	4	376	451	1
CAMBODIA	102	84	1	353	315	1
LAOS	206	90	2	297	552	1
MALAYSIA	90	92	1	221	278	1
MYANMAR	--	--	--	19	91	0
THE PHILIPPINES	8	5	2	7	42	0
THAILAND	--	--	--	2	4	1
India's OFDI	**23,143**	**2,121**	**11**	**54,224**	**11,889**	**5**

Source: Based on compilation of OFDI data by RBI.

accounted for an average of 94% compositional share of total OFDI from India. From 2007 to 2020, with total investments of USD 72.8 billion, the pre-FTA period investment of USD 22 billion increased to the post-FTA to USD 51 billion with a growth of 130%. Countries like Malaysia (0.4%) and Vietnam (1.6%) with relatively low compositional shares.

Investment impact on Singapore from India after the AIFTA can be judged based on firms' investment activities and the average investment. Firm-wise investment numbers increased by six times from 1,535 in the pre-FTA to 9,086 in the post-FTA period. However, value only increased by two times, which impacted the average size per firm, falling from USD 14 million to USD 6 million in Singapore. The only ASEAN country that showed a rise in average firm-wise Investment in Indonesia increased 1.5 times (see Table 8.9).

Singapore the Dominant Investment Destination for India

India's OFDI flows to ASEAN are highly skewed towards Singapore. Singapore accounts for a significant share of 94% of India's total OFDI flows. India's direct investment by firms was highly concentrated in Singapore with a share of 90% in 2007, which got catapulted to 96% in 2010. It has witnessed an oscillation between 94% and 96% (see Table 8.10). Therefore, it indicates only a marginal increase in investment by Indian firms in ASEAN economies. It could be further analysed in detail to understand the actual dynamics involved in such investments. Investment flows also should increase with increased confidence, and an FTA should ideally do this task. These need to be assessed using three modes of assessment in terms of average flows, investment types, organisational structure (JVs and WOS) and sectors.

AIFTA effectively expanded the sectoral scope and coverage for India's investments across AIFTA-10 countries. However, the post-FTA has seen only marginal increases across dominant trading partners like Indonesia, Malaysia, the Philippines, Thailand and Vietnam. Singapore absorbed a significant amount of OFDI flows both in value terms and several firm-wise investment acts.

In Singapore, investments by Indian firms were valued at USD 73 billion from 10,621 firm-level for 2007 to 2020 (Table 8.11). The acquisitions, new investments and forex flow to Singapore in the post-FTA period increased by 146% in the number of firms than the pre-FTA; the values showed a sharp fall of 35%. Of the nine sectors, the wholesale, retail trade, restaurants and hotels; agriculture, hunting, fishing, forestry and mining; community, social and personal services; and construction had the most significant gains in the value of OFDI flows. In terms of investment by the number of firms, top performers were agriculture, hunting, fishing, forestry and mining, wholesale, retail trade, restaurants and hotels, transport, storage and communication services and community, social and personal

Table 8.10 ASEAN Centric OFDI Flows from India (Number and Values)

SINGAPORE	*Number*	*USD Mn.*	*Average (Inv.)*
	10,533	*72,822*	*6.91*
Pre-FTA	**1,535**	**22,040**	**14.36**
% Share	**14.6**	**30.3**	**207.8**
Agriculture, Hunting, Fishing, Forestry and Mining	**78**	**1,145**	**14.68**
Community, Social and Personal Services	71	144	2.03
Construction	76	207	2.72
Electricity, Gas and Water	20	166	8.31
Financial Insurance, Real Estate and Business Services	**521**	**2,766**	**5.31**
Manufacturing	**453**	**5,985**	**13.21**
Miscellaneous	31	133	4.29
Transport, Storage and Communication Services	**94**	**10,792**	**114.81**
Wholesale, Retail Trade, Restaurants and Hotels	191	701	3.67
Post-FTA	**8,998**	**50,782**	**5.64**
% Share	**85.4**	**69.7**	**81.6**
Agriculture, Hunting, Fishing, Forestry and Mining	**807**	**10,884**	**13.49**
Community, Social and Personal Services	497	949	1.91
Construction	341	1,306	3.83
Electricity, Gas and Water	115	647	5.63
Financial Insurance, Real Estate and Business Services	**3,047**	**13,420**	**4.4**
Manufacturing	**1,399**	**6,078**	**4.34**
Miscellaneous	98	472	4.82
Transport, Storage and Communication Services	**757**	**10,036**	**13.26**
Wholesale, Retail Trade, Restaurants and Hotels	**1,937**	**6,990**	**3.61**
OFDI Flows to ASEAN Countries (No. and Value)	13,891 76	77,368 94	5.57 124.06

Source: Authors' calculation based on a compilation of RBI data on OFDI.

services. The manufacturing sector had negative growth in value terms, and the number of investments was the ninth rank. However, the service sectors did suggest a healthy trend and the unidirectional flow from India to Singapore with OFDI pointing increases in value and number terms.

Singapore's impact in terms of surge seen in the participation in numbers with no increase in the value is a direct impact of the AIFTA and not associated with the double taxation avoidance agreement as it was signed and put into operation since 1994 (Table 8.12).

Table 8.11 OFDI from India to Singapore

Sectors	*Increased OFDI – Pre-FTA*		*Increased OFDI – Post-FTA*		*% of Increased (Post- over Pre-FTA)*	
	USD million	*No.*	*USD million*	*No.*	*USD million*	*No.*
1	*2*	*3*	*4*	*5*	*6 =(4/2)%*	*7 =(5/3)%*
Agriculture, Hunting, Fishing, Forestry and Mining	**2,290.6**	**156**	**9,738.9**	**733**	**325.2**	**369.9**
Community, Social and Personal Services	**288.6**	**142**	**804.4**	**429**	**178.7**	**202.1**
Construction	413.5	152	1,099.1	266	165.8	75.0
Electricity, Gas and Water	332.2	40	481.3	95	44.9	137.5
Financial Insurance, Real Estate and Business Services	5,532.9	1,042	10,653.5	2,572	92.5	146.8
Manufacturing	11,969.9	906	93.2	954	-99.2	5.3
Miscellaneous	265.7	62	339.2	70	27.7	12.9
Transport, Storage and Communication Services	21,583.7	188	-755.9	665	-103.5	253.7
Wholesale, Retail Trade, Restaurants and Hotels	1,402.8	382	6,288.3	1,767	348.3	362.6
Total Value and Numbers	**44,080.1**	**3,070**	**28,742.0**	**7,551**	**-34.80**	**146**

Source: Authors' calculation based on a compilation of RBI data on OFDI.

Empirical Analysis: OLS-Based Determinants of OFDI Flows[3]

The ASEAN–India FTA, signed to build a robust economic partnership, was a significant and essential step for both. It is often the case that with FTAs, positive interlink of trade and investment is viewed as a desired objective. However, as seen above in the previous section, our finding based on RBI data indicates that in the post-FTA period, in 9 out of 10 ASEAN trading partners, India's outward FDI has seen a downward trend. To further establish our findings, we attempt to analyse the impact of FTA on Indian firms' OFDI flows empirically.

The equation below indicates the regression model used for the analysis:

$$OFDI_{i,j,t} = \beta_0 + \beta_1\left(FTA_{i,j,t}\right) + \beta_2\left(EcoActivity_{i,t}\right) + \beta_3\left(InvType_{i,t}\right) + \beta_4\left(OwnershipType_{i,t}\right) + \mu_{i,j,t} + \tau_t + \varepsilon_{i,j,t}$$

where '*i*' represents the home country (India in this case), '*j*' represents the destination country (ASEAN in this case), '*t*' represents the year. $OFDI_{i,j,t}$, the dependent variable in our regression equation, represents the outward FDI flow from India to the ASEAN group.

Additionally, the equation entails four independent variables included based on data availability. $FTA_{i,j,t}$, our primary explanatory variable of interest, is a dummy variable that takes the value of 1 after an FTA is signed between the regions i and j. In other words, it represents the post-FTA period and takes the value of 0 otherwise. $EcoActivity_{i,t}$ is the second independent variable representing four economic activities like agriculture, manufacturing, services etc, carried out in the country i. $InvType_{i,t}$. represents the various components of investment such as bank guarantee and loan to name a few. The last explanatory variable $Ownership_{i,t}$ is another dummy variable that takes the value of 1 if it's WOS and 0 otherwise.

The empirical analysis, which was based on panel data consisting of approximately 67,000 observations, used country fixed effects ($\mu_{i,j,t}$) and time fixed effects (τ_t) to take into account any variability that would arise across the countries and over time. Further description of each variable undertaken is summarised in Table 8.13.

The regression results are reported in Table 8.14, which presents the OLS estimation results for all destination countries where India invested.

Table 8.12 India's Double Taxation Avoidance Agreement with ASEAN Countries

S. No.	*ASEAN Partner: Agreement Name*	*Date of Signing*	*Date of Implementation*
1	Brunei Darussalam: Tax Information Exchange Agreement (TIEA)	28th February 2019	30th January 2020
2	Indonesia: Comprehensive Agreements	27th July 2012	5th February 2016
3	Malaysia: Comprehensive Agreements	26th December 2012	1st April 2013
4	Myanmar: Comprehensive Agreements	2nd April 2008	1st April 2010
5	The Philippines: Comprehensive Agreements	21st March 1994	21st March 1994
6	Singapore: Comprehensive Agreements (Synthesised Text)	27th May 1994 (29th June 2005, 24th June 2011 and 30th December 2016)	27th May 1994 (7th June 2017)
7	Thailand: Comprehensive Agreements	29th June 2015	13th October 2015
8	Vietnam: Comprehensive Agreements	2nd February 1995	2nd February 1995

Source: Various DTAA agreements of the Government of India.

Table 8.13 Data of Description of the Dependent and Independent Variables

Variables	*Categories*	*n (#)*	*Per Cent*	*Average*	*St. Dev*
FTA	Post-FTA	58,823	88.19	5.1	58.2
	Pre-FTA	7,878	11.81	5.2	38.8
Economic Activities	Agriculture	4,848	7.27	7.6	69.1
	Manufacturing	19,744	29.6	5.3	42.7
	Services	41,440	62.13	3.6	17.6
	Miscellaneous	669	1	4.8	60.9
Investment type	All Three Modes	43	0.06	57.1	96.8
	Bank Guarantee Alone	4,092	6.13	34.1	185.1
	Equity and Bank Guarantee	289	0.43	79.6	233.4
	Equity and Loan	1,491	2.24	9.7	60.4
	Equity Alone	40,743	61.08	2.2	26.6
	Loans and Bank Guarantee	457	0.69	47.7	110.8
	Loans Alone	18,836	28.24	2.6	18
	No of Investments	749	1.12	--	--
	Total Alone	1	0	--	--
Ownership Type	JV	18,522	27.77	4.6	81
	WOS	48,179	72.23	5.3	43.2
FTA with India	No?	147	89.09	52,310	5
	Yes?	18	10.91	13,891	6
OFDI (USD Mn.)					
Mean (OFDI Value)	5.13				
St. Dev.	56.26				

Note: # = Investments by firms.
Source: Authors' calculation based on a compilation of RBI data on OFDI.

Whereas Table 8.15 shows the OLS estimates for OFDI flow from India to ASEAN countries. As mentioned above, the four independent variables ('FTA', 'Economic Activity, 'Investment type' and 'Ownership Type') are standard for both tables. However, we have considered one more variable in the first table, i.e. India's FTA with other countries. Since our primary independent variable of interest is $FTA_{i,j,t}$, we observe in Table 8.14 a significant negative impact of the post-FTA period on OFDI.

In order to verify our results, we conduct a robustness check wherein, as seen in Table 8.15, we perform four different OLS estimations as we now define the FTA period from 2010 to 2011, 2013 and 2018, respectively, to identify the more accurate impact of FTA on the OFDI flow. In this way, we would capture the Agreement on OFDI with a lag and meet the tariff liberalisation dates in the latter periods, after 2010. Additionally, it would allow us to recognise the year of implementing the deal to boost India's OFDI. As previously seen, we still observe a significant negative impact of the post-FTA period in our latter model. Here the investment diversion is kept in the post-FTA period. However, it was found that the negative impact has

Table 8.14 OLS for OFDI from India to the Other Countries

Model 1 – Study Variable: [OFDI Flow]			
Independent Variables		*FTA = 2010*	
		Co-eff.	*t*
FTA (Base Category: Pre-FTA)		-1.63**	-2.43
Economic Activity (Base Category: Agriculture)	Manufacturing	-3.43***	-3.83
	Services	-2.81***	-3.33
	Miscellaneous	-4.73**	-2.05
Investment Type (Base Category: Bank Guarantee)	Equity	-32.26***	-35.31
	Loan	-31.59***	-33.03
	All Modes	22.73**	2.68
	Equity and Bank Guarantee	45.37***	13.46
	Loan and Bank Guarantee	13.69***	5.01
	Equity and Loan	-24.71***	-14.71
Ownership Type (Base Category: JV)		0.88*	1.80
India's FTA (Base Category: No FTA)		1.82***	3.93
Constant		37.76***	27.84
Statistics			
F Statistics		166.02	
R Sq.		0.03	
n(#)		65,952	

Note: *** = 1%, ** = less than 5%, and * = 10%.
Source: Authors' calculation based on a compilation of RBI data on OFDI.

reduced over the years. A significant adverse effect is observed for every economic activity like manufacturing, services and miscellaneous for both models. Only equity-bank guarantees and loan-bank guarantees have a positive impact on OFDI flows.[4] While the latter is positive but insignificant in the second model, the first one shows a similar impact as the earlier model. The movement from WOS to JV has a positive effect on OFDI in the first model. Still, a significant impact is not observed for the model for ASEAN.

Moreover, the impact is harmful to the ASEAN countries. The post-FTA period showed adverse and weaker effects across all the post-FTA period models starting from 2011, 2013 and 2018, respectively (see Table 8.15). However, variable India's FTA, which represents FTA with India and others, positively impacts OFDI. The result implies that the agreement signs between the countries with the hope of gaining trade and investment opportunities.

Going by the theoretical understanding of trade and investment linkages, there should have been increased OFDI flows in the ASEAN market through investment flows across any active economic market. But ironically, the expectation of an increased investment flow as tariffs were eliminated was

Table 8.15 OLS for OFDI from India to the ASEAN

Model 2 – Study Variable: [OFDI Flow]									
Independent Variables		*FTA = 2010*		*FTA = 2011*		*FTA = 2013*		*FTA = 2018*	
		Co-eff.	*t*	*Co-eff.*	*T*	*Co-eff.*	*t*	*Co-eff.*	*t*
FTA (Base Category: Pre-FTA)		-4.05**	-2.24	-3.93**	-2.69	-1.64	-1.31	-0.37	-0.33
Economic Activity (Base Category: Agriculture)	Manufacturing	-6.22***	-3.01	-6.07***	-2.94	-5.89***	-2.86	-5.86**	-2.84
	Services	-4.13**	-2.21	-3.98**	-2.13	-3.96**	-2.12	-4.02**	-2.16
	Miscellaneous	-9.25*	-1.63	-9.00	-1.59	-8.72	-1.54	-8.73	-1.55
Investment Type (Base Category: Bank Guarantee)	Equity	-33.14***	-15.22	-33.21***	-15.25	-32.95***	-15.15	-32.88***	-15.11
	Loan	-31.41***	-13.58	-31.54***	-13.62	-31.37***	-13.55	-31.28***	-13.51
	All Modes	16.18	0.84	14.92	0.77	15.40	0.80	15.80	0.82
	Equity and Bank Guarantee	70.97***	9.25	70.57***	9.19	70.93***	9.24	71.10***	9.26
	Loan and Bank Guarantee	3.51	0.48	3.62	0.50	3.36	0.46	3.47	0.48
	Equity and Loan	-21.08***	-4.84	-21.34***	-4.90	-20.78***	-4.77	-20.51***	-4.71
Ownership Type (Base Category: JV)		-0.21	-0.17	-0.25	-0.21	-0.23	-0.18	-0.12	-0.09
Constant		43.01***	12.85	42.63***	13.65	40.28***	13.47	39.18***	13.39
Statistics									
F Statistics		41.86***		42.07***		41.55***		41.40***	
R Sq.		0.03		0.03		0.03		0.03	
n(#)		13,828		13,828		13,828		13,828	

Note: *** = 1%, ** = less than 5%, and * = 10%.
Source: Authors' calculation based on a compilation of RBI data on OFDI.

not seen under the AIFTA. For the period analysed, the firm-level investment flows from India to the ASEAN market do not suggest an increase after the FTA in 2010 and 2013 and full liberalisation in 2018. What needs to be analysed further is the impact of tariff decreases seen in India; this could have impacted the investment flows from India to ASEAN.

Conclusion

The India-ASEAN FTA led to tariff elimination of up to 91 per cent of tariff lines and increased market access for both parties. Ideally, it should have led to enhanced investment flows too. It is observed that in terms of FDI inflows and outflows, the Southeast Asian countries were active even before the AIFTA. India's firm-wise analysis of OFDI revealed that the equity portion of OFDI decreased in its share. At the same time, the percentage of both loans and guarantees issued increased in proportion to total OFDI flows from India. The positive impact of loans and guarantees is observed in the OLS also. For the trade with ASEAN countries, the equity and guarantees have a significant effect on OFDI. In a limited way, this result implied that AIFTA helped Indian firms and banks build a strong confidence level in the potential of the ASEAN markets. AIFTA also expanded the reach of many Indian firms, clearly shown in the increased participation. There was a three-fold increase in the number of total firms in the post-FTA period, resulting in a decrease in the average value of the investment. The negative impact of the post-FTA period on OFDI establishes this proposition. The AIFTA did provide a stabilising effect on the region and gave countries like Singapore a boost in the OFDI flows from India. Investments were mainly concentrated in primary and service sectors like transportation, storage and communication services with nearly 39 per cent share in the increased OFDI. It is followed by insurance, real estate and business services with 22.6 per cent and agriculture, hunting, fishing, forestry and mining with 22.3 per cent shares. The post-FTA firm-level OFDI flows from India are concentrated in Singapore alone. Thus, the surges services sector, Singapore in particular, needs to be analysed to establish the facilitative role of India's exports or imports of goods.

The AIFTA agreement considers it fit for preferential access only those products which undergo a value addition of 35% along with a change in tariff sub-heading (CTSH). However, it ignores the substantial value addition under the ASEAN Free Trade Area, which supports local trade and manufacturing across all ASEAN countries and facilitates economic integration with regional and international allies. The OLS model clearly shows the significant negative impact of FTA on OFDI. Suggesting that India did not gain by way of investment in the post-FTA period. Hence, evidence may point to Singapore as the main attraction of OFDI flow to avoid double taxation. With FTAs with China, Japan and Korea, the ASEAN has little interest to build GVCs with India.

The AIFTA did provide a stabilising impact, but it was limited to the boost of Singapore shares in India's total OFDI flows to ASEAN. The production networks in Singapore were mainly concentrated in primary and service sectors like transportation, storage and communication services with nearly 39 per cent share in the increased OFDI. It is followed by insurance, real estate and business services with 22.6 per cent and agriculture, hunting, fishing, forestry and mining with 22.3 per cent shares. The post-FTA firm-level OFDI flows from India are concentrated in Singapore alone and were spread across five Southeast Asian countries, namely Indonesia, Malaysia, Myanmar, Thailand and Vietnam. Therefore, it suggested an increase in confidence in these FTA partners by Indian firms. Thus, the ODFI in the services sector needs to be analysed to establish its role to facilitate Indian exports or imports into India. It is evident from the empirical analysis (descriptive and analytical) that FTAs do not by any yard-stick lead to increased firm-level investments. The AIFTA has established this fact. The study suggested that the the liberization only in the manufacturing sector will not create regional or global value chains. Hence it indicated the need for the liberalization of the supportive services sector as well.

Driven by Global Production Networks, the new trade theories have suggested a positive linkage between trade and investment. Ironically, the expectation of an increase in investment flows from India is not observed under the AIFTA. For the period analysed, the firm-level investment flows from India to the ASEAN market do not suggest an increase after the FTA in 2010 and almost full liberalisation in 2018. Future research work needs to analyse this linkage by accounting for the gaps in applied tariffs under an FTA- and the MFN-applied rates of partners.

Notes

1 Kahouli & Kadhraoui (2012) explores extent regional economic integration affects growth. The study concludes that implementation of a policy of openness with an integration process must be at the heart of public intervention to promote growth and improve social welfare.

2 The general (ROO) rule is that local ASEAN content must be at least 40% of the FOB value of the good. The local ASEAN content can be cumulative, that is, the value of inputs from various ASEAN members can be combined to meet the 40% requirement.

3 The authors would like to acknowledge Ms Simran Khosla, Research Fellow at the Centre for WTO Studies.

4 Given that India's banking sector is under severe strain of NPAs, all such decisions were made in a period wherein there was a highly competitive environment, clouding the decision-making capacities of India's banks. Therefore, it suggested towards a need to conduct further studies on the clear delineation of the cause for this positive result between the two channels the 'equity and loans' with that of the 'bank guarantees'. Khan in 2012 has shown that the bank guarantees invoked is almost negligible when analysed on annual basis, suggesting that the firms mostly used them as a means to enhance market price of shares.

References

Aitken, B., Hanson, G. H., & Harrison, A. E. (1997), Spillovers, foreign direct investment and export behaviour, *NBER working paper no. 4967*, National Bureau of Economic Research, Massachusetts, United States.

Baier, S. L., & Bergstrand, J. H. (2007), Do free trade agreements actually increase members' international trade?, *Journal of International Economics*, *71*(1), pp. 72–95.

Banga, R., & Abhijit, Das (2012), *Twenty years of india's liberalization: Experiences and lessons*, UNCTAD and Centre for WTO Studies, IIFT, https://unctad.org/system/files/official-document/osg2012d1_en.pdf.

Bengoa, M., Sanchez-Robles, B., & Shachmurove, Y. (2020), Do trade and investment agreements promote foreign direct investment within Latin America? Evidence from a structural gravity model, *Mathematics*, *8*(11), p. 1882.

Blonigen, B. A. (2005), A review of the empirical literature on FDI determinants, *Atlantic Economic Journal*, *33*(4), pp. 383–403.

Caves, R. E. (1996), *Multinational enterprise and economic analysis*, 2nd edition, Cambridge University Press, Cambridge.

Chakrabarti, A. (2001), The determinants of foreign direct investments: Sensitivity analyses of cross-country regressions, *kyklos*, *54*(1), pp. 89–114.

Chantasasawat, B., Fung, K. C., Iizaka, H., & Siu, A. (2010), FDI flows to Latin America, East and Southeast Asia, and China: Substitutes or complements?, *Review of Development Economics*, *14*(3), pp. 533–546.

Chaudhry, N. I., Mehmood, A., & Mehmood, M. S. (2013), Empirical relationship between foreign direct investment and economic growth, *China Finance Review International*, *3*(1), pp. 26–41.

Dhar, B. & Kallummal, M. (2002), *Capital inflows an market driven investments: A focus on South Asian Crisis*, RIS Occasional Paper, 66, Research and Information Systems, New Delhi.

Du, L., Harrison, A., & Jefferson, G. H. (2012), Testing for horizontal and vertical foreign investment spillovers in China, 1998–2007, *Journal of Asian Economics*, *23*(3), pp. 234–243.

Duong, M., Holmes, M. J., & Strutt, A. (2020), The impact of free trade agreements on FDI inflows: the case of Vietnam, *Journal of the Asia Pacific Economy*, *26*(3), pp. 1–23.

Endoh, M. (1999), Trade creation and trade diversion in the EEC, the LAFTA and the CMEA: 1960–1994, *Applied Economics*, *31*(2), pp. 207–216.

Francis, S. (2010), Foreign direct investment concepts: Implications for negotiations, *Economic and Political Weekly*, *45*(22), May 29.

Francis, S. (2019), *Industrial policy challenges for india global value chains and free trade agreements*, March 19, Routledge India, ISBN 9780367343415.

Francis, S., & Kallummal, M. (2009), The new regionalism in the Southeast Asian Trade Policy and issues in market access and industrial development: An analysis of the ASEAN-China free trade agreement, *The Journal of Economic Policy and Research* (IISN 0975 8577), *4*(2), April to September 2009.

Francis, S., & Kallummal, M. (2006), US bilateralism in South East Asia: A sectoral analysis of market access issues in the proposed Thai-US free trade agreement, https://www.networkideas.org/feathm/aug2006/ft19_Abstracts_Bangkok.htm.

Francis, S., & Kallummal, M. (2013), India's comprehensive trade agreements: Implications for development trajectory, *Economic and Political Weekly*, *48*(31), August 03.

Francis, S., & Kallummal, M. (2018), Creeping financialisation through the FDI route: Implications for India's manufacturing sector, Paper presented at the *sixth IIFT conference on empirical issues in international trade & finance*, 13th & 14th December, http://eiitf.iift.ac.in/eiitf6/.

Fukao, K., Okubo, T., & Stern, R. M. (2003), An econometric analysis of trade diversion under NAFTA, *The North American Journal of Economics and Finance*, *14*(1), pp. 3–24.

García, E. C., Navarro Pabsdorf, M., & Gómez Herrera, E. (2013), The gravity model analysis: An application on MERCOSUR trade flows, *Journal of Economic Policy Reform*, *16*(4), pp. 336–348.

Harrison, A. E. (1994), Productivity, imperfect competition and trade reform: Theory and evidence, *Journal of International Economics*, *36*(1–2), pp. 53–73.

Helpman, E., Melitz, M. J., & Stephen, R. Y. (2004), Exports versus FDI with heterogeneous firms, *American Economic Review*, *94*(1), pp. 300–316.

Kahouli, B., & Kadhraoui, N. (2012), Consolidation of regional groupings and economic growth: Empirical investigation by panel data, *International Journal of Euro-Mediterranean Studies*, *5*(1), pp. 71–92.

Kahouli, B., & Maktouf, S. (2013), Regional trade agreements in Mediterranean area: Econometric analysis by static gravity model, *Journal of East-West Business*, *19*(4), pp. 237–259.

Kallummal, M. (2021), Import surge of agricultural products under the FTAs: Protection of substitutable products to address livelihoods concerns, *Seminar on Kerala and the World Economy*, 4th and 5th February 2021, organised by Centre for Development Studies (CDS), Thiruvananthapuram.

Kallummal, M., Zaki, H., & Parkhi, V. (2018), AIFTA goods liberalisation and investments: Is there a scope for value chain creation for India?, *Sixth IIFT conference on empirical issues in international trade & finance*, 13th & 14th December, http://eiitf.iift.ac.in/eiitf6/.

Kepaptsoglou, K., Karlaftis, M. G., & Tsamboulas, D. (2010), The gravity model specification for modelling international trade flows and free trade agreement effects: A 10-year review of empirical studies, *The Open Economics Journal*, *3*, 1–13.

Kox, H. L., & Rojas-Romagosa, H. (2020), How trade and investment agreements affect bilateral foreign direct investment: Results from a structural gravity model, *The World Economy*, *43*(12), pp. 3203–3242.

Li, Q., Scollay, R., & Gilbert, J. (2017), Analysing the effects of the regional comprehensive economic partnership on FDI in a CGE framework with firm heterogeneity, *Economic Modelling*, *67*, pp. 409–420.

Mun, H. W., Lin, T. K., & Yee, K. M. (2008), FDI and economic growth relationship: An empirical study on Malaysia, *International Business Research*, 1(2), pp. 11–18.

Nguyen, C. (2018), *Foreign direct investment, productivity and export participation: The case of Vietnam's manufacturing sector*, Department of Economics, Colombo University, Colombo, Sri Lanka.

Nguyen, V. C. (2020a), Trade liberalisation, economic reforms and foreign direct investment–A critical analysis of the political transformation in Vietnam (April 2). Research papers, SSRN's eLibrary, Rochester, New York, US. http://dx.doi .org/10.2139/ssrn.3566751.

Nguyen, V. C. (2020b), Energy consumption, income, trading openness, and environmental pollution: Testing environmental Kuznets curve hypothesis, *Journal of Southwest Jiaotong University*, *55*(1), pp. 1–10. https://doi.org/10.35741/issn.0258-2724.55.1.6.

OECD (2002), *Foreign direct investment for development maximising benefits, minimising costs*, Organisation for Economic Co-operation and Development, Paris.

Parakkal, R. (2021), Foreign investments in emerging economies: Do competition laws help or hinder?, *NLS Business Law Review*, 100–120, Accessed from f10044_3ad5576a7d734449ba487e172ec09af5.pdf (nlsblr.com) on July, 2021

Plummer, M. G., & Cheong, D. (2009), FDI effects of ASEAN integration, *Region et Developpement*, *29*, pp. 49–67.

Sasatra, S., & Prasopchoke, M. (2007), Go with the Gang, ASEAN!, *ASEAN Economic Bulletin*, *24*(3), pp. 339–335.

Sonam, C., Kallummal, M., & Verma P. (2012), Trade creation and trade diversion in the India-Sri Lanka free trade agreement: A sector-specific analysis, *Journal of Economic Policy and Research*, *8*(1), pp. 36–61.

Sudsawasd, S., & Mongsawad, P. (2007), Go with the Gang, ASEAN!, *ASEAN Economic Bulletin*, *24*(3), 339–356.

Takkar, I., & Nataraj, G. (2014), India-ASEAN FTA in services: Leading to enhanced trade prospects, Observer Research Foundation, Commentary. October 14, https://www.orfonline.org/research/india-asean-fta-in-services-leading-to-enhanced-trade-prospects/.

Tybout, J. R. (2000), Manufacturing firms in developing countries: How well do they do, and why?, *Journal of Economic Literature*, *38*(1), pp. 11–44.

Veeramani, C., & Saini, G. K. (2011), Impact of ASEAN-India preferential trade agreement on plantation commodities: A simulation analysis, *Economic and Political Weekly*, *10*, pp. 83–92.

Vogiatzoglou, K. (2007), Vertical specialisation and new determinants of FDI: Evidence from South and East Asia, *Global Economic Review*, *36*(3), pp. 245–266.

Wahyuningsih, D. (2021), Trade flow of manufacturing sector and foreign direct investment in ASEAN economic integration: The gravity model of trade, *Jurnal Perspektif Pembiayaan dan Pembangunan Daerah*, *8*(6), pp. 619–630.

Wang, J.-Y. (1990), Growth, technology transfer, and the long-run theory of international capital movements, *Journal of International Economics*, *29*(3–4), pp. 255–271, November.

9 Mergers and Acquisitions and Antitrust Implications

Evidence from the High-Tech Manufacturing Sector

P L Beena and Smruti Ranjan Sahoo

Introduction

Implementation of Trade-Related Aspects of Intellectual Property Rights (TRIPS) as part of the World Trade Organization (WTO) expects to boost the technological capabilities of the industry, attracts more Foreign Direct Investments (FDI) and creates a competitive environment. However, it is argued that middle-income countries do not benefit from stronger IPR regimes like high- and low-income countries as the positive effects from FDI and trade get offset by the negative effects due to the inability of these countries to imitate and use knowledge (Falvey et al., 2006). TRIPS can also impose a lot of additional costs on developing countries in the form of increased royalty payments, the theft of traditional knowledge and abuse of dominance (Chang, 2003; Fabre, 2015). Though there are many empirical studies on Innovation and Intellectual property, most of those studies either looked at the association of R&D and patents within manufacturing sector (Griliches, 1979; Arora, 2001; Kanwar and Evenson, 2003; Kanwar, 2012; Mani and Nelson, 2013; Basant, 2021; Dhar and Joseph, 2019) or on the technological transfer through FDI inflows and its impact on productivity (Kathuria, 2010; Kachoo, Ruchi and Madan, 2018). Given this context, the present chapter attempts to understand the recent trends and patterns of mergers and acquisitions in the Indian corporate sector and addresses the antitrust issues related to innovation and competition in the High Technology (HT) industries.

The chapter is divided into five sections. Section I discusses the trends and patterns of mergers and acquisitions in the Indian corporate sector from 2004 to 2018. Section II highlights the significance of the study and sets an analytical framework in light of the theoretical and empirical literature. Section III analyses the distribution of size of the firms across seven HT sectors in terms of sales. The impact of M&As on the market structure, price and non-price competitive strategies of seven HT industries during the new IPR regime (2006 to 2020) has been analysed in section III. Section IV presents the results of an econometric model that is employed to examine the determinants of price cost margin (PCM) of HT industries. The last section V sums up the major findings and suggests policy implications.

DOI: 10.4324/9781003343998-9

Trends and Pattern of Mergers and Acquisitions

Trends and patterns of M&As have been analysed in this section based on the monthly data extracted, both in terms of number and value of the deal, from the Venture Intelligence Database for the period 2004 to 2018. The data consists of the M&A deals between Indian firms (Domestic), Indian firms that are acquired by foreign firms (Inbound) and Indian firms that are involved in overseas acquisitions (Outbound). Distribution of the number and value of M&A deals across sectors such as resource based, manufacturing and services is further estimated at two-digit level. An attempt has also been made in this chapter to classify the deals in the manufacturing sector in terms of technological classification of industries, as defined by OECD.[1] Particularly, we looked at the high-technology industry group, which covers both High-technology and Medium-high-technology industries. There are seven industries in these groups. They are Manufacture of chemicals and chemical products (NIC 20); Manufacture of pharmaceuticals, medicinal chemical and botanical products (NIC 21); Manufacture of computer, electronic and optical products (NIC 26); Manufacture of electrical equipment (NIC 27); Manufacture of machinery and equipment n.e.c. (NIC 28); Manufacture of motor vehicles, trailers and semi-trailers (NIC 29); and Manufacture of other transport equipment (NIC 30).

Although there are 7877 M&A deals that took place in the Indian corporate sector during 2004 to 2018, only 4033 deals have reported their deal values. The total number of M&A deals that took place in 2004 was 131 which consistently increased to 646 in 2010 and 648 in 2018. Figure 9.1 depicts that the total value of deals is on the rise and reached its peak in

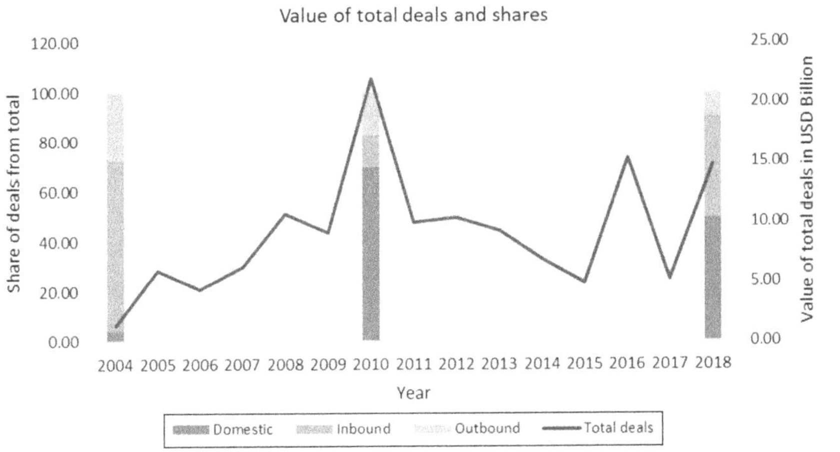

Figure 9.1 Value and distribution of M&As in terms of ownership

2010. Further the data reveals that the share of the M&A deals between Indian firms is much higher than the inbound and outbound deals, especially during the peak year.

From Table 9.1, it is observed that the service sector accounted for the largest share (71.75 per cent) of M&A deal values that took place in the Indian corporate sector from 2004 to 2018. Another 26 per cent of the M&A deals are engaged in the manufacturing sector, while the resources-based sector accounted for 2.67 per cent of the total M&A deals. Extraction of crude petroleum and natural gas accounted for a major share (43%) within the resource-based sector. Computer programming, consultancy and related activities are the leading sectors within the service sector accounting for 48.5 per cent of the total deal value of the service sector (Appendix 1). Similarly, six leading industries within manufacturing sector such as Manufacture of chemicals and chemical products (13%), Manufacture of pharmaceuticals, medicinal chemical and botanical products (12%), Manufacture of other non-metallic mineral products (18%), Manufacture of computer, electronic and optical products (15%), Manufacture of machinery and equipment n.e.c.(4%) and Manufacture of motor vehicles, trailers and semi-trailers (6%) together accounted for major share (68%) of M&A values (Table 9.2). Our analysis further reveals that 82 per cent of M&A deals that took place in the manufacturing sector are horizontal. Vertical mergers in the manufacturing sector accounted for 14 per cent, while conglomerate mergers accounted for only 4.5 per cent (Beena 2021). Some of these horizontal mergers could be vertical as well if we could disaggregate the industry classification of both acquirer and target firms in terms of detailed product activities, as observed by the earlier studies (Beena, 2001).[2] Similarly, 45 per cent of the total M&A deals in the service sector are vertical, while horizontal mergers accounted for 55 per cent of the total M&A deals (Beena 2021). It is also evident that the Indian corporate sector has seen a large share of inward FDI through cross-border M&As (CBM&As), which is a replacement of the existing investments/production capacity (Beena, 2014; Saraswathy, 2019; Dhar and Rao 2021). Many of the firms in Indian industries such as Drugs and Pharmaceutical, Automobiles, Iron and Steel, IT&ITEs and energy are also acquired by foreign-owned firms. Further, it is observed that most of the acquiring firms were either domestic leaders or global leaders in the respective industries. Such a pattern is also

Table 9.1 Sectoral distribution of number and value of M&A deals

Sector	*Number*	*Value (Billion US Dollar)*
Resource based	207 (2.63)	14.17 (2.67)
Manufacturing	2674 (33.94)	135.88 (25.58)
Services	4996 (63.42)	381.10 (71.75)
Total	7877 (100)	531.16 (100)

Note: Figure in the parenthesis represents percentage share to the total M&A deals.

Table 9.2 Industry-wise distribution of M&A deals during 2004–2018 (%)

NIC	*Industry*	*Number Domestic*	*Amount Domestic*	*Number Inbound*	*Amount Inbound*	*Number Outbound*	*Amount Outbound*	*Number Total*	*Amount Total*
10	Manufacture of food products	7.86	1.12	9.33	4.39	8.28	5.98	8.34	3.19
11	Manufacture of beverages	2.67	0.54	3.85	1.82	4.22	4.51	3.37	1.81
12	Manufacture of tobacco products	0.00	0.00	0.30	0.07	0.29	0.00	0.15	0.02
13	Manufacture of textiles	4.65	2.70	4.44	7.14	6.40	10.5	5.05	5.78
14	Manufacture of wearing apparel	3.05	1.35	2.67	1.42	2.62	1.63	2.84	1.43
15	Manufacture of leather and related products	0.53	0.61	1.48	1.75	0.00	0.00	0.64	0.82
16	Manufacture of wood and products of wood and cork, except furniture; manufacture of articles of straw and plaiting materials	0.76	0.11	0.59	1.15	0.15	0.00	0.56	0.40
17	Manufacture of paper and paper products	0.53	1.84	0.44	0.28	0.87	0.10	0.60	0.98
18	Printing and reproduction of recorded media	0.15	0.60	0.15	0.12	0.00	0.00	0.11	0.32
19	Manufacture of coke and refined petroleum products	1.14	1.04	0.44	0.00	0.73	0.05	0.86	0.51
20	Manufacture of chemicals and chemical products	11.7	11.2	12.0	21.7	12.5	4.23	12.0	12.8
21	Manufacture of pharmaceuticals, medicinal chemical and botanical products	14.6	8.15	16.0	18.2	20.3	13.3	16.4	12.3
22	Manufacture of rubber and plastics products	2.90	1.10	2.96	0.49	1.31	0.45	2.51	0.77
23	Manufacture of other non-metallic mineral products	7.86	26.7	5.33	13.4	3.92	4.99	6.21	17.8
24	Manufacture of basic metals	6.41	1.43	4.89	2.95	4.07	14.9	5.42	4.89

(*Continued*)

Table 9.2 Continued

NIC	*Industry*	*Number Domestic*	*Amount Domestic*	*Number Inbound*	*Amount Inbound*	*Number Outbound*	*Amount Outbound*	*Number Total*	*Amount Total*
25	Manufacture of fabricated metal products, except machinery and equipment	1.14	0.14	0.59	0.24	4.22	22.2	1.80	5.07
26	Manufacture of computer, electronic and optical products	4.35	28.1	3.41	1.60	5.67	5.65	4.45	15.1
27	Manufacture of electrical equipment	4.65	0.88	4.89	3.14	3.63	0.88	4.45	1.56
28	Manufacture of machinery and equipment n.e.c.	8.09	4.70	7.85	4.39	8.87	2.24	8.23	4.06
29	Manufacture of motor vehicles, trailers and semi-trailers	11.1	1.93	14.3	13.2	9.16	4.27	11.4	5.87
30	Manufacture of other transport equipment	1.68	0.29	2.22	0.80	1.02	1.94	1.65	0.81
31	Manufacture of furniture	0.15	0.00	0.00	0.00	0.29	0.29	0.15	0.07
32	Other manufacturing	2.90	2.45	1.33	0.72	1.45	1.78	2.13	1.77
33	Repair and installation of machinery and equipment	0.99	2.86	0.44	0.91	0.00	0.00	0.60	1.64
II	Manufacturing	100	100	100	100	100	100	100	100

Table 9.3 Technology-wise distribution of M&A deals in terms of number and value during 2004–2018

Distribution of M&A Deals	*Number*	*Value (Billion US Dollar)*
LT	591 (43.78)	64.32 (47.33)
HT	759 (56.22)	71.56 (52.66)
Total	1,350 (100)	135.88 (100)

Note: Figure in the parenthesis represents percentage share to total. Low technology (LT) industry includes both medium low and low technology industries.

observed in other industries such as the Drugs and Pharma, Platform industry, automation industry, fast-growing Indian inverter and secured power market; Crane, Elevator and Escalator markets and Electronics industry (Chaudhuri, 2012; Saraswathy 2018; Rao and Dhar, 2021). It is further evident that the high and medium-tech industries dominated the merger deals in terms of value (53%) and number (56%) compared to the low-tech industries during 2004 to 2018 (Table 9.3). Such observation is made in earlier studies as well in the context of the US economy (Chadhuri and Tabriz, 1999; Kohers and Kohers, 2000).

Acquisition of start-ups, including those initiated by serial entrepreneurs[3] by domestic or multinational firms, is also observed in the recent past. For instance, 37 per cent of the total sample of 356 Indian firms were acquired before attaining the age of 10 years. Six per cent of such acquired Indian firms were in the age of more than 40 years (Saraswathy, 2016). Our analysis further reveals that out of total start-up acquisitions that took place during 2018, 22 per cent of them were Enterprise related and 15 per cent were fintech-related deals, and Consumer services (14%), entertainment (7%), online travel (5.9%), E-commerce (5%)[4] and Edtech (4%) together accounted for 36 per cent (Beena 2021). It should be kept in mind that these acquisitions can also reduce the incentives to innovate or change the innovative and competitive dynamics in the relevant market, as argued elsewhere (Gonzalo, Marcos & Camila, 2017; Parsheera, Shah & Bose, 2017). It is also important to note that the 'lock-in effects' are a common phenomenon in many high-tech markets where a particular customer cannot readily switch to a substitute if it is not compatible with the current standard. Innovation arises at both the 'architectural' (standard) level and the 'modular' level (the sub-systems which comprise a standard) and raises questions, inter alia, about standard-setting and access to set standards (Glader, 2002).

TRIPs, Mergers and Acquisitions and Implications

Although the ultimate objective of competition and intellectual property policy is to raise social welfare by promoting the supply of new and existing products and services at low prices, many would argue that the TRIPS regime increases rather than reduces barriers (Edmund & Cantwell, 2012).

While the defenders of TRIPS argue that stronger protection of intellectual property rights is essential for innovation, knowledge generation and therefore economic development, the linkages between the TRIPS regime and economic development are difficult to measure (Maskus, 2008). The origin of IPR goes back to many centuries; however, it matured as an institution and took its current configuration in the first half of the nineteenth century. Under IPR, patents are considered as a device to provide monopoly power to the inventor to appropriate the returns to the invention. On the contrary, in the nineteenth century itself, an anti-monopoly movement referred to as antitrust practice was strengthened to address consumer surplus, which worsens due to monopoly. That is, the creation of a patent or IPR regime had coexisted with antitrust legislation (Beena & Siddik, 2019). For instance, to protect the interests of the consumer, a series of Acts such as the Sherman Act of 1890, the Clayton Act of 1914 and the Federal Trade Commission Act of 1914 were enacted in the United States and the United Kingdom. In the case of India, the Monopolies and Restrictive Trade Practices Act 1969 which was replaced by Competition Commission of India (CCI) Act in 2002 was on the same lines.

Debates on Competition policy and merger regulation across countries and in India have attracted scholarly attention during the WTO regime (Basant & Morris, 2000; Bhattacharjea, 2001; Bhattacharjea, 2016; Beena, 2014; 2021; Saraswathy, 2019; 2021; Chakrabarthy, 2005; Parsheera, Shah & Bose, 2017; Joseph, 2021; Francis, 2018). The major provisions of the Competition Act are to prohibit anti-competitive agreements, merger regulations and abuse of dominance. Such regulations were introduced to check the anti-competitive practices or market power and possible mark-up issues while analysing the post-merger outcome of mergers and acquisitions. The threshold limits for applying a combination of domestic firms or between domestic and foreign firms are fixed based on the turnover or total assets of the firms. However, it should be kept in mind that many mergers might not come under the purview of the merger review due to the existing thresholds level, although such deals might create negative externalities. For instance, the acquisition of a start-up by a large-sized incumbent player could be anti-competitive if it buys the technology and discontinues the technology path of that start-up based on the contestability principle (Francis, 2018). Although there are some studies on entrepreneurship and competition policy or start-up acquisitions and innovation dynamics, a lack of scholarly attention is given to address the anti-competitive effect of start-up acquisitions. There are studies in the context of developed and developing countries pointing out the limitation of the existing approach and suggesting broadening enough to include issues such as consumer privacy, personal data protection, consumer choice, switching costs, lock-in effects and market structure (Gonzalo, Marcos &Camila, 2017). This issue has become even more important due to the emergence of the new digital economy, which is globally controlled by the United States and China

(UNCTAD, 2019). A recent report of the competition law review committee has suggested introducing an additional threshold such as transaction value or deal value of M&As to review the combination. This is done in light of the observation made by many available studies (GOI, 2019; Bhattacharjea, 2019).

It is quite evident in the literature that one of the immediate effects of a merger is to increase the degree of concentration as it reduces the number of firms and generates barriers to entry (Bain, 1969; OECD, 2005). Artificial barriers can also be formed if the merger results in a strengthening of product differentiation through legal rights in designs, patents and know-how. It is argued that the cost-reducing effect of a particular proposed merger might probably outweigh its collusion-enhancing effects (Schmalensee, 1987). However, a small efficiency gain would generally be offset by a large increase in market power, which creates a situation that sets prices above the competitive levels (Williamson, 1968). Farrell and Shapiro (1990) argue that a merger that generates no synergy can exercise market power by cutting down the output or sales by keeping the price artificially high. The active market for corporate control might encourage managers to 'empire build', not only increasing their monopoly power but also strengthening the controlling block to progressively shield them from takeover (Beena, 2014).

The motives behind cross-border acquisitions differ from those, which drive purely domestic acquisitions. An acquiring firm might decide on an international merger to take advantage of cheap raw materials and labour, to capture profits from exchange rates or to invest its surplus cash (Weston, Chung and Haog, 1996). International differences in technology generate incentives for cross-border mergers in which low-cost firms from one country take over the high-cost firms from another country (Peter, 2007). The entry and subsequent activities of Multinational firms affect the structure of markets for goods and services in host countries in several different ways. Numerous studies for individual 'developing' countries as well as 'developed' economies indicate a positive association between Multinational Corporations' (MNCs) activities and the concentration of producers in host country industries (UNCTAD, 1997). 'Merger or takeover results in increased sales for the newly created foreign affiliates; or leave it unchanged if its size is the same as that of the incumbent firm acquired' (UNCTAD, 1997). The actual impact of an acquisition on competition depends upon the marketing strategies of MNCs, as well as on industry and country-specific circumstances. The risk that cross-border M&As may reduce competition tends to be greater in those industries in which shrinking demand and excess capacity are important motivations for M&As and in countries in which competition policy does not exist or where its implementation is weak (Zhan & Ozawa, 2001). Thus M&As can enhance concentration and build oligopolistic market power internationally. International mergers or combinations can raise consumer surplus and social welfare if and only if products are sufficiently differentiated. However, it is felt that international mergers and acquisitions should be discouraged where firms have an incentive to merge, but such mergers reduce social welfare (Qiu, Larry & Zhou, 2006).

Market Structure and Performance of High-Tech Industries

In light of the existing theoretical and empirical debates on the motives and consequences of mergers and acquisitions in the framework of structure-conduct-performance (SCP) developed by Bain (1951), this section analyses the impact of M&As on market structure and behaviour of seven HT industries. Before getting down to such an exercise, the following section tries to analyse the size distribution of the firms in these seven industries in terms of sales.

Table 9.4 indicates that very few firms control two-thirds of sales in these HT industries. Majority of the firms across all those industries are having a size of less than <1000 million sales. Our exploratory analysis further reveals that the ten leading firms in the chemical industry (NIC 20) control more than one-third of the total market share. This share is even more when we disaggregate the chemical industry at three-digit level. While ten leading firms in NIC 201 and NIC 202 control more than 40 per cent of the total market share, a single firm, i.e. Grasim industry in NIC 203, controls 71 per cent of the total sales. In the case of Drugs and Pharmaceutical industry (NIC 21), ten firms control 36 per cent of the total sales. It is further evident that these leading firms such as Hindustan Unilever, Asian Paints, Dabur India in chemical industry and Lupin, Aurobindo pharma, Dr Reddy's, Cipla, Glenmark and Sun Pharma in Drugs and Pharmaceutical industries were also engaged in M&A activities. Many of the Indian start-ups in this industry are also acquired by international market leaders. For instance, R&D-based pharmaceutical company Laurus Labs, which was founded in 2005, was acquired by US-based firm Aptuit in 2008. A recent study on market structure and pricing based on a representative sample of 135 molecules in the pharmaceutical industry (Chaudhury, 2018) observed that patented products accounted for almost two-thirds of the total sales of monopoly products and those products were largely produced by Multinational Corporations (MNCs). This industry has also experienced abuse of dominance by firms that hold patents in the formulation as it becomes dominant under statutory protection.[5] For instance, Biocon Ltd. and Mylan Pharmaceuticals private Ltd. filed a complaint against Roche for its pricing and non-pricing abuse concerning its biological cancer drug Trastuzumab (Org. for Econ. Cooperation & Dev, 2005). Subsequently an investigation was initiated by CCI against Roche and its two subsidiaries for anti-competitive conduct and denial of market access.

Four firms in the Manufacture of computer, electronic and optical products (NIC 26) control 75 per cent of total sales. Again, the top ten leading firms in the electronic components (NIC 261) control almost 60 per

Table 9.4 Size distribution of firms in HT firms as on 2020

NIC Code of Industries	*Size of Firms*	*0 to <250 Million*	*250 to < 500 Million*	*500 to < 1000 Million*	*1000 to < 5000 Million*	*5000 to < 10000 Million*	*>= 10,000 Million*	*Total Firm Listed in PROWESS Database*
20	No. of firms	133	83	92	240	71	86	1,332
	Percentage to total sales	0.29	0.68	1.53	13.18	11.48	72.84	
21	No. of firms	54	37	47	92	27	35	547
	Percentage to total sales	0.23	0.73	1.86	11.22	9.79	76.17	
26	No. of firms	106	32	45	83	10	14	580
	Percentage to total sales	0.60	0.77	2.15	12.37	5.19	78.92	
27	No. of firms	124	44	74	141	32	38	758
	Percentage to total sales	0.63	0.93	3.05	17.40	11.53	66.45	
28	No. of firms	203	74	86	179	52	59	949
	Percentage to total sales	0.78	1.06	2.45	15.13	15.03	65.56	
29	No. of firms	34	22	39	162	51	77	539
	Percentage to total sales	0.08	0.16	0.51	7.51	6.27	85.48	
30	No. of firms	2	5	1	14	1	3	35
	Percentage to total sales	0.23	2.36	0.73	34.37	9.41	52.90	

Source: Calculated using PROWESS Database, CMIE; industry sales are considered for the size distribution.

cent of the total sales. The two leading firms in Computers and Peripheral equipment (NIC 262) control 66 per cent of the total sales. Similarly, in the case of Communication and equipment industry (NIC 263) three leading firms such as Samsung India, Oppo India and Vivo India control 91 per cent of the total sales. A single firm, i.e., Dixon technologies, dominates 70 per cent of the sales in the consumer electronics industry (NIC 264). Five firms control 58 per cent of the total sales of the manufacture of irradiation, electromedical and electrotherapeutic equipment industry (NIC 266).

The leading ten firms in the manufacture of electrical equipment (NIC 27) industry control 40 per cent of the total sales. Two firms such as LG electronics and whirlpool in the Manufacture of domestic appliances (NIC 275) control almost 45 per cent of the sales while four firms control 44 per cent of the total sales in other electrical equipment (NIC 276) industry. While top 11 firms in the manufacture of machinery industry (NIC 28) control 30 per cent of the industry sales, top 12 firms control 40 per cent of the total sales of the manufacture of general purpose machinery (NIC 281). And in the case of Manufacture of special-purpose machinery (NIC 282), 10 firms control 48 per cent of the total sales.

In the case of Manufacture of motor vehicles, trailers and semi-trailer (NIC 29), top 10 out of 539 firms control 56 per cent of the total industry sales. In the case of Manufacture of motor vehicles (NIC 291), Maruti, Tata Motors and Hyundai control 52 per cent of the total sales while 10 firms control 30 per cent of the sales of the manufacture of parts and accessories for motor vehicles (NIC 292) industry. Thus market concentration is relatively more visible in the Motor vehicles compared to the Automobile component industry. Similarly, three firms in the Manufacture of railway locomotives and rolling stock (NIC 301) control 55 per cent of the total sales. Thus the analysis provides enough evidence to argue that the leading firms in these industries in terms of market share have also engaged in M&A activities during the new IPR regime.

The following section analyses the behaviour or performance of seven industries in HT sector in terms of price and non-price competitive strategies and check whether these industries performed relatively better than their counterparts, i.e., the Indian manufacturing sector. For this purpose, ratios such as Price cost margin (Profit after tax to net sales), R&D intensity (R&D expenditure/ Industry sales), Foreign technology intensity which consists of (Import of capital goods + Royalty paid for technology acquisition/ Industry sales), Export intensity (Export/Industry Sales), Import intensity (Import/Industry sales), Advertising and marketing intensity, Compensation to employees, Outsourcing of manufacturing job intensity and Outsourcing of professional job intensity are computed for two phases 1990–2005 and 2006–2020. The data related to these variables in the respective industries and for the entire manufacturing sector are extracted for the years 1990 to 2020 from the PROWESS database as of March 2021.

Table 9.5 reveals that the price cost margin of the manufacturing sector has sharply declined during the new IPR regime as compared to the earlier phase (1990–2005). A similar trend is noticed in most of the HT sectors except Drugs and Pharmaceutical industry. The import of technology by the manufacturing sector in the form of capital goods and royalty payments during the second phase (2005–2020) has marginally declined and a similar pattern is observed in five out of seven industries. Drugs and Pharmaceuticals and Manufacture of machinery and equipment did show a marginal increase in the foreign technology import intensity. However, in-house R&D intensity for the manufacturing sector as a whole and all the seven HT industries considered in this study has shown a consistent increase during the new IPR regime. The level of in-house R&D intensity is relatively high for HT industries as compared to the manufacturing sector, especially during the second phase (2006–2020). The intensity of advertisement and marketing expenditure for the manufacturing sector has also shown a consistent increase while similar trends were observed in only three out of seven industries such as Chemical (NIC 20), Manufacture of computer, electronic and optical products (NIC 26) and Manufacture of machinery industry (NIC 28). Further the analysis reveals that although export intensity of the manufacturing sector has increased significantly compared to the import intensity, the level is much lower than the import intensity. The similar pattern is observed in the case of industries such as NIC 26, NIC 27 and NIC 28. The level of export intensity in the case of Chemical (NIC 20) and Railway and Locomotive industry (NIC 30) is much lower than import intensity which has declined in the second phase. Once again, the export intensity of the Drugs and Pharmaceutical industry (NIC 22) and Automobile industry (NIC 29) did perform well in contrast with the manufacturing sector. These sectors have not only shown an improvement in the second phase but also quite high as compared to the import intensity. Further it is evident that the expenditure on personnel for all high-tech industries and the manufacturing sector has declined during the second phase, although the personal expenditure intensity is quite high for high-tech industries as compared to their counterparts (i.e., Indian manufacturing sector). Moreover, the Indian manufacturing sector and the high-tech industries were trying to cut down their personnel expenditure by outsourcing their manufacturing and professional jobs.

Impact of M&As on Price Cost Margin

An attempt has been made in this section to analyse the impact of M&As on price cost margin in Indian HT industries during the new IPR regime by reviewing the existing literature. In the context of India, studies such as Kamphampati and Parikh (2003), Goldar and Aggarwal (2005), Goldar and Kato (2008), Athreye and Kapur (2006) and Bhattacharjea and Sindhwani (2014) show that firms' market share, square of market share, research and

Table 9.5 Economic performance of HT industries (ratios)

Year	*NIC*	*Price Costs Margin*	*Foreign Technology Intensity*	*RD Intensity*	*Export Intensity*	*IRM Intensity*	*AMD Intensity*	*Outsourcing of Manufacturing Jobs Intensity*	*Outsourcing of Professional Jobs Intensity*	*Compensation to Employees*
1990–2005	20	0.47	0.015	0.002	0.08	0.10	0.07	0.003	0.001	0.06
2006–2020	20	0.34	0.013	0.002	0.10	0.13	0.07	0.005	0.004	0.05
1990–2005	21	0.57	0.010	0.020	0.19	0.11	0.08	0.004	0.003	0.10
2006–2020	21	0.50	0.014	0.056	0.34	0.10	0.08	0.010	0.016	0.11
1990–2005	26	0.36	0.027	0.008	0.07	0.13	0.05	0.001	0.001	0.08
2006–2020	26	0.31	0.018	0.012	0.12	0.19	0.05	0.004	0.006	0.07
1990–2005	27	0.44	0.019	0.003	0.06	0.11	0.06	0.003	0.001	0.08
2006–2020	27	0.28	0.012	0.003	0.14	0.14	0.05	0.01	0.008	0.06
1990–2005	28	0.45	0.015	0.004	0.08	0.06	0.03	0.01	0.002	0.12
2006–2020	28	0.34	0.016	0.004	0.10	0.10	0.04	0.01	0.010	0.08
1990–2005	29	0.39	0.032	0.005	0.07	0.07	0.03	0.00	0.001	0.08
2006–2020	29	0.28	0.032	0.009	0.09	0.08	0.03	0.01	0.005	0.06
1990–2005	30	0.39	0.010	0.001	0.13	0.08	0.03	0.01	0.002	0.20
2006–2020	30	0.25	0.007	0.002	0.08	0.09	0.03	0.02	0.011	0.08
1990–2005	All MFG	0.507	0.017	0.002	0.089	0.132	0.059	0.004	0.001	0.068
2006–2020	All MFG	0.366	0.013	0.004	0.140	0.177	0.040	0.007	0.004	0.047

development intensity, intensity of advertisement, marketing and distribution, export intensity and size play important roles in explaining Price cost margin (PCM) of firms. It has also been highlighted in the literature that R&D and advertising intensity are not only related to PCM contemporaneously, but their past values tend to affect PCM as well (Hanel and St-Pierre 2002, Majumdar, 1997). These studies however did not consider the role of M&As on market structure and its consequent impact on profit margin. M&As facilitate firms to raise their monopoly power, inculcate advanced technology in the process of production, and lastly it minimises the production cost by increasing the size of firms (Steiner, 1975; Porter, 1985; Chatterjee, 1986; Shelton, 1988; Mishra, 2010; Rossi, Tarba & Raviv, 2013). For the aforementioned reasons we may expect higher M&As leading to better financial performance of firms. However, Mueller (2004) argued that the majority of mergers reduced social welfare as such mergers led to declining efficiency and increase market power. Mishra and Chandra (2010) and Mishra (2019) examined the relationship between M&As and profitability of Indian firms. And these studies did not find any significant association between M&As and PCM in the case of Pharmaceutical industries as well as in the case of manufacturing sector. Based on the theoretical and empirical literature discussed in this section, the econometric model is estimated in order to analyse the impact of M&As on PCM in HT industries, along with other firm-specific variables.

$$PCM_{it} = \alpha + \beta_1 MERG_t + \beta_2 X_{it} + \varepsilon_{it} \tag{1}$$

where

i, t : Represents firm and year respectively.
PCM_{it} : Price cost margin of firm i in year t.
$MERG_t$: Value of M&As in year t
ε_{it} : Random disturbance term.
X_{it} : Set of explanatory variables. The construction of these variables is explained in Table 9.6.

For our empirical model, we considered the firm-level data for the period 2004–2018. The reason for considering this period is that this period suffices with our objective to analyse firms' profitability during the new IPR regime. We collected the firm-level information in HT industries from the Centre for Monitoring Indian Economy's PROWESS database. Though prowess provides detailed data on manufacturing firms, we observed that a large number of HT firms have missing values for their sales, net sales and profit after tax. We dropped those firms for consistency in our analysis. Cleaning the data in such a manner left us with an unbalanced panel of 30,209 observations.

There are four major issues that arise while estimating model 1. The first one is the firm-specific fixed effects and the second one is the year-specific random effects. To resolve the first issue, we considered an Ordinary Least

Table 9.6 Definition and construction of variables

Variables	*Abbreviations*	*Definition*
Price cost margin	PCM_{it}	Profit after tax/Net sales
Mergers and acquisitions	$MERG_t$	Total value of mergers and acquisitions in HT industries in time t
Market share	$MSHARE_{it}$	Firms sales/Industry sales
Market share square	$MSHARESQR_{it}$	(*Firms sales/Industry sales*)^2
Research and development expenditure intensity	$RDINT_{it}$	Expenditure on research and development/Sales
Lag of research and development expenditure intensity	$LRDINT_{it}$	Previous year expenditure on Research and development/Sales
Advertisement, marketing and distribution intensity	$AMDINT_{it}$	Expenses on advertisement, marketing and distribution/Sales
Lag advertisement, marketing and distribution intensity	$LAMDINT_{it}$	Previous expenses on advertisement, marketing and distribution/Sales
Export intensity	$EXPINT_{it}$	Export/Sales
Size	$SIZE_{it}$	Ln(Sales)

Square, Fixed Effect model (OLS, FE). The FE model performs a within transformation of the data, thus removing unobserved firm-specific effects that are fixed over time. To capture the year-specific random effects, we resort to the dummy variable approach. Year dummies are incorporated in our model for the unobserved factors that vary across time. The third issue is about collinearity among explanatory variables. Since we are considering both current and lagged values of some variable, one can expect collinearity. Before estimating the fixed effect model, we computed the variance inflation factor (VIF) and found that it is less than five for all independent variables. This implies no collinearity among variables. The last issue is pertaining to the variable MERGE. The information on M&As is difficult to obtain. For this reason, the MERGE variable is constructed by summing up the value of all M&As deals in HT indtry in each year. Thus, the variable MERGE remains the same for all firms in a particular year, whereas our dependent variable PCM varies across firms and year. Our final model is explained below.

$$\begin{aligned} PCM_{it} &= \alpha + \beta_1 MERG_t + \beta_2 MSHARE_{it} + \beta_3 SMSHARE_{it} \\ &+ \beta_4 RDINT_{it} + \beta_5 LRDINT_{it} + \beta_6 AMDINT_{lt} + \beta_7 LAMDINT_{it} \\ &+ \beta_8 EXPINT_{it} + \beta_9 SIZE_{it} + \vartheta_t + \varepsilon_{it} \end{aligned} \quad (2)$$

wheregression results are presented in

ϑ_t: Year dummy

ε_{it}: Random disturbance term.

The regression results are presented in Table 9.7. Columns 2 and 3 of this table show the results of OLS and OLS FE models, respectively. The probability values of Wald and F statists are zero, suggesting the rejection of the null hypothesis, that is coefficients of the model are simultaneously equal to zero. Thus, we can say that our models are valid.

Coming to the estimated coefficients of OLS, FE model (Table 9.7), we found that M&As (MERG) are significant and positive in explaining PCM of firms at one per cent level. However, its explanatory power is low. A one per cent increase in the values of merger in a year results in 0.0003 per cent increase in PCM of firms. This finding is in line with the existing studies. For instance, Beena (2021) found that the high-technology industries such as Drugs and Pharmaceutical industry and software industry that are engaged in more M&A achieve higher profit margin than the manufacturing sector as a whole.

Table 9.7 Determinants of PCM

Variables	*OLS* (*Model 1*)	*OLS, FE* (*Model 2*)
MERG	0.000267**	0.000335**
	(2.10)	(2.46)
MSHARE	-72.92*	-105.7**
	(-1.88)	(-2.09)
MSHARESQR	155.4*	207.5**
	(1.81)	(2.00)
RDINT	-3.542***	-3.073**
	(-2.98)	(-2.32)
LRDINT	0.416***	0.572***
	(3.12)	(2.61)
AMDINT	0.00117	0.00271**
	(1.64)	(2.41)
LAMDINT	0.000987*	0.00173*
	(1.73)	(1.88)
EXPINT	0.000493	0.00052
	(1.20)	(0.87)
SIZE	0.911**	1.958***
	(2.18)	(2.79)
Constant	-8.727**	-16.97***
	(-2.39)	(-2.97)
Observations	24,704	24,704
R-squared	0.003	0.013
Time effects	YES	YES
Wald chi2	69.55	
	(0.00)	
		0.0023
F Stat		(2.578)

Cluster robust z-statistics in parentheses. For Wald chi2 it is probabilities,
*** p<0.01, ** p<0.05, * p<0.1

We found the coefficient of market share is negative, but its square is positively significant in determining firms' PCM (Profit after Tax). This indicates that the market share of firms yields positive profit only after it crosses certain threshold values. Otherwise, it affects profitability negatively. Firms having larger market share produce efficiently under scale economies or keep price artificially high due to market power. Such externalities can only be accrued after a certain production threshold, and our findings on market share is not surprising. In the context of Indian manufacturing firms, Kambhampati and Parikh (2003) arrived at the same conclusion. They found that market share is negative and significantly causing PCM. On the contrary, Bhattacharjea and Sindhwani (2014) analysed firms of pharmaceutical industry and showed that market share is positive and significant while its square is negatively significant in explaining PCM.

The coefficient of R&D intensity (RDINT) is found to be significantly negative; however, its first lag (LRDINT) is positive and significant in determining PCM. Since spending on R&D takes time to realise in the process of production, in the current year this expenditure by firms may not affect their profit margin. However, once the benefits of R&D get actualised, profit tends to increase. Further, this finding is consistent with the existing studies. For example, Athreye and Kapur (2006) found that for the firms of nine manufacturing industries, R&D intensity in the same period is either negative or negative and significant. Similarly, Bhattacharjea and Sindhwani (2014) for pharmaceutical firms showed that R&D intensity is negatively related to PCM, but its third lag is positively significant.

Another variable that determines firms' PCM is the intensity of advertisement, marketing and distribution (AMD). Firms spend on AMD to differentiate their products and to reach out to the customers, both in domestic and foreign countries. Thus, it is expected that firms spending on AMD will have higher sales and will be more profitable. From our econometric analysis we found that the coefficients of AMDINT and its first lag are positive and significant, lying in the line of previous studies (see Kambhampati and Parikh, 2003).

Similarly, we found that Export intensity (EXPINT) of firms is positively related to the PCM. However, its coefficient is insignificant implying that exporting in the HT industry does not add to firms' profitability. This may be due to higher competition from developed countries in the export market of HT products and smaller size of HT export market.

The last variable in our analysis is SIZE which is measured in terms of sales. We found that size is significantly positive in explaining firms' PCM. Larger size firms are generally considered to be more efficient as they can exploit economies of scale in the production process and can operate under short-term market shocks. Because of these reasons, bigger firms stay in the production process consistently and incur positive profit. Our findings validate this hypothesis.

Conclusion

The Indian industrial sector has witnessed a large number of M&A deals. A significant number of firms, especially in the technology-oriented industries, including start-ups, are acquired by either domestically owned incumbent firms or by foreign-owned firms. Such aggressive growth strategies are adopted by leading firms owned by Indian business groups or multinationals operating in India as well (Chandrasekhar, 1999; Beena 2014; Mazumdar, 2012; 2015). Firms in the HT industries are also acquiring firms abroad. The large incidents of M&As, including CBM&As in the services sector, especially IT products and online services, financial services, advertising, travel agencies, and other business services, are notable. Similarly, Drugs and Pharmaceutical products, Automobiles and components, Food and beverages, Iron, steel and metals, construction goods are the leading industries within the manufacturing sector. Energy-related firms accounted for the largest share of total resource-based M&A deals. The M&As in the manufacturing sector are predominantly horizontal rather than vertical, as in the case of IT&ITEs. The chapter further observed that leading firms in terms of market share in the seven high-tech sectors are also engaged in mergers and acquisitions. And those firms control a major share of sales in the respective industries. A large number of target firms in these industries are found to be private limited firms. Most of these HT industries were spending relatively more on in-house R&D while its intensity on import of technology and expenditure on personnel has declined marginally after 2005. Net export of these industries was very low and it worsened during the new IPR regime, except in the case of Drugs and Pharmaceuticals and Automobile industries. It is evident from our econometric model that there is a strong association between M&As and Price cost margin in the HT industries. The other firm-specific variables such as size of the firm, market share, R&D intensity, marketing and advertisement intensity did play a significant role in determining price cost margin. Anti-competitive practices in terms of pricing or abuse of dominance are visible in most of these industries (Beena 2021; Chaudhuri 2018; Joseph 2021). Based on available evidence, the chapter argues that enhancing size in terms of corporate control of equity, product market share and innovation market share could be the motivations for the M&A phenomenon in the HT industries and that has had a direct impact on price cost margin. The study argues for introducing regulatory mechanisms that could address the antitrust implications of M&As in HT and knowledge-based firms including start-ups which are small in size as such acquisitions can change the innovative and competitive dynamics in the relevant product and geographic market.

Notes

1 OECD classified industries into four groups based on their R&D intensity. Those groups are High-technology; Medium-high-technology, Medium-low-technology and Low-technology industries. For detail on these industry groups see OECD (2011).

2 Out of 119 consolidations that took place from 2001 to 2013, 50 per cent of them have horizontal overlap. Thirteen per cent of them have vertical overlap while 24 per cent of them have conglomerate overlap. And another 7 per cent of them were horizontal and vertical overlap (see Bhattacharjea*2016*).

3 These are entrepreneurs who start a company with a new innovative idea and sell it to the established counterparts and start a new *venture* with the same purpose in mind and the trend continues.

4 US-based retail giant Walmart acquired Indian e-commerce unicorn Flipkart in a deal worth $16 Bn in 2018.

5 However, establishing the dominance in a relevant or geographic market is a difficult task as this industry is divided into therapeutic segments such as antibiotics, cardio ailments and vitamins.

References

Arora, A., Fosfuri, A., & Gambardella, A. (2001), *Markets for Technology: The Economics of Innovation and Corporate Strategy*, MIT Press.

Athreye, S., & Kapur, S. (2006), Industrial concentration in a liberalising economy: A study of Indian manufacturing, *The Journal of Development Studies*, 42(6), 981–999.

Bain, J. S. (1969), A note on pricing and monopoly and oligopoly, *American and Economic Review*, 39(2), 448–464.

Basant, R. (2021), *The Black Box Innovation and Public Policy in India*, Penguin.

Basant, R., & Morris, S. (2000), Competition policy in India: Issues for a globalising economy, *Economic and Political Weekly*, 36, 51.

Bhattacharjea, A. (2001). Competition policy: India and the WTO. *Economic and Political Weekly*, 4710–4713.

Bhattacharjea, A. (2016), Recent trends in mega-mergers in India and lessons for competition policy: Insights from merger cases under the Competition Act, in Veeramani, C. & Nagaraj, R. (Eds.), *International Trade and Industrial Development in India: Emerging Trends, Patterns and Issues*, Orient BlackSwan Private Limited

Bhattacharjea, A., & Sindhwani, F. (2014), *Competition Issues in the Indian Pharmaceuticals Sector*, Center for Development Economics, Delhi School of Economics, CUTS-CIRC.

Beena, P. L. (2001), Intangibles and finance: Motives and consequences of mergers in the Indian corporate sector, in Parthasarathi, B. & Frank, J. R. (Eds.), *Intangibles in Competition and Cooperation: Euro-Asian Perspectives*, Palgrave Macmillan.

Beena, P. L. (2014), *Mergers and Acquisitions: India under Globalisation*, Routledge.

Beena, P. L. (2021), IPR regime and antitrust implications of mergers and acquisitions: With a focus on software and pharmaceutical sector, *The Antitrust Bulletin*, 66(2), 203–213.

Beena, P. L., & Rabiyath, S. (2019), IPR institutions, innovation activities and developmental implications of IP asset intensive industries, https://papers.ssrn.com/sol3/cf_dev/AbsByAuth.cfm?per_id=868232.

Chakravarthy, S. (2005), Competition Act, 2002: The approach, in Mehta S. P. (Ed.), *Towards a Functional Competition Policy for India: An Overview*, Academic Foundation.

Chang, H.-J. (2003), *Globalisation, Economic Development and the Role of the State*, Zed Books and Third World Network.

Chandrasekhar, C. P. (1999), Firms, markets and the state: An analysis of Indian oligopoly, in Bagchi, K. A. (Ed.), *Economy and Organisation: Indian Institutions under the Neo-Liberal Regime*, SAGE Publications Pvt. Ltd.

Chaudhuri, S. (2012), Multinationals and monopolies: Pharmaceutical industry in India after TRIPS, *Economic and Political Weekly*, 4712, 46–54.

Chaudhuri, S. (2018, September), *Impact of Product Patents on Pharmaceutical Market Structure and Prices in India*, Working Chapter No. 813, IIM.

Chaudhuri, S., & Tabriz, B. (1999), Capturing the real value in high-tech acquisitions, *Harvard Business Review*, 77, 123–130.

Chatterjee, S. (1986), Types of synergy and economic value: The impact of acquisitions on merging and rival firms, *Strategic Management Journal*, 7(2), 119–139.

Dhar, B., & Chalapati Rao, K. S. (2021), Inbound M&As in India: Issues and challenges, *The Antitrust Bulletin*, 66(2), 158–183.

Dhar, B., & Reji, K. J. (2019), The challenges, opportunities and performance of the Indian pharmaceutical industry post-TRIPS, in K.-C. Liu & U. S. Racherla (Eds.), *Innovation, Economic Development, and Intellectual Property in India and China*, ARCIALA Series on Intellectual Assets and Law in Asia. https://doi.org/10.1007/978-981-13-8102-7_1.

Edmund, A., & Cantwell, J. (2012), *Innovative Firms in Emerging Market Countries*, Oxford University Press, Oxford.

Faber, G. (2015), The diversion of public health: Intellectual property regime: Innovation and access to medicines, Paper presented in *BRICS SEMINAR*, CDS, Trivandrum, May 4–5.

Falvey, R., Foster, N., & Greenaway, D. (2006), Intellectual property rights and innovation in developing countries, *Review of Developing Economies*, 10(4), 700–719.

Farrell, J., & Carl, S. (1990), Horizontal mergers: An equilibrium analysis, *The American Economic Review*, 80(1), 107–126.

Francis, S. (2018), *Evolution of Technology in the Digital Arena: Theories, Firm-Level Strategies and State Policies*, Working Chapter No. CWS/WP/200/47, IIFT Centre for WTO Studies.

Glader, M. (2002), *Innovation Markets and Competition Analysis: EU Competition Law and US Antitrust Law*, Edward Elgar Publishing, Incorporated.

Goldar, B., & Aggarwal, S. C. (2005), Trade liberalization and price-cost margin in Indian industries, *The Developing Economies*, 43(3), 346–373.

Goldar, B., & Kato, A. (2008), Import penetration and price-cost margins in Indian manufacturing industries, *The Indian Economic Journal*, 56(2), 166–192.

Gonzalo, M., Lyra, M., & Alves, C. (2017), Knowledge-based startups or small companies' takeovers in Latin America: An antitrust issue? Recent cases from US, EU and Brazil, *IE-UFRJ Discussion*. www.ie.ufrj.br/index.php/index-publicacoes/textos-para-discussao.

Government of India. (2019), *Competition Law Review Committee.*

Griliches, Z. (1979), Issues in assessing the contribution of research and development to productivity growth, *The Bell Journal of Economics*, 10(1), 92–116.

Hanel, P., & St-Pierre, A. (2002), Effects of R & D Spillovers on the Profitability of Firms, *Review of Industrial Organization*, 20(4), 305–322.

Joseph, K. R. (2021), Innovation, patents, and competition in modern agriculture: A case study of Bayer and Monsanto Merger, *The Antitrust Bulletin*, 66(2), 214–224.

Kambhampati, U. S. & Parikh, A. (2003), Disciplining firms: The impact of trade reforms on profit margins in Indian industry, *Applied Economics*, 35(4), 461–470.

Kanwar, S. (2012), Intellectual property protection and technology licensing: The case of developing countries, *Journal of Law and Economics*, 55(3), 539–564.

Kanwar, S., & Evenson, R. (2003), Does intellectual property protection spur technological change?, *Oxford Economic Papers*, 55(2), 235–264.

Kathuria, V. (2010), Does the technology gap influence spillovers? A post-liberalization analysis of Indian manufacturing industries, *Oxford Development Studies*, 38(2), 145–170.

Khachoo, Q., Sharma, R., & Dhanora, M. (2018), Does proximity to the frontier facilitate FDI-spawned spillovers on innovation and productivity?, *Journal of Economics and Business*, 97, 39–49.

Kohers, N., & Kohers, T. (2000), The value creation potential of high-tech mergers, *Financial Analysts Journal*, 56(3), 40–51.

Majumdar, S. K. (1997), The impact of size and age on firm-level performance: Some evidence from India, *Review of Industrial Organization*, 12(2), 231–241.

Mani, S., & Nelson, R. R. (Eds.) (2013), *TRIPS Compliance, National Patent Regimes, and Innovation: Evidence and Experience of Developing Countries*, Edward Elgar.

Maskus, K. E. (Ed.), (2008), Incorporating a globalized intellectual property rights regime into an economic development strategy, in *Intellectual Property, Growth and Trade*, Emerald Group publishing.

Mazumdar, S. (2012), The Indian corporate structure and the 'Theory' of emerging market business groups, *History and Sociology of South Asia*, 6(2), 87–109.

Mazumdar, S. (2015), Monopoly and Indian industry, in C. P. Chandrasekhar (Ed.), *Indian Industrialisation*, Vol. 1, OUP.

Mishra, P. (2019), How have mergers and acquisitions affected financial performance of firms in Indian manufacturing sector?, *Eurasian Journal of Business and Economics*, 12(23), 79–96.

Mishra, P., & Chandra, T. (2010), Mergers, acquisitions and firms performance: Experience of Indian pharmaceutical industry, *Eurasian Journal of Business and Economics*, 3(5), 111–126.

Moulton, B. R. (1990), An illustration of a pitfall in estimating the effects of aggregate variables on micro units. *The review of Economics and Statistics*, 334–338.
Mueller, D. C. (2004), Efficiency versus market power through mergers, in Manfred Nuemann and Jurgen Weigand (Eds.), *The International Handbook of Competition* (pp. 65–87). Edward Elgar Publishing.
Organization for Economic Co-operation and Development. (2005), *Excessive Pricing in Pharmaceutical Markets: Note by India*, DAF/COMP/WD.
Parsheera, S., Shah, A., & Bose, A. (2017), *Competition Issues in India's Online Economy*, Chapter No. 194, NIPF Working Papers.
Peter, J. N. (2007), Cross border mergers as instruments of comparative advantages, *Review of Economic Studies*, 4, 1229–1257.
Porter, M. E. (1985), *Competitive Advantage: Creating and Sustaining Superior Performance*, Free Press.
Qiu, L. D. & Zhou, W. (2006), International mergers: Incentives and welfare, *Journal of International Economics*, 68(1), 38–58.
Rossi, M., Tarba, S. Y., & Raviv, A. (2013), Mergers and acquisitions in the hightech industry: A literature review, *International Journal of Organizational Analysis*, 21(1), 66–82.
Saraswathy, B. (2016), *An Analysis of Foreign Acquisitions in India's Manufacturing Sector*, (ISID Working Chapter No. 193), Institute of Studies in Industrial Development. http://isid.org.in/working-chapters/.
Saraswathy, B. (2018), *The Globalisation of Indian Business: Cross Border Mergers and Acquisitions in Indian Manufacturing*, Routledge.
Saraswathy, B. (2019), The Flipkart- Walmart deal in India: A look into competition and other related issues, *The Antitrust Bulletin*, 64(1), 136–147.
Saraswathy, B. (2021). Economic Reforms and Market Competition in India: An Assessment. *The Antitrust Bulletin*, 66(2), 184–202.
Schmalensee, R. (1987), Horizontal merger policy: Problems and changes, *Journal of Economic Perspectives*, 1, 41–54.
Shelton, L. M. (1988), Strategic business fits and corporate acquisitions: Empirical evidence, *Strategic Management Journal*, 9(3), 279–287.
Steiner, P. O. (1975), *Mergers, Motives, Effects and Policies*, The University of Michigan Press.
UNCTAD (1997), *Transnational Corporations, Market Structure and Competition Policy*.
UNCTAD (2019), *Value Creation and Capture: Implications for Developing Countries*, Digital Economy Report.
Weston, J. F., Chung, K. S., & Hoag, S. (1996), *Mergers, restructuring, and corporate control*, Englewood Cliffs, NJ: Prentice Hall.
Williamson, O. E. (1968), Economics as an antitrust defence: The welfare trade-offs, *The American Economic Review*, 58(1), 18–36.
Zhan, J., & Ozawa, T. (2001), *Business Restructuring in Asia: Cross Border M&As in the Crisis Period*, Copenhagen Business School.

A. Appendix

Table A1

Table A1 Industry-wise distribution of M&As for the period 2004 to 2018

NIC	*Number Domestic*	*Amount Domestic*	*Number Inbound*	*Amount Inbound*	*Number Outbound*	*Amount Outbound*	*Number Total*	*Amount Total*
1	0.65	0.11	1.00	0.63	1.03	3.57	0.83	1.15
3	0.00	0.00	0.06	0.00	0.05	0.01	0.03	0.00
5	0.07	0.13	0.55	0.05	0.44	0.12	0.28	0.10
6	0.55	0.08	1.00	0.10	0.44	4.36	0.62	1.15
7	0.50	0.07	0.44	0.05	0.24	0.12	0.42	0.08
8	0.55	0.21	0.66	0.32	0.10	0.00	0.46	0.19
Resource based	2.31	0.59	3.71	1.14	2.30	8.18	2.63	2.67
10	2.56	0.34	3.49	0.99	2.79	1.36	2.83	0.82
11	0.87	0.16	1.44	0.41	1.42	1.03	1.14	0.46
12	0.00	0.00	0.11	0.02	0.10	0.00	0.05	0.01
13	1.51	0.81	1.66	1.60	2.15	2.40	1.71	1.48
14	0.99	0.40	1.00	0.32	0.88	0.37	0.96	0.37
15	0.17	0.18	0.55	0.39	0.00	0.00	0.22	0.21
16	0.25	0.03	0.22	0.26	0.05	0.00	0.19	0.10
17	0.17	0.55	0.17	0.06	0.29	0.02	0.20	0.25
18	0.05	0.18	0.06	0.03	0.00	0.00	0.04	0.08
19	0.37	0.31	0.17	0.00	0.24	0.01	0.29	0.13
20	3.82	3.38	4.49	4.88	4.21	0.96	4.08	3.30
21	4.77	2.44	5.98	4.09	6.85	3.03	5.59	3.16
22	0.94	0.33	1.11	0.11	0.44	0.10	0.85	0.20
23	2.56	8.00	1.99	3.02	1.32	1.14	2.11	4.57
24	2.09	0.43	1.83	0.66	1.37	3.41	1.84	1.25
25	0.37	0.04	0.22	0.05	1.42	5.07	0.61	1.30
26	1.42	8.45	1.27	0.36	1.91	1.29	1.51	3.87

27	1.51	0.26	1.83	0.70	1.22	0.20	1.51	0.40
28	2.63	1.41	2.94	0.99	2.98	0.51	2.79	1.04
29	3.62	0.58	5.37	2.97	3.08	0.97	3.88	1.50
30	0.55	0.09	0.83	0.18	0.34	0.44	0.56	0.21
31	0.05	0.00	0.00	0.00	0.10	0.07	0.05	0.02
32	0.94	0.73	0.50	0.16	0.49	0.40	0.72	0.45
33	0.32	0.86	0.17	0.20	0.00	0.00	0.20	0.42
Manufacturing	32.55	29.96	37.40	22.45	33.66	22.79	33.95	25.58
35	3.40	0.57	1.55	0.64	2.94	0.87	2.86	0.67
36	0.30	0.11	0.22	0.28	0.24	0.23	0.27	0.20
38	0.07	0.02	0.00	0.00	0.34	0.09	0.13	0.03
41	0.05	0.01	0.11	0.58	0.15	0.05	0.09	0.22
42	1.96	0.54	1.16	2.14	1.37	8.73	1.62	3.13
43	0.10	0.01	0.00	0.00	0.00	0.00	0.05	0.00
45	0.20	0.35	0.06	0.00	0.05	0.02	0.13	0.15
46	0.25	0.12	0.11	0.03	0.00	0.00	0.15	0.06
47	2.95	1.15	2.44	0.98	1.86	2.52	2.55	1.43
49	0.15	0.01	0.33	0.09	0.00	0.00	0.15	0.04
50	0.02	0.01	0.11	0.01	0.05	0.02	0.05	0.01
51	0.05	0.00	0.00	0.00	0.05	0.00	0.04	0.00
52	2.43	0.91	4.38	1.83	1.96	0.29	2.75	1.07
55	1.27	2.19	1.33	1.35	2.05	1.91	1.49	1.83
56	0.62	0.03	0.89	0.13	0.88	0.09	0.75	0.08
58	2.58	1.01	3.32	3.83	7.05	3.21	3.91	2.53
59	0.15	0.01	0.39	0.06	0.64	0.46	0.33	0.14
60	0.67	0.10	0.78	1.96	1.47	0.27	0.90	0.78
61	0.74	0.17	0.61	0.33	2.84	1.03	1.26	0.44
62	22.22	38.18	17.84	42.27	16.49	18.91	19.73	34.80
64	2.68	0.67	3.32	3.63	2.10	0.94	2.68	1.76
65	0.62	0.36	0.83	0.08	0.88	0.50	0.74	0.30
66	1.66	0.89	1.66	1.89	4.06	4.81	2.29	2.21
68	0.12	0.00	0.17	0.03	0.05	0.04	0.11	0.02

(Continued)

Table A1 Continued

NIC	*Number Domestic*	*Amount Domestic*	*Number Inbound*	*Amount Inbound*	*Number Outbound*	*Amount Outbound*	*Number Total*	*Amount Total*
69	0.10	0.01	0.06	0.59	0.44	0.90	0.18	0.44
70	0.50	1.90	0.89	3.91	2.20	1.02	1.03	2.37
71	0.30	0.14	0.22	0.25	0.29	0.20	0.28	0.19
72	0.37	1.90	0.17	0.03	0.68	0.59	0.41	0.93
73	1.91	0.68	1.88	2.87	2.64	1.22	2.09	1.57
74	0.57	0.46	0.28	0.82	0.98	0.39	0.61	0.57
77	0.07	0.05	0.00	0.00	0.15	0.03	0.08	0.03
78	0.60	1.58	0.06	0.29	0.68	1.05	0.50	1.00
79	0.62	1.96	0.44	0.19	0.49	0.14	0.55	0.89
80	0.20	0.41	0.44	0.40	0.00	0.00	0.20	0.30
82	5.06	6.66	6.26	2.21	1.96	1.01	4.53	3.72
84	0.00	0.00	0.00	0.00	0.05	0.04	0.01	0.01
85	1.71	0.23	1.44	0.52	0.88	0.22	1.43	0.33
86	3.18	1.15	2.33	0.45	2.35	12.91	2.77	3.83
87	0.05	0.02	0.00	0.00	0.05	0.00	0.04	0.01
90	0.37	0.08	0.11	0.06	0.39	1.28	0.32	0.37
92	0.05	0.02	0.00	0.00	0.05	0.00	0.04	0.01
93	1.14	0.23	0.89	0.93	0.49	2.04	0.91	0.92
95	0.74	0.47	0.28	0.16	0.15	0.43	0.48	0.35
96	1.91	4.04	1.16	0.49	0.98	0.38	1.50	1.91
99	0.40	0.06	0.39	0.09	0.64	0.18	0.46	0.10
Service Sector	65.14	69.45	58.89	76.41	64.04	69.03	63.43	71.75
Total	100	100	100	100	100	100	100	100

Note: 1 – Crop and animal production, hunting and related service activities, 3 – Fishing and aquaculture, 5 – Mining of coal and lignite, 6 – Extraction of crude petroleum and natural gas, 7 – Mining of metal ores, 8 – Other mining and quarrying, 9 – Recourse based, 10 – Manufacture of food products, 11 – Manufacture of beverages, 12 – Manufacture of tobacco products, 13 – Manufacture of textiles, 14 – Manufacture of wearing apparel, 15 – Manufacture of leather and related products, 16 – Manufacture of wood and products of wood and cork, except furniture; manufacture of articles of straw and plaiting materials, 17 – Manufacture of paper and paper products, 18 – Printing and reproduction of recorded media, 19 – Manufacture of coke and refined petroleum products, 20 – Manufacture of chemicals and chemical products, 21 – Manufacture of pharmaceuticals, medicinal chemical and botanical products, 22 – Manufacture of rubber and plastics products, 23 – Manufacture of other non-metallic mineral products, 24 – Manufacture of basic metals, 25 – Manufacture of fabricated metal products, except machinery and equipment, 26 – Manufacture of computer, electronic and optical products, 27 – Manufacture of electrical equipment, 28 – Manufacture of machinery and equipment n.e.c., 29 – Manufacture of motor vehicles, trailers and semi-trailers, 30 – Manufacture of other transport equipment, 31 – Manufacture of furniture, 32 – Other manufacturing, 33 – Repair and installation of machinery and equipment, 35 – Electricity, gas, steam and air conditioning supply, 36 – Water collection, treatment and supply, 38 – Waste collection, treatment and disposal activities; materials recovery, 41 – Construction of buildings, 42 – Civil engineering, 43 – Specialised construction activities, 45 – Wholesale and retail trade and repair of motor vehicles and motorcycles, 46 – Wholesale trade, except of motor vehicles and motorcycles, 47 – Retail trade, except of motor vehicles and motorcycles, 49 – Land transport and transport via pipelines, 50 – Water transport, 51 – Air transport, 52 – Warehousing and support activities for transportation, 55 – Accommodation, 56 – Food and beverage service activities, 58 – Publishing activities, 59 – Motion picture, video and television programme production, sound recording and music publishing activities, 60 – Broadcasting and programming activities, 61 – Telecommunications, 62 – Computer programming, consultancy and related activities, 64 – Financial service activities, except insurance and pension funding, 65 – Insurance, reinsurance and pension funding, except compulsory social security, 66 – Other financial activities, 68 – Real estate activities, 69 – Legal and accounting activities, 70 – Activities of head offices; management consultancy activities, 71 – Architecture and engineering activities; technical testing and analysis, 72 – Scientific research and development, 73 – Advertising and market research, 74 – Other professional, scientific and technical activities, 77 – Rental and leasing activities, 78 – Employment activities, 79 – Travel agency, tour operator and other reservation service activities, 80 – Security and investigation activities, 82 – Office administrative, office support and other business support activities, 84 – Public administration and defence; compulsory social security, 85 – Education, 86 – Human health activities, 87 – Residential care activities, 90 – Creative, arts and entertainment activities, 92 – Gambling and betting activities, 93 – Sports activities and amusement and recreation activities, 95 – Repair of computers and personal and household goods, 96 – Other personal service activities, 99 – Miscellaneous

10 Industrialisation and Role of MSMEs in India

With a special Reference to Punjab

Jatinder Singh

Introduction

The micro, small and medium enterprises sector is one of the most vibrant and dynamic sectors that has been contributing significantly to the growth and development of developing and advanced countries on the one hand and playing a pivotal role in reducing regional and social inequalities on the other hand (Mohan, 2002; Das, 2011; ILO, 2017; OECD, 2016, 2018a; UN-DESA, 2020). MSMEs accounted for around 90 per cent of the total business worldwide and up to 40 per cent of the national income in emerging economies[1]. China is a giant exporter, and about 70 per cent of its exports are directly or indirectly contributed by MSMEs. A similar trend has been noticed in developing nations like Bangladesh and Thailand where MSMEs command approximately 50 per cent of the industrial output. In the case of OECD countries, small and medium enterprises accounted for 50 to 60 per cent of value addition (OECD, 2017). Besides, these enterprises are very accommodative in absorbing workers with diverse skill sets and varied skill levels including highly skilled, low skilled and unskilled workers. According to ILO (2017), the number of full-time workers in this sector has increased from 79 million to 156 million across 132 countries during 2003 and 2016. On average, more than 50 per cent of worldwide employment is generated by these enterprises, and this figure is as high as 70 per cent in the case of some OECD countries in recent years (OECD, 2016 and 2018b).

This sector has been receiving a considerable policy support from the government in India post-independence. It is evident in the form of announcements of various policies and programs specifically for strengthening the MSME sector. India came up with its first industrial policy in 1948 wherein small industry and village and cottage industry were encouraged with financial support to generate employment with small capital investment and to facilitate rehabilitation. In the early 1950s, product reservation, whereby some items were specifically reserved for the manufacturing of small units[2], was initiated for the protection of small industrial units from large-scale industries. Over the years, the number of products

DOI: 10.4324/9781003343998-10

reserved for small units increased to more than 800 (Mohan, 2002; Shankaran, 2015)[3]. Further, various organisations[4] were established for providing assistance, specifically, to small units for ensuring their smooth growth and development (Mohan, 2002; Das, 2006, 2011; Bhavani, 2011, 2016). On the market front, small units were assisted through procurement policy. Besides national-level initiatives, sub-national governments in India also announced various measures for strengthening this sector (Prakash, 1956; Sandhu and Singh, 1984; Subrahmanian, 2003, Singh and Kumar, 2020b). For instance, the government of Punjab provided liberal financial assistance by modifying the State Aid to Industries Act 1935, established testing centres specifically for small units, assisted in ensuring the supply of quality inputs, etc. (Gupta, 1982; Pandit, 1984; Singh, 1994). These national and sub-national measures continued to support the MSME sector till the mid-1990s.

A new policy setup of the early-1990s brought a paradigm shift in the operating environment around the industrial sector by eliminating restrictions on the entry of new firms, liberalising the restrictions on the imports of goods and services, de-reservation of exclusive product list for small industrial units, abolition of tax exemptions for industrially backward regions, etc. Partial or complete elimination of these measures exposed the business firms including small units to international competition. The opening up of the economy provided unparalleled new opportunities and also posed survival risks to small units. On the one hand, liberal policy regime provided opportunities for these units to enter into new markets through vertical and horizontal collaborations with large firms including multination corporations. Whereas the new business environment has also been pressurising the industrial units to restructure in order to remain competitive in the market.

Existing studies have analysed the impact of the new policy regime on the operations of small units (Tendulkar and Bhavani, 1997; Mohan, 2002; Das, 2006, 2011; Bhavani, 2011, 2016; Kumar, 2014; Shankaran, 2015). The views of these scholars are not uniform. Some scholars have argued that the new regime has improved the performance of small-scale units whereas others have reported a negative impact on the survival and operations of MSMEs[5].

Against this understanding, the proposed chapter intends to analyse the issues and concerns of the small-scale enterprises under the new policy regime in India in general and industrial units in Punjab in particular. Punjab is a fit case to analyse this issue as a large number of small industrial units have become unviable and closed their businesses in the recent period (Ghuman and Singh, 2017; Singh and Cheema, 2021).

The chapter is organised into six sections including introduction. The second section provides a discussion on the review of literature. Details on data and methodology are provided in the third section. The fourth section presents the empirical results at all India level. The fifth section outlines the experience of the MSME sector in Punjab. The last section summarises the main findings emerging from the analysis.

Insights From the Existing Literature

The importance of the MSME sector in the economic and social growth of India and other parts of the world has attracted considerable attention from scholars and policymakers. The scholars have analysed different aspects related to the development of MSMEs, viz. impact of different policy regimes on the growth and development of MSMEs, contribution of MSMEs in terms of various national-level indicators, performance of MSMEs in pre- and post-reform period, problems and challenges faced by these enterprises especially under globalisation, etc. (Nagaraj, 1985; Sandesara, 1993; Subrahmanian, 1995; Subrahmanian and Pillai, 1994; Bhavani, 2002; 2016; Sathe, 2002; Subrahmanya, 2004; 2011; Mohan, 2002; Kumar, 2011; ILO, 2017; OECD, 2016a, 2018a; Mukherjee, 2018; UN-DESA, 2020).

The first argument pertains to the performance of the small-scale sector under the protective policy regime. It is argued that the small-scale industrial sector could not realise its potential under a closed policy regime (Ramaswami, 1994; Tendulkar and Bhavani, 1997; Mohan, 2002; Subrahmanian and Pillai, 1994; Subrahmanya, 2004; Kumar, 2011; Bhavani, 2016). The policy initiatives adopted in the early years of independence dampened the developmental potential of small industrial units by isolating them from any kind of competition. The policy measures provided a protected space to the small-scale industrial units by exclusively reserving items for their manufacturing and also by ensuring a captive market for their products through governmental and other departmental purchases. Thus, there was no pressure on these units to work with commercial motives and upgrade them technologically. Resultantly, the majority of micro and small units continued to supply low-quality products that confined these units to serve just the local markets (Subrahmanya, 1995; Tendulkar and Bhavani, 1997; Bhavani, 2002; 2011). However, some studies held the opposite view and stated that a protective regime has helped in developing a strong and dynamic industrial base including the ancillary sector (Narayana, 1989; Pingle, 1999; Singh, 2019).

The second argument emerging from the existing studies relates to the impact of change in policy regime in 1991 on the operations of small-scale industrial units (Bhavani, 2002; 2016; Subrahmanya, 2004; Das, 2011; Kumar, 2011). The abolition of various benefits extended to small units on the one hand and allowing imports of goods and entry of foreign direct investment on the other hand have exposed small-scale units to open market competition. The unregulated supply of imports and continuous entry of large firms including MNCs have intensified the competition and posed challenges for survival to small-scale units. Unlike large firms, these units are unable to realise the economies of scale which is critical to ensure the supply of products at competitive prices. Further, MSMEs lack in terms of forward and backward linkages. Due to this, these units face challenges in the procurement of raw materials at a competitive price and also to sell products in best price market. It is evident as less than 6 per cent of micro units in India advertise their products online (RBI, 2019). Accordingly, MSMEs, particularly micro units, are not able to sell their products to the actual buyers (Singh and Kumar, 2020a).

Various factors have been reported for the slowdown of small-scale units under globalisation. The important ones include low quality of products, absence of usage of modern technology, low scale of production, etc. It is argued that small-scale units should restructure and upgrade themselves in terms of technology and management to strengthen their position. Upgradation would facilitate these firms in improving the quality of their products and also enable small firms to enter into the value chain by forming linkages with large firms.

The third set of studies relate to the constraints faced by the small-scale enterprises in achieving their potential (Sandesara, 1993; Subrahmanian, 1995; Subrahmanian and Pillai, 1994; Das, 2011, Singh and Kumar, 2020a and 2020b). (i) A major constraint faced by the MSME sector is the availability of financial resources at their disposal. The problem becomes more serious as banks are unwilling to lend money to these units, especially micro units, that constitute 95 per cent of the total MSME sector. According to different estimates, finances received from formal sources are just around 15 to 20 per cent of the total credit requirement of this sector (Das, 2011; IFC, 2018). Thus, around 80 per cent of the total credit requirement of this sector is met from informal sources. It is worth highlighting that the highest dependence on informal sources is in the case of micro units (90 per cent) and the lowest is in the case of medium units[6]. There are several reasons behind the high dependence of the MSME sector on informal sources of finance (RBI, 2019). (a) Due to capital scarcity and the absence of buffers, lending to this sector involves a high risk of repayment that discourages banks from lending money. (b) 70 to 80 per cent of MSME units are unregistered and also do not maintain a regular record of the payments and receipts. Thus, it becomes cumbersome and a time-taking process for the formal financial institutes to assess their creditworthiness.

Another constraint faced by the MSME sector relates to technological upgradation. As technology is changing every day and is a key input in production function (Narayanan, 1998; Blalock and Gertler, 2009; Mani, 2011; Singh, 2019), MSMEs are under pressure to equip themselves with the latest technology. With some exceptions, micro and small enterprises are, in general, characterised by a low level of technology upgradation (Subrahmanian, 1995; Subrahmanya, et al., 2002; Singh and Jain, 2006; Bhavani, 2016). It works as a major hurdle for these units in marking their footprint in a globalised world. According to Singh and Kumar (2020b), around 60 per cent of micro and small units in Punjab have not upgraded technology during the last decade and those who have upgraded have not adopted the latest technology. Various reasons have been reported for using obsolete technology including the indivisible character of technology, financial constraint, lack of awareness, lack of access to advanced technology, etc.

Existing studies have revealed that the micro and small units do not receive payments from buyers on time (Kumar, 2011; Singh and Kumar, 2020b). The payments are mostly delayed by more than 90 days on an average. It severely reduces their cash flow and adversely affects their working capital and business. To solve the problem, steps have been taken under the MSME Act, 2006. A Micro and Small Enterprises Facilitation Council (MSEFC) has been established. But MSMEs are afraid of taking help from this council that their buyers may retaliate to this. Up to June 14, 2019, 11,015 cases involving an amount of Rs. 3,7653.1 million have been filed with MSEFC but only 3,899 cases involving Rs. 1,1717.4 million have been disposed (RBI, 2019). It shows that the process is slow.

Specific studies pertaining to Punjab state have also confirmed that the MSME sector in the state has been witnessing downfall in the post-reform period (Singh, 2005; Ghuman and Singh, 2017; Singh and Kumar, 2020a and 2020b; Singh and Cheema, 2021). As reported by Singh and Kumar (2020b), more than 65 per cent of operating units have witnessed either absolute decline or stagnation in production during the last decade. Among commonly reported factors (policy change in 1991, competition, etc.) behind the deceleration of the MSME sector, there are some factors which specifically worked against the development of the sector in the case of Punjab during the last couple of decades. First, in the late 1990s, the Government of India announced a series of benefits to the neighbouring states of Punjab, namely Himachal Pradesh, Jammu and Kashmir and Uttarakhand, for the development of the industrial sector. These benefits were announced in the form of capital investment subsidies on plant and machinery, transportation costs, exemption on excise duty, etc. (Singh and Kumar, 2020a). These benefits would be continuing till 2027. To avail benefits, a large number of small units from Punjab have fully or partially shifted their production base to these states during the last couple of decades. Second, socio-economic disturbances in the 1980s and early 1990s have played a crucial role in decelerating the industrialisation process in the state. The disturbances have not only created panic among the business firms but also created a negative perception about the responsibility of the government towards business entities. The lagged effect of the disturbances has even been observed during the 1990s and afterwards (Bawa, Raikhy and Dhindsa, 2007; Ghuman and Singh, 2017).

Data Sources and Definitional Changes of MSME

To analyse the above-said objective, both primary and secondary information have been used. The important secondary data sources include (i) Statistical Abstract of Punjab; (ii) Economic Survey of Punjab and India; (iii) National Accounts Statistics; (iv) Various Annual reports published by the Ministry of MSME and (v) National Sample Survey Organization (NSSO). From these sources, we have collected data related to the number and type of industries, output and investment in the industrial sector, etc.

Primary information was collected from four industrial centres of Punjab, namely Amritsar, Jalandhar, Ludhiana and Fatehgarh Sahib (Mandi Gobindgarh)[7]. A total of 408 industrial units spread across four selected industrial locations were surveyed. Both qualitative and quantitative information were collected through field surveys. Information collected through field surveys covered different aspects such as growth, opportunities and challenges faced by the MSME units in Punjab. For this paper, we have mainly used qualitative information to discuss the concerns pertaining to the sector in recent times.

Defining Small-Scale Industries in India

The classification of industrial units in India has been done on the basis of investment in plant and machinery. Definition of small-scale sector has been revised from time to time by raising the upper limit of investment (Table 10.1). With the enactment of the MSME Act 2006, a discernible change was observed in defining the industrial sector. For the first time in 2006, medium enterprises were incorporated and the sector is now defined as MSME sector. In 2020, the Government of India again revised the definition of MSME sector, wherein an MSME is defined on the basis of two criteria: (i) investment in plant and machinery and (ii) annual sales turnover of the unit.

Growth Trends of MSMEs at National Level

As discussed in the preceding section, the definition of small-scale enterprises has been revised from time to time and it renders data before and after 2006, incomparable in a true sense. Before analysing the growth trends, it is important to discuss about the main characteristics of MSME

Table 10.1 Definitional investment ceilings for SSIs in India – 1980-2006 (Rs. in millions)

		Manufacturing enterprises			*Enterprises providing services*		
		Upper limit of the investment in plant and machinery (Rs. in million)			*Upper limit of the investment in plant equipment (Rs. in million)*		
		Medium	*Small*	*Tiny*/micro*	*Medium*	*Small***	*Micro*
1980		-	2.0	0.2	-	-	-
1985		-	3.5	0.2	-	0.2	-
1991		-	6.0	0.5	-	0.5	-
1997		-	30.0	2.5	-	0.5	-
1999		-	10.0	2.5	-	0.5	-
2001		-	10.0$	2.5	-	1.0	-
2006		100.0	50.0	2.5	50.0	20.0	1.0
2020	Investment	500	100	10	500	100	10
	Turnover	< 1000	< 500	< 50	< 1000	< 500	< 50

Source: Mohan (2002); Das (2011) and GoI (2020).

notes: '-' indicates not defined formally.

* *In 1980, these referred to units located in the rural areas or towns with a maximum population of 50,000 as per Census of India, 1971. By 1985, the population limit increased to 0.5 million as per Census of India, 1981. However, by 1991, the locational conditions were dropped.*

** *SSSE – Small Scale Service Enterprise; introduced in 1985.*

SSSBE – Small Scale Service and Business Enterprise; this category replaced SSSE in 1991.

$ *Since October 2001, for 41 items of Hosiery and Hand Tools; since June 2003, for 23 more items of Stationery and the Drugs and Pharmaceutical industry; and since October 2004, for 7 more items of Sports goods, the upper limit for investment has been raised to Rs. 50 million.*

units[8]. First, as per the latest NSSO estimates in 2015-16, the total number of MSMEs in India stood at around 63 million. The distribution of these units is extremely skewed since micro units account for 99.47 per cent of total units, and 0.52 per cent are small in size, the remaining (0.01 per cent) are medium-sized units. Second, it is interesting to note that MSMEs are involved in a range of activities such as manufacturing, trade and other services. The highest percentage of units (36.34 per cent) are involved in the trade of goods; it is followed by other services (32.63 per cent) such as repairing and maintenance, and around 31 per cent are engaged in manufacturing activities. Third, more than 6000 products are being produced by MSMEs in India and these products range from traditional to high-tech items[9]. The third salient character of these units is their organisational structure of these units. A majority of these units are run by family members (79 per cent), and this proportion is as high as 84 per cent in the case of micro units[10]. Further, a majority of these units are operating in an informal setup. According to NSSO estimates, the proportion of MSMEs operating in the informal sector is as high as around 70 per cent of total MSME units. Fourth, more than 50 per cent of these enterprises are based in rural India and supply products according to local requirements. Around 66 per cent of total MSMEs are owned by the socially backward castes (SC, BC and OBC). Alternatively, 32.95 per cent of MSMEs are owned by the upper caste households.

Growth Trends of MSMEs

MSMEs are analysed on the basis of certain key indicators including fixed investment, production, employment, and number of units (Table 10.2). It is interesting to note that the MSME sector has consistently grown over the years in the post-reform period in terms of all the selected indicators[11]. The number of units increased from 7.06 million in 1991-92 to 10.11 million in 2000-01 and then stood at 12.34 million in 2005-06. The increase in the number of units continued in the following period. Similarly, the number of workers employed in the sector has increased continuously during the reference period. It increased from 16.6 million in 1991-92 to 22.91 million in 1999-2002 and further reached around 30 million in 2005-06. In 2016-17, the number of workers employed in the MSME sector stood at around 129.42 million. The growing presence of MSMEs is also visible in terms of production and fixed investment (Table 10.2). At current prices, the volume of MSMEs production has increased from Rs. 730720 million in 1991-92 to Rs. 4978420 million in 2005-06 and the increase in production continued in the following period. The production of the MSME sector increased to Rs. 18981330 million in 2016-17 (Table 10.2).

Table 10.2 Growth of SSIs/MSMEs in India: Major indicators

Year	*Total SSI units (in million)*		*Fixed investment (Rs. in million)*		*Production (Rs. in million)*		*Employment (in million)*	
1990-91	6.79		935550		635180		15.83	
1991-92	7.06	(3.98)	1003510	(7.26)	730720	(15.04)	16.6	(4.86)
1992-93	7.35	(4.11)	1096230	(9.24)	855810	(17.12)	17.48	(5.30)
1993-94	7.65	(4.08)	1157950	(5.63)	988040	(15.45)	18.26	(4.46)
1994-95	7.96	(4.05)	1237900	(6.90)	1222100	(23.69)	19.14	(4.82)
1995-96	8.28	(4.02)	1257500	(1.58)	1482900	(21.34)	19.79	(3.40)
1996-97	8.62	(4.11)	1305600	(3.83)	1684130	(13.57)	20.59	(4.04)
1997-98	8.97	(4.06)	1332420	(2.05)	1891780	(12.33)	21.32	(3.55)
1998-99	9.34	(4.12)	1354820	(1.68)	2129010	(12.54)	22.06	(3.47)
1999-2000	9.72	(4.07)	1399820	(3.32)	2342550	(10.03)	22.91	(3.85)
2000-01	10.11	(4.01)	1473480	(5.26)	2612890	(11.54)	23.91	(4.36)
2001-02	10.52	(4.06)	1543490	(4.75)	2822700	(8.03)	24.93	(4.27)
2002-03	10.95	(4.09)	1623170	(5.16)	3148500	(11.54)	26.02	(4.37)
2003-04	11.34	(3.56)	1702190	(4.87)	3645470	(15.78)	27.14	(4.30)
2004-05	11.86	(4.59)	1786990	(4.98)	4297960	(17.90)	28.26	(4.13)
2005-06	12.34	(4.05)	1881130	(5.27)	4978420	(15.83)	29.49	(4.35)
2006-07	36.17	(193.11)	8685430	(361.71)	13513830	(171.45)	80.52	(173.04)
2007-08	37.73	(4.31)	9204590	(5.98)	14351790	(6.20)	84.2	(4.57)
2008-09	39.37	(4.35)	9771140	(6.16)	15242340	(6.21)	88.08	(4.61)
2009-10	41.08	(4.34)	10385460	(6.29)	16193550	(6.24)	92.17	(4.64)
2010-11	42.87	(4.36)	11059340	(6.49)	17215530	(6.31)	96.51	(4.71)
2011-12	44.76	(4.41)	11827570	(6.95)	18343320	(6.55)	101.16	(4.82)
2012-13	44.75	(-0.02)	12687630	(7.27)	18099760	(1.20)	106.14	(4.92)
2013-14	48.84	(9.14)	13637000	(7.48)	18316240	(1.20)	111.42	(4.97)
2014-15	51.06		14719120	(7.94)	18535310	(1.20)	117.13	(5.12)
2016-17	55.78		-		18981330	(1.20)	129.42	(5.12)

Source: (i) Various Annual Reports of the Ministry of MSMEs (ii) Post 2006-07 data has been accessed from the Statistical year book India, 2018, available at https://mospi.gov.in/web/mospi/reports-publications/-/reports/view/templateTwo/8411?q=TBDCAT). (iii) Data on fixed investment is entirely from MSME annual reports.

Notes: Figures in brackets show the percentage growth over the previous year

The growth rate of MSMEs' production as compared to overall industry is presented in Figure 10.1. Except for a few years, the MSME sector has registered a considerably high growth as compared to the overall industrial sector in India during 2000-01 to 2015-16. It is interesting to note that the sector has recorded a double-digit growth rate from 2004-05 till 2008-09. Post 2008 crisis, the growth of the MSME sector has witnessed a downfall and hovered around 4 to 7 per cent since 2009-10. It remained below the growth of the overall industrial sector (Figure, 10.1).

Another view on the importance of MSMEs is depicted in terms of their contribution to the national aggregates (Table 10.3). It is analysed in terms of the share of MSMEs in the gross domestic product, manufacturing and the country's total exports (Table 10.3). In general, it appears that MSMEs have a sizeable presence in India. It is evident as the contribution of this sector to GDP ranged between 30 and 37.54 per cent during 2006-07 to 2018-19. Though the share of the MSME sector in GDP has started declining in recent years, it is still around 30.27 per cent (Table 10.3). Further, the share of the MSME sector in total industrial output is quite significant, but it has consistently declined from 42.02 per cent to 33.00 per cent during 2006-07 to 2018-19. Contrarily, the share of MSMEs in total exports has increased over the years. It stood around 32 per cent in 2006-07 and then reached above 40 per cent in 2012-13 and stood at 45 per cent in 201718. The significant contribution of this sector in national-level aggregates implies

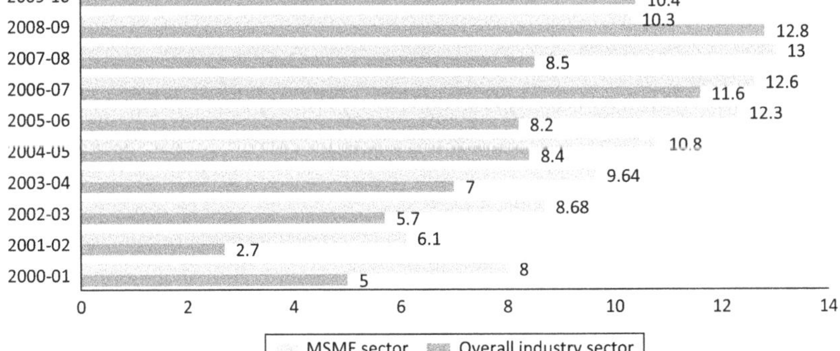

Figure 10.1 Growth rate of MSME and overall industrial sector production *Source: RBI (2019).*

Table 10.3 Contribution of the MSME sector to national aggregates

	Share in GDP	*Share in manufacturing output*	*Share in total exports*
2006-07	35.13	42.0	31.92
2007-08	35.41	42.0	30.8
2012-13	37.54	37.3	40.06
2018-19	30.27	33.0	45.00

Source: Different annual reports of MSMEs.

that the MSME sector is playing a critical role in India's overall economic growth and development.

To sum up, it appears that the role of the MSME sector is very significant in India's development. However, the recent decline in its growth has raised serious concerns for policymakers.

MSME Sector in Punjab

This section analyses the development of small-scale industry in Punjab since 1980-81. The analysis is based on secondary information gathered from the Statistical Abstract of Punjab and the primary data collected from four major industrial districts of Punjab. Various parameters have been used to understand growth and development of the selected industrial group (Table 10.4). The number of small-scale industrial units in the state has increased from 43338 to 206095 during 1980-81 to 2017-18, it increased by 4.76 times. The decadal growth rate of the number of units was above 12 per cent during 1980-81 to 1990-91. It slowed down during 1990-91 to 2000-01 and then turned negative in the first decade of the 21st century (Table 10.4). The negative growth indicates that the number of units has declined in absolute terms in the early years of this century. Further, trends in production and fixed investment in small-scale industry have also recorded a consistent increase in the state during the period of 35 years from 1980-81 to 2014-15. The increase remained higher during the 1980s as compared to the later period (Table 10.4). In absolute terms, the volume of production of small scale industry has increased from Rs. 28590.9 million in 1980-81 to Rs. 328322.3 million in 2014-15. Correspondingly, the volume of fixed investment has increased from Rs. 8490 million to Rs. 20440 million.

The importance of the SSI sector in Punjab's industrial development has remained considerably high in terms of all the key indicators (Table 10.5). An interesting point to note here is that the share of small units in total registered industrial units has remained above 99.5 per cent throughout the reference period. However, on the basis of production, the share of these

Table 10.4 Trends in small-scale industry in Punjab (at 1993-94 prices)

Year	*Small industrial units (nos.)*	*Employment (nos.)*	*Production* (Rs. in million)*	*Fixed investment * (Rs. in million)*
1980-81	43338	264869	28590.9	8490
1991-92	176378	711417	53044	17910
1996-97	193332	821170	89276.5	20020
2001-02	201736	909266	140949.4	30310
2006-07	191639	938684	185258.5	30580
2012-13	154421	1077616	257591.2	46930
2013-14	156518	1112858	297101.3	51510
2014-15	156518	1139126	328322.3	54990
2017-18	206095	1487843	-	-
Compound annual growth rate (in %)				
1980-81 to 1990-91	12.63	8.79	5.93	7.04
1990-91 to 2000-01	2.06	2.71	8.29	4.46
2000-01 to 2010-11	-2.46	1.01	5.61	2.54
1991-92 to 1995-96	1.61	2.43	8.48	0.30
1996-97 to 2000-01	0.74	1.80	7.69	7.69
2001-02 to 2005-06	0.27	0.91	5.25	-0.22
2006-07 to 2010-11	-4.46	1.33	4.94	4.56
2011-12 to 2014-15	0.59	2.46	6.73	6.78
2014-15 to 2017-18	9.6	9.31	-	-

Source: (i) Directorate of Industries, Government of Punjab, Chandigarh.

units never crossed 50 per cent of total industrial production in Punjab; it varied between 34.18 per cent and 49.49 per cent during 1980-81 to 2014-15. The results are quite surprising in terms of the share of small-scale units in investment and employment (Table 10.5). These units accounted for 31.35 per cent of total fixed investment in the registered industrial sector in Punjab in 1980-81 and it declined to 20.44 per cent in 2014-15. Correspondingly, the proportion of workers employed in the small-scale sector has increased consistently over the years. In 1980-81, 70.7 per cent of total industrial workers in Punjab were employed in the small-scale sector and this figure stood at 82.4 per cent in 2014-15. With minimal capital investment, this sector is able to generate huge employment and contribute a significant share of production.

Table 10.5 Share of small-scale sector in registered industrial sector

Year	*Small industrial units*	*Employment*	*Production*	*Fixed investment*
1980-81	99.48	70.7	49.49	31.35
1991-92	99.78	78.6	36.53	24.76
1996-97	99.70	78.9	34.18	20.36
2001-02	99.69	79.7	42.88	19.83
2006-07	99.82	82.5	47.50	19.12
2012-13	99.72	81.8	45.44	18.59
2013-14	99.73	82.2	49.67	19.44
2014-15	99.72	82.4	48.15	20.44
2017-18	99.76	81.6	-	-

Source: Same as Table 10.4.

The direction of change in the growth of MSMEs in Punjab is presented in Table 10.6. As per NSSO estimates, 268485 out of 1465032 units have reported an expansion of their units during the preceding three years of 2015-16, which turns out to be less than 20 per cent. On the other hand, about half of total MSMEs (48.4 per cent) have reported stagnation in their growth in 2015-16 and 15.4 per cent have reported a decline in their business (Table 10.6).

The direction of change in the growth of MSME units during the last decade is analysed on the basis of primary data collected from 408 industrial units located in four industrial centres of Punjab (Amritsar, Jalandhar, Ludhiana and Mandi Gobindgarh). Around 35 per cent of units have recorded an expansion both in terms of production and manufacturing capability during the last decade. The remaining 65 per cent of the surveyed units have observed either no change in production and manufacturing capacity or witnessed a decline in both the indicators. 28.4 per cent of units have reported stagnation whereas 28.2 per cent (115 out of 408) of units have recorded a decline in their production volume during the last decade. Corresponding figures for manufacturing capacity turned out to be 43.4 per cent and 20.4 per cent.

Based on the above results, it appears that the MSME sector in India has started witnessing a downfall. The downfall is visible in terms of both the growth rates and the declining contribution of the sector in national aggregates. The situation is even worse in the case of Punjab. The downfall in Punjab is confirmed by both secondary and primary data. Recent studies have reported that around 18770 units in Punjab have completely wound up their production during 2007 to 2014, and a large number of small industrial units are on the verge of closure (Ghuman and Singh, 2017; Singh and Ghuman, 2018; Singh and Kumar, 2020b; Singh and Cheema, 2021). The declining presence of MSMEs is a serious cause of concern for the policymakers of the country.

Table 10.6 Status of MSMEs in Punjab in terms of production and manufacturing capacity

Direction of change	*During the preceding 3 years of survey**		*Preceding 10 years of survey***	
	2010-11	*2015-16*	*Production*	*Manufacturing capacity*
Expanding	2,31,359 (16)	2,68,485 (18.3)	145 (35.5)	144 (35.3)
Stagnant	7,99,434 (55.4)	7,08,486 (48.4)	116 (28.4)	177 (43.4)
Contracting	1,50,415 (10.4)	2,25,438 (15.4)	115 (28.2)	84 (20.6)
Operated for less than three years	2,61,823 (18.1)	1,93,262 (13.2)	-	-
Fluctuating	-	-	32 (7.6)	-
No information	-	69,362 (4.7)	-	3 (0.7)
Total	14,43,031 (100)	14,65,032 (100)	408 (100.0)	408 (100.0)

Source: (i) based on NSSO. (ii) ** Primary survey carried out during October 2018 to January 2020.*
Note: Figures in brackets are percentage of respective total.
'-' indicates no information.

To deal with the downfall of the industrial sector including MSME, the government of Punjab has taken various steps in recent years. It is evident as the government of Punjab has announced three industrial policies (2003, 2009 and 2017) during the last two decades. Wherein the emphasis was to revive the MSME sector by providing various types of incentives, particularly financial incentives in the form of direct subsidies, tax deferment/exemption to industrial units, stamp duty, property tax, etc. (for details, see Ghuman and Singh, 2017; Singh and Kumar, 2020b). Besides, the government of Punjab organised three industrial summits in 2013, 2015 and 2019 wherein a number of financial incentives were offered to new units. Despite these efforts, the industrial sector, particularly the MSME sector, has been continuously reporting a slowdown and a sizeable number of micro and small units have closed their production activities in Punjab during the last one and a half decades. These trends imply that financial incentives alone may not be enough to keep the industrial sector growing and woo the private investment. Besides fiscal and other incentives, it is equally important to provide a congenial business climate by strengthening the institutes dealing with the industrial sector. The study by Singh and Kumar (2020b) reported that the lack of inter-departmental coordination and the lack of clear and transparent policy have played an instrumental role in derailing the industrial sector in Punjab. Further, the poor business conditions of Punjab are visible as the state has been continuously placed at the bottom in various business indicators. For instance, on the basis of ease of doing business, Punjab was placed on 16th rank in 2015 and 19th rank in 2019. Further, NITI Aayog (2019) ranked states on the basis of business environment wherein Punjab was positioned at number 10.

Conclusion

The MSME sector in India has passed through different regulatory regimes, ranging from complete protection to openness, to reach its present stage of development. The paradigm shift in the business environment in 1991 and afterwards posed serious challenges for the existence of small-scale units and forced these units to restructure and upgrade. Despite intense competition, the MSME sector continuously expanded its footprint by entering into diversified product lines. Presently, 63.3 million MSMEs in India are manufacturing more than 6000 products and providing employment to around 11 million people in the country. The contribution of the MSME sector in national aggregates (GDP, industrial output and exports) is quite significant. In 2018-19, this sector accounted for 30 per cent of India's GDP, 33 per cent of manufacturing output and around 45 per cent of exports. In line with the overall scenario, the importance of the small-scale sector in Punjab is considerably high. More than 99.5 per cent of total industrial units in Punjab are small in size. In recent years, this sector has generated around 48 per cent of industrial production in Punjab and accounted for around 82 per cent of total industrial sector employment and 20 per cent of fixed investment.

Though this sector is still managing to make its strong presence felt at the national level as well as in Punjab, recent trends are not encouraging. The contribution of the MSME sector in India's GDP and manufacturing output has been declining in recent years. In the case of Punjab, only around one-third of small units have expanded their business and remaining two third units have either witnessed contraction or stagnation in their businesses during the last decade.

The downfall reported by the MSME sector in recent years has far-reaching implications for the social and economic development of the country on the one hand and it may also hurt the progress of India in realising the SDGs set for 2030. SDG goal number 8 aims at promoting sustainable inclusive economic growth with full employment and decent work for all and the goal number 9 aims to promote sustainable industrialisation and foster innovation. Though these enterprises are small in size, they are a big performer in terms of all economic and social parameters. Further, reducing any type of inequalities is listed under SDG number 10. Ubiquitous presence of MSMEs in India can help in reducing social, economic and gender inequalities. In India, around 20 per cent MSMEs are owned by females and around two-third MSMEs belong to socially backward caste households. Formalisation of the MSME sector and technological upgradation of these units would enable India to achieve most of the goals under SDGs 2015.

For materialising the potential of this sector, it is important to address the issues and concerns faced by the MSME by drafting a long-term road map. Some of the concerns of MSMEs are age-old whereas others have cropped up with the implementation of new economic policies.

Notes

1 https://www.worldbank.org/en/topic/smefinance
2 Development Commission (MSME), Ministry of MSMEs, GoI, New Delhi. Available at: http://laghu-udyog.gov.in/policies/preseve.htm.
3 The list of reserved products expanded from 180 to 807 products by May 1978. It further stood at 821 in 1998-99.
4 For instance, Small Industries Development Organisation was established in 1954, National Small Industries Corporation in 1955, Khadi and Village Industries Commission in 1956 and so on.
5 Detailed discussion is provided in the review of literature section.
6 http://intellecap.com/wp-content/themes/intellecap/pdf/micro_smal.pdf
7 For detail on the selection of districts and respondents, see Singh and Kumar (2020b).
8 Discussion in this section is drawn from 4th All India Census of Small Scale Industries, 73rd round of NSSO survey and different documents of the Ministry of Micro, Small and Medium Enterprises, Government of India, New Delhi.
9 Around 64 per cent of total products produced by MSME sector are related to six major products categories such as (i) Food products (22 per cent); (ii) Chemical and chemical products (22 per cent); (iii) Basic metal industry (10 per cent); (iv) Metal products (8 per cent); (v) Electrical and machinery parts (6 per cent); (vi) Rubber and plastic products (6 per cent) and remaining 36 per cent are unclassified.
10 Such enterprises are termed as own account manufacturers. OEMs are those enterprises which are run by a household without any hired worker.
11 Due to change in definition of MSMEs in 2006, a sudden jump was recorded in all the indicators such as output, investment and employment in 2006-07.

References

Bawa, R. S., Raikhy, R. S., & Dhindsa, P. K. (2007). *Globalization and Punjab Economy: Issues in Agriculture and Small Scale Industry*. Amritsar: Guru Nanak Dev University.

Bhavani, T. (2002). Small-Scale Units in the Era of Globalisation: Problems and Prospects. *Economic and Political Weekly*, *37*(29), 3041–3052.

Bhavani, T. (2011). Dynamic Business Environments: What These Mean for Indian Small Enterprises. In K. Das (Ed.), *Micro and Small Enterprises in India: The Era of Reforms* (pp. 27–45). New Delhi: Routledge.

Blalock, G., & Gertler, P. J. (2009). How Firm Capabilities Affect Who Benefits from Foreign Technology. *Journal of Development Economics*, *90*(2), 192–199.

Das, K. (2006). Micro and Small Enterprises. In Alternative Economic Survey (Ed.), *India 2005–2006: Disempowering Masses* (pp. 111–120). Delhi: Daanish Books.

Das, K. (2011). *Micro and Small Enterprises in India: The Era of Reforms*. New Delhi: Routledge.

Ghuman, R. S., & Singh, J. (2017). *Status of Industrial Development in Punjab: A Case Study of Mandi Gobindgarh Industrial Cluster*. Chandigarh: Centre for Research in Rural and Industrial Development.

Government of Punjab (1998). *Statistical Abstract of Punjab*. Chandigarh: Economic and Statistical Organization, Government of Punjab.

Gupta, D. B. (1982). *Rural Industry in India: The Experience of Punjab Region*. Delhi: Hindustan Publishing Corporation.

IFC (2018). *Financing India's MSMEs: Estimation of Debt Requirement of MSMEs in India*. International Finance Organisation, World Bank Group.

ILO (2017). *World Employment and Social Outlook 2017: Sustainable Enterprises and Jobs: Formal Enterprises and Decent Work*. Geneva: International Labour Office.

Kumar, N. P. (2011). Policy Reforms and Small Enterprises: Entrepreneur Perceptions from Uttar Pradesh. In K. Das (Ed.), *Micro and Small Enterprises in India: The Era of Reforms* (pp. 292–315). New Delhi: Routledge.

Kumar, P. (2011). Policy and Performance of MSME: A Critical Appraisal. *Amity Business Review*, *12*(2), 47–60.

Kumar, P. (2014). An Empirical Study on Performance of Indian MSME. *Asia-Pacific Journal of Management Research and Innovation*, *10*(4), 367–375.

Mukherjee, S. (2018). Challenges to Indian Micro Small Scale and Medium Enterprises in the Era of Globalization. *Mukherjee Journal of Global Enterpreneurship Research*, 8, 1–19.

Nagaraj, R. (1985). Some Aspects of Small Scale Indutries in India: Findings Based on Two All-India Sample Surveys. *Economic and Political Weekly*, *20*(41), 1741–1746.

Narayana, D. L. (1989). *The Motor Vehicle Industry in India (Growth within a Regulatory Policy Environment)*. Delhi and Trivandrum: Oxford & IBH Publishing Co. Pvt. Ltd.

Narayanan, K. (1998). Technology Acquisition, De-regulation and Competitiveness: A Study of Indian Automobile Industry. *Research Policy*, *27*(2), 215–228.

NITI Aayog (2019). *India Innovation Index*. New Delhi: NITI Aayog, Government of India.

OECD (2016). *Fostering Markets for SME Finance: Matching Business and Investor Needs*. Paris: OECD Working Party on SMEs and Entrepreneurship.

OECD (2017). *Financial Education for Micro, Small and Medium-Sized Enterprises in Asia*. Paris: OECD Publishing.

OECD (2018a). *Financing SMEs and Entrepreneurs 2018: An OECD Scoreboard*. Paris: OECD Publishing.

OECD (2018b). *Strengthening SMEs and Entrepreneurship for Productivity and Inclusive Growth*. Mexico City: Key Issues Paper SME Ministerial Conference, 22–23 February.

Pandit, M. L. (1984). *Industrial Development in the Punjab and Haryana: Domination of fooTloose Industry*. Delhi: B R Publishing Corporation.

Pingle, V. (1999). *Rethinking the Developmental State*. New York: St. Martin's Press.

Prakash, V. (1956). Small Scale Cottage Industries in Punjab. *The Economic Weekly*, December 8.

RBI (2019). *Report of the Expert Committee on Micro, Small and Medium Enterprises*. Mumbai: Reserve Bank of India.

Sandesara, J. C. (1993). Modern Small Industry, 1972 and 1987–88: Aspects of Growth and Structural Change. *Economic and Political Weekly*, *28*(6), 223–229.

Sandhu, J. S., & Singh, A. (1984). Industrial Development in Punjab: Some Features. In S. Johar and J. S. Khanna (Eds.), *Studies in Punjab Economy* (pp. 111–120). Amritsar: Guru Nanak Dev University.

Sathe, D. (2002). Industrial Slowdown and Small-Scale Sector. *Economic and Political Weekly*, *37*(29), 2990–2992.

Singh, J. (2019). *Global Players and India's Car Industry: Technology Trade and Structure Change*. New Delhi, India: Routledge.

Singh, J., & Cheema, M. D. (2021). Regional Industrial Development under Economic Regime in Punjab. *Indian Journal of Economics and Development*, *17*(2), 339–349.

Singh, J., & Ghuman, R. S. (2018). Industrialization in Punjab: Status, Constraints and Policy Intervention. *Man and Development*, *40*(3), 1–19.

Singh, J., & Kumar, V. (2020a). *Constraints and Prospects of Industrial Development: A Study of Two Industrial Districts of Punjab* [Unpublished report]. Department of Planning, Government of Punjab.

Singh, J., & Kumar, V. (2020b). *What Ails Industrial Development: A Study of Major Industrial Centre in Punjab* [Unpublished report]. New Delhi: Indian Council of Social Science Research.

Singh, L. (2005). Deceleration of Industrial Growth and Rural Industrialization Strategy for Indian Punjab. *Working Paper No. 799*, Munich Personal RePEc Archive.

Singh, L., & Jain, V. (2006). Unorganised Manufacturing Industry in the Era of Globalisation: A Study of Punjab, *Working Paper No. 197*, MPRA.

Singh, S. (1994). Refugees as Entrepreneurs: The Case of the Indian Bicycle Industry. *The Journal of Entrepreneurship*, *3*(1), 81–95.

Sinha, S., & Pental, K. (2018). Study on Demand for Skilled Labour in Unregistered MSMEs of India. *Report No. 87*, South Asia Region, Education Global Practice.

Subrahmanya, M. B. (2004). Small Industry and Globalisation: Implications, Perfromance and Prospects. *Economic and Political Weekly*, *39*(18), 1826–1834.

Subrahmanian, K. K. (1995). Technology Dimensions of Small Scale Industry. *Productivity*, *36*(1), 26–30.

Subrahmanian, K. K. (2003). *Regional Industrial Growth under Economic Liberalization: A Study of Selected Issues with Reference to Kerala State*. New Delhi: Manak Publications.

Subrahmanian, K., & Pillai, P. M. (1994). Liberalisation and Small Industry: Need for New Growth Strategy in Kerela. *Economic and Political Weekly*, *29*(33), 2168–2174.

Subrahmanya, B. H. M. (1995). Rservation Policy for Small-Scale Industry: Has It Delivered the Goods? *Economic and Political Weekly*, *30*(21), M51–M54.

Subrahmanya, B. H. M. (2011). Small-Scale Industry Development for Export Promotion: India's Experience under Liberalization. In K. Das (Ed.), *Micro and Small Enterprises in India: The Era of Reforms* (pp. 46–66). New Delhi: Routledge.

Subrahmanya, M. B., Mathirajan, M., Balanchandra, P., Srinivasan, M., & Prasad, L. (2002). *R&D and Technological Innovations in Small Scale Industries.* Mumbai: Allied Publishers Pvt. Ltd.

UN-DESA (2020). *Micro, Small and Medium-Sized Enterprises and Their Role in Achieving the Sustainable Development Goals.* Department of Economic and Social Affairs. Available at: https://sdgs.un.org/sites/default/files/2020-07/MSMEs_and_SDGs.pdf.

11 Bridging the Gap

A Critical Assessment of the Digital Divide in India

Gautam Kumar Jha

Introduction

As we enter the 30th year of economic reforms, we cannot deny that Information and Communication Technology (ICT) and ICT-enabled services have played an important part in the overall development process of the Indian economy. As per the International Trade Administration (ITA), ICT contributes over 13 per cent to India's Gross Domestic Product (GDP) (ITA, 2020). National Association of Software and Service Companies (NASSCOM), in its strategic review, pegged the industry to grow at around 8 per cent, much faster than the GDP growth rates (Phadnis, 2020). ICT is a broad term which refers to all communication technologies, including the internet, wireless networks, mobile phones, computers, software, middleware, video-conferencing, social networking and other media applications and services enabling users to access, retrieve, store, transmit and manipulate information in a digital form. It refers to technologies that provide access to information through telecommunications. It is similar to Information Technology (IT) but focuses primarily on communication technologies such as the internet, wireless networks, mobile phones and other communication mediums. It helps in reducing and/or removing the barriers created by distance and time.

The contribution of the IT sector to the Indian economy has increased significantly over the years. During the last decade, the industry has shown a five-fold growth in revenue terms, and its relative share in India's GDP has increased from around 1.2 per cent in 1998 (Mehta, 2020) to around 8 per cent in 2020-21(E) (MEITY, 2021). In India, the main focus has traditionally been on the increased productivity effects. New technologies and their implementation in productive activities are accelerated by the diffusion of ICT-enabled services. Additionally, the increased usage of ICT has helped in boosting productivity across sectors, enhancing employment opportunities both within the broad IT sector and also outside of it, and in elevating exports. It has helped reduce geographical barriers in a vast country like India, not only in terms of access to markets and commodities, but also connecting family and friends. Greater penetration of ICT-enabled services has

DOI: 10.4324/9781003343998-11

also improved the provision and implementation of government services. It may be argued that they have reduced the incidence of corruption, brought more transparency and efficacy in the provision of essential services, social benefit schemes and financial inclusion. The relevance of growth of the ICT sector and telephony growth in economic development in developed and developing countries has been well documented in Mehta (2020); Edquist et al. (2018); Chakraborty and Nandi (2014); Singh (2010); Sridhar and Sridhar (2007) among others. However, the penetration of ICTs has largely been concentrated in urban areas and among males thereby creating a digital divide. This chapter is divided into six sections. While the first section gives introductory remarks, the second section defines the concept of digital divide. The third and fourth sections look at the nature and extent of this divide globally and within India respectively. The fifth section analyses the policy measures to bridge the divide, and finally, the sixth section provides the concluding remarks and some policy suggestions.

Defining the Digital Divide

ICTs not only positively contribute to the facets mentioned above, they also act as a medium to bridge the digital divide. According to the Organisation for Economic Co-operation and Development (OECD), the term digital divide

> refers to the gap between individuals, households, businesses and geographic areas at different socio-economic levels with regard to both their opportunities to access ICTs, and to their use of the Internet for a wide variety of activities. It reflects various differences among and within countries.
>
> (pg. 5, OECD, 2001)

Compaine (2001) defines the digital divide in terms of the perceived gap between those who have access to the latest information technologies and those who do not. The Digital Opportunity Task Force (DOT Force) calls it

> a reflection of existing broader socio-economic inequalities and can be characterized by insufficient infrastructure, high cost of access, inappropriate or weak policy regimes, inefficiencies in the provision of telecommunication networks and services, lack of locally created content, and uneven ability to derive economic and social benefits from information-intensive activities.
>
> (DOT Force, 2001)

To put it simply, the term is used to describe situations where there is a marked gap in accessing ICT services through devices, with communications infrastructure, computer availability and internet access being the important indicators. They are generally measured in terms of fixed-line phones per inhabitant or number of mobile phones per inhabitant or number of internet connections and/or users per inhabitant.

The term digital divide is argued to have gained importance when it became a part of the title of the second National Telecommunications and Information Agency (NITA), USA, survey in 1998. While its origin has not been attributed to any particular author, it caught up as a catchy label for different agencies to study its causes and measure it (Compaine, 2001). While the term might be recent, it signifies a concept that has been around for ages – a difference between 'haves' and 'have-nots' – albeit in a technological sense. While the key focus is on the technological inequality in access and use of ICTs, there are social, economic, political, cultural and at times ethical dimensions to it. Another salient aspect of this divide is the distinction between the problem of access to ICTs and the inability to effectively use such services (particularly in terms of ability and skills) by a large section of the population, especially in developing countries.

While there has been an argument for looking at the concept of digital divide with suspicion in the sense that with time and innovation any such kind of divide diminishes (Compaine, 2001), in my contention, the concept needs to be analysed and the 'gap' measured, particularly when ICTs play a significant role, not only in the development of an economy but also in the everyday life of common people. The role of ICTs in our day-to-day activities has suddenly seen a massive increase during the global Covid-19 pandemic. As governments asked their citizens to stay at home, maintain social distance and undertake extreme precautions, more and more people are turning to their laptops, computers, smartphones and other devices as a substitute for their 'in-person activities' (Devara, 2020). While the realisation of dependency on digital connectivity is hitting home, especially as more and more people are encouraged to work from home and students are required to attend online classes, this is true for those who are connected to the internet. Be it earning a livelihood or access to online education, those at the other end of the digital spectrum have been hit hard by the increasing digitisation.

Wherein the globally connected population is concerned, this pandemic has brought to the forefront the gap between 'technology haves' and 'technology have-nots'. Ostensibly, it appears to be a binary classification, there is a much deeper understanding that is required. Many authors have talked about the many aspects of the digital divide (Singh, 2010). In my view, this concept can be categorised at three different levels. First is the divide between geographical areas – developed and developing countries, mainland and hinterland areas within a country, etc. Second is the divide in terms of means and more importantly access to ICT devices. And, finally, the divide between people who have the knowledge and capabilities to use them and those who do not.

The Global Digital Divide

As mentioned earlier, ICTs have played a significant role in the economic development of an economy. In modern times, almost all of the essential activities can be performed with the press of a few 'keys' or a screen on a handheld device. ICT and ICT-enabled services have radically changed the way of conducting businesses, not only for the large enterprises but also for the small entrepreneurs. It has brought into the fold those markets which were earlier not accessible due to the constraints of distance and time and even awareness. As India embarks on the path of economic progress, it can be safely said that ICTs will play a crucial role in the social, economic and political developments as well as in changing the lives of millions in the way they conduct their day-to-day activities.

However, the potential to exploit the benefit of ICTs, particularly for developing countries, not only depends on access to them but also on their adoption which varies extremely across regions. This is evident from Table 11.1, which gives a snapshot of the access to ICTs across different regions across the globe. It shows a north–south divide in access to ICTs, with the access being much larger in the developed areas as compared to the developing and less developed areas. The numbers for Sub-Saharan Africa are abysmal in this regard. While there is a remarkable reduction in the gap for numbers when we look at mobile cellular subscription, when we analyse the fixed broadband connections we again see the gap widening. Even for the South Asian economies, the numbers are marginally better than in Sub-Saharan Africa.

If we look at the numbers across the years, by broadly classifying economies into income groups, the 'access gap' for ICTs becomes more clear. Figures 11.1–11.4 show the gap between the indicators (shown in Table 11.1) across broad income categories for various years. Low-income countries (LIC) are those in which 2020 Gross National Income (GNI) per capita was $1,045 or less. Lower-middle-income countries (LMC) are those in which 2020 GNI per capita was between $1,046 and $4,095. Upper-middle-income countries (UMC) are those in which 2020 GNI per capita was between $4,096 and $12,695. Middle-income countries (MIC) are those in which 2020 GNI per capita was between $1,046 and $12,695. High-income countries (HIC) are those in which 2020 GNI per capita was $12,696 or more[1]. LICs and MICs largely form the developing nations, while the HICs are developed ones[2].

If we look at the figures, we can see that there is a significant gap across income groups across all indicators. While the gap for fixed telephone lines (Figure 11.1) has reduced, it has occurred due to reduction in the numbers for HICs and UMCs. On the other hand, in Figures 11.2 and 11.3, the gap

Table 11.1 Access to ICTs Across Regions

Area	*Year*	*Individuals Using the Internet (% of Population)*[a]	*Year*	*Fixed Broadband Subscriptions (per 100 People)*[b]	*Year*	*Fixed Telephone Subscription (per 100 People)*[c]	*Year*	*Mobile Cellular Subscriptions (per 100 People)*[d]
World	2017	49	2019	15.68	2019	13	2019	109
Arab World	2018	63	2019	8.59	2019	9	2019	105
Caribbean Small States	2017	60	2019	16.16	2019	18	2019	117
Central Europe and the Baltics	2019	80	2019	26.5	2019	19	2019	123
East Asia and Pacific	2017	55	2019	25.31	2019	15	2019	129
East Asia and Pacific (excluding high income)	2017	51	2019	24.21	2019	11	2019	127
Euro Area	2019	87	2019	37.8	2019	43	2019	122
Europe and Central Asia	2019	84	2019	29.13	2019	29	2019	126
Europe and Central Asia (excluding high income)	2019	78	2019	19.6	2019	17	2019	130
European Union	2019	85	2019	35.6	2019	37	2019	122
Fragile and Conflict Affected Economies	2017	19	2019	1.63	2019	3	2019	75
Heavily Indebted Poor Countries (HIPC)	2017	19	2019	0.67	2019	1	2019	77
Latin America and Caribbean	2018	66	2019	14.11	2019	15	2019	100
Latin America and Caribbean (excluding high income)	2018	66	2019	13.8	2019	16	2019	98
Least Developed Countries: UN Classification	2017	17	2018	1.39	2019	1	2018	76
Middle East and North Africa	2018	65	2019	10.41	2019	16	2019	116
Middle East and North Africa (excluding high income)	2018	60	2019	8.54	2019	15	2019	112
North America	2018	88	2019	35.35	2019	33	2019	130
OECD Members	2018	83	2019	31.85	2019	34	2019	124

(*Continued*)

Table 11.1 Continued

Area	*Year*	*Individuals Using the Internet (% of Population)*[a]	*Year*	*Fixed Broadband Subscriptions (per 100 People)*[b]	*Year*	*Fixed Telephone Subscription (per 100 People)*[c]	*Year*	*Mobile Cellular Subscriptions (per 100 People)*[d]
Other Small States	2017	50	2019	9.02	2019	12	2019	120
Pacific Island and Small States	2017	33	2018	0.98	2018	5	2017	86
Small States	2017	51	2019	10.06	2019	13	2019	118
South Asia	2018	20	2019	1.7	2019	2	2019	85
Sub-Saharan Africa	2017	19	2019	0.58	2019	1	2019	87
Sub-Saharan Africa (excluding high income)	2017	19	2019	0.58	2019	1	2019	87
High Income	2018	87	2019	34.65	2019	37	2019	130
Low and Middle Income	2017	42	2019	11.89	2019	8	2019	105
Low Income	2017	16	2017	0.41	2018	1	2018	60
Lower Middle Income	2017	33	2019	3.21	2019	3	2019	98
Middle Income	2017	45	2019	12.6	2019	8	2019	108
Upper Middle Income	2017	59	2019	24.49	2019	14	2019	121

Note:

a: Internet users are individuals who have used the Internet (from any location) in the last 3 months. The Internet can be used via a computer, mobile phone, personal digital assistant, games machine, digital TV, etc.

b: Fixed broadband subscriptions refers to fixed subscriptions to high-speed access to the public Internet (a TCP/IP connection), at downstream speeds equal to, or greater than, 256 Kbit/s. This includes cable modem, DSL, fibre to the home/building, other fixed (wired)-broadband subscriptions, satellite broadband and terrestrial fixed wireless broadband. This total is measured irrespective of the method of payment. It excludes subscriptions that have access to data communications (including the Internet) via mobile cellular networks. It should include fixed WiMAX and any other fixed wireless technologies. It includes both residential subscriptions and subscriptions for organisations.

c: Fixed telephone subscriptions refers to the sum of active number of analogue fixed telephone lines, voice-over-IP (VoIP) subscriptions, fixed wireless local loop (WLL) subscriptions, ISDN voice-channel equivalents and fixed public payphones.

d: Mobile cellular telephone subscriptions are subscriptions to a public mobile telephone service that provide access to the Public Switched Telephone Network (PSTN) using cellular technology. The indicator includes (and is split into) the number of postpaid subscriptions, and the number of active pre-paid accounts (i.e. that have been used during the last three months). The indicator applies to all mobile cellular subscriptions that offer voice communications. It excludes subscriptions via data cards or USB modems, subscriptions to public mobile data services, private trunked mobile radio, telepoint, radio paging and telemetry services.

Source: Compiled by the author from ITU World Telecommunication/ICT Indicators Database as accessed from https://data.worldbank.org/ .

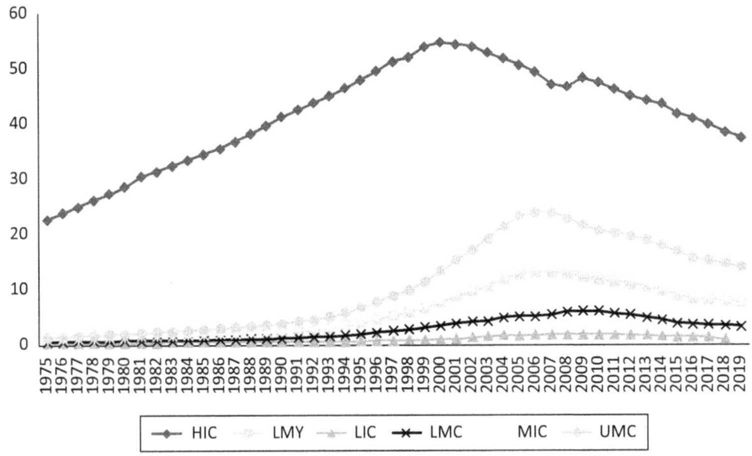

Figure 11.1 Fixed Telephone Subscription (per 100 People) Across Income Groups Note: Data of LICs for 2019 was not available. Source: Compiled by the author from ITU World Telecommunication/ICT Indicators Database as accessed from https://data.worldbank.org/.

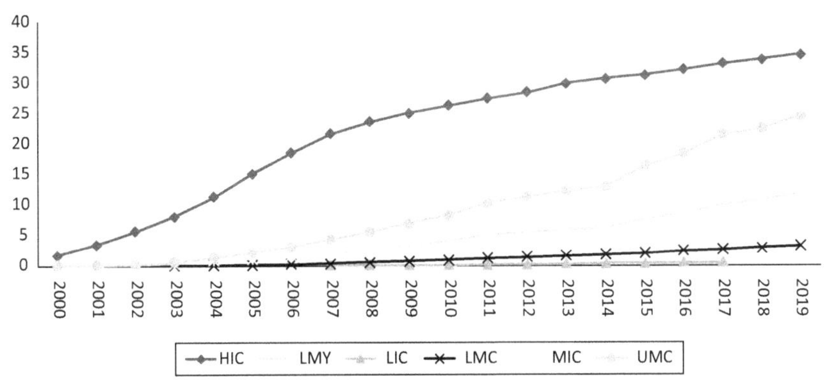

Figure 11.2 Fixed Broadband Subscriptions (per 100 People) Across Income Groups Note: Data of LICs for 2018 and 2019 was not available. Source: Same as Figure 11.1.

has remained almost the same over the years. A significant reduction in the gap can be seen in mobile cellular subscription data (Figure 11.4), particularly from 2004. This can be attributed to the diffusion of wireless technology in most of the developing countries, largely due to reduction in costs. However, across all the four indicators, the gap between LICs and HICs is significantly large, implying that while some parts of the developing world

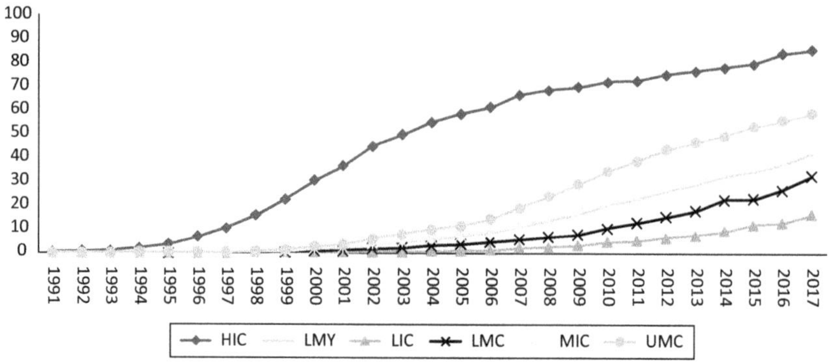

Figure 11.3 Individuals Using the Internet (% of population) Across Income Groups
Source: Same as Figure 11.1.

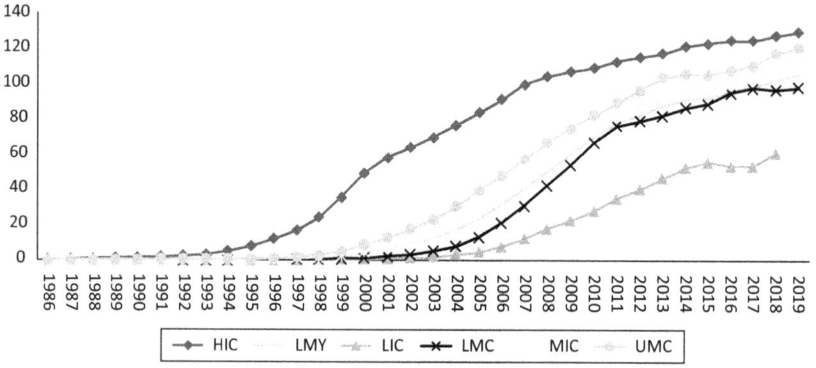

Figure 11.4 Mobile Cellular Subscriptions (per 100 People) Across Income Groups
Note: Data of LICs for 2019 was not available. Source: Same as Figure 11.1

have had reasonable success in mitigating the 'access gap' to ICTs, other parts, particularly the economies with low per capita real income, have not had the same success.

While the main focus of this chapter is to look at the 'divide' in India, it would be useful to look at India's performance vis-à-vis its neighbours. As evident from Figures 11.5–11.8, there are significant gaps in accessing different ICT indicators across the region itself. While the Maldives has consistently been the standout performer in all but one of the indicators, Bangladesh has consistently maintained pace with India in almost all the indicators. War-torn Afghanistan and Pakistan are at the lower end of the ICT spectrum.

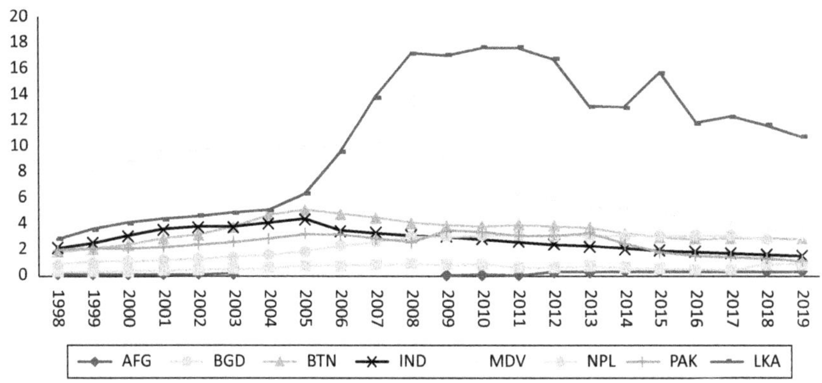

Figure 11.5 Fixed Telephone Subscription (per 100 People) Across South Asia Note: AFG: Afghanistan, BGD: Bangladesh, BTN: Bhutan: IND: India, MDV: Maldives, NPL: Nepal, PAK: Pakistan and LKA: Sri Lanka. Source: Same as Figure 11.1.

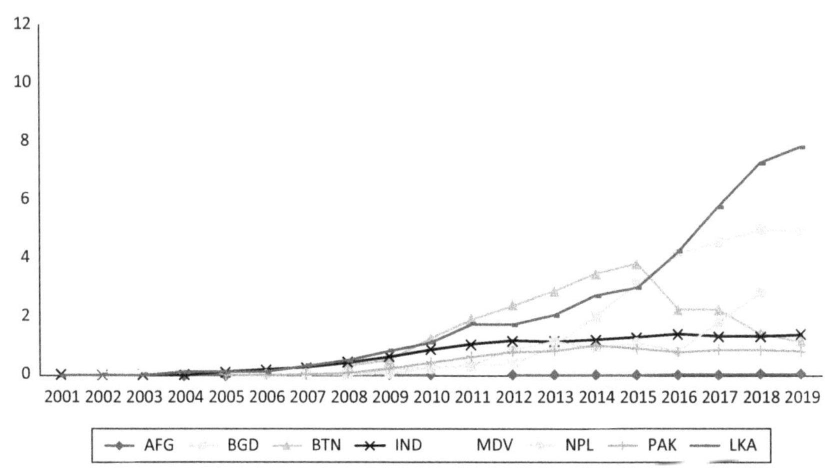

Figure 11.6 Fixed Broadband Subscriptions (per 100 People) Across South Asia Source: Same as Figure 11.1.

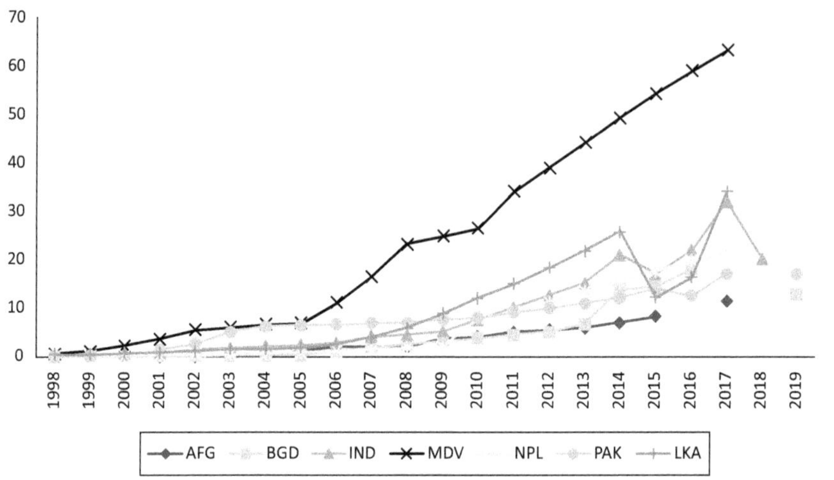

Figure 11.7 Individuals Using the Internet (% of Population) Across South Asia
Source: Same as Figure 11.1.

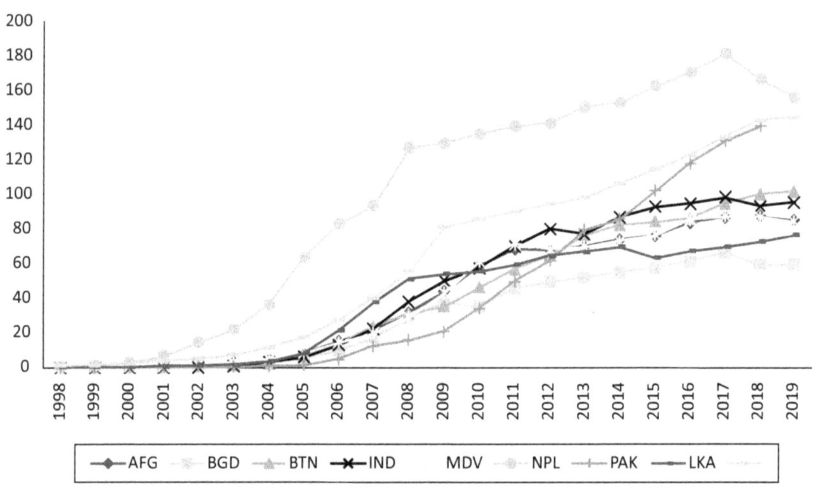

Figure 11.8 Mobile Cellular Subscriptions (per 100 People) Across South Asia
Source: Same as Figure 11.1.

Digital Divide: The Indian Case

The discussion above highlights the north–south and the south–south divide in accessing ICTs. We now turn our attention to India. Being the second most populous nation with a significant demographic advantage in terms of age and an English-speaking populace, India has become a major player in the global economy. It was the second fastest growing nation (after China), with more than 50 per cent contribution to growth coming from the services sector (GoI, 2021). Over the past two decades, there has been a concerted push for wider adoption of digitisation and greater access to ICT services among its citizens, particularly for the rural population.

Providing information link between urban and rural areas and among rural residents helps in overcoming the distance barrier that hampers rural development. It is widely agreed that access to information is crucial for development activities, including agriculture. If information is critical to the development process, then ICTs, as a medium of sharing information, do not just connect people, but are a vital link in the development process. ICTs can play a significant role in rural areas where alternative means of obtaining and conveying information, like personal contact, transport and postal services, are likely to be less accessible.

Rural Indian population face the double jeopardy of not only having inadequate roads and public transport facilities and other infrastructure, as compared to urban areas, but also being deprived of many ICT services. Economic imbalances are not only intensified but also inequalities, which have achieved staggering proportions, increases. Low-cost technologies, like wireless, are now available at reasonable prices in the rural areas. The advent of low-cost wireless technologies and business innovations such as pre-pay options have reduced the entry price at the lower end of the market and enabled easy access to multiple services, especially in rural areas, where fixed telephone infrastructure is poor.

However, this was not always the case. Providing every village in India with a single connection used to be a continuing target of policymakers. Prior to the 1980s, the policymakers were of the view that ordinary citizens had no need of telecommunication utilities and thus investment in telecommunications should be restricted to serve government and few other essential needs. With economic reforms, this sector was opened up to private players. Through competition and regulation, the accessibility of telecommunication services has improved in the urban areas. It was not until the Eight Five Year Plan (1992–1997) that there was some attention given to roll out of rural telephone lines. The Department of Telecommunications (DoT) was tasked with covering every village with at least one telephone. For a detailed discussion on the political economy behind providing telecommunications services in rural areas, one can refer to Dossani (2003), Desai (2006) and Tangirala (2019) among others.

There has been a significant improvement in provision of telecommunication services in rural areas. As per the data provided by the Telecom Regulatory Authority of India (TRAI), the rural subscriber base has increased significantly from 4.57 million in March 2007 to 521.51 million by March 2020 and to 525.92 million at the end of December 2020[3]. Out of the total subscribers in India, as of December 2020, rural wireless subscribers were 44.65 per cent while the urban wireless subscribers were 53.64 per cent. The same for wireline subscribers was 0.15 per cent and 1.55 per cent for rural and urban subscribers, respectively[4]. It is widely believed that the main growth in terms of access to telecommunications and other ICT services has largely come from the wireless segment in the rural areas.

Overall teledensity[5] is on the lower side among most of the South Asian countries. India is the biggest economy among the South Asian economies and has the second largest telecommunications network (after China)[6]. The total subscriber base, combination of both wireline and wireless subscribers, has reached 1203.47 million by April 2021 with a monthly growth rate of 0.19 per cent for April 2021. The urban subscriber base was 664.34 million while the rural subscriber base was 539.14 million by April 2021. The distinguishing feature in this data is that the monthly growth rate for urban areas was 0.08 per cent whereas that for rural areas was 0.32 per cent during April 2021[7]. A similar trend in growth rate has been seen across various months where rural monthly growth rates have outstripped urban growth rates[8]. While some may attribute this to the global pandemic, even if we look at the data in the pre-pandemic period in India, we find that monthly growth rates of rural subscribers have surpassed the growth rate of urban subscribers.

Rural monthly growth rate surpassing urban monthly growth rate augurs well for the provision of ICT services. However, it cannot be denied that there are significant disparities extant within India. The large number of telecommunication subscribers in India masks a disconcerting reality in India – there exists, at times huge, gaps in the penetration of ICT services across India. The evidence of this can be seen in the access to telecommunication services across India. Table 11.2 shows the number of telephone subscribers and teledensity across the length and breadth of this country as of December 2020. While for most states total subscribers in urban areas exceed those in rural areas, it is interesting that for three most populous states in India – Uttar Pradesh, Bihar and Rajasthan – among some other small states, rural subscribers are greater than urban subscribers. This is largely due to the higher concentration of rural population in these states. It also shows the lack of uniform access to telecommunication services across India. To mitigate the difference in absolute numbers due to size and/or population of a particular area, we use teledensity data. The difference across states can also be seen in teledensity numbers. The urban teledensity is higher than rural teledensity across states and union territories across India with the exception of Goa, Kerala, Mizoram, Nagaland, Sikkim and Dadra and Nagar Haveli & Daman and Diu. For states like Bihar, Jharkhand and Uttar Pradesh, there is significant scope in improving the accessibility of ICTs through telecommunication services. The overall teledensity numbers highlight the inequality between rural and urban India in terms of access to telecommunication services.

Data shown in Table 11.2 gives a panoramic view of the difference in access to telecommunication services across India. The numbers have

Table 11.2 State-Wise Telephone Subscribers and Teledensity (as of December 2000)

	Telephone Subscribers (Million)			*Teledensity (%)*		
	Total	*Rural*	*Urban*	*Total*	*Rural*	*Urban*
State						
Andhra Pradesh	46.48	26.11	20.37	88.14	129.86	240.41
Arunachal Pradesh	1.34	0.85	0.49	87.7	74.32	127.54
Assam	24.17	15.19	8.98	69.1	51.28	167.79
Bihar	62.88	43.77	19.11	51.21	40.55	128.58
Chhattisgarh	20.61	10.07	10.54	70.04	46.53	135.47
Goa	2.74	0.94	1.8	175.81	226.46	157.51
Gujarat	67.97	27.05	40.92	97.6	74.21	123.3
Haryana	33.34	12.1	21.24	113.35	69.53	178.88
Himachal Pradesh	11.14	7.52	3.62	150.86	113.45	478.12
Jharkhand	22.22	11.83	10.4	57.9	41.54	104.96
Karnataka	69.41	27.57	41.84	103.97	72.92	144.51
Kerala	45.89	21.2	24.69	129.42	203.66	98.57
Madhya Pradesh	55.59	24.33	31.25	65.92	40.5	128.9
Maharashtra (incl. Mumbai)	129.81	43.89	85.92	104.48	67.85	144.25
Manipur	2.37	1.08	1.28	74.95	50.33	127.66
Meghalaya	2.36	1.41	0.95	81.8	54.07	140.37
Mizoram	1.39	0.65	0.74	114.29	117.25	111.82
Nagaland	1.67	0.97	0.7	76.3	77.59	74.57
Odisha	33.72	21.91	11.81	76.63	61.08	145.27
Punjab	36.71	13.13	23.57	121.15	73.51	189.59
Rajasthan	65.63	35.56	30.07	82.96	60.99	144.5
Sikkim	0.99	0.58	0.41	146.17	153.7	136.79
Tamil Nadu	81.23	23.54	57.68	106.4	65.22	143.32
Telangana	42.51	18.29	24.22	112.82	90.4	138.81
Tripura	3.19	1.58	1.61	78.47	61.61	107.43
Uttar Pradesh	156.73	84.51	72.23	68.02	48.08	132.18
Uttarakhand	12.97	6.52	6.45	114.04	88.06	162.53
West Bengal (incl. Kolkata)	80.58	35.19	45.39	82.2	55.99	129.04
Union Territories						
Andaman & Nicobar Islands	0.42	0.16	0.26	105.27	68.93	153.65
Chandigarh	1.7	0.04	1.66	140.73	-	-
Dadra and Nagar Haveli & Daman and Diu	0.78	0.25	0.53	73.16	107.66	63.65
Delhi	42.09	2.19	39.9	205.22	-	-
Jammu & Kashmir and Ladakh	11.96	5.58	6.38	89.32	59.47	159
Lakshadweep	0.09	0.04	0.047	125.88	-	-
Puducherry	1.16	0.33	0.83	74.17	70.2	75.89
Total	**1173.83**	**525.92**	**647.9**	**86.38**	**59.05**	**138.34**

Note: For Chandigarh, Delhi and Lakshadweep, there is no distinction between urban and rural areas.
Source: TRAI, The Indian Telecom Services Performance Indicators – Oct-Dec 2020.

improved significantly. However, if we look at teledensity data over the years, we can see that it is only in the last few years that the overall rural-urban gap in access to telecommunication services has declined. Figure 11.9 shows the overall teledensity as well as rural and urban teledensity for the period of 1996–2021. Figure 11.10 plots the gap in urban and rural teledensity over the same period.

The overall teledensity in India has improved from 0.2 in 1948 to 3.95 in 1996, reaching a high of 93.27 in 2018. Ever since then there has been

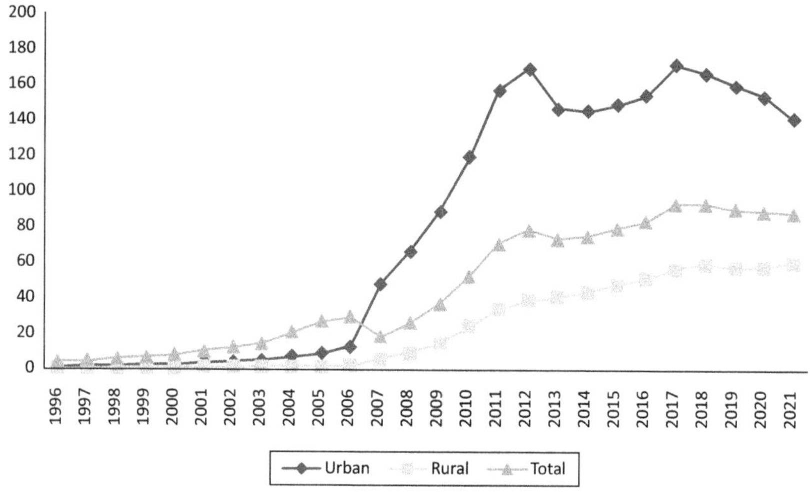

Figure 11.9 Teledensity in India: 1996-2021 (%) Source: Compiled by the author from Annual Reports of DoT and TRAI, various years.

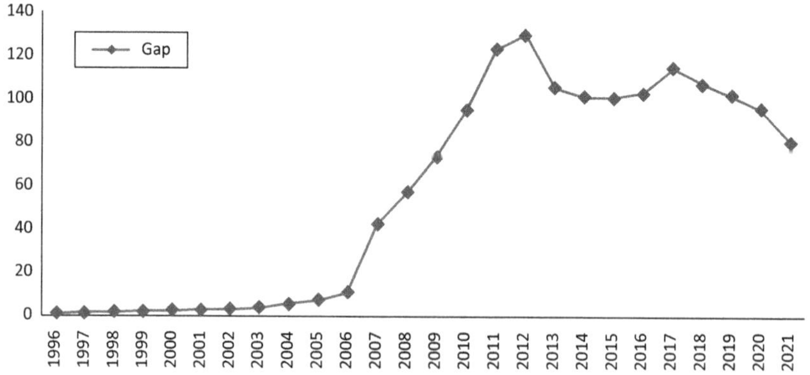

Figure 11.10 Rural-Urban Teledensity Gap 1996-2021 (%) Source: Same as Figure 11.9.

a marginal fall in the overall teledensity. Urban teledensity saw a sharp increase from 2006, where it overtook the overall teledensity figures, up until 2012. This has generally been attributed to increasing affordability of telecommunication services across the nation. Incoming calls became free, call rates also fell and more and more service providers started offering low-cost pre-paid schemes for a wide range of customers. There was some volatility from 2012; however, teledensity had again started to increase and reached a maximum of 171.5 per cent in 2017. Since then, there has been a secular decline in the urban teledensity numbers. This can be attributed to the saturation among the urban consumers in terms of mobile devices. With services like mobile number portability (MNP),[9] customers are not changing their mobile numbers, just their operator. This has also contributed to the decline in urban teledensity.

Better affordability of telecommunication services and devices and access to low-cost wireless technologies for the service providers have resulted in a secular increase in rural teledensity numbers. Rural teledensity also improved significantly from 2006. However, the rate of improvement has not been in the same league as their urban counterparts. Despite several policy initiatives to promote greater penetration of telecommunication service in rural areas, growth in teledensity has been skewed in favour of urban areas. This is highlighted in Figure 11.10. The graph in Figure 11.10 almost follows the same trajectory as the urban teledensity graph in Figure 11.9. The gap in accessing telecommunication services increased significantly since 2006. It's only over the last few years that we see that the inequities have been reducing.

One of the fundamental reasons for this deficiency in telecommunication services in rural areas was the lack of seriousness on part of policymakers. The incumbent used the pretext of connecting rural areas with telephones to counter attempts to introduce competition. Even with the advent of economic reforms, the focus of policymakers remained largely on improving urban connectivity, particularly in the wireless segment. It is generally agreed that diffusion of wireless technology is less costly than wireline technology in reducing the last mile connectivity issues. Being a natural monopoly, the provision of wireline services incurs a huge sunk cost. With low population density and lack of demand in rural areas, they were not attractive to private players. While the government stepped in to connect all villages, it used to cross-subsidise from the revenue earned from long-distance calling. With the formation of TRAI and the introduction of the New Telecom Policy, 1999, (NTP 99) the ability of incumbent to generate sufficient revenue to cross-subsidise rural telephones was reduced.

As an alternative source of revenue, Universal Service Obligation Fund (USF)[10] was established. Government set up the USF within DoT by amending the Indian Telegraph Act of 1985, in 2003, which became operational on April 1, 2004, making USF a non-lapsable fund. Earlier the expenditure on rural connections relied entirely on the incumbent, now it would have a steady source of finance. The other source for generating revenues for financing building of infrastructure was the Access Deficit Charge (ADC). ADCs were essentially the fees paid by private entrants to the incumbent presuming that the basic service providers face unprofitable social service obligations and should therefore be compensated by private entrants who are free to seek out a profitable subscriber base. ADCs, which were considered to be inefficient and used to put additional burden on a new entrant, were gradually phased out and removed by October 2008[11].

Support to the incumbent is necessary for their rural wireline operations as about 95.19 per cent of lines belong to Bharat Sanchar Nigam Limited (BSNL) – corporate arm of DoT. They are largely unprofitable for the incumbent as the population density is low in rural areas and, more often, there is non-payment of bills and political compulsions in rural areas don't allow for penal provisions like disconnection of telephone lines. In the wireless segment, it's the private operators who hold the edge. Since most of the customers are in the pre-paid category, the profitability of private players in providing rural wireless services is not affected much by sunk costs. The only variable that affects costs in the wireless segment is the low population density in rural areas. Hence, setting up infrastructure to provide wireless services to the entire population in a village requires more expenditure per head than in urban areas. Nonetheless, three factors have been crucial in proliferation of wireless technology in rural areas. One is the saturation occurring in the urban segment which has forced service providers to look at smaller towns and towards rural areas. Second is the increased competition to capture this untapped market and fear of losing market share. And third is the reduction in costs of setting up telecom towers[12]. Of course, there has been a concerted policy push from the policymakers in this regard. As a result, we are witnessing an increasing trend in the penetration of telecommunication services in rural areas.

Table 11.3 provides a breakup of subscribers in terms of wireless and wireline subscribers for urban and rural areas across states and union territories. The table shows that for the majority of the states, the share of rural wireless subscribers is less than the share of urban wireless subscribers. Even in the wireline segment, not only does the same trend continue, but is more dominant. Only in Himachal Pradesh and Kerala do we find that the share of rural wireline subscribers is greater than their urban counterparts. However, over the years, the share of rural subscribers in the wireless segment has been increasing while that of the wireline subscribers has been falling (Figures 11.11 and 11.12). This shows that more and more residents in the rural areas are adopting wireless technology to access telecommunication services. While this augurs well for rural penetration of telecommunication services, the fall in share of rural wireline subscribers might create hurdles in providing broadband internet connection in rural areas.

As argued earlier, the entire world is increasingly becoming online. Lack of access to the internet implies being left behind in the development

Table 11.3 State-Wise Wireless and Wireline Subscribers and Teledensity (as of December 2020)

	Wireless Subscribers (in Millions)			*% of Rural Wireless Subscribers*	*Wireless Teledensity (%)*			*Wireline Subscribers (in Millions)*			*% of Rural Wireline Subscribers*	*Wireline Teledensity (%)*		
	Total	*Rural*	*Urban*		*Total*	*Rural*	*Urban*	*Total*	*Rural*	*Urban*		*Total*	*Rural*	*Urban*
State														
Andhra Pradesh	45.74	26.02	19.72	56.89	86.72	76.1	106.29	0.75	0.09	0.65	12.00	2.61	0.34	6.8
Arunachal Pradesh	1.32	0.85	0.47	64.39	86.38	73.98	123.31	0.02	0.00	0.02	0.00	1.32	0.34	4.23
Assam	24.05	15.18	8.87	63.12	68.74	51.23	165.72	0.13	0.02	0.11	15.38	0.36	0.05	2.07
Bihar	62.78	43.75	19.03	69.69	51.13	40.54	128.00	0.10	0.02	0.09	20.00	0.08	0.01	0.58
Chhattisgarh	20.47	10.07	10.40	49.19	69.54	46.50	133.70	0.15	0.01	0.14	6.67	0.49	0.04	1.77
Goa	2.66	0.91	1.75	34.21	170.88	220.90	152.81	0.08	0.02	0.05	25.00	4.98	5.56	4.70
Gujarat	67.01	26.98	40.03	40.26	96.23	74.03	120.62	0.96	0.07	0.89	7.29	1.88	0.18	2.68
Haryana	33.02	12.07	20.96	36.55	112.27	69.32	174.52	0.32	0.03	0.28	9.38	1.08	0.20	2.86
Himachal Pradesh	11.05	7.47	3.58	67.60	149.66	112.74	472.52	0.09	0.05	0.04	55.56	1.21	0.71	5.59
Jharkhand	22.11	11.82	10.29	53.46	57.61	41.51	103.90	0.11	0.01	0.11	9.09	0.29	0.02	1.06
Karnataka	67.23	27.48	39.75	40.87	110.71	72.69	137.28	2.18	0.09	2.09	4.13	8.26	0.23	7.23
Kerala	44.60	20.50	24.10	45.96	125.77	196.89	96.21	1.29	0.70	0.59	54.26	8.65	6.77	2.86
Madhya Pradesh	55.04	24.32	30.72	44.19	65.27	40.48	126.68	0.55	0.01	0.54	1.82	0.65	0.02	2.21
Maharashtra (incl. Mumbai)	125.60	43.75	81.85	34.83	101.09	67.63	137.42	4.21	0.14	4.07	3.33	8.89	0.22	6.83
Manipur	2.35	1.08	1.27	45.96	74.30	50.21	126.16	0.02	0.00	0.02	0.00	0.56	0.12	1.50
Meghalaya	2.34	1.41	0.93	60.26	71.19	54.00	137.67	0.02	0.00	0.02	10.00	0.61	0.07	2.70
Mizoram	1.38	0.65	0.73	47.10	113.32	117.12	110.15	0.01	0.00	0.01	10.00	0.97	0.13	1.67
Nagaland	1.66	0.97	69.00	58.43	75.95	77.56	72.79	0.01	0.00	0.01	0.00	0.85	0.03	0.78
Odisha	33.51	21.88	11.64	65.29	76.16	60.99	143.15	0.21	0.03	0.17	14.29	0.47	0.10	2.21
Punjab	36.18	13.03	23.15	36.01	119.41	72.93	186.19	0.53	0.10	0.42	18.87	1.74	0.58	3.40
Rajasthan	65.16	35.53	29.64	54.53	82.36	60.93	142.40	0.47	0.03	0.44	6.38	0.59	0.05	2.10
Sikkim	0.98	0.58	0.41	59.18	145.49	153.64	135.34	0.00	0.00	0.00	0.00	0.68	0.06	1.45
Tamil Nadu	79.34	23.33	56.01	29.41	103.93	64.63	139.17	1.88	0.21	1.67	11.17	2.47	0.59	4.15

(Continued)

Table 11.3 Continued

	Wireless Subscribers (in Millions)			*% of Rural Wireless Subscribers*	*Wireless Teledensity (%)*			*Wireline Subscribers (in Millions)*			*% of Rural Wireline Subscribers*	*Wireline Teledensity (%)*		
	Total	*Rural*	*Urban*		*Total*	*Rural*	*Urban*	*Total*	*Rural*	*Urban*		*Total*	*Rural*	*Urban*
Telangana	41.88	18.26	23.62	43.60	111.14	90.28	135.33	0.63	0.02	0.61	3.17	1.68	0.12	3.48
Tripura	3.17	1.58	1.59	49.84	77.91	61.54	106.05	0.02	0.00	0.02	0.00	0.55	0.07	1.38
Uttar Pradesh	156.07	84.46	71.61	54.12	67.73	48.05	131.04	0.67	0.05	0.62	7.46	0.29	0.08	1.14
Uttarakhand	12.87	6.52	6.36	50.66	112.16	87.94	160.24	0.10	0.01	0.09	10.00	0.88	0.11	2.30
West Bengal (incl. Kolkata)	79.69	35.12	44.57	44.07	81.30	55.88	126.70	0.89	0.07	0.82	7.87	0.91	0.11	2.34
Union Territories														
Andaman & Nicobar Islands	0.4	0.15	0.25	37.50	101.06	65.95	147.8	0.02	0.01	0.01	50.00	4.21	2.98	5.85
Chandigarh	1.53	0.04	1.5	2.61	127.1	-	-	0.16	0.001	0.16	0.63	18.68	26.08	13.59
Dadra and Nagar Haveli & Daman and Diu	0.78	0.24	0.53	30.77	72.73	106.84	63.33	0.005	0.002	0.003	40.00	0.48	0.82	0.32
Delhi	38.8	2.19	36.61	5.64	189.19	-	-	3.29	0	3.29	0.00	16.03	0.18	16.13
Jammu & Kashmir	11.33	5.39	5.94	47.57	84.61	57.45	148.05	0.16	0.01	0.15	6.25	0.59	0.05	1.85
Ladakh	0.47	0.18	0.29	38.30	163.48	89.82	332.56							
Lakshadweep	0.08	0.04	0.04	50.00	119.48	-	-	0.004	0.002	0.003	50.00	6.4	79.62	3.99
Puducherry	1.12	0.33	0.8	29.46	71.72	69.02	72.88	0.04	0.01	0.03	25.00	2.46	1.18	3.01
Total	1153.77	524.11	629.67	45.43	84.9	58.85	134.44	20.05	1.81	18.24	9.03	1.48	0.2	3.89

Note: For Chandigarh, Delhi and Lakshadweep, there is no distinction of urban and rural areas.
Source: Same as Table 11.2 and authors own calculations.

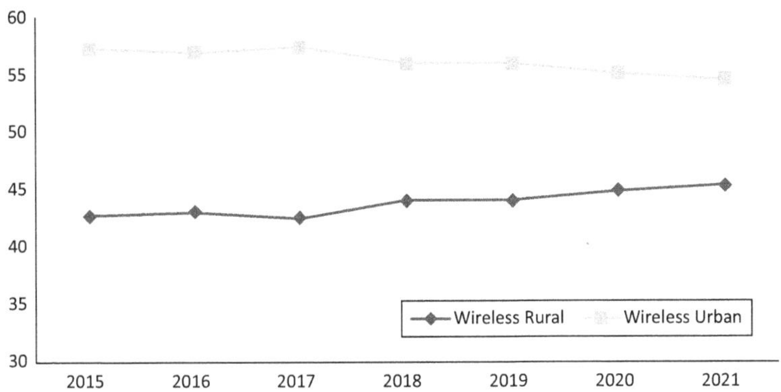

Figure 11.11 Share of Wireless Subscribers (%) Note: Date pertains to financial years. Source: Compiled by the author from TRAI, Annual Report, various years.

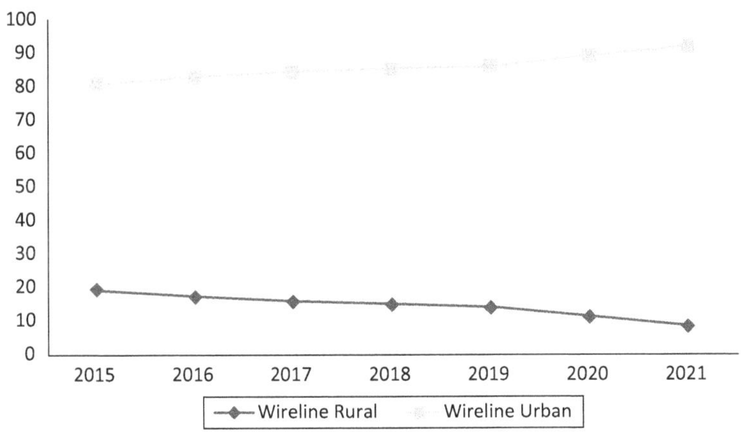

Figure 11.12 Share of Wireline Subscribers (%) Note: Date pertains to financial years. Source: Same as Figure 11.11.

process. This is particularly true for rural areas. However, there has been a lack of affordable and quality internet services within rural areas in India for a long period of time. Disaggregated data for urban and rural internet subscribers is available only from 2015 (Table 11.4). The total number of internet subscribers in India has more than doubled as of March 2020 as compared to March 2015. The same is true for numbers in urban and rural areas. However, if we look at the number of internet subscribers per 100 population, we see that while there has been a tremendous growth in urban areas where the value has reached almost 100, in rural areas approximately only one in three subscribers have internet subscriptions.

Table 11.4 Internet Subscribers in India

Year (as of 31 March)	*Total Internet Subscribers (in Million)*			*Internet Subscribers (per 100 Population)*		
	Total	*Urban*	*Rural*	*Total*	*Urban*	*Rural*
2015	302.35	194.79	107.57	24.09	50.15	12.41
2016	342.65	230.71	111.94	26.08	58.28	12.8
2017	422.19	285.68	136.52	32.86	70.83	15.49
2018	493.96	348.13	145.83	38.02	84.74	16.41
2019	636.73	409.72	227.01	48.48	97.94	25.36
2020	743.19	457.23	285.97	55.12	99.12	32.24

Source: Compiled by author from TRAI, Annual Reports, various years.

According to the Indian Telecom Services Performance Indicators, October–December 2020, published by TRAI, as of December 2020, 96.71 per cent of subscribers are using mobile devices for accessing the internet whereas the share of wired internet subscribers was 3.21 per cent of total internet subscribers. While 93.99 per cent of total internet subscribers are using broadband services[13] for accessing the internet, 6.01 per cent were narrowband subscribers. Among the total broadband subscribers, 96.93 per cent constituted mobile device (phone + dongle) users. The corresponding figure among narrowband subscribers was 93.2 per cent. Considering these facts along with those given in Tables 11.3 and 11.4, we can safely conclude that most of the internet subscribers in rural areas are wireless broadband subscribers. There is a very small presence of wireline internet access in rural areas.

Numbers vary hugely across India. This can be seen from Figure 11.13 which shows the rural-urban gap in internet subscribers in absolute numbers as well as per 100 population across different service areas in the country. The variations in access to the internet in urban and rural areas are visible not only at the absolute level but also in percentage terms. While there exist considerable variations in the extent of the gap in the absolute sense, with states like Bihar and Odisha showing better access to the internet in rural areas, the variations in percentage terms seem to be relatively uniform across states with Delhi, Kerala and Himachal Pradesh as the outlier states. Absolute numbers in themselves hide the extent of the gap between rural and urban areas owing to the difference in population numbers across the states. In percentage terms, this difference comes to the forefront.

The above discussion highlights the 'teledensity divide' between rural and urban areas. As discussed earlier, one of the fundamental causes of the digital divide is the lack of accessibility to ICTs. The National Sample Survey 75th Round Report on Household Social Consumption on Education[14] (NSS 75th Round) in India illustrates the lack of accessibility to ICTs among households in India. Figure 11.14 shows that a significantly higher number

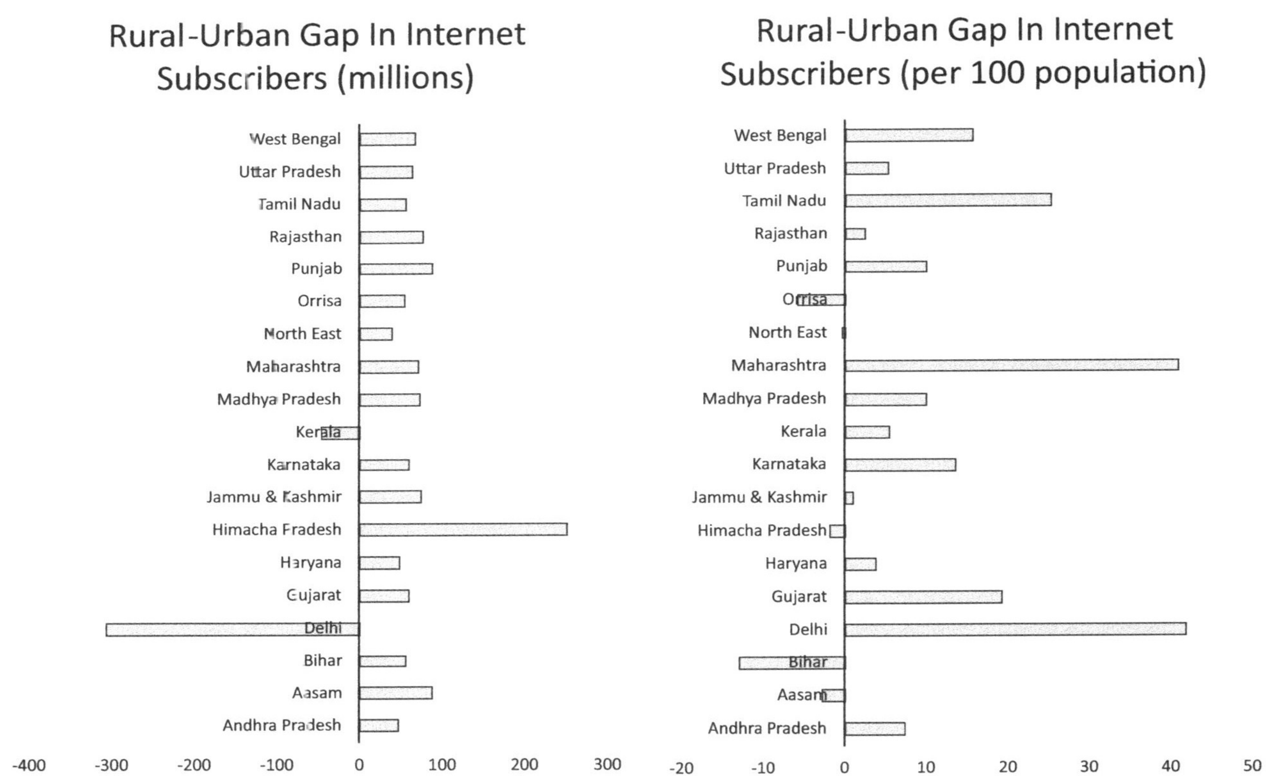

Figure 11.13 Service Area Wise Rural-Urban Gap in Internet Subscribers (as of December 2020) Note: West Bengal includes Kolkata; Maharashtra includes Mumbai and Uttar Pradesh is UP (East) and UP (West) combined. The difference is of urban–rural values. Source: Computed by author from TRAI, Indian Telecom Services Performance Indicators, October–December 2020.

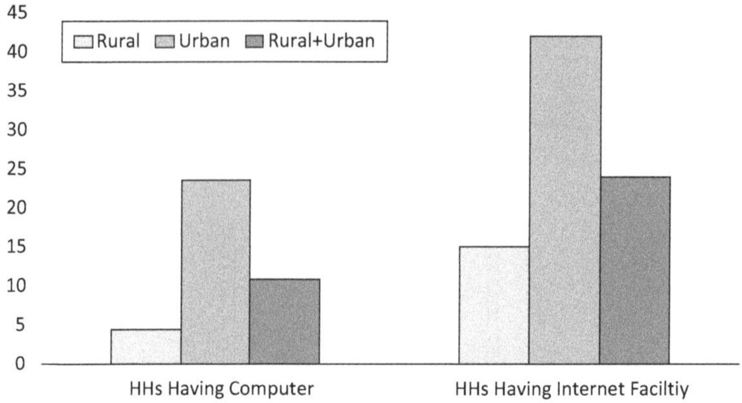

Figure 11.14 Households With Computer and Internet Facilities (All India) (%) Note: HHs stands for households. Source: NSS Report No. 585: Household Social Consumption on Education in India.

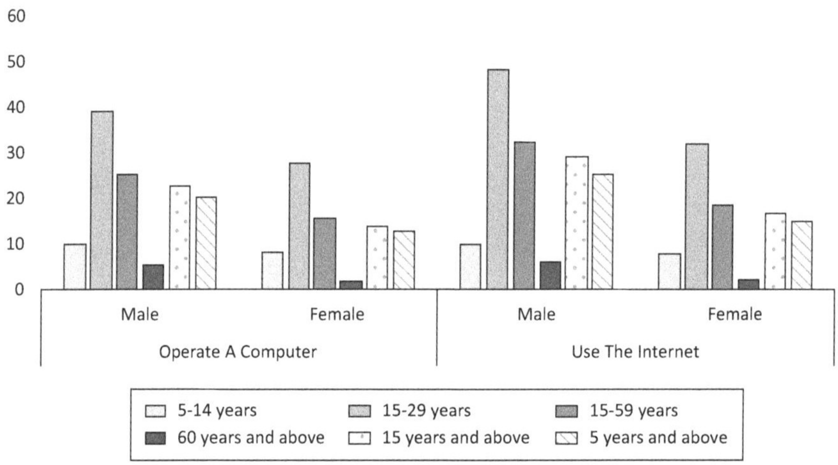

Figure 11.15 Persons Across Age Groups Who Are Able to Operate a Computer and Use the Internet for Males and Females (%) Source: Same as Figure 11.14.

of households in urban areas own a computer and have access to internet facilities. As we move up the income level, we find that for both rural and urban areas the percentage of households with a computer and having access to the internet increases, with the increase more significant in the urban areas[15].

Accessibility is one aspect, ability to use is another. After all, if you have a computer with internet and do not know how to use it, its availability amounts to nothing. Figure 11.15 highlights this lack of inability to use

ICTs, not only across age groups but also across gender. Males are more adept in using the internet as well as operating a computer than females. For both males and females, the 15–29 age group had the highest values. The 60+ age group had a much lower ability to use ICTs than the younger generation. This difference becomes more stark when we analyse the rural-urban variations. The urban male has a significantly higher ability to use ICTs as compared to females across all age groups. The above analysis puts into context the 'gender divide' within the digital divide in access to ICTs in India where females neither have proper access to ICTs nor are trained and educated in their use. Similar trends are also seen across different states of India with regard to the above-mentioned indicators[16].

For the first time, the National Family Health Survey (NFHS) collected data on variations in access to ICTs across 22 states and union territories in its 5th Round of survey for the period 2018–2020 (NFHS-5) as shown in Table 11.5. The data further highlights the gender divide in access to ICTs in India. Across the sample, we see that a significant number of women have not used the internet even once. In some states, like Bihar, close to 80 per cent of women and more than 80 per cent of rural women have never used the internet. The numbers for females are again lower than their urban counterparts across the sample. For many states and union territories, exclusive ownership and usage of a mobile phone by women is less than their urban counterparts. It is not only the fact that they have never used an internet facility, females and particularly rural females are much lower in the pecking order within a family, when it comes to even owning a mobile phone.

Government Policies to Bridge the Digital Divide: A Critical Analysis

The analysis so far has brought out the digital divide at the global level and across India. We now focus on analysing the policy initiatives to reduce this divide in India. For a very long time, providing telephones to the larger public was not a priority of the governments. With policy changes starting from the 1980s, public provisioning of telephones improved. However, due to technology constraints, the number of telephones installed was not able to keep pace with the demand. In 1990, the waiting time for telephones was 50 months (Desai, 2006). While the waiting time came down to 13 months by 1996 (Desai, 2006), it was realised that the public sector will not be able to keep up with the demand. This ushered in an era of private players in the telecommunications market thus breaking the government monopoly in telecommunication services.

While licenses allotted to private players and their related conditions got embroiled in legal disputes, the government went ahead and established a regulator – TRAI – in March 1997, notwithstanding the opposition by the incumbent (DoT). Attempts by TRAI to discipline the incumbent and

Table 11.5 Access to ICTs

State/UTs	*Women Who Have Ever Used the Internet (%)*			*Men Who Have Ever Used the Internet (%)*			*Women Having a Mobile Phone That They Themselves Use (%)*		
	Urban	*Rural*	*Total*	*Urban*	*Rural*	*Total*	*Urban*	*Rural*	*Total*
Andaman and Nicobar Islands	44.1	27.9	34.8	54.6	41.1	46.6	80.8	80.9	80.8
Andhra Pradesh	33.9	15.4	21	65.1	41.5	48.8	67.4	40.9	48.9
Assam	49	24.4	28.2	67.4	37.8	42.3	75.4	53.9	57.2
Bihar	38.4	17	20.6	58.4	39.4	43.6	61.8	49.3	51.4
Dadra & Nagar Haveli and Daman & Diu	49.4	23.8	36.7	76.2	61.3	68.3	75.4	45.5	60.5
Goa	78.1	68.3	73.7	86.1	76.6	82.9	94.5	87.1	91.2
Gujarat	48.9	17.5	30.8	72.9	48	58.9	66	36.2	48.8
Himachal Pradesh	78.9	45.2	49.7	83.7	65.1	67.9	90.9	77.8	79.5
Jammu & Kashmir	55	38.9	43.3	79.4	68.8	72	80.4	73.3	75.2
Karnataka	50.1	24.8	35	71.5	55.6	62.4	74.2	52.4	61.8
Kerala	64.9	57.5	61.1	78.3	74.2	76.1	86.2	86.9	86.6
Lakshadweep	61.8	36	56.4	81.5	77	80.3	85.1	80.1	84
Ladakh	66.5	54	56.4	82.9	64.3	67.8	80.8	81.2	81.2
Maharashtra	54.3	23.7	38	76.8	47.2	61.5	68.2	43.1	54.8
Meghalaya	57.8	28	34.7	59.2	38.5	42.1	78.2	64.3	67.5
Manipur	50.8	40.4	44.8	81.5	68.2	73.9	77.8	68.2	72.2
Mizoram	83.8	48	67.6	92.7	63.9	79.7	91.8	70.6	82.3
Nagaland	66.5	40.3	49.9	81	55.2	64.6	93	76.3	82.5
Sikkim	90	68.1	76.7	94.2	69.5	78.2	96.9	83.3	88.6
Telangana	43.9	15.8	26.5	72.3	46.7	57.4	75.2	50.6	60
Tripura	36.6	17.7	22.9	47	45.2	45.7	66.2	48	53.1
West Bengal	48.1	14	25.5	64.6	38.3	46.7	71.9	39.1	50.1

Source: Compiled by the author from NFHS-5, 2019-20, State/Union Territories Fact Sheets, Phase-I.

provide a more level-playing field for the new entrants were thwarted by unfavourable verdicts from the Delhi High Court in favour of the incumbent. With the private operators in a perilous financial position, the government came out with the NTP 99, which superseded the National Telecom Policy 1994 (NTP 94)[17]. It restored the powers of TRAI. However, it lacked legislative sanction and could be challenged in courts. To counter such possibilities, the government, through an ordinance, set up a Telecom Disputes Settlement and Appellate Tribunal (TDSAT) to hear appeals against the directions of TRAI and adjudicate disputes. The verdict of TDSAT could only be appealed in the Supreme Court. It also brought DoT under TRAI's directive powers and gave statutory instructions to the government to consult TRAI on matters relating to licensing.

The ordinance breathed new life into TRAI. It went about trying to increase competition in the telecommunications sector. While the role of policymakers cannot be undermined, it was the development and introduction of second-generation wireless technology[18] that provided a major fillip to the penetration of ICT services across India. The growth rate in the subscriber base of private operators increased from 38.64 per cent in 1999 to 64.32 per cent in 2008[19]. While that of public operators decreased from 21.29 per cent to 11.41 per cent over the same period. As of December 2020, the share of private operators has increased to 88.74 per cent, and that of public operators has remained almost stagnant at 11.26 per cent[20]. As has been discussed earlier, most of the increase in subscribers has come in the wireless segment, dominated by private players.

While the penetration of ICTs increased substantially, most of the growth still remains concentrated in urban areas. In the rural areas, the objective of earlier policies has been to connect every village with a Village Public Telephone (VPT). It was only after the NTP 99 that the percentage of villages covered by VPTs increased and by 2005 around 88.7 per cent of villages in India were covered by at least a VPT. With the replacement of old, inefficient and high-maintenance technologies by more efficient one and financing from USF, more and more VPTs were being installed in villages mostly by BSNL. With access to cheaper and more efficient wireless technology, rural wireless numbers have increased while that of rural wireline has decreased. Out of the 5,93,731 inhabited villages in India as per the census 2021, only 68,606 villages have VPTs[21].

NTP 99 had targeted to provide internet access to all district headquarters by 2000. It also aimed to provide high-speed data and multimedia capability using technologies including ISDN[22] to all towns with a population greater than 0.2 million by 2002[23]. Both of these targets were not achieved[24]. Acknowledging the 'potential of ubiquitous Broadband service in growth of GDP and enhancement in quality of life' (Broadband Policy, 2004, Preamble), the government finalised the Broadband Policy in 2004 to accelerate the growth of broadband services. It targeted 40 million internet subscribers and 20 million broadband subscribers by 2010. Both these targets were not achieved[25]. Realising the importance of ICTs in economic development, TRAI first came out with a consultation paper regarding broadband penetration in India in 2010[26] followed by its recommendations in December 2010[27]. Most of its recommendations were incorporated in the National Telecom Policy, 2012 (NTP 12).

With an aim to connect all the 2,50,000 Gram Panchayats (GPs) in the country through optical fibre using which the telecom service providers like mobile operators, Internet Service Providers (ISPs), cable TV operators and content providers can launch various services in rural areas government launched the National Optical Fibre Network (NOFN) in October 2011[28]. This project was to be funded by USF and project implementation was to be done through a special purpose vehicle, Bharat Broadband Network Limited (BBNL), which was incorporated in February 2012[29]. NOFN was renamed BharatNet in 2015. All the GPs were to be provided broadband connectivity by using existing fibre of central public sector undertakings – BSNL, RailTel Corporation Limited (RailTel) and Power Grid Corporation of India Limited (PGCIL)[30]. With 0.1 million GPs connected, Phase-I of the implementation of the programme was completed in December 2017 and the remaining GPs are being connected under Phase-II. By December 2020, under BharatNet (Phase-I and II) 0.163 million GPs have been connected by an optical fibre network and around 0.15 million GPs have been made service ready by laying down 0.485 million km of optical fibre cable across India. The last mile connectivity is being provided through Wi-Fi or any other suitable broadband technology at public places and government institutions. Wi-Fi hotspots have been installed at about 0.1 million GPs and 0.5 million Fibre to the Home (FTTH) have been provided with a combined data usage of over 1400 TB/month by the end of December 2020[31]. As on June 21, 2021, out of the 1,32,600 GPs for which the agencies decided to install Wi-Fi/FTTH, Wi-Fi was installed in 1,04,208 GPs with 65,074 active whereas 5,09957 FTTH connection were installed with 3,05,498 active. There were 15,71,598 active users with a data consumption of over 2700 TB for May 2021[32].

One of the main reasons for low internet penetration in India has been lack of supporting infrastructure. If you want a nation to go online, you need to provide adequate ICT facilities for it to exploit. During the 1990s, policy impetus was on providing fixed wireline telephones to people. The emphasis of this policy was mainly on urban areas. With increased competition, regulation and advancement in technology, there was wider penetration of telecommunication services, largely of wireless services and again concentrated in urban areas. This created a huge digital divide between urban and rural areas. With various policies and with some success, the government has tried to reduce this gap. However, one needs to realise that this gap is reducing largely due to saturation and a decline in the urban markets than due to rural growth of subscribers outstripping urban growth.

This gap widens when we come to internet subscribers with rural India lagging behind. Attempting to connect districts and villages through optical fibres, though a commendable effort, does not take into cognisance one very important fact – rural India is not ready for the internet revolution. According to a report by Internet and Mobile Association of India (IAMAI)[33], in 2015, only 12 per cent of the rural population had used the internet at least once per month (monthly active users) while 14 per cent had at least used the internet once in their life (ever users). Compared to 2014, when 26 per cent of users accessed the internet using the Community Service Centres (CSCs) facilitated by the government, the number had come down to only 6 per cent. The list of services utilised in CSCs in rural areas and their relative percentage is as follows: Education (27%), Government Service (22%), Commercial Services (17%), IT/Telecom Services (15%), Finance (5%), Travel (4%), Health (2%) and Agriculture Services (1%). One of the most important aspects of the IAMAI Report is that it also asked reasons for not using the internet for urban and rural areas. This has been depicted in Figures 11.16 and 11.17. More than 20 per cent of non-users in both urban and rural India believe that there is no need for the internet. 76 per cent of non-users in rural areas are unaware of the internet. The same is 19 per cent for urban areas. Apart from the lack of awareness, affordability and ownership of ICT devices is also a main reason for non-use of the internet, particularly for rural areas.

Whereas the data pertained to 2015, can we expect similar trends in the following years? Although such a report was not published in the subsequent years, IAMAI and Nielsen brought out a report, India Internet 2019, which articulates some interesting figures. Among the internet users in India, around four per cent used the internet 4–6 days a week, 11 per cent 1–3 days a week, seven per cent once a week and 13 per cent less than once a

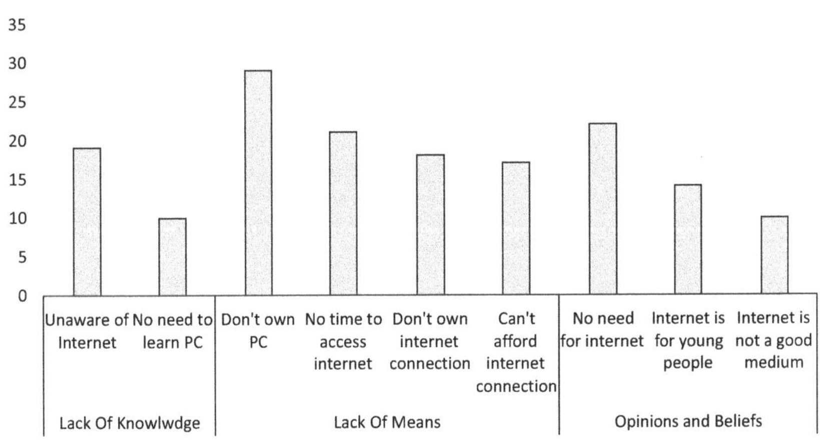

Figure 11.16 Reasons for Not Using Internet – Urban (%) Source: IAMAI, Internet in India 2015.

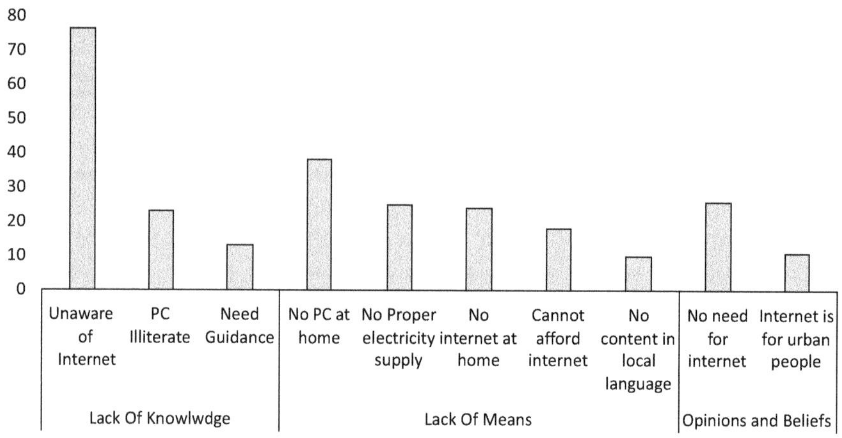

Figure 11.17 Reasons for Not Using Internet – Rural (%) Source: Same as Figure 11.16.

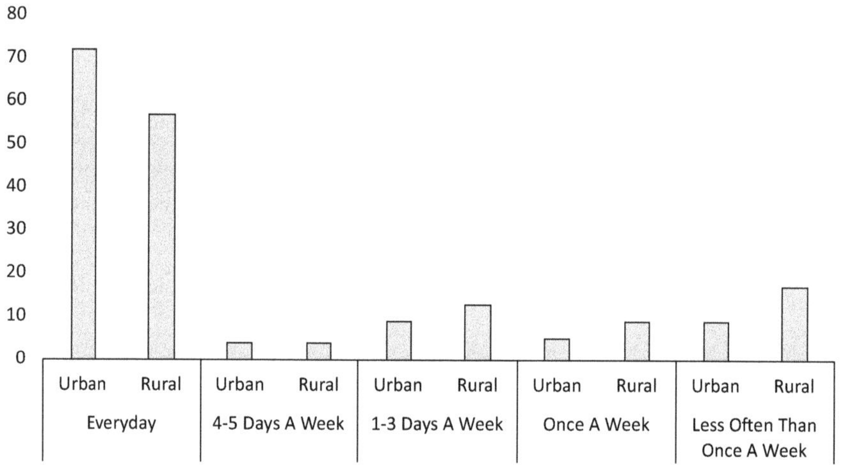

Figure 11.18 Frequency of Usage Among Internet Users – Urban–Rural (%) Source: IAMAI, India Internet 2019.

week. Sixty-five per cent of the Indian population was online every day. The details of the frequency of usage among internet across rural and urban area users are shown in Figure 11.18. India has completely bypassed the desktop-laptop generation of internet users, with 4G[34]-enabled mobile phones becoming the preferred source of accessing internet in both urban and rural India. While most of the internet consumption happens at home, urban consumers also access the internet while travelling. The use of internet cafes for accessing the internet is low across India. A significant section of both urban and rural areas spends less than one hour accessing the internet every day.

The data tells us that a very small proportion of the rural population accesses the internet. Out of the small number of rural internet subscribers, most of them access the internet through their mobile phones. Either due to lack of awareness or due to affordability issues, a large section of rural India either is not aware of the internet or cannot afford to use the internet. Moreover, it does not use the internet every day and is 'online' for less than one hour on the days the internet is accessed. The connection of GPs with optical fibre will not contribute much in improving internet penetration simply because the rural population does not own desktop PCs, laptops or tablets. While one can argue that they can be used to create Wi-Fi hotspots, as the earlier strategy of leaving the last mile connectivity to private players did not have desired results, we have seen that not everyone accesses them. This is true particularly for the rural females who are generally not allowed to move out and about. In certain areas, there is a strict aversion to providing mobile phones to females as it is perceived to lead to moral corruption.

Even among those who can access these Wi-Fi hotspots, the main purpose is for entertainment or social media. They are either unaware of the other benefits that can be exploited from being online or are apprehensive and at times distrust some benefits, particularly those relating to financial matters. Then there is the matter of literacy. As per the NSS 75th Round, the rural literacy rate was 73.5 per cent in India. Only 24 per cent of the people in the age group of 15–29 years know how to operate a computer and around 25 per cent know how to use the internet in rural areas. If we consider all people of over five years, the numbers fall down to 9.9 per cent and 13 per cent respectively. Thus, while literacy rates are indicative numbers, they do not imply proficiency in using ICT devices and/or services.

There is also an issue of affordability. This aspect is not just in terms of being able to afford ICT devices but in terms of the costs involved in being connected. A significant section of India's rural population is not well-off. Mostly dependent on agriculture or working as contractual workers, their income levels are not high enough for them to own and operate ICT-enabled devices and be connected to the internet. A study has also shown that the broadband tariffs are higher than in rural areas largely due to higher rental fees (Kayum, 2018). Therefore, the real test of the sustainability of the Bharat Net programme lies in the adoption of this infrastructure by the rural population which goes beyond just entertainment and social media. Furthermore, low population density and lack of enough profits (due to high costs) have also led to a token presence of the private sector. ICT devices require uninterrupted power supply. While the government claims 100 per cent rural electrification, continuous power supply of sufficient wattage still needs to be fulfilled. In the absence of this, most rural populations access the internet through their mobile phones for only a small length of time as they need to save the power in their devices.

In rural areas and even in smaller towns and cities, not everyone owns a smartphone. Generally, it's the earning member of the household that owns a smartphone while others either own a feature phone or a basic phone, if any. Accessing the internet on the latter category of phones is difficult and the owners are not technically adept to handle them. In order to tackle this problem, most governments, both at the centre and states, have been distributing mobile tablets, particularly to meritorious students. While this is a good initiative, until the internet becomes affordable its usefulness is limited. While there are not many studies following up such initiatives of different governments, one such study on the much touted Aakash Tablet points out the main deficiency of such projects – poor quality of hardware with unreliable software, short life span and pedestrian content (Bapna, et al., 2020).

IAMAI conducted a review of the various digital initiatives of the government through the prism of four parameters – rise in the beneficiary of the schemes, improving increase in savings to beneficiaries and government in terms of money and time through the implementation of these schemes, improving efficiency and transparency for the people and ability of the scheme to increase welfare and employment generation[35]. While for most of the parameters there has been an improvement, the extent of the impact has been less than desirable with considerable opportunity for improvement.

Conclusion

India has the second largest telecommunications network in the world. It also has one of the lowest tariff structures globally. While there has been a spectacular increase in the subscriber base across the country, it has also created a digital divide. In the global context, India is still behind the advanced nations and even some of its neighbours. If we look within our country, we find that the divide exists not only between urban and rural areas but also among men and women in access and use of ICTs. The divide is skewed in favour of urban areas and towards the male population, particularly the urban male populace in the 15–29 age group.

The main focus of policymakers has been to improve the teledensity numbers. However, teledensity does not always give a correct picture. In urban areas, consumers own multiple devices, which pushes up the teledensity numbers but does not show the actual access to ICTs. The rural values of teledensity, though giving a clearer picture of penetration of ICT, cloaks the socio-economic divide in rural areas. The provision of VPTs largely excluded those at the lower end of the spectrum in rural areas. Most of the benefits were appropriated by either the rich or the upper caste population in villages. It was only when wireless technologies became affordable and urban markets reached a saturation point, that we see and uptick in rural penetration of telecommunication services.

With regard to internet and broadband subscribers, this study finds that more and more Indians are getting connected and going online, but largely for entertainment or for using social media. Even here, the values are higher for urban areas. However, we also see that even for urban areas there is either lack of access or knowledge or just reluctance to embrace the benefits of ICTs. In absolute numbers, more of rural India is online, but similar issues pertain there too. In order to tackle this hurdle, governments have taken many policy initiatives. Though these initiatives appear to have created a foundation for improving digitisation and increasing the penetration of ICTs across India and particularly rural India, there is a lack of supporting infrastructure as well as affordability issues for a large part of our country.

India has a demographic advantage compared to other emerging economies. In order to fully exploit this advantage, the populace must be given an impartial opportunity to become part of this increasingly digitised world. While efforts are underway to improve the level of digital education among the young, a cursory glance at the different schemes launched by the government tells us that it is highly skewed in favour of technical education in English language. With around 98 per cent of students enrolled in general courses[36], the need of the hour is to provide content that helps them successfully incorporate and take advantage that ICTs provide and in vernacular languages. The infrastructure across schools and colleges also needs to be ramped up and teachers, who are not adept in communicating via digital mediums, trained properly.

The Government of India recently launched the National Digital Communications Policy (NDCP) in 2018 with the aim to unlock the transformative power of digital communications networks - to achieve the goal of digital empowerment and improved well-being of the people of India; and towards this end, attempts to outline a set of goals, initiatives, strategies and intended policy outcomes. (GoI, 2018, para 11, pg. 15)

It aims to accomplish the following Strategic Objectives by 2022[37]:

- Provisioning of broadband for all.
- Creating four million additional jobs in the digital communications sector.
- Enhancing the contribution of the digital communications sector to eight per cent of India's GDP from ~6% in 2017.
- Propelling India to the top 50 nations in the ICT Development Index of ITU from 134 in 2017.

- Enhancing India's contribution to global value chains.
- Ensuring digital sovereignty.

Whether the targets mentioned in the NDCP, 2018 will be achieved or not remains to be seen. The policy itself states:

> It has been broadly estimated that a 10% increase in broadband penetration in a country could potentially lead to an over 1% increase in GDP. However, studies in India estimate that the impact could be significantly higher for the country, given the increased productivity and efficiency gains that are likely to accrue to the economy.
>
> (GoI, 2018, para 11, pg. 15)

The policymakers must realise that availability and access to ICTs, proliferation of telecommunication services and provisions of access and ability to use the internet are not just mere services that will help propel India farther at the global level. They should be treated as public goods and even as merit goods, particularly in rural areas, where the benefits far outweigh the costs of providing them in the long run and where, due to lack of profitability, private participation might remain muted. The State has to intervene in order to eradicate this digital divide. This is of particular significance in the present scenario where the world is under a global pandemic and with the associated conditions digitisation is increasing not only globally but also in India, accompanied with loss of employment and employment opportunities and rising income inequalities. One of the areas that has been severely affected is the education sector where the digital divide has not only raised its ugly head but also increased. Analysing the digital divide in access to education is in itself a separate topic of study and should be taken up in future.

Notes

1 International Telecommunication Union (ITU) World Telecommunication/ICT Indicators Database as accessed from https://data.worldbank.org/.
2 Some HICs are categorised as other HICs as their social indicators are not at par with the advanced countries.
3 TRAI, Annual Report – Various Years and TRAI (2021a).
4 TRAI (2021a).
5 Teledensity is defined as the number of telephone connections (fixed lines and mobile phone subscribers) per 100 inhabitants within a geographical area.
6 DoT (2021). DoT (2021b).
7 TRAI (2021d).
8 This can be seen from various telecom monthly subscription data released by TRAI.
9 Mobile number portability is a facility that allows a telecom service user to move from one operator to another operator irrespective of geographical area (e.g. Delhi to Mumbai). If a subscriber is not satisfied with the services of his current operator, he can port his mobile number to another service provider of his choice

(https://www.trai.gov.in/faqcategory/mobile-number-portability) as accessed on July 18, 2021.

10 'As per the Indian Telegraph Act 1885 (as amended in 2003 and 2006), Universal Service Obligation is defined as access to telegraph services to people in rural and remote areas at affordable and reasonable prices. In the present context, it may be said that Universal Service Obligation means providing telecommunication service to all users everywhere with a defined minimum service of specified quality at an affordable price' (pg. 32, TRAI, Annual Report 2019-20).

11 TRAI (2008a).

12 https://www.moneycontrol.com/news/business/companies/-2003597.html (as accessed on July 19, 2021)

13 Broadband connectivity is defined as 'An "always-on" data connection that is able to support interactive services including Internet access and has the capability of the minimum download speed of 256 kilo bits per second (Kbps) to an individual subscriber from the Point Of Presence (POP) of the service provider intending to provide Broadband service where multiple such individual Broadband connections are aggregated and the subscriber is able to access these interactive services including the Internet through this POP. The interactive services will exclude any services for which a separate licence is specifically required, for example, real-time voice transmission, except to the extent that it is presently permitted under ISP licence with Internet Telephony' DoT (2004). The present minimum speed is >512 Kbps for broadband connections and a speed of <512 Kbps is called a Narrowband connection (GoI, 2013).

14 All the terms are as per the definition specified in the Report.

15 NSS 75th Round.

16 *Ibid.*

17 DoT (1999).

18 As per the international telecommunications union (ITU), second-generation (2G) digital cellular systems were first developed at the end of the 1980s. These systems digitised not only the control link but also the voice signal. The new system provided better quality and higher capacity at lower cost to consumers. https://www.itu.int/osg/spu/ni/3G/technology/ accessed on July 21, 2021.

19 Computed by author from TRAI, Annual Report 2007-08.

20 TRAI (2021a).

21 *Ibid.*

22 ISDN is a circuit-switched telephone network system that transmits both data and voice over a digital line. It was designed to replace outdated landline technology to digital.

23 DoT (1999).

24 TRAI (2011a)

25 TRAI (2011a)

26 TRAI (2010a)

27 TRAI (2010b)

28 https://pib.gov.in/newsite/PrintRelease.aspx?relid=76838 and DoT, Annual Report 2012-13.

29 DoT (2013).

30 DoT (2013).

31 *Ibid.*

32 http://bbnl.nic.in/usage2.pdf as accessed on July 21, 2021.

33 IAMAI (2015).

34 4G stands for fourth-generation wireless technology, which builds upon the earlier second-generation (2G) and third-generation (3G) technologies, but is faster than the earlier 3G technology.

35 IAMAI (2018).
36 NSS 75th Round.
37 GoI (2018) para 11, page 15.

References

Bapna, A., et al. (2020). Digital Divide and the Aakash Tablet: Technology Intervention in Education. *Economic and Political Weekly*, Vol. LV, No. 10, March 7, pp 27–34, 2020.

Chakraborty, C. and Nandi, B. (2014). Privatization, Telecommunications Adoption and Growth in Developing Countries: A Cointegration Approach. Retrieved July 15, 2021, from https://www.researchgate.net/publication/240640495_Privatization_Telecommunications_and_Growth_in_Selected_Asian_Countries_an_Econometric_Analysis.

Compaine, B. M. (Ed.). (2001). *The Digital Divide: Facing a Crisis or Creating a Myth?* The MIT Press, Cambridge, MA.

Desai, A. V. (2006). *India's Telecommunications Industry: History, Analysis, Diagnosis*. Sage Publications, New Delhi.

Devara, R. (2020). Broadband Internet Access: A Luxury or a Right? *Economic and Political Weekly*, Vol. LV, No. 48, December 5, pp 21–25, 2020.

Dossani, R. (2003). *Telecommunications Reform in India*. Viva Books Private Limited, New Delhi.

DoT (1999). New Telecom Policy, 1999, New Delhi. Retrieved July 15, 2021, from https://dot.gov.in/new-telecom-policy-1999.

——— (2004). Broadband Policy, 2004, New Delhi. Retrieved July 15, 2021, from https://dot.gov.in/broadband-policy-2004.

——— (2005). Annual Report, 2006–07, New Delhi.

——— (2010). Annual Report, 2009–10, New Delhi.

——— (2012). National Telecom Policy, 2012, New Delhi. Retrieved July 15, 2021, from https://dot.gov.in/relatedlinks/national-telecom-policy-2012.

——— (2013). Annual Report, 2012–13, New Delhi.

——— (2015). Annual Report, 2014–15, New Delhi.

——— (2018). Annual Report, 2017–18, New Delhi.

——— (2020). Annual Report, 2019–20, New Delhi.

——— (2021a). Annual Report, 2020–21, New Delhi.

——— (2021b). Telecom at a Glance. Retrieved July 21, 2021, from https://dot.gov.in/sites/default/files/Telecom%20at%20a%20Glance-2019.pdf?download=1.

DOT Force (2001). Digital Opportunities for All: Meeting the Challenge. Report of the Digital Opportunity Task Force, May 11, 2001. Retrieved July 21, 2021, from http://www.g7.utoronto.ca/summit/2001genoa/dotforce1.html.

Edquist, H., et al. (2018). How Important Are Mobile Broadband Networks for the Global Economic Development? *35th IARIW General Conference*, Copenhagen, Denmark, August 20–25, 2018.

GoI (2013). Government of India, Ministry of Communication and Information Technology, Department of Telecommunications, S.O. No. 4-4/2009-Policy-I, July 18, 2013, New Delhi.

——— (2018). Government of India, Ministry of Communication and Information Technology, Department of Telecommunications, F. No. 2-14/2018-Policy-I.(Pt.-I) Preamble, New Delhi.

——— (2021). Government of India, Economic Survey 2020–21, Vol. 2, Chapter 9 Services, New Delhi.

IAMAI (2015). Internet in India 2015, Mumbai.

——— (2018). Digital India: 2014–2018 – Mapping the Impact of Key Schemes under Digital India, Mumbai.

——— (2019). India Internet 2019, Mumbai.

ITA (2020). India – Information and Communication Technology, 25-08-2020. Retrieved July 14, 2021, from https://www.trade.gov/knowledge-product/india-information-and-communication-technology.

ITU (2021). World Telecommunication/ICT Indicator Database. Accessed from https://data.worldbank.org/.

Kayum, A. (2018). Sustainability Assessment of BharatNet Project. Study Paper. Telecommunication Engineering Centre, August 1, 2018, New Delhi.

Mehta, B. S. (2020). Inter-Industry Linkages of ICT Sector in India. *Indian Journal of Human Development*, Vol. 14, No. 1, 42–61. Sage Publication, New Delhi.

MEITY (2021). Ministry of Electronics & Information Technology. Government of India. Software and Services Sector. Retrieved July 15, 2021, from https://www.meity.gov.in/content/software-and-services-sector.

NFHS (2020). Fact Sheets, National Family Health Survey-5, 2019–20, Key Indicators, 22 States/UTs, Phase-I, July 2020, New Delhi.

NSS (2020). Household Social Consumption on Education in India, NSS Report No. 585(75/25.2/1), July 2020, New Delhi.

OECD (2001). Understanding the Digital Divide, OECD Publications, *Paris Cedex* 16, France.

Phadnis, S. (2020, February 13). IT Industry Grows at 8.5 %, Much Faster than GDP. *The Times of India*. Retrieved July 14, 2021 https://timesofindia.indiatimes.com/business/india-business/it-industry-grows-at-8-4-much-faster-than-gdp/articleshow/74109191.cms

RBI (2021). Handbook of Statistics on Indian Economy. New Delhi. Retrieved July 15, 2021 from https://www.rbi.org.in/scripts/AnnualPublications.aspx?head=Handbook%20of%20Statistics%20on%20Indian%20Economy.

Singh, S. (2010). Digital Divide in India: Measurement, Determinants and Policy for Addressing the Challenges in Bridging the Digital Divide. *International Journal of Innovation in the Digital Economy*, April 2010. Retrieved July 14, 2021, from https://www.researchgate.net/publication/220136939_Digital_Divide_in_India_Measurement_Determinants_and_Policy_for_Addressing_the_Challenges_in_Bridging_the_Digital_Divide.

Sridhar, K. S. and Sridhar, V. (2007). Telecommunications Infrastructure and Economic Growth: Evidence from Developing Countries. *Applied Econometrics and International Development*, Vol. 7–2, pp 37–61.

Sridhar, V. (2012). *The Telecom Revolution in India*. Oxford University Press, New Delhi.

Tangirala, M. P. (2019). *Telecom Sector Regulation in India: An Institutional Perspective*. Routledge Publications, New York.

TRAI (2006). Annual Report, 2005–06, New Delhi.

——— (2007). Annual Report, 2006–07, New Delhi.

——— (2008a). Press Release No. 29/2008, March 27, 2008, New Delhi.

——— (2008b). Annual Report, 2007–08, New Delhi.

——— (2010a). Consultation Paper No. 09/2010, Consultation Paper on National Broadband Plan, June 10, 2010, New Delhi.
——— (2010b). Recommendations on National Broadband Plan, December 8, 2010, New Delhi.
——— (2011a). The Indian Telecom Services Performance Indicators – January–March 2011, July 28, 2011, New Delhi.
——— (2011b). Annual Report, 2010–11, New Delhi.
——— (2014). Quality of Service of Broadband Service (Second Amendment) Regulations, 2014, 05/2014, June 25, 2014, New Delhi.
——— (2015). Annual Report, 2014–15, New Delhi.
——— (2016). Annual Report, 2015–16, New Delhi.
——— (2017). Annual Report, 2016–17, New Delhi.
——— (2018). Annual Report, 2017–18, New Delhi.
——— (2019). Annual Report, 2017–18, New Delhi.
——— (2020). Annual Report, 2019–20, New Delhi.
——— (2021a). The Indian Telecom Services Performance Indicators – October–December 2020, April 27, 2021, New Delhi.
——— (2021b). Press Release No. 27/2021, May 11, 2021, New Delhi.
——— (2021c). Press Release No. 33/2021, June 18, 2021, New Delhi.
——— (2021d). Press Release No. 34/2021, July 12, 2021, New Delhi.

12 Liberalisation of Petroleum Product Prices in India

Expectation and Reality

Animesh Kumar

Introduction

The Indian economy has gone through three significant phases as far as petroleum policy is concerned. The three phases differ in the degree to which they favoured the private sector vis-à-vis the public sector. The pre-APM period can be categorised as the first phase when the Government control was minimum, and the private companies were in charge of major decision-making related to the pricing and supply of petroleum products in the country. The situation soon altered with the adoption of APM when almost all the petroleum industry was brought under the control of the public sector. During this phase, the public sector was in control of all segments of the petroleum industry, from exploration and production to marketing and distribution. The third phase or post-APM period was driven by the reform philosophy, which called for a gradual withdrawal of the Government from the petroleum sector. This phase, which is continuing, has witnessed increasing dominance of the private sector. Given India's vulnerability to international oil prices, the Government's stated policy objectives have been, among others, to reduce import dependency, ensure price stability and secure the financial viability of the domestic firms. The deregulation and privatisation of the petroleum sector were considered a panacea for all ills and were expected to increase competition in order to ensure better prices for consumers, reduce import dependency and provide safeguards against future fluctuations.

In this context, the present study intends to analyse the impact of liberalisation on transforming the structure of the petroleum industry, with an emphasis on import dependency and price stability. The chapter is arranged along the following lines. First, the theoretical approaches to price petroleum products are discussed. Then it looks into the changes in the pricing regimes that took place in India after liberalisation. Next, the impacts of changes in pricing policies on the performance of public and private sectors are discussed. The changing pattern of under-recoveries, indigenous production and sales and distribution of petroleum products is looked at to draw policy conclusions.

DOI: 10.4324/9781003343998-12

Petroleum Pricing in India: Theoretical Background

Pricing is one of the most important aspects of petroleum policy. It is perhaps the most effective policy tool available to policymakers to manage the supply-demand balance and control the distribution of oil resources. An optimal pricing policy helps the Government in achieving many important objectives such as promoting economic growth, satisfying the minimum energy needs of every citizen, including that of low-income groups, securing the financial viability and autonomy of the oil industry, energy conservation, ensuring price stability, etc. (Munasinghe, 1980). To ensure price stability, the price should be regulated to protect consumers from unforeseen price fluctuations, which implies that there cannot be a complete alignment of international and domestic prices. In addition, the pricing policy should incorporate the need to subsidise the consumption of less well-off sections. However, a reasonable return to the oil companies, in the long run, is also necessary to ensure the financial viability of domestic oil firms. Often, there is a conflict between different objectives, and hence some of the objectives are prioritised over others. As we shall see, during the Administered Pricing Mechanism (APM) period, price stability and equity were the principal objectives, while during the post-reform period, there is more stress on financial performance and profit in the name of increasing efficiency.

The adopted oil prices should try to achieve a balance between various objectives of the Government. Given its implications, the goals of price stability, social equity, oil security and financial viability of oil firms are particularly important for the oil sector. Since the poorer sections of society predominantly use kerosene for cooking and lighting purposes while pricing kerosene, Government should consider the purchasing power of such consumers. The other objective of a good oil pricing policy is to promote the use of merit goods in the form of clean fuels like LPG, natural gas and kerosene to replace hazardous fuels like firewood and cow dung. Government's intervention is also required to insulate domestic prices, particularly because of the volatile nature of international petroleum prices. A complete pass-through of world oil price increases may cause undesired inflation in the domestic economy. So, a pricing system that results in wide fluctuations in domestic prices is not desirable (Dasgupta, 1968, 1971).

The structure of petroleum pricing in India has been widely debated and has undergone significant changes over the years. Arguments have been made both for and against market-determined prices for petroleum products. On the one hand, it is said that in the absence of domestic price control, increases in world oil prices may lead to high inflation and generate uncertainty which may persist even when the oil price comes down. Further, market competition in refining and distribution can at most affect trading margins since much of domestic consumption is met with imports. On the other hand, opponents of regulation argue that price caps, subsidies and taxes create distortions that may not be desirable. Heavily under-priced natural resources may encourage wastage, while overpricing may lead to reduced access for less well-off groups. An appropriate pricing mechanism is also necessary for the Government to generate revenue and ensure a smooth supply of oil resources to different groups of people.

Both types of positions have influenced the policy. The regulation dominated the immediate post-Independence policy. However, the Government has gradually deregulated the petroleum sector and allowed the entry of private players over the last two decades. Free-market pricing and easier norms for exploration and marketing for private companies were finally introduced. While investment and efficiency are desirable, it is doubtful that a free-market mechanism can best care for oil security and distribution.

Nevertheless, it is convenient for the Government to use the international free-market price rather than the actual cost of production for two reasons. First, free-market price information is readily available. And second, using international market prices as domestic prices preempts domestic cost-inflating inefficiencies from pushing domestic prices above international prices. However, if the global price does not represent market fundamentals properly, its adoption can mislead the domestic market. In the international oil market, political economy and cartels are known to play a significant role in determining market price.

The Transition from APM to Current Pricing Mechanism

In India, the need for changing the pricing system was recognised after the oil crisis that led to a spike in petroleum prices. The pre-APM pricing systems were all dependent on the world price for determining domestic petroleum prices. They only tried to find ways to decrease petroleum products' domestic price and enhance energy security without disturbing the import parity pricing principles. This was mainly done by setting lower profit margin limits for oil companies or asking them to get higher discounts while importing oil from abroad. However, broadly international prices remained the primary determinant of domestic petroleum prices, and therefore, the sharp price fluctuations at the time of the oil crisis had a significant impact on the domestic economy. After the oil crisis in the seventies, it became apparent that the global price would not be stable in future, and if India wanted any stability in the domestic oil prices, it had to necessarily evolve its own pricing mechanism. Further, the oil shocks exposed the vulnerability of the economy to external oil prices. India's experience from the wars fought with neighbouring countries in the 1960s and 1970s also demonstrated the importance of oil security.

Such increases in oil price questioned the sustainability of any pricing regime that used world prices to determine the domestic price. The pricing system was neither good from an economic growth point of view nor did it serve the purpose of social equity. Hence, a need for a pricing system independent of free international prices was felt necessary. Thus, after the 1973 oil crisis, the Oil Prices Committee (OPC) under the chairmanship of K. S. Krishnaswamy was constituted. The objective was to recommend a flexible and practicable pricing policy that would meet any extraordinary situations that may arise later. The other objective was to reduce import dependency by increasing the production of indigenous crude and expanding refining capacity. The committee concluded that import parity price was not the proper basis for pricing crude oil or refined products and instead recommended that the price should be linked to the cost of producing a product (Krishnaswamy Committee, 1976). Thus, the APM came into existence on 16 December 1977 and was in operation till 1997. The committee estimated the long-run marginal cost (LRMC) of onshore and offshore[1] crude separately. The "pooled price" of crude oil was fixed as the weighted average of indigenous and imported crude oil prices. It was also decided that the price of refined products would be linked to the cost of production after allowing a reasonable return to the refineries.

The APM was criticised on the ground that it led to distorted pricing of petroleum products due to various subsidies given by the Government. It was argued that grants were often provided in a non-transparent manner and were financed through cross-subsidisation (Singh, Parekh, & Joshi, 2018). Therefore, the consumer prices did not reflect their true economic values and led to inefficient use[2]. But the so-called free-market price in the international market was also not the actual free-market competitive price. Also, to some extent, the price distortion was necessary to protect the interest of poor consumers. In the absence of electricity, many consumers used kerosene primarily for lighting purposes and hence a subsidy on the product was necessary to keep the prices low. However, the need to control inefficiencies in the use of the product cannot be ignored. It was also argued that the provision of guaranteed profit under APM worked in favour of inefficient refineries as it did not provide enough incentive for technological upgradation and cost reduction. APM, it was argued, failed to create a modern and internationally competitive oil industry in India. However, this problem could be minimised if an adequate monitoring system had been in place to examine the benefits obtained by refiners under the cost-plus formula. Also, the inadequate technological up-gradation and cost reduction could be attributed to Government decisions as the sector was under the control of the Government. The retail prices were not revised to match the increasing cost of production, and hence it caused a heavy financial burden for the Government and the oil PSUs. But the lack of revision of the retail price was mainly a political decision and was not a consequence of the APM pricing system. Furthermore, APM was designed for an oil industry dominated by public sector firms and not for promoting private firms and competition.

After 1991, the structure of the domestic petroleum industry started to change with increased liberalisation and privatisation policies. The entry of many new private players and joint ventures in the petroleum industry made it challenging to administer the APM in the same form. Doubts were also raised regarding the sustainability of APM as it resulted in significant deficits in the pool accounts (Bandyopadhyay, 2010). The controlled price under APM was generally lower than the free-market price offered by the private players. Also, the free-market price was prone to fluctuate in sync with an international price. Thus, the APM made it difficult for private sector companies to compete with the public sector in the domestic market even when their entry was allowed. But the Government was very keen on increasing private sector participation in the oil industry, and it considered APM as the main barrier to their entry. Accordingly, dismantling of the APM was carried out in a phased manner over the period 1998-2001 as per the recommendation of the R-group (R-Group, 1996). It was finally dismantled in March 2002. The Market-Determined Pricing Mechanism was notified, which paved the way for complete deregulation of the petroleum sector.

The Market-Determined Pricing Mechanism (MDPM) was operationalised from 1 April 2002 to decontrol petroleum prices. Import parity price (IPP)[3] was adopted as a shortcut to the free-market price. The import parity price of petroleum products was the notional landed cost of import from the Arab Gulf. Thus, under import parity, the retail selling prices of petroleum products were based on a notional price at which these products would have been imported into the country, i.e. conceptual landed cost and not on the basis of the actual ex-refinery price of these products[4]. Thus, IPP tends to overestimate the cost of oil. In an attempt to rationalise the price, Rangarajan Committee recommended trade parity pricing (TPP) for pricing petrol and diesel, which was a weighted average of IPP and an EPP. The weights were to be taken in the ratio of 80:20 for IPP and EPP, respectively, to reflect India's dependency on imports of crude oil (Rangarajan Committee, 2006). No other concrete basis was given to justify such a high weightage to IPP. The objective was to bring the oil price below IPP and thereby reduce the rent earned by oil companies. Based on the recommendations, the refinery gate price (RGP) of petrol and diesel was linked to TPP in 2006, while the RGP of PDS kerosene and domestic LPG was still based on IPP.

Effective from 26 June 2010, the price of Petrol was made market determined. However, the revisions made in the price did not fully reflect the changes in international oil prices because the public sector OMCs absorbed a part of the increase as under-recoveries. Retail selling prices (RSPs) of other sensitive petroleum products, viz. diesel, PDS kerosene and domestic LPG, continued to be modulated by Government to shield the domestic consumer from rising international prices and possible domestic inflation. Later, reversing the old decision again, the price of diesel was also completely decontrolled with effect from 19 October 2014, taking advantage of declining international oil prices. Subsequently, the price of all four sensitive products has been made market determined with provisions of subsidies for PDS kerosene and domestic LPG through direct benefit transfer schemes.

Further, starting 16 June 2017, petrol and diesel prices are subject to a daily revision across the country rather than fortnightly revision. Also, a cap of six subsidised cylinders per year was introduced on domestic consumers with effect from 14 September 2012, which was later modified to nine on 18 January 2013. From the year 2014-15, the cap has been increased to 12 subsidised domestic cylinders.

Under-Recovery

"Loss" and "under-recovery" are often used interchangeably to indicate the losses of oil companies due to lower market prices than the cost of production. However, the two terms are different in their meaning. The actual loss or profit of oil marketing companies takes into account the actual cost of production, including income from all sources like dividend income, profits from freely priced products, pipeline income, inventory changes, etc. On the other hand, under-recoveries represent the difference between the estimated product price based on TPP/IPP and the actual selling price of the product (excluding taxes, dealer commission, etc.). Thus, for the purpose of calculating under-recoveries, the product price based on IPP/TPP is assumed to be the cost of production which includes costs such as ocean freight, insurance and port dues. But these costs are not actually incurred as these products are not directly imported by the oil companies. Thus, under-recoveries are purely notional in nature, and it does not represent the actual loss of oil companies. The concept of under-recovery helps the domestic producers as long as they are fully compensated.

After the dismantling of APM, no provision was made for fiscal subsidies on petrol and diesel as these products were soon to be brought to the market-determined level. However, the price of petrol and diesel could not be adjusted fully to take account of sharp increases in international oil prices. As a result, the difference between retail selling price (RSP) and cost price per unit (on an import parity basis) kept on increasing. The resulting under-recoveries on account of the sale of subsidised petroleum products since 2002-03 can be seen in Table 12.1. It shows that the under-recovery on the sale of petrol and diesel was zero after 2011-12 and 2015-16, respectively, because the price of these products was made market determined. Total under-recovery reached its peak of Rs. 1,610 billion in 2012-13, and after that, the under-recovery decreased substantially. diesel accounted for the largest component of under-recovery for most of the years before 2014-15. Since 2016-17, the under-recovery has become very low, and other subsidies under the schemes of direct benefit transfer of LPG and PDS kerosene (DBTL & DBTK) and Pradhan Mantri Ujjwala Yojana (PMUY) are provided.

Soon after the dismantling of APM, the price of the Indian basket of imported crude increased from $24.99 per barrel in May 2003 to $132.47 per barrel in July 2008, i.e. more than five times over a five-year period. During the same period, the price of diesel increased from Rs 19.18 per

Table 12.1 Under-recoveries/ DBTL subsidy on sale of sensitive petroleum products (Rs. in million)

Year	*Under-Recovery*					*Other Subsidies (DBTLPMUY+ DBTK)*
	*Petrol**	*Diesel**	*Domestic LPG ^*	*PDS Kerosene*	*Total*	
2002-03	-	-	33630	20670	54300	-
2003-04	-	-	55230	37520	92740	-
2004-05	1500	21540	83620	94800	201460	-
2005-06	27230	126470	102460	143840	400000	-
2006-07	20270	187760	107010	178830	493870	-
2007-08	73320	351660	155230	191020	771230	-
2008-09	51810	522860	176000	282250	1032920	-
2009-10	51510	92790	142570	173640	460510	-
2010-11	22270	347060	217720	194840	781900	-
2011-12	-	811920	299970	273520	1385410	-
2012-13	-	920610	395580	294100	1610290	-
2013-14	-	628370	464580	305740	1398690	39120
2014-15	-	109350	365800	247990	723140	39710
2015-16	-	-	180	114960	115150	220110
2016-17	-	-	-	75950	75950	159150
2017-18	-	-	-	46720	46720	235770
2018-19	-	-	-	59500	59500	368800

Source: Petroleum Planning and Analysis Cell, GoI
**Under-recovery on petrol is only up to 25 June 2010 and under-recovery on diesel is only up to 18 October 2014*

litre to Rs 34.88 per litre, and the price of petrol increased from Rs 30.4 per litre to Rs 50.62 per litre, which was an increase of 82 per cent and 67 per cent, respectively. This naturally resulted in high and mounting under-recoveries on account of all the sensitive products, particularly diesel, PDS kerosene and domestic LPG, which needed the urgent attention of the Government. The fiscal subsidies given under the PDS kerosene and domestic LPG Subsidy Scheme, 2002 were not sufficient to recover even 10 per cent of total under-recoveries on these two products by 2007-08. The rise in international oil prices and consequent under-recoveries adversely affected the fiscal situation and the Government's budget. The Government had to find a way to balance between the price increase and maintaining the budget deficit. Three major steps were taken by the Government for this purpose. First, an oil bond scheme was devised in 2005-06; and second, the taxes and duties on crude and refined products were rationalised to neutralise some of the impacts of the rising price of crude. Further, the under-recovery burden was handled through an arrangement to share it among the upstream oil companies, OMCs and the Government (Table 12.2).

The oil bonds were special securities issued by the Government of India to OMCs in lieu of cash subsidies. These were usually long-dated securities, maturity periods extending over 15-20 years, and carried a marginally

Table 12.2 Burden sharing of under-recovery on sale of sensitive petroleum products (Rs. in million)

Year	*Oil Bonds/Cash Subsidy (%)**	*Borne by OMCs (%)*	*Upstream Companies (%)#*	*Total Under-Recovery*
2002-03	0	54300 (100)	0	54300
2003-04	0	61510 (66.33)	31230 (33.67)	92740
2004-05	0	141990 (70.48)	59470 (29.52)	201460
2005-06	115000 (28.75)	145000 (36.25)	140000 (35)	400000
2006-07	241210 (48.84)	47590 (9.64)	205070 (41.52)	493870
2007-08	352900 (45.76)	161250 (20.91)	257080 (33.33)	771230
2008-09	712920 (69.02)	0	320000 (30.98)	1032920
2009-10	260000 (56.46)	56210 (12.21)	144300 (31.33)	460510
2010-11	410000 (52.44)	68930 (8.82)	302970 (38.75)	781900
2011-12	835000 (60.27)	410 (0.03)	550000 (39.7)	1385410
2012-13	1000000 (62.1)	10290 (0.64)	600000 (37.26)	1610290
2013-14	746840 (51.94)	20760 (1.44)	670210 (46.61)	1437810
2014-15	312790 (41.00)	21840 (2.86)	428220 (56.13)	762850
2015-16	322560 (96.21)	180 (0.05)	12510 (3.73)	335260
2016-17	235100 (100)	0	0	235100
2017-18	282490 (100)	0	0	282490
2018-19	428300 (100)	0	0	428300

Source: Indian Petroleum and Natural Gas Statistics (various years)
* *Oil bonds replaced with cash subsidy since 2009-10*
# *OIL, ONGC and GAIL*

higher coupon over the securities of comparable maturity. The oil companies were supposed to sell them for liquid cash in the secondary market or use them as collateral to raise funds. Unlike cash subsidies, there was no direct cash flow in issuing oil bonds, and hence they were not accounted for in fiscal deficit calculations for the issuing years. Thus, it helped Government to pay for under-recoveries while window-dressing its fiscal deficit. Also, oil bonds allowed the Government to make payments in a deferred manner. Compared to this, direct fiscal transfers in the form of subsidies financed by borrowing from the domestic capital market would have been more transparent. However, this would have made maintaining fiscal discipline more difficult, more so after the enactment of the Fiscal Responsibility and Budget Management (FRBM) Act.

Several attempts were made by the Government to decrease the subsidy burden. The direct benefit transfer of LPG (DBTL) was launched with the objectives of reducing the Government's burden and making it easier for the Government to target beneficiaries based on income criteria. The direct benefit transfer schemes to domestic LPG and PDS kerosene consumers were implemented in a phased manner as per the recommendations of a task force constituted by the Government in February 2011 *(Task Force Report, 2011)*. After the complete implementation of the DBTL scheme, the under-recovery on account of the sale of subsidised LPG has been close to zero. This is because the OMCs sell the LPG to the consumers at the market price and therefore do not incur under-recovery on the sale of the LPG. The eligible consumers receive the subsidy from the Government directly in their account. Table 12.1 also shows a gradual increase in DBTL subsidy from Rs. 39.12 billion in 2013-14 to Rs. 368.80 billion in 2018-19. Presently, those with an annual income of more than 1 million per annum are not eligible for subsidies. As on 14 July 2017, out of total 207.5 million LPG consumers, 181.8 million consumers were getting subsidies in their bank accounts under the DBTL scheme[5]. The Government has been trying to lower the income eligibility criteria further to Rs. 500 thousand to reduce its expenditure (Jacob & Roychoudhury, 2019). Further, there has been a sharp decline in the consumption of subsidised kerosene during the last few years. This has led to substantial savings for the Government in the form of falling under-recovery.

Exploration and Production

During the 1980s, significant augmentation of indigenous crude production was observed, which was mainly due to the discovery of Bombay high (Table 12.3). A few more discoveries were made in the pre-liberalisation period, due to which the known reserves and the corresponding reserve/production (R/P) ratio[6] increased. This resulted in a threefold increase in crude production between 1980-81 and 1985-86. But still, the total reserve was not sufficient to service future expected domestic demands. To augment the exploration further, New Exploration and Licensing Policy (NELP) was adopted in 1997 which placed a lot of trust on the private sector. Even after the adoption of NELP, the production of crude oil has been stagnant

Table 12.3 Reserve and production of crude oil in India (MMT)

Year	*Balance of Recoverable Reserve*	*Indigenous Production*	*Reserve/Production Ratio (R/P)*
1970-71	127.84	6.82	18.74
1975-76	143.90	8.45	17.03
1980-81	366.33	10.51	34.86
1985-86	499.51	30.17	16.56
1990-91	739.00	33.02	22.38
1995-96	732.00	35.17	20.81
2000-01	703.00	32.45	21.66
2005-06	756.00	32.20	23.48
2010-11	660.04	37.69	17.51
2015-16	621.28	36.94	16.82
2018-19	618.95	34.20	18.10

Reserve as on 31 March of each year
Source: Compiled from Indian Petroleum and Natural Gas Statistics (various years)

at between 30 and 40 MMT for the last 25 years. A reasonably stable R/P ratio of around 23 between 1990-91 and 2009-10 indicates that new discoveries and technological up-gradation were only sufficient to compensate for the loss of reserves due to production. However, the R/P ratio has been continuously falling after that due to the failure of exploration companies to add significant new reserves. The estimated reserve had decreased from 775 MMT in 2010 to 594 MMT in 2018, and the corresponding R/P ratio had decreased from 23.2 in 2009-10 to 16.66 in 2017-18. This means if indigenous production continues at the current level and no more reserves are added, the current level of reserves will last only for the next 16 years, i.e. the current level of production can be sustained only for 16 years. This points to the immediate need to accelerate the exploration of activities.

NELP allowed for 100 per cent Foreign Direct Investment (FDI) to attract foreign players in E&P activities. Incentive in the form of lower royalty and cess was given under NELP. To promote exploration in offshore blocks, a lower rate of royalty was charged for offshore areas and deep-water sites. Also, the blocks awarded under NELP were exempted from the cess levied under the Oil Industry Development Act. Further, public sector companies were given the same contracts as private companies. A total of 140 oil and gas hydrocarbon discoveries were made, most of which were in offshore and deep-water blocks. The participation of exploration and production (E&P) companies increased from 35 (15 Foreign, 15 Private and 5 PSUs) to 117 (48 foreign, 58 Private and 11 PSUs) after the conclusion of the ninth round of NELP (Directorate General of Hydrocarbons, 2015). Major private and foreign companies like British Petroleum, British Gas, Cairn Energy, RIL, Essar and Jubilant participated in various rounds of bidding. However, not much success was achieved during the post-liberalisation period in increasing the known recoverable reserves of crude oil. NELP was successful in increasing the participation of foreign companies but could not contribute much to increasing indigenous production. The failure of the liberalised regime to augment the crude oil reserves and reduce import dependency prompted the Government to come out with corrective measures. The Government announced a new policy named the Hydrocarbon Exploration and Licensing Policy (HELP) in March 2016, replacing NELP, which had been in existence for 18 years. The HELP regime for exploration and production further attempted to make the activities more attractive to corporates. So far, only Reliance Industries has submitted an Expression of Interest (EOI). No foreign company has submitted an Expression of Interest under HELP. The production of crude oil in India has been largely stagnant. The Government has not succeeded in either increasing the output or attracting sufficient interest from major players even after adopting a more liberalised regime.

The quantity of known recoverable reserves of crude oil and the level of production determine the country's self-reliance on oil energy. As shown in Table 12.3, the total crude oil production has been stagnant around 35 MMT per year for a long period of time. The steps taken in the pre-liberalisation period resulted in an increase in the production of indigenous crude from 6.82 million metric tons (MMT) in 1971 to 30.17 MMT in 1986, i.e. or by five times in a span of 15 years (MoSPI, 2007). However, the production of crude oil did not increase much after that, and production stood at 36.01 MMT in 2017 (MoSPI, 2018). That reflects a compound annual growth rate (CAGR) of 3.68 per cent during a period of 50 years. The data also reveals a decreasing trend in the production of indigenous crude since 2014, which might be a deliberate decision of the Government. The recent cut in the crude production can be attributed to two main factors; first, the recent decline in the international price of crude, and second, the absence of discovery of new oil reserves and consequent decrease of the R/P ratio.

The contribution of the public and private sectors to total production has been shown in Table 12.4 and Figure 12.1. While the production of the private sector has increased significantly, not much increase in the total production of crude has been observed in the post-reform period. It seems that the production of the private sector increased only at the cost of the public sector. The increase in the private sector output was roughly compensated by the corresponding decline in public sector output. As far as total production is concerned, during the last 20 years (since 1997), the level of crude production has been near stagnant with a CAGR of 0.45 per cent. But the share of the private sector has been increasing continuously without any significant addition to total production. During the last 20 years, the private sector's share in total production has increased to approximately 30 per cent, and therefore, the public sector share has declined to around 70 per cent. ONGC has been the market leader in crude oil production, but its share has continuously declined since the 1990s.

The share of upstream public company ONGC has decreased from 80.7 per cent in 1998-99 to 60.22 per cent in 2018-19, and the share of the private sector has increased from 9.24 per cent to 29.64 per cent (Figure 12.1). The share of other public sector company OIL has remained constant at around 10 per cent of total production. Since total production has been stagnant, this means that the increasing participation of the private sector in upstream activities has not resulted in an increase in total production. Only the share of the public and private sectors in total production has been altered with increasing share given to the private sector. Further, indigenous crude oil is sold at the import parity price, which is generally much higher than the cost of extraction, this means a higher profit share of the private sector. Hence, with the increasing share of the private sector in total production, the profit of public sector companies has declined without any significant impact on total production. With the increasing requirement of crude and the inability to produce the crude domestically, India's oil import dependency increased considerably over the time period. In 1971, India was producing 37.11 per cent of its crude consumption requirement domestically, but that gradually reduced to 14.7 per cent in 2017 due to a relative increase in consumption compared to production.

Table 12.4 Indigenous crude oil production in India since 1970-71 (MMT)

	ONGC	OIL	PSU Total	JVC/Private@	Total Crude Oil	Condensate*	Total (Crude Oil + Condensate)
1970-71	3.79	3.08	6.87		6.87		6.87
1975-76	5.35	3.10	8.45		8.45		8.45
1980-81	9.26	1.24	10.51		10.51		10.51
1985-86	27.51	2.65	30.17		30.17		30.17
1990-91	29.51	2.65	32.16		32.16		32.16
1995-96	30.94	2.88	33.82	0.65	34.47		34.47
2000-01	25.07	3.29	28.36	4.09	32.45		32.45
2005-06	24.41	3.24	27.65	4.55	32.20		32.20
2010-11	22.52	3.55	26.08	9.51	35.59	2.10	37.69
2015-16	21.08	3.23	24.31	11.19	35.50	1.44	36.94
2020-21 (P)	19.10	2.90	22.00	7.10	29.10	1.40	30.50

Source: PPAC and MoPNG

*Condensate production is available separately from 2006-07 onwards.

@ Joint ventures were allowed in production from 1995-96 onwards

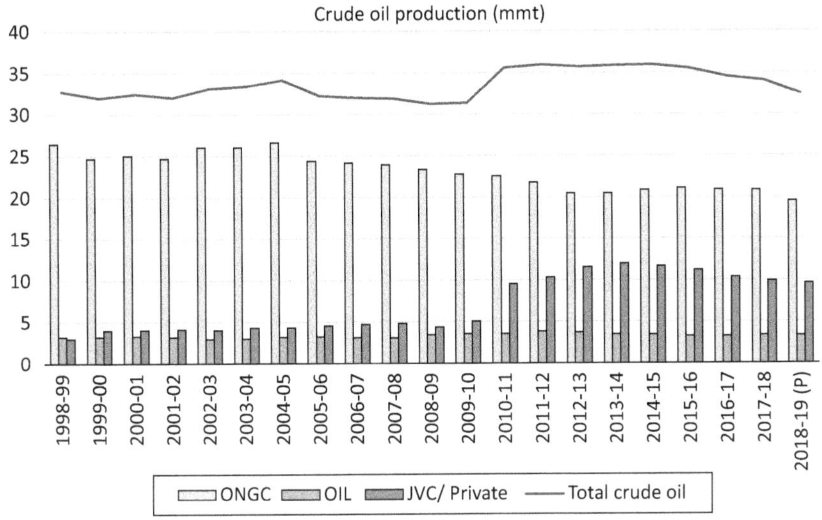

Figure 12.1 Indigenous crude oil production by public and private sector *Source: Data from PPAC*

Sales and Distribution

The marketing and distribution segment is dominated by three public sector companies, namely IOCL, HPCL and BPCL, with the private sector also emerging as a significant player. In 2019-20, IOCL accounted for 38.3 per cent of the domestic market share, followed by BPCL and HPCL with 19.5 per cent and 17.5 per cent share, respectively. The private sector contributed 22.6 per cent of total domestic sales in terms of volume (Table 12.5). Between 1994-95 and 2019-20, the share of the public sector in total sales has gradually declined to 77 per cent with a corresponding increase in the private sector. On average, public sector sales volume grew at 3.98 per cent per year, while the average rate of growth of private sector sales was 17.20 per cent during the period. Figure 12.2 also shows the changes in the sales volume of the public and private sectors separately (private sector measured on the secondary axis). The gradual increase in the share of the private sector in total sales can also be seen from the widening gap between the lines representing total sales and public sales. The compound annual growth rate (CAGR) of the public and private sectors over the past 24 years was 3.7 per cent and 13.9 per cent, respectively, while the combined growth (CAGR) was 4.7 per cent.

The rapid increase in the private sector's sales started in 1998, the year in which the dismantling of APM started. During the next ten years, i.e. between 1997-98 and 2006-07, the average rate of growth (per year) of private sector sales was more than 30 per cent. The growth slowed after

Table 12.5 Annual domestic sales and market share (%) of public and private sector companies (MMT)

Year	*Public Sector*	*Private Sector*	*Total Sales/Consumption*
1994-95	65.48 (96.99)	2.02 (3.00)	67.51
1999-00	90.65 (93.37)	6.43 (6.62)	97.09
2004-05	94.59 (84.73)	17.04 (15.26)	111.63
2009-10	116.77 (84.73)	21.03 (15.26)	137.81
2014-15	137.58 (83.39)	27.40 (16.60)	164.99
2019-20 (P)	165.70 (77.39)	48.42 (22.61)	214.13

Source: Indian Petroleum and Natural Gas Statistics, MoPNG (various years)

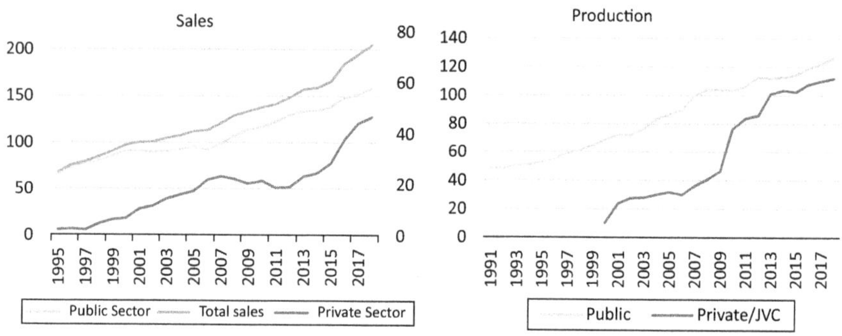

Figure 12.2 Domestic production and sales of petroleum products by public and private sector companies (MMT) *Source: Data from MoPNG and CEIC *Private sector on the secondary axis*

2006-07, mainly because of subdued demand after the financial crisis. The private sector sales in the domestic market fell from 22.8 MMT in 2006-07 to 18.54 MMT in 2010-11, which was a decrease of 18 per cent of the initial volume. Consequently, the market share of private companies in total sales declined by approximately 5 per cent. Since the production continued to grow, this resulted in growing surplus production in the private sector (Table 12.6). The surplus was either sold to the public sector companies for selling to final consumers or exported. The domestic sales volume started to grow again and it took only six years (2013-14 to 2019-20) to double the sales volume. As a result, the share of the private sector in total sales has increased from 15.23 per cent in 2013-14 to 22.56 per cent in 2019-20. This resulted in the growing presence of the private sector in marketing and sales business in the domestic market.

Table 12.6 shows the production from private and public sector companies separately. After liberalisation, the private sector production has grown much faster than that of the public sector. Over the last 12 years, the private sector has expanded its production by close to three times while the public

Table 12.6 Domestic production (MMT) of petroleum products in the public and private sector and its percentage share in domestic consumption/sales

Year	*Public*	*Private*
1994-95	52.92 (80.80)	
1999-00	69.14 (76.27)	10.26 (159.44)
2004-05	86.67 (91.62)	31.90 (187.19)
2009-10	103.64 (88.75)	76.12 (361.94)
2014-15	114.46 (83.17)	102.67 (367.94)
2019-20 (P)	137.21 (82.80)	120.98 (249.83)

Source: Indian Petroleum and Natural Gas Statistics, MoPNG (various years)

sector has expanded by just 31.9 per cent. Hence, the public sector contribution in total production fell from 71 per cent in 2007-08 to 53 per cent in 2019-20, while the private sector contribution increased from 30 per cent to 47 per cent during the same period. The private sector has recorded surpluses of production over sales since the establishment of the first refinery in Jamnagar (Gujarat) by Reliance Petroleum Limited in 2000. This increase in surplus production was experienced despite faster growth of sales by the private sector compared to the public sector. This extraordinary growth of production in the private sector was mainly due to the establishment of four new refineries in the private sector and joint venture companies.

On the other hand, the public sector did well in satisfying the consumer demand during the APM period, but the performance worsened after liberalisation. Between 1971-72 and 1999-2000, total consumption and public sector sales both grew at the average rate of approximately 5.7 per cent per year. But, after the abolition of APM, the public sector sales growth fell to 3.31 per cent per year while the consumption grew at more than 4 per cent per year. This meant giving more space to the private sector in the marketing and distribution segment. This might have been done deliberately as per privatisation policy of the Government. After the adoption of economy-wide liberalisation programmes, the Government was under pressure to privatise the petroleum industry. In the post-APM period, the private sector received massive investments in the refining segment, but no new refinery was set up in the public sector. In addition, the public sector continued to operate from old sites while the private sector made use of the latest available technologies to augment their production. The result of these policy initiatives is quite evident if we look at the trends in domestic production of the public and private sectors separately.

The public sector marketing companies have been facing a shortage of petroleum products and thus relying significantly on imports or private sector production for its sales. Except for the year 2007, when there was a marginal surplus of domestic production over sales (1.7 MMT), the public sector has always been in a deficit. Though the production in the public sector has increased consistently over time, it failed to match the growth of sales, and therefore resulted in the increasing deficit over time. In 2017-18, only 80 per cent of the total public sector sales was produced indigenously by public sector companies (Table 12.6). This is the case when India, in aggregate, has more than 25 per cent surplus production overconsumption. This means that it is the private sector that is mainly responsible for the export of petroleum products and also supplies to the public sector to sell to final consumers.

Figure 12.3 shows the sales of petroleum products at a more disaggregated level. The behaviour of the top four products in terms of sales volume has been shown for both public and private sectors. A significant difference between public and private companies in sales patterns has been observed. In the public sector, middle distillates played the dominant role in sales, while the private sector depended mostly on heavy and light distillate products for domestic sales. As expected, most of the sales in the public sector are attributed to the four sensitive products. The sale of all sensitive products except kerosene has followed an increasing trend. Further, the sale of diesel oil by public sector companies has been stagnant for the last 5 years. It has grown at an average rate of only 1.5 per cent per year after 2013 despite consumption growth of about 3.5 per cent per year. On the other hand, most of the domestic sale by the private sector consists of free-market petroleum products (i.e. products not classified as sensitive products). Even though the private sector accounts for only 22 per cent share in total sales, it has still managed to sell more than the public sector domestically in the heavy-end category since 2014. The highest contribution is from petroleum coke which is a by-product of the oil refining process and is mainly used as industrial fuel. Only exception here is HSD whose sale has risen to 4.5 million tonnes in 2017 from an insignificant level in 2014. This might be the result of the Government's decision to decontrol the diesel price w.e.f. 19 October 2014.

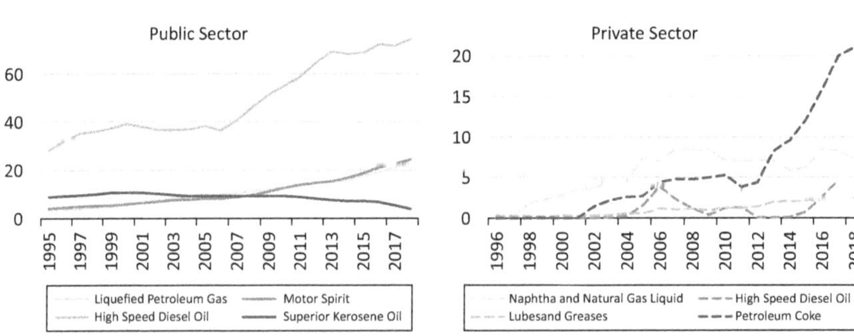

Figure 12.3 Total sales of light, middle and heavy distillates by the public and private sector companies (MMT) *Source: Data from MoPNG and CEIC*

The size of the private sector has now become almost equal to the public sector in refining and production but is lagging behind in sales. Most of the sales in the public sector are attributed to the four sensitive products. With the recent changes in the "Guidelines for Granting authorisation to market Transportation Fuels", the private sector is set to dominate the domestic marketing in the sphere of sensitive products also. On 23 October 2019, the Cabinet Committee on Economic Affairs (CCEA) approved the new guidelines which relaxed the fuel retailing norms to allow private firms, including foreign players, to set up petrol pumps in India (Mukul, 2019; Press Information Bureau, 2019). Under the new norms, the private entities seeking authorisation would need to have a minimum net worth of Rs. 2.5 billion, much lenient than the previous requirement of Rs. 20 billion prior investment in exploration and production, refining, pipelines or terminals.

Among the private sector, only Reliance and Essar (now Nayara Energy Ltd) have a noticeable presence in the retail segment with 2.2 per cent and 7.9 per cent of market share, respectively (Expert Committee Report, 2019). The three central public sector enterprises (CPSE), viz. IOCL, HPCL and BPCL, still account for approximately 90 per cent of retail outlets for transportation fuel. As of 1 April 2019, there were 64,624 retail outlets operating throughout the country, of which 57,944 were operated by the three CPSEs, and the remaining 6,680 outlets were operated by private companies. The following diagram shows the change in the number of retail outlets operated by public and private sector oil companies over time in India.

The growth rate of public sector retail outlets has been relatively stable as compared to the private sector over the period. On average, the number of retail outlets operated by public sector companies has grown at the average rate of 7 per cent per annum between 2003 and 2019. The rate of growth has slowed in recent years, particularly after 2014. During the last five years (2014-15 to 2018-19), the number of public retail outlets grew at an average rate of only 3.41 per cent, while the private retail outlets grew at an average rate of 18.89 per cent (Figure 12.4). Before that, the number of retail outlets in the private sector remained stagnant at around 3000. The sudden swap in growth performance between public and private companies after 2014 raises doubts that public sector growth was curtailed deliberately at the instruction of the Government as an additional benefit to the private sector. The sudden fall in growth after 2014 is observed for all the three public sector OMCs.

One of the reasons for stagnancy in the number of private retail outlets before 2015 was the Government policy regarding the pricing of sensitive petroleum products. Prices of common products like petrol and diesel were controlled by Government and were generally lower than the IPP price. The difference between market price and sale price, known as under-recovery, was borne by Government, upstream companies and oil marketing companies. There was no provision to compensate private companies in case of

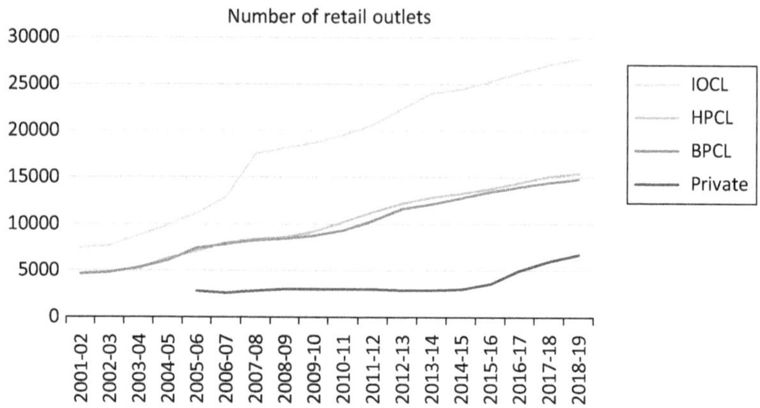

Figure 12.4 Number of retail outlets in public and private sectors *Source: Data from Indian Petroleum and Natural Gas Statistics, MoPNG (various years) and (Expert Committee Report, 2019)*

under-recovery. So, during the period of high international oil price compared to the domestic price, which was the case during most of the duration before 2014, the private oil companies were not able to compete with the public sector marketing companies. However, the private companies established some retail outlets in areas where the supply was less or irregular. Further, with the Government giving a strong push to liberalisation, it was expected that sooner or later, the Government will decontrol the petroleum price completely, which raised profit expectations of the private retailer. This drove additional investment in the retail business by private players.

After July 2014, the international price started to fall, and the domestic price started to increase due to the complete deregulation of petrol and diesel. Further, the norms for private entry were relaxed, and the expansion of public sector retail outlets was stalled to give more space to private sector expansion. The private sector responded and registered a double-digit growth rate since 2016. However, the combined growth of retail outlets actually slowed down even after accommodating the high growth of private sector outlets. Among the public sector companies, the highest growth in the number of retail outlets has been observed in the case of IOCL. The sharp increase in 2007-08 was due to the merger of IBP with IOCL, as a result of which more than 3500 retail outlets of IBP Corporation Limited were taken over by IOCL. As of 1 April 2019, 42.9 per cent of retail outlets belong to IOCL, 23.9 per cent HPCL, 22.9 per cent BPCL and the remaining 10.3 per cent were in the private sector. The Government took two decisions in 2019 which will significantly affect the oil marketing and retail sector. The first was to privatise BPCL and the second decision was to relax the norms for setting up private retail petroleum outlets. The privatisation of BPCL will increase the private share of retail outlets to 33.2 per cent. Further, with easier norms for private sector entry, the share of private outlets will increase at an even higher rate. Given the current trend of growth, the private sector is expected to dominate in the marketing and retail business also. With this, the characteristics of the Indian petroleum industry is going to be altered from a public sector-dominated industry to a private sector-dominated industry. However, the past experience of India under the private petroleum industry was quite different. The lack of continuous supply during the 1960s and 1970s was the main reason behind the Government's decision to bring the entire oil industry under its control. In addition to this, private companies engaged in profit-making behaviour during high international prices after the oil crisis, which led to even higher prices and uncertainty. Now with the continuous push to liberalisation in the petroleum industry, the Government is actually trying to reverse its own decision.

The share of public and private sectors in different segments of the petroleum industry can be seen in Figure 12.5. The size of the public and private sectors is almost equal in terms of installed capacity and production of petroleum products. However, the difference is relatively high in the case of sales and retail outlets. With an increase in the number of retail outlets, sales are also expected to jump proportionally. It is also observed that the share of the private sector in total domestic sales is more than 22 per cent despite just 10 per cent share in total retail outlets. The relatively higher contribution to sales was mainly because of higher sales to industrial buyers. The performance of the public and private sectors in different segments of operation during the last ten years has been compared in Figure 12.6. The figures show the changes in the share of public and private sectors in production, sales, installed capacity and distribution network during the last ten years.

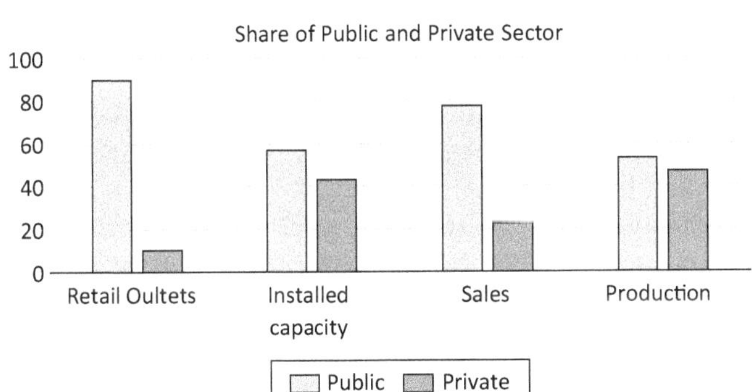

Figure 12.5 Share of the public and private sectors in total production, sales, installed capacity and retail outlets in 2017-18 *Source: Data from MoPNG and CEIC Note: *Retail outlets and installed capacity as of 1st April 2019*

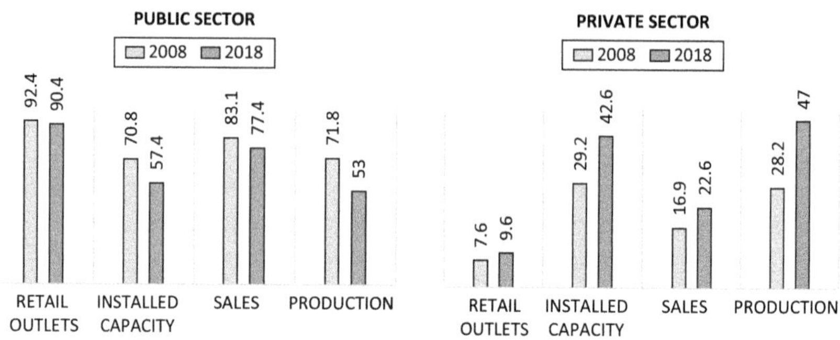

Figure 12.6 Change in production, sales, installed capacity and distribution network under public and private sectors during the last ten years *Source: Data from MoPNG and CEIC*

It can be seen from the diagram that the share of the public sector has been decreasing in all four areas of its operation. On the other hand, the share of the private sector has been increasing.

Conclusion

The policy measures adopted in different phases of development reflect the Government's priorities. After economic liberalisation, the priority of the Government changed, and it started to prioritise private sector participation in the oil sector. Before the reforms, the APM system focussed more on price stability, affordability and availability of petroleum products. Even though APM delivered well in terms of social equity principle, the success of APM was questioned on the basis of efficiency. Further, the APM was not well suited for private players as it did not allow free pricing of products. The private players were in favour of removing all the restrictions on pricing and rather promoted the free-market pricing. The Government accepted the view that the increasing participation of the private sector would lead to a more competitive and efficient petroleum industry. This changing focus of the Government called for the dismantling of APM, though it was well known that doing so would make the domestic price vulnerable to international price fluctuations. The APM system worked well for two and a half decades, after which it was dismantled to make way for the market-determined pricing system in 2002. Thus, once again, the domestic prices were made dependent on international prices. Some provisions for subsidies and under-recoveries were made initially to maintain price stability but were later withdrawn gradually.

A comparison of price variation between the APM and post-APM periods shows that the APM was more successful in insulating consumers from international oil price fluctuations. Even though severe fluctuations in crude oil prices were experienced after the second oil crisis in 1979, the effect of this was minimal. In addition, the performance of the industry in reducing import dependency in the pre-liberalisation period was much better than in the post-liberalisation period. In the areas of exploration and production of crude, which is really important for the Government to reduce import dependency, the private sector has not been successful. The reform in the form of the introduction of NELP and HELP has failed to attract enough investment and has not resulted in the substantial discovery of crude.

Despite the stagnant level of total indigenous crude production during the post-liberalisation period, the share of the private sector in the total production has increased by approximately 20 per cent. Further, in the post-APM period, the private sector performed better in terms of adding new refining capacity. In 2019, the private sector accounted for 43 per cent of total refining capacity. This helped the private sector to increase the production of refined products at a faster rate during the post-APM. Thus, though private sector participation (both domestic and foreign) has increased by a substantial amount in the post-APM period, no success was achieved either in reducing import dependency or maintaining price stability. Thus, we can only expect the growing dominance of the private sector in both refining and production of petroleum without gaining much with respect to price stability and import dependency.

After liberalisation, a faster pace of growth in the private sector vis-à-vis the public sector is seen in terms of refining capacity, production, sales and export. Also, the public sector marketing companies have been facing a continuous shortage of petroleum products in the post-reform period, and thus, they are dependent on imports and private sector production for their sales. The private sector, on the other hand, has recorded a surplus of production over sales since 2000 despite faster growth of sales compared to the public sector. The extraordinary growth was because of changes in Government policies towards promoting private investment after liberalisation. The dismantling of APM was also part of the overall liberalisation agenda which further facilitated the shift from the public to the private sector. In the post-liberalisation period, four new refineries in the private sector and joint venture companies were established, while no new refinery was added in the public sector.

In the marketing segment also, the private sector has emerged as a significant player. In the post-APM period, the growth rate of public sector sales declined, which gave more space to the private sector. The private sector accounted for 22.61 per cent of total sales in 2019-20. As far as the number of retail outlets is concerned, the private sector has started to grow extraordinarily at an average rate of 19 per cent per year after remaining stagnant for ten years (2006-15). On the other hand, the public sector OMCs growth has slowed from an average of eight per cent to 3.5 per cent since 2015. The fall in the international price of petroleum products, deregulation of domestic petroleum prices, relaxation of norms for private investment in retail business and reduction of investment by public sector firms have been the factors that helped the private sector to expand at a higher rate. It could be concluded that the private sector seems to have grown at the expense of the public sector.

Notes

1 Onshore oil refers to oil extracted from under the earth's surface (land) whereas offshore oil relates to oil extracted from underneath the seabed. Extracting offshore oil is much more difficult than the onshore oil and therefore the cost associated with the production of offshore crude oil is more than that of onshore crude oil.
2 For example, the low price of kerosene encouraged fuel adulteration and its diversion to many unintended uses.
3 IPP is the price paid by the importer at the Indian ports and includes free on board (FOB) price, insurance, ocean freight, custom duties, port dues, etc.
4 Other elements of cost were added to the landed cost or import parity price to arrive at the ex-storage point selling price for petrol and diesel. These components included costs such as cost of marketing, marketing margins, return on working capital, stock loss, retail pump outlet (RPO) charges, etc.
5 Rajya Sabha unstarred question no.450 answered on 19 July, 2017.
6 Reserve/production (R/P) ratio means that at current level of production, the known reserves will last for "R/P" no. of years.

References

Bandyopadhyay, K. R. (2010). *Petroleum Pricing in India: Transition from APM to MDPM*. Asian Institute of Transport Development, New Delhi.

Dasgupta, B. (1968). Pricing oil products: Its economic consequences. *Economic & Political Weekly*, *3*(35), 1337–1340.

Dasgupta, B. (1971). *The Oil Industry in India: Some Economic Aspects*. Frank Cass & Company, London.

Directorate General of Hydrocarbons. (2015). *Chronology of E&P Events in India*. National Data Repository, DGH, MoPNG, GoI. Retrieved from https://www.ndrdgh.gov.in/NDR/.

Expert Committee Report. (2019). *Report of the Expert Committee to Review Guidelines for Granting Authorisation to Market Transportation Fuels*. MoPNG, GoI, New Delhi. Retrieved from http://petroleum.nic.in/sites/default/files/expertcomm_0.pdf.

Jacob, S., & Roychoudhury, A. (2019). Govt mulling options to lower income cut-off level for LPG subsidy. *Business Standard*.

Krishnaswamy Committee. (1976). *Report of the Oil Prices Committee (Chairman, K.S. Krishnaswamy)*. Ministry of Petroleum, Govt. of India, New Delhi.

MoSPI. (2007). *Energy Statistics*. CSO, Ministry of Statistics and Programme Implementation, Government of India, New Delhi.

MoSPI. (2018). *Energy Statistics*. CSO, Ministry of Statistics and Programme Implementation, Government of India, New Delhi.

Mukul, J. (2019, October 24). Govt relaxes fuel retailing norms, private firms can set up petrol pumps. *Business Standard*. Retrieved from https://www.business

-standard.com/article/economy-policy/india-relaxes-fuel-retailing-norms-private-firms-can-set-up-petrol-pumps-119102301067_1.html.

Munasinghe, M. (1980). An integrated framework for energy pricing in developing countries. *The Energy Journal, International Association for Energy Economics, 1*(3), 1–30. https://doi.org/10.5547/issn0195-6574-ej-vol1-no3-1.

Press Information Bureau. (2019). *CCEA Approves Review of Guidelines for Granting Authorization to Market Transportation Fuels*. MoPNG, Government of India. Retrieved from https://pib.gov.in/PressReleasePage.aspx?PRID=1588855

R- Group. (1996). *Report of the Strategic Planning Group on Re-structuring of Oil Industries (Chairman, V.L. Kelkar)*. Ministry of Petroleum & Natural Gas, Govemment of India, New Delhi.

Rangarajan Committee. (2006). *Pricing and Taxation of Petroleum Products*. Ministry of Petroleum and Natural Gas, Government of India, New Delhi.

Singh, S., Parekh, S., & Joshi, M. (2018). Pricing in India's oil and gas sector. In A. Goswami (Ed.), *Fuel Pricing in India* (pp. 55–92). TERI, New Delhi.

Task Force Report. (2011). *Report of the Task Force on "An IT Strategy for PDS and an implementable solution for the direct transfer of subsidy for Food and Kerosene" (Chairman, Nandan Nilekani)*. Ministry of Finance, Government of India, New Delhi.

13 An Enquiry into India's Labour Market Flexibility

Learning from the Literature

Devangana Jha

Introduction

An acute sense of dissatisfaction with the existing labour-law regime has informed the neo-liberal vision of the Bharatiya Janata Party (BJP) Government that came to power in 2014. This vision is of course not unique to the new party in power, but is in line with the long-held mainstream view that India's poor industrial performance (output and employment) may be attributed to its restrictive labour laws. While it is true that this view has been shared by parties of all colours, and the labour-reform agenda has been on their minds for quite some time, a watershed moment occurred in 2014 with the BJP Government in the state of Rajasthan enacting three major labour amendments.[1] In continuation of this initiative, the Union Government sought to promulgate in 2019 an even more thoroughgoing labour legislation by consolidating 29 Central Labour Laws into four New Labour Codes. Only the first of these (the Code of Wages) could be enacted before India was hit by the Covid-19 pandemic. But such is the perceived urgency of the labour market reform question that in the very midst – indeed as a part – of the economic recovery after the first wave of the pandemic, one of the first acts of the Government was to enact the remaining three labour codes (the Industrial Relations Code, the Social Security Code, and the Occupational Safety, Health and Working Conditions Code) in September 2020.

It is thus only pertinent to wonder if labour laws have had such a profound bearing on our economic performance, so that we may accordingly expect these recent *legal* reforms to bring about the desired *economic* turnaround. In this chapter, we make a modest attempt to review the empirical rationale of the question in the available economic literature.

Labour Market Flexibility: Genesis and Evolution

The history of economic liberalism and labour legislation has had a long and tortuous course, but it was only during the neo-liberal offensive in the 'Crisis Decades' since the late 1970s following the end of 'the Golden Age of Capitalism' about 1973[2] that the concept of labour flexibility began to be

DOI: 10.4324/9781003343998-13

developed in earnest by professional economists. In the Indian context, it is not correct to suppose, as is usually done, that 'the earliest contribution in this *genre*'[3] was made as late as 1991 by Peter Fallon and Robert Lucas in their paper 'The Impact of Changes in Job Security Regulations in India and Zimbabwe'. A benchmark study as it no doubt was, the paper was preceded by a series of studies dating back at least to 1986, when for the World Bank, Lucas did 'An Overview of the Labour Market in India', and in the same series of the Bank the next year Fallon published a piece entitled 'The Effects of Labour Regulation upon Industrial Employment in India' (Lucas 1986; Fallon 1987). They were accompanied by yet another set of the Bank's economists (Ian Little, Vijay Joshi and John Page), underlining the adverse implications of the restrictive regulations and pointing out how the laws reserving a number of industries for small-scale enterprises were preventing productivity growth through economies of scale and technological improvement (Little, Joshi, and Page 1987, cited in Little and Joshi 1994: 37-38, 364n17; also in Zagha 1998: 412). In 1988, Lucas undertook a detailed analysis of the Indian economy between 1960 and 1980 and attributed the sluggish employment growth to two factors, namely high wages (due to union power) and job security legislation:

> rising industrial wage has been a significant factor in the observed move towards more capital intensive techniques ... . Since the scope and coverage of these job security laws has increased through time, it again seems likely that they have contributed to the trend towards reliance on more capital-intensive techniques within many manufacturing industries. (Lucas 1988)

The reason why the aforementioned 1991 paper (and its revised 1993 version) by Fallon and gained such prominence was its startling conclusion that employment in India fell by a massive 17.5 per cent due to labour legislation (in particular the amendment of 1976 that was incorporated as Chapter V-B in the Industrial Disputes Act) and union power. It was followed by an equally influential paper by Isher Judge Ahluwalia in 1992 which again attributed the poor employment record of India to its restrictive and rigid labour laws. In the 'Discussion Paper' on economic reforms by Government of India in 1993, it figures in a matter-of-fact way as received wisdom that must form the basis of policy:

> we must review and reform the current legislations for employment and industrial disputes to ensure that excessive rigidities are removed and long-term growth facilitated. The operation of the current Industrial Disputes Act (in particular, the requirement for prior approval by government for closure of sick units and retrenchment of labour) needs to be reviewed as it affects incentive for investment and (*sic*!) as well as increased employment. ... Rigid rules limiting the flexibility with which

labour can be hired and retrenched have the effect of pushing entrepreneurs into more capital-intensive technology and reduce the number of workers they have to deal with.

(GOI 1993: 34)

It was thus that the labour flexibility theory acquired the status of what was aptly dubbed (by R. Nagaraj in 1994) as the 'orthodox' view (Nagaraj 1994: 177, 184). With heavy backing from the collective opinion of institutions such as the World Bank, International Monetary Fund (IMF), and Organisation of Economic Co-operation and Development (OECD),[4] it would routinely find unqualified support in the official publications of Government of India.

However, even as it was becoming orthodoxy, informed sceptical voices could be heard. It would indeed be no exaggeration to say that over the long course of their development in India, neo-liberal claims about the labour market rigidities have been *met with rebuttals and alternative interpretations of the evidence* at every step. We thus have Nagaraj (among others) countering, as early as 1994, the first onrush of the theses that blamed labour market rigidities for the many ills of the Indian economy. In a move 'towards an alternative explanation' [Nagaraj 1994: 182-184 (section IV)], he was able to show that the observed outcomes were to be understood very differently; for example, it was 'mainly in response to the macro-economic compulsions of the 70s and the discovery of appropriate natural resources ... [rather than to some legal obstacle that] ... the composition of output changed in favour of less labour intensive industries' (Nagaraj 1994: 184). The same irrelevance of the regulatory legal framework in understanding economic outcomes was brought out in a rigorous study by Roberto Zagha [Zagha 1998: 419 (for the concluding remarks)].

The critics' point has in fact been compellingly simple: the many twists and turns of the Indian economy can hardly be understood in terms of the laws that have remained unchanged on the whole since 1991, or in terms of the pressure tactics of a progressively weakening trade union movement under an undisguised state offensive. In the balanced judgement of Jayati Ghosh: 'in the ultimate analysis, labour laws, significant as they are, are perhaps far less significant as factors in affecting private investment, than more standard macroeconomic variables and profitability indicators' (Ghosh 2004: 29).

It remains true nevertheless that we have a very large number of empirical studies for India that support the case for the reforms by seeking to demonstrate the adverse effect of the laws on economic outcomes in various ways. Each of these studies is important in itself and merits separate treatment, but in terms of shared methodology and assumptions, it is possible to divide them in two broad groupings. The first is best represented by the Fallon and Lucas piece, and the second by an article that Timothy Besley and Robin Burgess published in 2004. The latter has by far been the more influential and has inspired the largest number of studies. Both the approaches have been subjected to sustained critiques. In the limited space of this chapter, we discuss these studies in terms of the twofold division.

Employment Protection Legislation and Employment

The question whether the Industrial Disputes Act (IDA) laws affected employment was investigated by Fallon and Lucas (1991, 1993) with reference to the 1976 amendment. They used the ASI data on formal manufacturing for the period 1959-1981. ASI data have two major division: the 'census' sector comprises factories (with power), employing 50 or more workers as well as those (without power) employing 100 or more workers; and the 'sample' sector, employing the remaining factories with power that employed 10 or more, and those without power employing 20 or more.[5] Fallon and Lucas examined 35 out of the 36 industries of the sample sector (one industry did not have the relevant information), which included their target group of factories with 300 or more workers to which the 1976 law applied. They checked their results further with cross-evidence from the sample sector:

> Thus no evidence is found to suggest that job loss in the census sector as a result of the 1976 amendment produced job gains in parallel sample sector factories through transfer of workers across establishments, through sub-contracting, through putting out of work, or through major adjustments in establishment size.
>
> (Fallon and Lucas 1991: 407; Fallon and Lucas 1993: 264-265)

Fallon and Lucas did not see any shift in the employment adjustment rate. However, they did see a reduction in labour demand after 1976 that is significant at 5% in 11 of 35 industries. The data further show, according to them, that the new law had a negative effect on labour demand in 25 out of 35 sectors using a 25% level of significance. (Fallon and Lucas 1993: 263). The conclusion is that, but for the 1976 amendment, employment would have been 17.5% higher in India in the formal sector. (Fallon and Lucas 1991: 412).

However, as Sonia Bhalotra points out, the figure of 17.5% was reached by them on the basis of the questionable method of averaging across insignificant coefficients. (Bhalotra 1998: 7n3). Second, their negative estimate for labour demand was significant at a very high level (25%) of significance. 'Clearly, they are drawing about the negative impact on employment of labour regulations that their estimates do not portray'. (D'Souza 2008: 270). The conclusion drawn was thus noted to be rather seriously overdrawn.

Fallon and Lucas, however, were perfectly aware that their estimation of dynamic labour demand for 35 industries in India showing a drop in employment does not hold for a majority of them, with the required confidence level of 90% being obtained only for 14 industries. One of their major conclusions, stated more than once, is also that 'the consequences of job security regulations ... vary considerably from one industry to another'.[6]

This outcome, that not all industries could be said to have suffered employment loss, was explained by them in terms of the following observations: the 1976 law applied only to factories with 300 or more employees; some of these big factories have strong union presence that will cushion the impact of the law; and a number of these factories are public sector enterprises with over-staffing and strong unions, and 'hence effectively immune to such changes in labour laws'. (Fallon and Lucas 1993: 269).

It is here that one may locate perhaps the most vulnerable points in their exercise (apart from the job adjustment rigidity point to be discussed presently), comprising a number of unverified, question-begging assumptions and statements. First, the overall decline in employment, calculated at the weighted average of 17.5%, is *assumed* to have been the effect of the 1976 legislation alone, although their data included an uncalculated number of firms that employed less than 300 workers, and could not have felt any impact of the law in question. The second assumption is that the projected loss of employment in the big firms (with 300 plus employees) percolated down to and characterised the smaller firms too, including those in the sample sector. This is begging the question. Why would the smaller firms allow themselves to be affected by a law that did not apply to them, and not take advantage of that fact instead?

The explanation for the observed variations of the negative coefficients among firms is similarly based on a series of unverified assumptions: that those less or little affected were either public sector enterprises (a special case with labour hoarding and all), or private firms with powerful unions, while those most affected were neither public sector enterprises nor private firms with powerful unions, nor – one may add in furtherance of their suppositions – firms with less than 300 employees. Fallon and Lucas state: 'In India, it is in the private sector, in plants employing more than 300 workers, and where union membership is low, that the greatest drop in employment is *observed*' (emphasis added) (Fallon and Lucas 1993: 269). This observation remains probably unsubstantiated and is actually contradicted by the very specific employment data in the formal sector for the period 1977-78 to 1988-89, which shows positive growth in employment in factories with less than 1000 workers, that is to say, in factories being covered by the twin IDA amendments (Nagaraj 1994: 180).

In 2004 Dutta Roy published her study on the impact of JSL on employment. She cast a much wider net, extending the period up to 1994 (1960-1994), thus studying the impact of both 1976 and 1982 legislation, and covering industry groups that formed more than 77% of total employment, and more than 84% of the value added, of the formal manufacturing sector.

Like Bhalotra had done previously on the basis of an industry-region panel for the 1980s, Dutta Roy established high employment adjustment rigidities in the Indian labour market. According to Bhalotra, 90% of the optimal-level adjustment in employment takes 5.8 years in the formal manufacturing sector (Bhalotra 1998: 18). Dutta Roy showed, for 1960-1994, that of the 16 industries, employment in 10[7] showed an insignificant response to a disequilibrium in the industry's own market in the preceding period; the average of four industries[8] showed a less than 40% correction of the disequilibrium; and only two – cement and non-ferrous basic metals – displayed approximately 90% correction of the disequilibrium in any period. On an average across all these industries, she concluded, it takes from five to six years for the completion of most of the employment adjustment.

The first implication that these results have for the studies of Fallon and Lucas is that their data terminating at 1980-81 are too premature to reflect employment adjustments due to the 1976 law.

How may then the observed rigidities in the industrial labour market be explained, and how significant are the two labour laws in this respect? Looking at her data across 1976 and across 1984 (when the 1982 amendment came into effect) and looking for a change in the adjustment coefficients, Dutta Roy discovered results that were rather too complex for any simple-minded explanation based on labour laws and that suggested that the answers will have to be mostly sought in industry-specific characteristics. She did separate estimation exercises for workers and for supervisors. In view of their immense bearing on our concerns, the results for the workers may be quoted in full:

1. Of the 16 industries in the sample, 10 reveal rigidities in adjustment even in the pre-JSR (job security regulation) period. Of these, the impact of JSR is statistically insignificant in the case of seven industries, probably indicating that the observed rigidities are attributable to their inherent characteristics. The impact of JSR is statistically significant for three industries, for two of which the net impact of IDA 1976 and IDA 1982 is ambiguous.
2. The estimated coefficients for six industries indicate flexibility in the pre-JSR period, with an average coefficient of –0.72. Of these, three do not reveal any significant impact of the IDA 1976 or IDA 1982. Only in the sole case of cement is flexibility found to have been impaired significantly as a result of labour market regulations. In the case of the remaining two industries, the impact of JSR on flexibility is found to be favourable. (Dutta Roy 2004: 245)

Aditya Bhattacharjea pointed to a more fundamental problem in the use of the dummy variable method for showing the impact of legislation on employment. The method can establish only the incidence of job loss, but not the cause of it. Thus, the job losses after 1976 could have been a result as much of the Emergency as of the labour-law amendment (Bhattacharjea 2006: 7-8; Roychowdhury 2018: 47-48), or *of none of these*. Equally to the point, 'Fallon and Lucas' result seems to suggest that the 1976 job security amendment had a one-shot effect in reducing employment *immediately* but no *sustained* effect in slowing down employment adjustments in the long run' (Roychowdhury 2018: 48, 99-100, citing the argument of Anant *et al* 2006).

State-Level Laws and Economic Performance: The BB Index and Its Derivatives

We know that Labour is a Concurrent subject, and States of the Indian Union have passed a large number of labour-related laws that add to and/or amend the Union legislation, thus superseding them. Permission for closure as per IDA was normally to be obtained from the State concerned. Since it is the state-level legislation and decision-making that really matter at ground level, a number of studies have focussed on labour laws as they operate at state levels, and their impact on the economies of the various states.

Besley and Burgess worked out a scheme, in which, depending on the differences in state-level amendments to IDA, the states were slotted as pro-worker, pro-employer, or neutral, and accordingly assigned scores of +1, −1, and zero. These scores were assigned for every year, depending on the net result of the existing laws. As the law(s) enacted by a state for any year could naturally not be expected to be necessarily in line with the overall nature of its laws till then, Besley and Burgess evolved an index for the state for that year by cumulating its annual scores up to that year, calling it a 'regulatory measure'. This index in turn became a regressor, together with some control variables, for explaining state-level outcomes, including employment, output, investment, and productivity in the formal industrial sector of the state.

Following this method for investigating the pattern of manufacturing development in the 16 states for the period 1958-1992, Besley and Burgess identified four (Gujarat, Maharashtra, Orissa, and West Bengal) as 'pro-worker' or 'control' states, six as 'pro-employer' (Andhra Pradesh, Karnataka, Kerala, Madhya Pradesh, Rajasthan, and Tamil Nadu); and six as neutral (Assam, Bihar, Haryana, Jammu and Kashmir, Punjab, and Uttar Pradesh). (Besley and Burgess 2004. 7). The conclusion they reached was that the impact of the respective labour regime had been decisive:

> Pro-worker states on average had high per capita registered manufacturing output in 1960 relative to control states and pro-employer states. However, by 1990, there is no statistically significant difference between pro-worker and pro-employer states. Moreover, registered manufacturing output in the pro-employer states has overtaken that in the control states.
>
> (Besley and Burgess 2004: 7)

The evidence amassed in the paper further points to the direction of labour regulation as a key factor in shaping the pattern of industrial development in India. Regulating in a pro-worker direction was associated with lower levels of investment, employment, productivity, and output in registered manufacturing. It also increased informal sector activity (Besley and Burgess 2004: 21).

The index of Besley and Burgess, called after them the BB index, became the basis, with changes here and there and with some updating, of a number of studies in state-level correlations of labour regime and economic performance. The BB index went up to 1992. It was updated through 1997 in Philippe Aghion et al, through 2002 in Purfield, and through 2005 in Dougherty, while Ahsan and Pages did a full re-scoring of the index. All the studies buttressed the conclusions of BB, except one by Purfield, which 'did not find significant detrimental effects of more pro-employer labour institutions on state-level growth' (Cited in Dougherty 2008: 15).

For instance, Aghion and his associates give the following scores to the various states for the period 1980-1997:

> There is heterogeneity in both the level and change of labour regulation across our 1980–1997 sample period. The most extreme pro-worker state, West Bengal, has labour regulation values that rise from 12 to 14 over the 1980–1997 period. Three other states (Gujarat, Maharashtra, and Orissa) are also recorded as beginning the period as pro-worker or amending in this direction. The most extreme pro-employer state, Andhra Pradesh, has a score that varies from 22 to 23 across our period. Four other states (Kerala, Rajasthan, Tamil Nadu, and Karnataka) begin the period as pro-employer or amend in that direction. There are six neutral states (Assam, Bihar, Haryana, Jammu and Kashmir, Punjab, and Uttar Pradesh) that begin the period at zero and do not amend in either direction. Finally, Madhya Pradesh is neutral in all years except for a pro-employer change in 1982, which is reversed by a 1983 pro-worker amendment.
>
> (Aghion et al 2008: 1400)

Then they proceed to study whether and how the progress of liberalisation in the various states corresponds to these scores. Their focus is on the impact of the delicensing dimension of the liberalisation: in 1985, around one-third of all three-digit industries were delicensed, and in 1991 all industrial licensing was practically done away with, with the exception of a small number due to strategic, safety, and such other concerns.[9] Their conclusion is as emphatic as that of Besley and Burgess:

> The actual delicense-labour regulation interaction is significant at the 5 percent level in 98 of the 100 regressions, whereas the placebo delicense-labour regulation interaction is significant at the 5 percent level

> in only 7 of the regressions. The results of both falsification exercises serve as compelling evidence that the actual timing of when industries are delicensed is central to our main empirical result.
>
> (Aghion et al 2008: 1409)

The methods and the results of these (and other such) analyses can and have indeed been comprehensively questioned. Technically, for instance, the analysis of Besley and Burgess remains defective (D'Souza 2008: 6), so that 'once the time trend is introduced, labour regulation is no longer a significant variable in explaining manufacturing output and employment' and 'instead now development expenditure which is state spending on social and economic services (health, education, infrastructure, and administration) is the driving variable that explains output growth amongst states' (D'Souza 2008: 7).

The problems with the slotting of states into the three categories are equally serious. For instance, calling Gujarat 'pro-worker' on the basis of a solitary amendment in 1973, whereby a penalty of Rs 50 a day was imposed on employers for not nominating representatives to firm-level joint management councils, is rightly criticised as 'strange' (Bhattacharjea 2006: 10). It has also been noted that application of more sensible criteria results in altogether different rankings:

> BB classify Gujarat and Maharashtra as pro-worker; they also designate Kerala as pro-employer. Drawing attention to a World Bank report on the investment climate in various states that provides evidence of actual implementation of labour legislation as indicated by the degree of over-manning and the frequency of inspections, Hasan et al reverse the classification of these three states for their own econometric analysis. … Madhya Pradesh, which BB had classified as pro-employer, is classified by Hasan et al as having inflexible labour markets, because pro-employer amendments in 1982 were offset by a pro-worker amendment the following year.
>
> (Bhattacharjea 2006: 19)

There are other problems too with identifying Gujarat and Maharashtra as pro worker and Kerala as pro-employer. For instance, it has been found in a study that factory inspectors visit small and medium enterprises in 'pro-employer' Kerala twice as many times as they do in 'pro-worker' Maharashtra and Gujarat. (Cited in D'Souza 2008: 5). Furthermore,

> states such as Andhra Pradesh, Rajasthan, and Tamil Nadu, which had been classified as pro-employer, have had declining secondary sector employment elasticities in the recent reforms period (1994-2000) compared to the 1984-94 period, whereas pro-employee states such as Maharashtra, Gujarat, and Orissa have witnessed an acceleration in

> secondary employment during this period (their employment elasticities have increased).
>
> (Cited in D'Souza 2008: 5)

In sum, BB's analysis suffers from the omission of 'far too many potentially relevant ... variables' (Bhattacharjea 2006: 18). Thus, the non-incorporation in the indices of the critically relevant portions of the court judgements could not but lead to proportionately critical errors in their conclusion.[10]

Although they note that Bhattacharjea's criticisms of Besley and Burgess 'could invalidate' their results, Ahsan and Pagés nevertheless follow their method. For example, on the basis of an amendment to IDA by Andhra Pradesh government in 1987 that put certain restrictions on parties in an industrial dispute, they encode it as 'minus one' (Ahsan and Pagés 2008: 7, 9).

In 2007 OECD came out with an altogether original scheme of indices to chart state-level economic performance in the light of their labour regimes. (OECD 2007: 130-132). Having notably contributed to the development of this different set of indices for state-level analyses, Sean Dougherty identified the regulatory framework, operating at the state level, as the common and the lone culprit for a series of economic ills: why employment has expanded everywhere except in the formal industrial sector; why the job dynamics are so uneven and so costly, and; how capital intensity in investment and informalisation in employment have grown because of the high labour costs of permanent employment. (Dougherty 2008).

The results from all these state-level analyses, however, suffer from a common, and most damaging, problem, which is the fact of enormous changes in the economy while the indices remained by and large the same, displaying very little change, if at all:

> although there had been little change in the BB index [this would apply to other indices too] in the late 1980s and none in the 1990s, there had been a substantial change in the industrial relations scenario during this period.
>
> (Bhattacharjea 2009: 4)

The critique has been considerably strengthened and enriched in the latest and an almost exhaustive critical survey of the literature by Bhattacharjea (June 2021). He has described in detail additional methodological and econometric errors in the BB index (and its various avatars). He showed that a mere 30 out of the 113 state amendments used in the construction of the BB index, either in its original or modified version, are relevant to the measurement of flexibility, even if we adopt an expansive definition of labour market flexibility. Apart from this selection/classification error where irrelevant amendments were included in the construction of the index, there is the problem of miscoding of individual amendments. He demonstrates several such cases; to cite just one, a non-zero score has been assigned (by BB) to five irrelevant state amendments to Chapter V-B which should have been coded zero. Further, there is a lamentable lack of differentiating between types of amendments with potentially very different implications for the labour market. Clubbing them all mechanically, a summary score of +1 or –1 would be assigned to a particular state that amended several sections of the IDA simultaneously, without taking into due account the actual character of the individual amendment in question. Still worse is the assigning of scores in terms of the duration of the legislation rather than the character per se of it: thus

> a state that passed a set of pro-worker amendments in one year would have its score changed by +1, whereas another state that passed the same amendments over several years would see its score progressively increased by +1 each time.
>
> (Bhattacharjea 2006: 12)

Much of these criticisms has also been shown to apply to later indices such as the 'OECD Index' of Sean Dougherty, and the composite index of Gupta et al. (Bhattacharjea 2021: 3-4). His considered judgement is unequivocal: 'The literature thus suffers from serious methodological deficiencies, as well as misunderstanding of both the law and the data. ... I can only conclude that this research programme is irrelevant as a guide to policy'.[11]

Conclusions

The question of labour flexibility has long been held to be of critical importance both in India and abroad, illustrated most recently by the labour reforms by GOI. The conceptual-ideological foundations of these reforms consist in the main in the labour market flexibility thesis, namely, that dismantling of India's restrictive and rigid labour laws is essential to improving output and employment outcomes in Indian manufacturing in the formal sector. This thesis goes back several decades, and draws upon a very distinguished, influential, and extensively argued and researched stream of economic thinking. However, the critiques of this thinking and vision have been almost as old as the advocacy of labour flexibility. The labour flexibility *controversy* that was thus born has been continuing till date, as arguments and evidence have been marshalled in an unceasing flow of research in innumerable lectures, seminars, essays in newspapers and research journals, etc. As a result, we have two contrasting and competing sets of views, each thickly backed with argument and evidence.

Here comes the nub of the matter. The 'orthodox' side has chosen by and large simply to ignore the very specific criticisms of its standpoint, of the theoretical and empirical grounds on which the labour reforms have been undertaken. 'Controversy' rather than 'debate' is thus the more precise word for describing the current state of the issue. This necessarily raises questions about the propriety of the reforms. The unfortunate failure of response has resulted in a loss of legitimacy for the reforms. It is incumbent upon the reformers to account for and/or accommodate the issues raised by the critics. There can be no justification for the reforms without a review of the whole question – that is to say, without a proper debate.

Notes

1 These pertain to the Industrial Disputes Act (IDA) of 1947; the Factories Act of 1948; and the Contract-Labour (Regulation and Abolition), or the CLRA.
2 For the 'Golden Age' and the subsequent crisis, see Hobsbawm 1994: Chapters 9 and 14.
3 Roychowdhury 2018: 44. See also Guha 2009: 46.
4 For instance, OECD's first-ever economic survey of India in 2007 devoted one chapter to 'Improving the Performance of the Labour Market', which lauds the reforms for having 'taken some of the bite out the core labour laws' and calls for 'more comprehensive reforms' for correcting the remaining 'distortions' in the labour market (OECD 2007: chapter 4). Gerry Rodgers reports a near consensus on the issue among these institutions, though 'other views can also be found in World Bank publications' (Rodgers 2006: 2).
5 The definitions and thus the coverage of these two categories (census and sample) have varied from time to time. For example, in 1987-88, the definition of the census sector was changed to the units employing 100 or more workers irrespective of their operation with or without power. For a complete discussion, see Manual on Annual Survey of industries: 11. Accessed at http://mospi.nic.in/mospi_new/upload/asi_manual-22.09.08.pdf.
6 Fallon and Lucas 1993: 242. This is repeated on p. 269 ('there is a good deal of variation in estimated impact across industries').
7 These include chemicals and chemical products, structural clay products, miscellaneous food products, sugar, paper and paper products, non-electrical machinery, electrical machinery, railroad equipment, and motor vehicles.
8 These include iron and steel, rubber and rubber products, textile products, and tobacco.
9 Aghion et al: 1398-1399. The 1985 delicensing allowed the automatic entry into about 25 broad categories of industries (Gupta and Kumar 2010: 13).
10 E.g. Bhattacharjea 2009: 9 ('While the amendments discussed above have been imperfectly incorporated into the BB analysis, none of the court judgments striking down various sections of chapter V-B has even been recognised, although they too have direct implications for the index'.)
11 Bhattacharjea 2021: 33-34. In an earlier piece of his, Bhattacharjea, after offering incisive critiques, would still call himself an 'agnostic' as to the merits of the case for labour-law reforms in India (Bhattacharjea 2009: 62). It needs to be said however that even then his own observations were sufficient enough to preclude any room for the agnosticism (Jha, Devangana 2013: 52-53).

References

Aghion, Philippe, Robin Burgess, Stephen J. Redding, and Fabrizio Zilibotti (2008). The Unequal Effects of Liberalization: Evidence from Dismantling the License Raj in India, *American Economic Review*, 98(4), 1397–1412.

Ahluwalia, Isher J. (1992). *Productivity and Growth in Indian Manufacturing*, Oxford University Press, New Delhi.

Ahsan, A., and C. Pagés (2008). Are All Labour Regulations Equal? Evidence from Indian Manufacturing, *IZA Discussion Paper No. 3394*.

Anant, T. C. A., R. Mohapatra, R. Nagaraj, and S. K. Sasikumar (2006). Labour Markets in India: Issues and Perspectives, in J. Felipe and R. Hasan (eds.), *Labour Markets in Asia: Issues and Perspectives*, pp. 205–300, Palgrave Macmillan, Basinstoke.

Besley, T., and R. Burgess (2004). Can Regulation Hinder Economic Performance? Evidence from India, *Quarterly Journal of Economics*, 119(1), 91–134.

Bhalotra, Sonia R. (1998). The Puzzle of Jobless Growth in Indian Manufacturing, *Oxford Bulletin of Economics and Statistics*, 60(1), 5–32.

Bhattacharjea, Aditya (2006). Labour Market Regulation and Industrial Performance in India: A Critical Review of the Empirical Evidence, *Indian Journal of Labour Economics*, 49(2), 211–232.

Bhattacharjea, Aditya (2009). The Effects of Employment Protection Legislation on Indian Manufacturing, *Economic and Political Weekly*, 44(22), 55–62.

Bhattacharjea, Aditya (2021). Labour Market Flexibility in Indian Industry: A Critical Survey of the Literature. Last revised 28 June, 2021. https://papers.ssrn.com/sol3/papers.cfm?abstract_id=3745120 (accessed July 18, 2021).

Dougherty, Sean (2008). Labour Regulation and Employment Dynamics at the State Level in India, *OECD Economics Department Working Papers*, No. 624, OECD Publishing.

D'Souza, Errol (2008). Labour Market Institutions in India—Their Impact on Growth and Employment, *ILO Asia-Pacific Working Paper Series*.

Dutta Roy, Sudipta (2004). Employment Dynamics in Indian Industry: Adjustment Lags and the Impact of Job Security Regulations, *Journal of Development Economics*, 73(1), 233–256.

Fallon, Peter (1987). *The Effects of Labor Regulation upon Industrial Employment in India*, World Bank Research Department Discussion Paper No 287.

Fallon, Peter R., and Robert E. B. Lucas (1991). The Impact of Changes in Job Security Regulations in India and Zimbabwe, *The World Bank Economic Review*, 5(3), 395–413.

Fallon, Peter R., and Robert E. B. Lucas. (1993). Job Security Regulations and the Dynamic Demand for Labor in India and Zimbabwe, *Journal of Development Economics*, 40(2), 241–275.

Ghosh, Jayati (2004). *Macroeconomic Reforms and a Labour Market Policy Framework for India*, Employment Strategy Papers, ILO, Geneva.

Guha, Atulan (2009). Labour Market Flexibility: An Empirical Inquiry into Neoliberal Propositions, *Economic and Political Weekly*, 44(19), 45–52.

Gupta, Poonam, R. Hasan, and U. Kumar (2009). Big Reforms but Small Payoffs: Explaining the Weak Record of Growth in Indian Manufacturing, in S. Bery, B. Bosworth, and A. Panagariya (eds.), *India Policy Forum*, volume 5, pp. 59–108. Accessed at http://mpra.ub.uni-muenchen.de/13496/ MPRA Paper No. 13496.

Hobsbawm, Eric J. (1994). *The Age of Extremes*, Abacus, London.

Jha, Devangana (2013). *Of Workers and Wages: Examining the Labour Flexibility Thesis for India's Formal Industrial Sector, 1981–2009*, Unpublished M.Phil. dissertation, CESP, JNU.

Joshi, Vijay, and Ian Malcolm David Little (1996). *India's Economic Reforms: 1991–2001*, Clarendon Press, Oxford.

Joshi, Vijay, and Ian Malcolm David Little (1994). *India: Macroeconomics and Political Economy, 1964–1991*, World Bank, Washington, DC.

Little, Ian Malcolm David, Vijay Joshi, and John Page (1987). *Small Manufacturing Enterprises. A Comparative Analysis of India and Other Economies*, World Bank and Oxford University Press, New York.

Lucas, Robert E. B. (1986). *An Overview of the Labour Market in India*, Development Research Department, Economics and Research Staff, World Bank, Original from Indiana University, Digitized Jul 14, 2011.

Lucas, Robert E. B., and Gustav F. Papanek (1988). India's Industrial Policy, in Robert E. B. Lucas and Gustav F. Papanek (eds.) *The Indian Economy: Recent Development and Future Prospects*, pp. 189–190, Oxford University Press, Delhi.

Ministry of Finance (1993). *Discussion Paper*, GOI.

Nagaraj, Rayaprolu (1994). Employment and Wages in Manufacturing Industries: Trends, Hypotheses and Evidence, *Economic and Political Weekly*, 29(4), 177–186.

OECD (2007). *OECD Economic Surveys: India.*

Roychowdhury, Anamitra (2018). *Labour Law Reforms in India: All in the Name of Jobs*, Routledge, India.

Zagha, Roberto (1998). Labor and India's Economic Reforms, *The Journal of Policy Reform*, 2(4), 403–426.

14 Female Employment in the Retail Trade Sector in India

Bindu Oberoi

Introduction

The Indian economy has undergone a significant structural shift in terms of sectoral shares in employment in recent years. An analysis based on the unit-level data from the NSS employment unemployment surveys shows that the share of agriculture in total employment (ps+ss) declined by 2.95 percentage points from 1993-94 to 1999-00 and by 3.15 percentage points from 1999-00 to 2004-05. It then declined drastically by 9.57 percentage points from 2004-05 to 2011-12. About 33.13 m workers (ps+ss) withdrew from agriculture during the period between 2004-05 and 2011-12. About 26.21 m of these were female workers in the rural areas (Table 14.1). Construction emerged as the most important sector in terms of employment generation during the period and employed about 4.51 m additional female workers in the rural areas (Table 14.1). However, overall, about 21.98 m female workers in the rural areas lost their work and could not be absorbed in any sector.

The recent decline in rural female employment has received considerable attention in the public debate. The decline is generally attributed to rising incomes and increasing participation of women in education (Chatterjee et al. 2015; Thomas 2012; Bhalla and Kaur 2011). A few studies have paid attention to absence of job opportunities, particularly in the rural non-farm sector (Ramesh and Srivastava 2014; Kannan and Raveendran 2012). There are studies that point to measurement fallacy and the problems of distinguishing between domestic duties and contributing family work (Mehrotra 2015). Role of sociocultural norms that discourage women's participation in the labour force is also highlighted (Srivastava and Srivastava 2010). It is in this context that the present chapter analyses trends in female employment in India's retail trade sector that has always been considered a refuge sector for those unable to find jobs in any other sector in the economy.

The post-liberalisation period had seen remarkable growth of the retail trade sector in India. The period was marked with a substantial increase in demand for various consumer goods, including food, fuel, clothing, goods

DOI: 10.4324/9781003343998-14

Table 14.1 Usual Status Employment of Rural Female Workers (m)

Sectors	*1993-94*		*1999-00*		*2004-05*		*2011-12*	
	PS	*PS+SS*	*PS*	*PS+SS*	*PS*	*PS+SS*	*PS*	*PS+SS*
Agriculture and Related Activities	56.08	79.95	65.41	85.75	69.85	96.7	49.58	70.49
Mining & Quarrying	0.31	0.35	0.27	0.29	0.33	0.34	0.25	0.28
Manufacturing	5.26	7.09	5.95	7.63	7.46	9.7	6.36	9.21
E, G & WS	0.07	0.09	0.13	0.15	0.09	0.11	0.06	0.06
Construction	0.65	0.73	0.97	1.06	1.49	1.69	3.38	6.2
Trade & Repair Including Retail	1.24	1.66	1.37	1.6	1.97	2.34	1.97	2.60
Retail	1.16	1.42	1.32	1.56	1.89	2.29	1.85	2.47
Transport & Post & Telegraph	0.04	0.05	0.05	0.05	0.11	0.12	0.07	0.1
Hotel & Restaurants	0.2	0.25	0.36	0.39	0.46	0.54	0.42	0.47
Other Services	2.24	2.49	3.25	3.53	4.05	4.51	4.48	4.94
Total	66.1	92.66	77.77	100.46	85.8	116.04	66.57	94.35

Notes: Following codes are used:
Agriculture and related activities: For 50th Round for 1993-94 based on NIC-1987 codes 00+01+03+04+05+06+230; For 55th and 61st Rounds for 1999-00 and 2004-05 based on NIC 1998 codes 01+02+03; For 68th Round for 2011-12 codes 01 to 03 based on NIC 2008.
Mining and Quarrying: For 50th Round for 1993-94 based on NIC-1987 – codes (10-101)+11+120+13+140+15+(19-199); For 55th and 61st Rounds for 1999-00 and 2004-05 based on NIC 1998 codes 10 to 14; For 68th Round for 2011-12 codes (05 to 09)+19204 based on NIC 2008.
Manufacturing: For 50th Round for 1993-94 based on NIC-1987 – codes (200 to 399-394-230-398)-(284+285)+964; For 55th and 61st Rounds for 1999-00 and 2004-05 based on NIC 1998 codes (15 to 36)-2211-2212-2213-2219; For 68th Round for 2011-12 codes (10 to 33)-19204 based on NIC 2008.
Electricity, Gas and Water Supply – For 50th Round for 1993-94 based on NIC-1987 – codes (400+401+410+420+430+431+432+439)+910; For 55th and 61st Rounds for 1999-00 and 2004-05 based on NIC 1998 codes 37+40-41+9000; For 68th Round for 2011-12 codes 35 to 39 based on NIC 2008.
Construction: For 50th Round for 1993-94 based on NIC-1987 – codes 101+199+(500 to 506)+(509 to 515)+519; For 55th and 61st Rounds for 1999-00 and 2004-05 based on NIC 1998 code 45; For 68th Round for 2011-12 codes 41 to 43 based on NIC 2008.
Wholesale and Retail Trade and Repair: For 50th Round for 1993-94 based on NIC-1987 – codes (680 to 689)+840+841+398+974; For 55th and 61st Rounds for 1999-00 and 2004-05 based on NIC 1998 codes (50 to 52)-5260; For 68th Round for 2011-12 codes (45 to 47)+92001+92002 based on NIC 2008.
Transport, Post and Telegraph: For 50th Round for 1993-94 based on NIC-1987 – codes (700 to 712)+720+721+730+731+732+(738+741)+(749 to 751); For 55th and 61st Rounds for 1999-00 and 2004-05 based on NIC 1998 codes (60 to 64)-6420-6304; For 68th Round for 2011-12 codes (49 to 53).
Hotel and Restaurants: For 50th Round for 1993-94 based on NIC-1987 – codes (690+691); For 55th and 61st Rounds for 1999-00 and 2004-05 based on NIC 1998 code 55; For 68th Round for 2011-12 codes (55+56) based on NIC 2008.
Other Services: For 50th Round for 1993-94 based on NIC-1987 – codes to (800 to 990)+(733 to 737)+284+285+752+759+394-910-964-974-840-841; For 55th and 61st Rounds for 1999-00 and 2004-05 based on NIC 1998 codes (2211+2212+2213+2219)+(6420+6304)+5260-9000; For 68th Round for 2011-12 codes (58 to 99)-92001-92002 based on NIC 2008.
Source: Computed based on unit-level data from the NSS 50th, 55th, 61st and 68th rounds on employment-unemployment.

for personal care, toilet articles, etc. (Oberoi, 2017). The retail sale grew in the economy at a high average annual rate of 13.6 per cent during 1994-95 to 1999-00. The growth declined during 2000-01 to 2002-03 but picked up again at about 11 per cent per annum during 2003-04 to 2006-07 (ICREAR, 2008). Retail sales grew at 14.29 per cent per annum from 2005 to 2010[1]. The growth of India's retail sector is vital as it provided a source of livelihood to the increasingly large number of persons when employment opportunities were shrinking in the rapidly growing economy since the 1990s. It is the second-largest sector, after agriculture, for generating self-employment in the economy and has always been considered a refuge employment sector. However, an analysis of the NSS employment-unemployment data indicates that the sector's potential to absorb surplus labour has decreased in recent years. The changing trend seems to have affected female workers more than their male counterparts.

The present chapter focuses on trends in female employment in the retail trade sector in India since the 1980s and examines the reasons that have affected the potential of this sector to absorb surplus female labour. It argues that the sector has experienced several significant structural changes since the 1990s. These changes have adversely affected the potential of the sector to serve as a refuge sector, especially for female workers in the rural areas which account for more than 80 per cent of the female workers in India. The chapter is divided into five sections. Section 2 analyses trends in employment in India's retail trade sector. Section 3 highlights changes in the structure of the retail trade sector in India and examines its impact on the nature of retail sector employment in general and on female employment in the retail sector in particular. Section 4 discusses the consequences of the continuance of a low degree of female labour absorption in the sector. Section 5 summarises the discussion by linking all the sections. The scope of the study is limited to the period since 1980-81, as the Indian retail trade has undergone significant structural changes during this period.

Estimates of employment (spa and ps+ss)[2], based on the usual status approach used to classify the activity status of the persons employed in the retail sector, are generated. The study is based on the unit-level data from the 38th, 43rd, 50th, 55th, 61st and 68th rounds of the NSS Surveys on Employment and Unemployment for the years 1983, 1987-88, 1993-94, 1999-00, 2004-05 and 2011-12. The concordance from three-digit levels of NIC-1987 to NIC-1970, from four-digit level of NIC-1998 to three-digit level of NIC-1987, from four-digit levels of NIC-2004 to NIC-1998 and from four-digit levels of NIC-2008 to NIC-2004 was used for ensuring comparability of employment data over time. Further, since the focus is to analyse female employment in the retail trade sector in the context of the overall industrial distribution of female workers, disaggregation of NIC-2008 at a five-digit level was also necessary.

Trends in Employment in Retail

According to the NSS data on employment unemployment, about 14.88 million persons were employed according to their usual status (ps+ss) in buying goods from the wholesaler or dealer and selling them to the consumers at the all-India level during 1983 (Table 14.2). Employment continued to increase in the sector during the period from the 1980s. While much of the increase in employment in the rural areas occurred after the 1990s; it took place during the 1990s itself in the urban areas. However, the gender-wise analysis of the growth of employment suggests that female employment continued to remain low in India's rural as well as urban retail sectors (Table 14.2)

Since the majority of the female workers have always been engaged in agriculture, the retail trade sector in India employed only a negligible percentage of female workers. For example, in 1993-94, the retail sector in

Table 14.2 Usual Status Employment in India's Retail Sector (m)

Year	*Rural*					
	Rural Male		*Rural Female*		*Rural Total*	
	PS	*PS+SS*	*PS*	*PS+SS*	*PS*	*PS+SS*
1983	4.91	5.85	1.14	1.53	6.05	7.38
1987-88	6.22	7.84	1.26	1.57	7.48	9.41
1993-94	7.01	8.67	1.16	1.42	8.17	10.09
1999-00	8.49	8.61	1.32	1.5	9.81	10.11
2004-05	11.14	13.2	1.89	2.29	13.03	15.49
2011-12	12.66	14.05	1.85	2.47	14.51	16.52
Year	*Urban*					
	Urban Male		*Urban Female*		*Urban Total*	
	PS	*PS+SS*	*PS*	*PS+SS*	*PS*	*PS+SS*
1983	6.29	6.59	0.73	0.91	7.02	7.5
1987-88	6.68	7.08	0.77	0.92	7.45	8
1993-94	8	8.22	0.9	0.94	8.9	9.16
1999-00	11.86	12.04	1.67	2.11	13.53	14.15
2004-05	11.87	12.19	1.48	1.54	13.35	13.73
2011-12	14.39	14.87	1.73	2.04	16.12	16.91

Notes: For 38th and 43rd Round for 1983 and 1987-88, respectively, based on NIC-1970 codes 650-659, 660-661, 670-679, 680-684 and 689 are used.
For 50th Round for 1993-94 based on NIC-1987, codes 650-659, 660-661, 670-679, 680-689 are used.
For 55th and 61st Round for 2004-05, codes 521-525 based on NIC-1998[3] were used.
For 68th Round for 2011-12, code 47 based on NIC-2008 was used.
Source: Computed based on unit-level data from NSS 38th, 43rd, 50th, 55th, 61st and 68th rounds on employment-unemployment.

India employed only about 2.21 per cent (ps+ss) of the female workers while about 78.08 per cent of them were engaged in the agriculture sector[4]. In the rural areas, which account for a majority of the female workers[5], the dependence on agriculture was even higher. However, it has been declining since the 1990s. It fell slowly from 86.28 per cent in 1993-94 to 85.36 per cent in 1990-00 and further to 83.33 per cent in 2004-05. It then declined drastically to 74.94 per cent in 2011-12 (Table 14.1). During this recent period, about 26.21 million female workers lost their work (ps+ss) in agriculture. And employment declined in other sectors, including manufacturing, mining and quarrying, electricity, gas and water supply, transport and post and telegraph (Table 14.1). Under these circumstances, a substantial increase in female employment in the rural retail trade sector was expected as the sector creates mainly self-employment, which is the preferred form of employment for female workers in the rural areas (discussed below). However, the data indicate that the much-expected increase in female employment in the rural retail sector didn't come about. The female labour absorption capacity of the retail sector, measured as the percentage of overall female workers employed in retail, continued to remain low at around 1.5-2.5 per cent in the rural areas throughout the period (Table 14.3).

Compared to the rural areas, the service and manufacturing sectors played a vital role in the industrial structure of the female workers in the urban areas (Table 14.4). In the year 1993-94, the service sector employed about 30.01 per cent of urban female workers (ps+ss). Manufacturing, agriculture and construction employed approximately 27.15 per cent, 24.87 per cent and 5.26 per cent, respectively (Table 14.5). The retail sector accounted for about 6.58 per cent. During the 1990s, when female employment (ps+ss) in the urban areas declined in the agriculture and manufacturing sectors; as expected, it increased in the urban retail sector at a high rate of 14.43 per cent per annum, and the increase in the retail sector more than compensated the fall in female employment. During 1999-00 to 2004-05, more of female workers got absorbed in agriculture, manufacturing and other services sectors. During this period, the growth rate of female employment in the retail sector, as expected, turned negative at –6.10 per cent per annum. During the later period from 2004-05 to 2011-12, female employment growth in the urban areas turned negative in the agriculture sector and slowed down in manufacturing and other services. However, female employment (ps+ss) in the retail sector increased only at a low rate of 4.10 per cent per annum. Unlike in the 1990s, the increase in retail sector employment could not compensate for the loss of 1.14 million female employment in the urban agriculture sector during this recent period (Table 14.4). The female labour absorption capacity of the urban retail sector increased from 6.58 per cent in 1993-94 to 13.22 per cent in 1999-00. It remained much lower thereafter at 7.75 per cent in 2004-05 and 9.24 per cent in 2011-12 (Table 14.5).

Overall, notwithstanding the fast growth of the retail trade sector in India during the post-liberalisation period, the female labour absorption

Table 14.3 Female Labour Absorption Capacity of Sectors in Rural Areas (Usual Status) %

	1993-94		*1999-00*		*2004-05*		*2011-12*	
Sectors	*PS*	*PS+SS*	*PS*	*PS+SS*	*PS*	*PS+SS*	*PS*	*PS+SS*
Agriculture and Related Activities	84.84	86.28	84.11	85.36	81.41	83.33	74.48	74.71
Mining & Quarrying	0.47	0.38	0.35	0.29	0.38	0.29	0.38	0.29
Manufacturing	7.96	7.65	7.65	7.60	8.69	8.36	9.55	9.76
E, G & WS	0.11	0.10	0.17	0.15	0.10	0.09	0.09	0.07
Construction	0.98	0.79	1.25	1.06	1.74	1.46	5.08	6.57
Trade & Repair Including Retail	1.88	1.79	1.76	1.59	2.30	2.02	2.96	2.76
Retail	1.75	1.53	1.70	1.55	2.20	1.97	2.78	2.63
Transport & Post & Telegraph	0.06	0.05	0.06	0.05	0.13	0.10	0.11	0.11
Hotel & Restaurants	0.30	0.27	0.46	0.39	0.54	0.47	0.63	0.50
Other Services	3.39	2.69	4.18	3.51	4.72	3.89	6.73	5.24
Total	100	100.00	100.00	100.00	100.00	100.00	100.00	100.00

Notes: Same as Table 14.1.
Source: Computed based on Table 14.1.

Table 14.4 Usual Status Employment of Urban Female Workers (m)

	1993-94		*1999-00*		*2004-05*		*2011-12*	
Sectors	*PS*	*PS+SS*	*PS*	*PS+SS*	*PS*	*PS+SS*	*PS*	*PS+SS*
Agriculture and Related Activities	2.19	3.55	1.92	2.75	2.36	3.55	1.64	2.41
Mining & Quarrying	0.07	0.11	0.05	0.06	0.04	0.04	0.06	0.06
Manufacturing	2.86	3.88	3.03	3.72	4.02	5.51	5.02	6.34
E, G & WS	0.12	0.13	0.08	0.09	0.1	0.12	0.23	0.24
Construction	0.54	0.75	0.72	1.17	0.71	0.94	0.81	0.86
Trade & Repair Including Retail	1.02	1.23	1.81	2.26	1.67	1.9	1.94	2.22
Retail	0.9	0.94	1.67	2.11	1.48	1.54	1.73	2.04
Transport & Post & Telegraph	0.14	0.15	0.19	0.2	0.16	0.17	0.15	0.16
Hotel & Restaurants	0.17	0.2	0.31	0.35	0.42	0.49	0.51	0.6
Other Services	3.9	4.29	5	5.37	6.5	7.14	8.51	9.19
Total	11.02	14.28	13.11	15.96	15.98	19.87	18.86	22.07

Notes: Same as Table 14.1.
Source: Computed based on unit-level data from the NSS 50th, 55th, 61st and 68th rounds on employment-unemployment.

Table 14.5 Female Labour Absorption Capacity of Sectors in Urban Areas – (Usual Status) Employment (%)

	1993-94		*1999-00*		*2004-05*		*2011-12*	
Sectors	*PS*	*PS+SS*	*PS*	*PS+SS*	*PS*	*PS+SS*	*PS*	*PS+SS*
Agriculture and Related Activities	19.87	24.86	14.65	17.23	14.77	17.87	8.70	10.92
Mining & Quarrying	0.64	0.77	0.38	0.38	0.25	0.20	0.32	0.27
Manufacturing	25.95	27.17	23.11	23.31	25.16	27.73	26.62	28.73
E, G & WS	1.09	0.91	0.61	0.56	0.63	0.60	1.22	1.09
Construction	4.90	5.25	5.49	7.33	4.44	4.73	4.29	3.90
Trade & Repair Including Retail	9.26	8.61	13.81	14.16	10.45	9.56	10.29	10.06
Retail	8.17	6.58	12.74	13.22	9.26	7.75	9.17	9.24
Transport & Post & Telegraph	1.27	1.05	1.45	1.25	1.00	0.86	0.80	0.72
Hotel & Restaurants	1.54	1.40	2.36	2.19	2.63	2.47	2.70	2.72
Other Services	35.39	30.04	38.14	33.65	40.68	35.93	45.12	41.64
Total	100.0	100.0	100.0	100.0	100.0	100.0	100.0	100.0

Notes: Same as Table 14.1.
Source: Computed based on Table 14.4.

capacity of the country's retail sector has been low, hovering around 2.21–3.88 per cent since the 1990s. This has been much lower than that of male workers, which stood at 7.69 per cent in 1993-94 and increased to 9.5 per cent by 2011-12. In the rural areas, the male labour absorption capacity of the retail sector fluctuated between 4.63 and 6.55 per cent (Table 14.1A); for female workers, it remained almost negligible (increasing from 1.53 to 2.63 per cent, Table 14.3). Similarly, in the urban retail, the male labour absorption capacity of the retail sector fluctuated between 15.5 and 19 per cent (Table 14.2A); for female workers, it remained much lower (fluctuating between 6.58 per cent and 13.22 per cent, Table 14.5) during the period.

Changing Structure and Its Impact on Female Employment

The continuing low female labour absorption capacity of India's fast-growing retail sector despite the substantial fall in female employment in agriculture seems to be the result of changing structure of the sector due to the spread of organised retail. The retail sector in India has traditionally been in the unorganised sector. It is dominated by small units stretching from Kirana stores to street vendors that work with a limited amount of fixed assets and face locational disadvantages. The NSSO surveys conducted in 34th Round (July 1979 to June 1980), 41st Round (July 1985 to June 1986), 46th Round (July 1990 to June 1991) and 53rd Round (January to December 1997) provide comparable information regarding basic characteristics of these small units, which include own account retail enterprises (OAREs) and non-directory retail establishments (NDREs). The own account retail enterprises are the units run by household workers only without any hired worker on a fairly regular basis. The OAREs are the units that have always been dominating the small trading units. According to the NSS 53rd survey, the OAREs formed about 92 per cent of the small trading units. The non-directory retail establishments are the units that employ fewer than six workers – household and hired workers taken together. According to the surveys, there were about 5.71 m small trading units in 1979-80. The number of these small trading units increased fast at an annual growth rate of 7.76 per cent during 1979-80 to 1985-86. However, the growth slowed down after that to 3.47 per cent per annum during 1985-86 to 1990-91. The growth rate of these small trading units slowed down further to 2.00 per cent per annum during 1990-91 to 1997. In addition to these small trading units, larger-sized retail units were operating in the unorganised sector, called Directory Trade Establishments (DTEs), which employ six or more workers. However, they were few in numbers. According to a survey conducted by CSO from October 1996 to September 1997, only 60,053 of such DTEs are operating in the unorganised sector.

Later, according to the unit-level data from the 67th Round of NSS survey on unincorporated non-agricultural enterprises conducted in 2010-11, about 18.19 million retail enterprises were operating in the unorganised sector at the all-India level. This survey grouped the unorganised retail enterprises into Own Account Retail Enterprises (OAREs) that did not employ regularly hired workers and Retail Establishments (REs) that did so. According to the survey, the OAREs continued to dominate unorganised retail in the economy. They accounted for about 89.28 per cent of the unorganised retail enterprises which employed about 78.62 per cent of the workers engaged in unorganised retail in the year 2010-11. According to the survey, these excessively small OAREs were based on more primitive non-hired labour forms of organisation. They faced a shortage of fixed assets which are held mainly in the form of land and building. According to the survey, most of these OAREs were either 'household units' located in household premises or units without a fixed location. About 39.3 per cent and 24 per cent of OAREs were located within household premises in the rural and urban areas, respectively. About 18.1 and 17.3 per cent of the OAREs in the rural and urban areas, respectively, had no fixed location being activities undertaken by street vendors or mobile markets. Although REs had a locational advantage over the OAREs, they constituted a small percentage of the total retail enterprises in the unorganised sector. As a result, overall, India's unorganised retail sector remained heavily biased in favour of small and organisationally primitive units that worked with a limited amount of fixed assets and faced locational disadvantages.

However, the structure of the retail sector in India started showing signs of change during the post-liberalisation period when several large corporate entities entered the Indian retail market leading to the spread of organised retail. Organised retail is usually chain stores, all owned or franchised by a central entity, or a single store larger than some cut-off point (ICREAR, 2008). Organised retail is a capital-intensive business involving significant investments in real estate, leasehold improvements and working capital that ultimately lead to economies of scale.

Till 1996 there had been no specific restrictions on the entry of foreign retailers into the Indian market. Under this regime, a few foreign players entered the Indian market for retail. In 1997 it was decided to prohibit FDI in retailing into the country. Later, foreign companies were allowed to own up to 51 per cent of single-brand retail in 2006 following partial liberalisation as approved by the Foreign Investment Promotion Board. Under the current rules, while there is a cap of 51 per cent in multi-brand retail, 100 per cent foreign ownership is allowed in cash-and-carry trade, wholesale trade and single-brand retail (ICREAR, 2008). In the current scenario, retail giants, Wal-Mart-Bharti and Future group (Pantaloon), are expanding their share of organised retail by investing more. Meanwhile, Indian retail chains like Reliance Retail, Croma, Aditya Birla group, S Kumars, Shoppers' Stop, Westside and Trinethra have all been consolidating their realty, brands, market shares and locations. Consequently, the percentage of organised retail in India's overall retail is increasing fast over the years.

It was estimated to be 3.5 per cent in 2005 (ICREAR, 2008). The share was estimated to be 8 per cent in 2015 and was expected to increase to 13 per cent by 2019 (IBEF, 2017).

Another significant structural change that the sector has experienced in recent years is the growth of online retailers due to the rising preference for online shopping. Amazon.in has become the most visited e-commerce site in the country. The increasing number of customers are getting attracted to e-tailers because of better deals, discounts and free shipping. Apart from the price cuts during the festival season, online players carry out off-season sales affecting the shopping pattern of the customers. The e-commerce players adopt competitive strategies and depend on least-cost sources. Competing with these e-commerce players is posing significant challenges for traditional retailers and organised brick and mortar retailers.

The structural changes in the sector have affected the nature of employment in India's retail sector (Table 14.6). Although self-employees continued to dominate, their share declined. The share of regular employees increased towards the end of the 1990s. An analysis of unit-level data from the NSS employment-unemployment surveys suggests that the share of self-employed retailers (ps+ss) (which has always been above 85 per cent) at the all-India level declined to 80.86 per cent by 1999-00 and then varied between 81.07 and 84.38 per cent. The share of regular employment (which has been around 10 per cent) at the all-India level increased to 14.53 per cent by 1990-00 and varied between 12.5 and 15.5 per cent thereafter. Casual employment continued to form a small percentage of the total retail employment.

Similar changes were observed concerning female employment in the retail trade sector. The absolute numbers and the percentage of regularly employed female workers in retail increased during 2004-05 to 2011-12 in the rural and as well as in the urban areas (Table 14.7). In rural areas, the percentage of regular female workers increased from 0.7 per cent in 1993-94 to 2.18 per cent in 2004-05 and further to 10.12 per cent in 2011-12. In urban areas, the percentage was higher at 6.38 in 1993-94, which increased to 11.11 per cent in 2004-05 and further to 14.78 per cent in 2011-12. Consequently, the percentage of self-employed female workers in rural retail declined from 99.3 per cent in 1993-94 to 96.94 per cent in 2004-05 and to 88.26 per cent in 2011-12. The percentage of self-employed female workers in the urban areas declined from 90.43 per cent in 1993-94 to 83.74 per cent in 2011-12.

This shift from self-employment to regular female employment in retail is a welcome sign. However, it has not favourably affected overall female employment in the sector as the increase in overall employment in the sector was limited. Since the capital-intensive organised retail sector used modern technology, the spread of this segment did not generate a huge demand for workers (Singh, 2011). The rising preference for online shopping has further affected the growth of employment in the retail sector. Since retail

Table 14.6 Category-wise Usual Status Employment (Male+Female) in Retail (m)

	1983	1987-88	1993-94	1999-00	2004-05	2011-12	1983	1987-88	1993-94	1999-00	2004-05	2011-12
	Rural-PS						*Rural-PS+SS*					
Self	5.58	6.89	7.55	8.72	11.39	12.47	6.87	8.75	9.4	9.07	13.73	14.2
Regular	0.31	0.4	0.44	0.7	1.25	1.55	0.33	0.43	0.46	0.7	1.31	1.73
Casual	0.15	0.19	0.18	0.4	0.4	0.48	0.19	0.23	0.21	0.41	0.45	0.58
Total	6.05	7.48	8.17	9.81	13.04	14.51	7.39	9.41	10.08	10.18	15.49	16.51
	Urban-PS						*Urban-PS+SS*					
Self	5.71	6.12	7.19	10.02	10.57	12.21	6.16	6.61	7.43	10.6	10.91	12.9
Regular	1.02	1.09	1.43	2.7	2.42	3.38	1.04	1.12	1.44	2.71	2.45	3.44
Casual	0.29	0.24	0.28	0.82	0.35	0.53	0.3	0.27	0.29	0.84	0.36	0.57
Total	7.02	7.45	8.9	13.53	13.34	16.12	7.5	8	9.16	14.15	13.72	16.91
	All-India – PS						*All-India – PS+SS*					
Self	11.3	13.01	14.74	18.74	21.96	24.68	13.03	15.36	16.83	19.68	24.64	27.1
Regular	1.33	1.49	1.87	3.39	3.67	4.93	1.37	1.55	1.9	3.41	3.76	5.17
Casual	0.45	0.43	0.45	1.21	0.75	1.01	0.49	0.5	0.5	1.25	0.81	1.15
Total	13.07	14.93	17.07	23.35	26.38	30.63	14.89	17.41	19.24	24.33	29.21	33.42

Notes: Same as Table 14.2.
Source: Computed based on unit-level data from the NSS 50th, 55th, 61st and 68th rounds on Employment-Unemployment.

Table 14.7 Category-Wise Employment in Retail Sector (m)

	1993-94	*1999-00*	*2004-05*	*2011-12*	*1993-94*	*1999-00*	*2004-05*	*2011-12*
Rural Male	*PS*				*PS+SS*			
OAWs	5.43	6.37	8.15	9.27	6.77	6.39	9.68	10.15
Employers	0.11	0.05	0.08	0.12	0.12	0.05	0.08	0.12
Helpers	0.86	1.03	1.33	1.44	1.1	1.13	1.75	1.75
Self	6.4	7.45	9.56	10.83	8	7.56	11.51	12.03
Regular	0.43	0.66	1.2	1.38	0.46	0.67	1.26	1.48
Casual	0.17	0.38	0.38	0.45	0.21	0.39	0.43	0.54
Total	7.01	8.49	11.14	12.66	8.66	8.62	13.2	14.04
Rural Female	*PS*				*PS+SS*			
OAWs	0.67	0.7	0.89	0.91	0.8	0.77	1.03	1.05
Employers	0	0	0	0	0	0	0	0
Helpers	0.48	0.56	0.93	0.73	0.61	0.74	1.19	1.12
Self	1.15	1.27	1.82	1.64	1.41	1.51	2.22	2.18
Regular	0.01	0.03	0.05	0.18	0.01	0.03	0.05	0.18
Casual	0	0.02	0.02	0.04	0.01	0.02	0.02	0.05
Total	1.16	1.32	1.89	1.85	1.42	1.56	2.29	2.41
Urban Male	*PS*				*PS+SS*			
OAWs	4.8	6.73	7.01	8.46	4.96	6.81	7.18	8.65
Employers	0.31	0.19	0.38	0.53	0.31	0.2	0.39	0.54
Helpers	1.26	1.71	1.9	1.82	1.31	1.77	2.01	2.01
Self	6.37	8.63	9.29	10.81	6.57	8.79	9.58	11.2
Regular	1.37	2.53	2.26	3.09	1.38	2.54	2.28	3.14
Casual	0.26	0.7	0.32	0.49	0.27	0.71	0.33	0.53
Total	8	11.86	11.87	14.39	8.22	12.04	12.19	14.88

Urban Female	PS				PS+SS			
OAWs	0.53	0.91	0.67	0.82	0.56	1.17	0.71	0.93
Employers	0.01	0.01	0	0.02	0.01	0.05	0	0.02
Helpers	0.28	0.47	0.6	0.57	0.29	0.6	0.62	0.74
Self	0.82	1.39	1.27	1.4	0.85	1.82	1.33	1.7
Regular	0.06	0.17	0.17	0.29	0.06	0.17	0.17	0.3
Casual	0.02	0.11	0.03	0.03	0.03	0.13	0.03	0.04
Total	0.9	1.67	1.47	1.73	0.94	2.12	1.53	2.03

Notes: 1. Industry codes same as Table 14.2.
2. Status codes 11, 12 and 21 are used for calculating the number of self-employed. Code 31 is used for regularly employed. Codes 41 and 51 are used for casual workers.
Source: Computed based on unit-level data from the NSS 50th, 55th, 61st and 68th rounds on Employment-Unemployment.

staff require qualified manpower with adequate soft skills to enable them to interact with customers, these limited jobs in the organised retail remained restricted to the workers with higher levels of education and the ability to provide a satisfactory experience to customers. A majority of the female workers in rural areas were not suitable for work in the organised retail sector. In spite of the expansion of women's education in the economy, nearly 69 per cent of the rural females are either illiterate or have educational attainment only up to the primary level (Sanghi, et al., 2015). These women are mostly employed as unpaid helpers, own account workers, or casual workers in agriculture. In addition to this, the limited jobs being created in the organised retail are not in line with the preference of the female workers, especially in the rural areas, as they need to attend to their domestic duties also and therefore prefer women-centric work which can be discharged from the household in the nature of self-employed (Sanghi et al., 2015).

Further, the changing structure of retail adversely affected the number of self-employed female workers in unorganised retail because the spread of organised retail adversely affected the incomes of small primitive OAREs as many of them could not compete with the capital-intensive, organised retailers and became less profitable. Various studies suggest that the small enterprises operating in the vicinity of the shopping malls experienced falling sales and incomes Kalhan (2007), ICREAR (2008), Singh and Singla (2011).

A detailed analysis of the unit-level data from the NSS employment-unemployment surveys suggests that among the self-employed workers[6] in household retail enterprises, the growth of helpers was affected the most during this period. They formed about 18-21 per cent and 21-24 per cent of the self-employed retail workers in the rural and the urban areas, respectively, since the 1990s[7]. The helpers in household retail enterprises are family members who do not receive any regular salary or wages in return for the work performed. They do not run the retail enterprise on their own but assist the own account workers living in the same household. Own account workers, by and large, carry out their work without hiring any labour. They dominated the self-employed retail workers accounting for about 80 per cent and 72-75 per cent of such workers in the rural and the urban areas, respectively.

In the rural areas, while the ROG of own account retail workers continued to grow, though, at a much lower rate, the ROG of helpers turned negative during 2004-05 to 2011-12. During this period, the number of helpers declined at –0.34 per cent per annum in the rural areas. In urban areas, the ROG of helpers declined continuously from 6.77 per cent during 1993-94 to 1999-00 to 0.64 per cent during 2004-05 to 2011-12. Falling incomes seem to have forced unpaid family workers to look for more remunerative work outside of the household's retail enterprise. Self-employed female workers in retail were affected more than their male counterparts in the rural and urban areas during 2004-05 to 2011-12 as a much higher percentage of female workers in retail were engaged as unpaid family workers. According to the data, unpaid female workers accounted for about 43-53 per cent of the self-employed female workers (ps+ss) in rural retail since the

1990s, while the percentage was only 14-15 for the male workers (14.7). Similarly, in the urban areas, unpaid female workers accounted for about 32-47 per cent of the self-employed female workers (ps+ss) in retail since the 1990s, while the percentage was only 17-20 for the male workers.

The other reason self-employed female workers in rural retail were affected more than their male counterparts seems to be the higher increase in wages/salaries for female workers compared to the male workers during the period. According to Sanghi et al. (2015), in rural areas, the female wages/salaries for a regular type of work increased by 30 per cent in 2011–2012 over 2004–2005 as compared to only 23 per cent for males. In the case of casual workers involved in works other than public works, the wages for female workers increased by 63 per cent against 50 per cent for the male counterparts in 2011–2012. For those involved in public works other than MNREGA also women workers experienced a better hike in their compensation/wages. Falling incomes of the households engaged in retail and higher wages seem to have shifted unpaid female workers in the rural areas to paid work outside household retail enterprises despite their preference for self-employment.

In urban India, the changing scenario lowered the growth rate of the male own account retail workers. In contrast, the growth rate turned negative for the female own account retail workers during 1999-00 to 2004-05 (Table 14.7). While the percentage of own account male workers fluctuated between 56.5 and 60.5, there was a substantial decline for female own account workers from 59.57 per cent in 1993-94 to 45.81 per cent in 2011-12. It seems to be due to unfavourable circumstances prevailing in the urban areas. In metropolitan India, the hawkers generally are treated as encroachers of public space and face harassment, constant eviction and lack of institutional credit. There are issues related to their safety as well as the security of their goods. They need to travel long distances and work for very long hours (Ghosh et al., 2007). These problems faced by hawkers in urban India seem to have affected female employment in retail more than their male counterparts.

Consequences

The overall trend which has emerged in the Indian economy in the recent period since 2004-05 is the one in which a substantial number of female workers (27.35 m), who moved out from low productivity agricultural sectors, were unable to get jobs in the manufacturing or service sectors, which are considered to be high productivity sectors. They could not even be absorbed by the fast-expanding organised retail or the low productivity petty retail sector. In other words, the retail sector no longer serves as the refuge employment sector for female workers since 2004-05. This changing trend in the Indian economy appears to have led to peculiar consequences.

An analysis of the NSS data suggests that the urban areas experienced a shift of female workers to other low productivity areas including private households with employed persons and manufacturing during 1999-00 to 2004-05. The highest increase in female employment occurred in the number of female workers of domestic personnel with private households[8]. In principal status, about 1.24 m female workers got employed as domestic personnel such as maids, cooks, gardeners, gatekeepers, secretaries, governess, babysitters, etc. Additional 0.04 m got employed in such low productivity jobs in their subsidiary capacity. The female labour absorption capacity of this category of services increased by 5.4 percentage points in principal and subsidiary status combined during this period.

The female labour absorption capacity of the manufacturing sector also increased by 4.42 percentage points (ps+ss) in the urban areas. However, of the 0.99 million female workers who got employed in urban manufacturing in principal status during the period majority (about 73.70 per cent) of them became self-employed in the unorganised manufacturing sector where, as reported by the NSS 2004-05 Survey, around half of self-employed women do not find their work to be remunerative. Another 8.31 per cent entered as casual workers in public works in the urban areas. The casual workers were completely flexible and had no job security or social security. However, overall, a setback to the growth of female employment in urban retail was more than compensated by an increase in other services, manufacturing and agriculture during 1999-00 to 2004-05. Overall female employment in the urban areas grew at 4.48 per cent per annum.

But, during the later period from 2004-05 to 2011-12, female employment growth in the urban areas slowed down in other services and manufacturing. Though the number of female workers of domestic personnel with private households declined[9], more females got absorbed in education as teachers, cooks or Anganwadi workers and human health and social welfare activities. The NSS data indicate that while the female labour absorption capacity (ps+ss) of private households declined by –2.28 percentage points, it increased in education[10] by 1.74 percentage points during the period. The degree of absorption of female workers (ps+ss) of health and social welfare activities[11] (ps+ss) increased by 1.02 percentage points during the period. However, the overall scenario became more unfavourable for female workers in the urban areas during this period as the growth rate of female employment declined in other services from 5.86 per cent per annum during 1999-00 to 2004-05 to 3.67 per cent per annum during 2004-05 to 2011-12. It declined in manufacturing also from 8.17 per cent per annum to 2.02 per cent per annum during the respective periods. Female employment growth turned negative in agriculture. Overall, there was a slowdown in the overall employment growth of female workers during the period 2004-05 to 2011-12 in the urban areas.

In the absence of even the limited employment opportunities that are available in the urban economy, the female workers in rural India started shifting to the so-called male-dominated construction sector for survival after the potential to absorb surplus labour declined in agriculture and the retail sector. This resulted in the highest growth of female employment in rural construction. According to the NSS employment-unemployment data, female employment in the construction sector grew at a high rate of 20.4 per cent per annum during 2004-05 to 2011-12 and absorbed about 4.51

million female workers in the rural areas (Table 14.1). The female labour absorption capacity of the construction sector in the rural areas which stood at a mere 0.79 per cent in 1993-94 and about 1.46 per cent in 2004-05 increased substantially to about 6.59 per cent by 2011-12. During the times, the movement of rural female workers was facilitated by social sector schemes such as MNREGA and rural road programmes, which led to a substantial increase of female workers in construction jobs (CRISIL, 2011). Demand for workers increased both in organised and unorganised construction. The growth of employment in the organised construction sector was due to the substantial growth of infrastructure investment projects during the Eleventh Five-Year Plan (2007-12). The remarkable increase in employment in the unorganised sector was mainly the result of private housing development (Mehrotra et al., 2013). Though employment increased both in the organised and unorganised construction, the jobs generated in the sector were informal in nature, and workers hardly had any kind of social security coverage (Mehrotra et al., 2013). Further, the sector created low productivity jobs since employment growth in the sector was more than the growth in value added by the sector. Employment elasticity of output in the sector increased from 0.78 during 1999-00 to 2004-05 to 1.19 during 2004-05 to 2009-10 (Mehrotra et al., 2013). The construction sector didn't have the potential to absorb the large number of female workers who lost their work in the agriculture sector. It created jobs that were not in line with the preference of the female workers in the rural areas. Overall, the upward swing of female employment in the construction sector could not reverse the broader picture of reduced employment for female workers in rural India. It led to a scenario where about 21.98 m female workers in usual status (ps+ss) lost their work in rural India during 2004-05 and 2011-12. The insufficient employment opportunities for female workers in the non-agricultural sector, including the retail sector, in rural India led to a substantial fall in female labour force participation rates in rural India after 2004.

Conclusion

The rapid growth of the retail trade sector during the post-liberalisation period was accompanied by an essential change in the structure of the sector. Though the fast expansion of organised retail generated more regular female employment, it adversely impacted the viability of the small traditional retail enterprises, reducing the sector's potential to absorb the vast number of surplus workers. Consequently, the labour-intensive petty retail sector has not been able to absorb surplus female workers and prevent a substantial decline in female work participation rates particularly in the rural areas. This calls for newer ways to productively engage female workers in the non-agricultural sector of the economy, encouraging non-farm activities undertaken by female workers in their household or nearby. It requires providing vocational and basic skills training and improving infrastructure and connectivity.

Appendix of Ch 14

Table A2.1 Male Labour Absorption Capacity of Various Sectors in Rural Areas (Usual Status) %

Sectors	*1993-94*		*1999-00*		*2004-05*		*2011-12*	
	PS	*PS+SS*	*PS*	*PS+SS*	*PS*	*PS+SS*	*PS*	*PS+SS*
Agriculture	73.77	73.43	71.24	71.40	66.22	66.50	59.16	59.36
Mining & Quarrying	0.71	0.68	0.58	0.58	0.65	0.64	0.55	0.54
Manufacturing	7.69	7.54	7.33	7.29	7.95	7.90	8.20	8.13
E, G & WS	0.35	0.34	0.29	0.28	0.29	0.29	0.31	0.31
Construction	3.25	3.16	4.52	4.47	6.92	6.84	13.07	13.01
Trade & Repair Including Retail	5.17	5.98	5.40	5.39	6.77	6.75	7.00	7.00
Retail	4.35	**5.19**	4.64	**4.63**	5.65	**6.55**	5.98	**6.53**
Transport & Post & Telegraph	2.20	2.16	3.06	3.04	3.68	3.62	4.10	4.06
Hotel & Restaurants	0.56	0.56	0.71	0.71	0.86	0.86	1.04	1.04
Other Services	6.30	6.16	6.87	6.84	6.65	6.61	6.57	6.56
Total	100	100	100	100	100	100	100	100

Notes: Same as Table 14.1
Source: Computed based on unit-level data from the NSS 50th, 55th, 61st and 68th rounds on Employment-Unemployment.

Table A2.2 Male Labour Absorption Capacity of Sectors in Urban Areas (Usual Status) %

Sectors	*1993-94*		*1999-00*		*2004-05*		*2011-12*	
	PS	*PS+SS*	*PS*	*PS+SS*	*PS*	*PS+SS*	*PS*	*PS+SS*
Agriculture	8.88	9.12	6.46	6.54	6.02	6.15	5.50	5.59
Mining & Quarrying	1.25	1.25	0.88	0.87	0.92	0.92	0.90	0.90
Manufacturing	25.00	24.81	22.19	22.04	23.35	23.26	22.40	22.38
E, G & WS	1.54	1.52	1.05	1.04	0.99	0.99	1.40	1.40
Construction	6.97	7.21	8.76	8.97	9.28	9.40	10.59	10.58
Trade & Repair Including Retail	20.59	20.58	23.96	23.99	22.98	22.88	22.04	22.04
Retail	**15.44**	**15.59**	**18.92**	**18.98**	**17.06**	**17.24**	**16.27**	**16.66**
Transport & P & Telegraph	9.47	9.35	9.80	9.71	9.61	9.53	9.10	9.03
Hotel & Restaurants	2.70	2.69	3.11	3.11	3.38	3.37	4.10	4.09
Other Services	23.60	23.48	23.79	23.74	23.47	23.49	23.97	23.96
Total	100	100	100	100	100	100	100	100

Notes: Same as Table 14.1
Source: Computed based on unit-level data from the NSS 50th, 55th, 61st and 68th rounds on Employment-Unemployment.

Notes

1 Source: http://www.nielson.com/
2 ps: Principal Status; ss: Subsidiary Status
3 The estimates for 1999-00 and 2004-05 based on NIC-1998 include the retail sale of second-hand goods which were not defined separately in previous years' NICs. The estimates also include the pawn shops as these cannot be separated from the sale of second-hand goods for 1999-00 and 2004-05.
4 Computed based on unit-level data from the NSS 50th round on employment-unemployment.
5 Rural areas accounted for about 85 per cent of the female workers in India in 1993-94.
6 Self-employed workers include own account workers, employers and helpers.
7 Computed based on figures from Table 7.
8 Following NIC 1998 code 9500 is used for 1999-00 and 2004-05.
9 Following NIC 2008, code 9700 is used for 2011-12.
10 For 2004-05 code 80 is used following NIC 1998 and for 2011-12 code 85 is used following NIC 2008.
11 Calculated based on figures from NSS Reports. For 2004-05 code 85 is used following NIC 1998 and for 2011-12 codes 86 to 89 are used following NIC 2008.

References

Bhalla, S., & Kaur, R. (2011). *Labour Force Participation of Women in India: Some Facts, Some Queries*. Working Paper No. 40, Asia Research Centre, London School of Economics. Economics. Retrieved November 15, 2018 from https://eprints.lse.ac.uk/38367/ARCWP40-BhallaKaur.pdf

Chatterjee, U., Murgai, R., & Rama, M. (2015). *Job Opportunities along the Rural-Urban Gradation and Female Labour Force Participation in India*. Working Paper No. 7412, World Bank, Policy Research. Retrieved August 20, 2021 from http://documents.worldbank.org/curated/en/732961468189870923/pdf/WPS7412.pdf

CRISIL. (2011). *Employment in India: Uneven and Weak*. Centre for Economic Research.

Ghosh, J., Sengupta, A., & Roychoudhury, A. (2007). *The Impact of Macroeconomic Change on Employment in the Retail Sector in India: Policy Implications for Growth, Sectoral Change and Employment*. International Labour Organization. Retrieved July 22, 2019 from https://www.ilo.org/public/libdoc/ilo/2008/108B09_248_engl.pdf

Govt. of India. (2000). *Directory Trade Establishment Survey, 1996–97: Report on Trade Sector*. Central Statistical Organisation, Ministry of Statistics and Programme Implementation, New Delhi.

Indian Brand Equity Foundation. (2017). Retrieved May 22, 2018 from https://www.ibef.org/download/Retail-January-2017.pdf

Indian Council for Research on International Economics Relations: Joseph, M., Soundararajan, N., Gupta, M., & Sahu, S. (2008). *Impact of Organized Retailing on the Unorganized Sector*, Working Paper 222.

Kalhan, A. (2007). Impact of Malls on Small Shops and Hawkers. *Economic and Political Weekly* 42: 2063–2066.

Kannan, K., & Raveendran, G. (2012). Counting and Profiling the Missing Labour Force. *Economic and Political Weekly* 47 (6): 77–80.

Mehrotra, S. (2013). Turnaround in India's Employment Story, Silver Lining Amidst Joblessness and Informalisation? *Economic & Political Weekly* 48 (35): 87–96.

Mehrotra, S. (2015). *Why the Female Labour Force Participation is Low and Falling?* Retrieved July 17, 2019 from https://www.researchgate.net/publication/29515719

National Sample Survey Organisation. (1998). *Surveys on Small Trading Unit in India and Their Basic Characteristics: 1997, 53rd Round.* Department of Statistics, Government of India.

Oberoi, B. (2017). *The Textile Industry in India: Changing Trends and Employment Challenges.* Oxford University Press.

Ramesh, C., & Srivastava, S.K. (2014). Changes in the Rural Labour Market and Their Implications for Agriculture. *Economic and Political Weekly* 49 (10): 47–54.

Sanghi, S., Srija, A., & Vijay, S.S. (2015). Decline in Rural Female Labour Force Participation in India: A Relook into the Causes. *VIKALPA, The Journal for Decision Makers* 40 (3): 255–268.

Singh, S. (2011). FDI in Retail: Misplaced Expectations and Half-Truths. *Economic and Political Weekly* 46 (51): 13–16.

Singh, S., & Singla, N. (2011). *Fresh Food Retail Chains in India: Organisation and Impacts.* New Delhi: Allied.

Srivastava, N., & Srivastava, R. (2010). Women, Work and Employment Outcomes in Rural India. *Economic and Political Weekly* 45 (28): 49–63.

Thomas, J. (2012). India's Labour Market during the 2000s: Surveying the Changes. *Economic and Political Weekly* 47 (51): 39–51.

15 Women's Workforce Participation and Spousal Violence

Insights from India

Arpita Biswas and Anjana Thampi

Introduction

Globally, 35 percent of women have reported experiencing sexual and/or physical violence, and in most cases by their partners (WHO, 2013). The south-east Asian region has the highest prevalence of intimate partner violence, and this region includes India as classified by the WHO (2013). In India, the number of women who experienced sexual violence by their husbands in 2005 has been estimated to be 40 times the number of women who experienced such violence from non-intimate perpetrators, though only about 1–2 percent of the acts of physical or sexual violence by the husband were reported to the police (Gupta, 2014). This chapter contributes to the existing literature on intimate partner violence by analysing the effect of married women's employment status on spousal violence in the Indian context.[1] The chapter examines this relationship within and across different socio-religious and economic groups. The study suggests that such intersectional analyses can further our understanding of the potential reasons as to why women's employment lowers or further aggravates the risks of intimate partner violence.

According to mainstream economic models on intra-household bargaining, women's economic activity could be a deterrent to spousal violence (Tauchen et al., 1991; Lundberg & Pollak, 1994; Farmer & Tiefenthaler, 1997). An employed woman may be less reliant on the spouse and her improved economic fallback position could enhance her bargaining power within the household.

However, the nature and quality of employment play a key role in deciding the fallback position of women, and not just whether they are employed or not (Panda & Agarwal, 2005; Bhattacharyya et al., 2011). Women who are employed on an occasional or seasonal basis and/or are unpaid or paid meagre wages or only in kind can hardly gain economic security. Even in the cases when they do, there are chances that, owing to the prevalent cultural norms and gender ideology, an enhanced fallback position may not translate into improved bargaining power at home (Katz, 1991; Agarwal, 1997). For instance, in societies where separation or divorce is stigmatised, women

DOI: 10.4324/9781003343998-15

would find it onerous to exit an abusive marriage even if they are financially capable of taking care of themselves, in turn affecting their ability to negotiate favourable changes in their male partners' behaviour. Bloch and Rao (2002: 1030) characterise a bride as a "potential hostage" as divorce is near-impossible in their region of study in the south Indian state of Karnataka.

Bloch and Rao (2002) model intimate partner violence as an instrument used by the husband to bargain with the wife's family for economic resources. In their model, the husband bargains by using the threat of separation as the abandoned wife would bear heavier costs. Their results suggest that spousal violence is linked to low dowry payments and that women from wealthy families are more likely to face spousal violence as their husbands attempt to extort additional payments even after marriage. If we were to extend their analysis to include the employment status of women, the findings could suggest that employed women who have access to economic resources may face higher spousal abuse as a bargaining tool used by the husband.

Sociologists have indeed argued that, instead of being a deterrent, women's economic independence may aggravate violence against them. In analysing the aetiology of intimate partner abuse, they emphasise the "symbolic" importance of women's employment as signifying a challenge to the cultural norms of male dominance and female dependence which can have strong effects on the self-esteem and mental health of the male partners (Kessler & McRae Jr., 1982; Thoits, 1992; MacMillan & Gartner, 1999). Perceiving women's employment as a threat to their traditional gender role and masculinity, men may resort to violence to reinstate control in the domestic sphere. This may be particularly true of men belonging to poorer and marginalised communities who use violence in response to their inability to control their partners through seclusion as well as to extract material resources from them (Anandhi & Jeyaranjan, 2002; Still, 2017). Moreover, the backlash effect can be especially critical in marital relations, for marriage in most societies is argued to operate as a hierarchical institution sustained through socially sanctioned authority and covert force (Goode, 1971; MacMillan & Gartner, 1999).

We locate ourselves in this debate by positing that the actual effect of women's workforce participation on spousal violence against them is context dependent. The theoretical models and empirical evidence pertaining to this link in one setting may not adequately reflect its state in a different context. The central question of this chapter is whether and how being employed affects an average married Indian woman's intimate life. In this case, the context is one of a country where the female labour force participation rate is appallingly low and declining in spite of higher educational enrolment and economic growth over time (Chandrasekhar & Ghosh, 2007; Himanshu, 2011; Naidu, 2016). Moreover, given that the specification "Indian woman" does not reveal much about one's immediate reality, we ask how the effect varies by her class and socio-religious identity. Thus, we focus on analysing how married women with similar socio-economic attributes fare in terms of the risks of facing spousal violence when they are employed vis-à-vis when they are not. And how do such risks faced by employed women from a certain economic or social group compare with the risks faced by employed women from other groups? This intersectional analysis will enable us to understand if, in a vastly heterogenous country such as India, the employment status of women from diverse social and economic backgrounds affects their chances of facing spousal violence differently, and why.

Bargaining Theory Versus Male Backlash Hypothesis

The findings of studies examining the effect of women's employment on the likelihood of intimate partner violence are mixed. Kalmuss and Straus (1982) find that unemployed married women in the US are exposed to significantly higher risks of severe spousal violence. Villarreal (2007) reports that employment significantly lowers women's risk of violence in Mexico. These studies suggest that being economically independent makes employed women less tolerant of abuse and more capable of negotiating changes in their partners' behaviour. Thus, they lend support to the household bargaining models in underscoring employment as an empowerment tool for women (see also Hadi, 2005 [Bangladesh]; Gage, 2005 [Haiti]).

In contrast, John (2020) finds that, in the traditional setting of Nepal, married women engaged in paid employment face a significantly higher risk of intimate partner violence as compared to their unpaid or non-working counterparts. Assessing the association between relative spousal employment status and violence, Macmillan and Gartner (1999) show that the effect of Canadian women's employment on spousal violence is inverse when their partners are also employed but adverse and substantial when they are not. These works validate the male backlash theory which argues that women's employment provokes their partners to coercively control them so as to prevent any perceived threat to prevalent gendered norms and hierarchy (see also Oduro et al., 2015 [Ecuador]; Owoo, 2020 [Nigeria]).

We expect these differences to have resulted from methodological and contextual variations in the studies. With regard to the former, differences in the reference period of the study (past 12 months before survey or long-term), the group of women examined (currently or ever partnered/married), and the set of control variables may have mattered. In addition, the treatment of potential endogeneity between women's employment and intimate partner violence could have been particularly important. The two main sources of such endogeneity are simultaneous causality and omitted variables. Researchers analysing the other direction of the relationship have suggested that spousal violence can have an adverse influence on women's likelihood of being employed, their work hours, and employment stability (Tolman & Wang, 2005; Kimerling et al., 2009; Crowne et al., 2011) or have a positive association with their paid and year-round employment (H. Bhattacharya, 2015). Furthermore, spousal abuse and women's workforce participation may both be affected by unobserved factors, like the presence of a controlling male partner or of orthodox in-laws, and that can bias the findings on the effect of abuse on women's employment.[2] However, much of the literature, with the notable exceptions of some studies by Gibson-Davis et al. (2005), Villarreal (2007), Bhattacharyya et al. (2011), and Lenze and Klasen (2017), does not control for endogeneity. While this may not be a relevant critique against studies that treat women's employment status only as a control variable, given the aim of our analysis, we recognise and tackle the issue by implementing a suitable instrumental variable logit model.

With respect to the other major source of wide variations in findings from the literature, contextual factors specific to the region under study may have counted. Oduro et al. (2015) indicate the relevance of cultural norms around women's workforce participation in Ecuador and Ghana, countries where the shares of employed men are high and very close (93 percent in Ecuador and 94 percent in Ghana). They find women's employment to increase spousal violence in Ecuador where only 60 percent of women are economically active, and to cause no significant effect for those living in Ghana where 90 percent of women are in the workforce. Bhattacharyya et al. (2011) show how norms and labour market patterns around women's occupational engagement also matter. They find employment in agricultural wage work to shield women of Kaushambi district of Uttar Pradesh [India] from spousal abuse whereas this is not the case with non-agricultural activities where women are minimally present. Panda and Agarwal (2005), by giving evidence of a protective effect of a regular job as against no significant effect of a seasonal one in Thiruvananthapuram district of Kerala [India], highlight the role of quality of women's employment in improving their bargaining power and escaping physical abuse from male partners.

These studies offer a meaningful framework that can help us analyse and understand the association between women's employment and risks of spousal violence against them in varied contexts. To reiterate, the framework conceptualises women's employment as an indicator of access to economic resources with the potential to increase their bargaining power (depending on the quality of employment) vis-à-vis a symbolic/cultural resource with the potential to attract male backlash when men perceive employed spouses as transgressing the norms around gender division of labour and identity.

Nonetheless, to the best of our knowledge, none of the earlier studies recognise women's employment as a signifier of compromised "reproductive" resources.[3] With women being the primary (if not the sole) caregiver, their participation in the workforce can constrain the energy, time, or other resources that they have available for reproductive labour. In societies where household work is perceived to be their principal responsibility, falling short of their male partner's or his family's expectations can trigger violence against women. Field research by Bhattacharyya et al. (2011) indeed reveals that a significant share of both married men and women (46 percent) consider women's "negligence" of housework (for instance, food not cooked properly or on time, children not taken care of, clothes not washed) as one of the most common reasons for their physical abuse.[4] Moreover, with neoliberal capitalism continually dislocating the burden of reproduction onto families and deepening the crisis of social reproduction (Bhattacharya, 2013; Fraser, 2016), we expect this additional channel of male backlash to have become particularly relevant in recent decades. Thus, we hypothesise that, by bolstering the possibilities of the backlash effect, intensive care burden can increase employed women's risks of witnessing intimate partner violence over those who are not employed. Also, as the intensification of reproductive labour appears to have been especially severe for households from socially and economically deprived sections (Bhattacharya, 2013; Naidu, 2016; Rao, 2018), we imagine this source of the backlash effect to be particularly strong for employed women from such households. By incorporating these socio-economic undercurrents of the contemporary system, our intersectional study aims to contribute to feminist political economic analyses of domestic violence in India.

Data

This study uses unit-level data from the 2015–6 National Family Health Survey 4 [NFHS-4], the latest in the series of Demographic and Health Surveys in India at the time of writing. Among a variety of questionnaires that the NFHS employs, our present analysis primarily concerns itself with the domestic violence module while supplementing it with relevant data collected on the spouse of the sampled woman through the men's questionnaire.

For the module on domestic violence, the NFHS randomly selected one woman between 15 and 49 years per household. The selected women can be classified into two broad categories: never married and ever married women. The latter consists of currently married women and women who were married earlier but are now separated, divorced, widowed, or have been deserted. To minimise underestimation bias, we only consider the subsample of currently married women who were cohabiting with their husband during the reference period. The surveyed women responded to questions on different forms of physical, sexual, and emotional abuse caused by their partners. As classified by the survey, physical violence includes cases where the respondent reported that her husband pushed, shook, or threw something at her; twisted her arm or pulled her hair; slapped her; punched her; kicked, dragged, or beat her up; tried to choke or burn her; or threatened or attacked her with a weapon. Sexual violence refers to the respondent reporting that the husband forced her to have sexual intercourse with him or forced her to perform sexual acts. In cases of emotional violence, the respondent reported that the husband humiliated her in front of others, threatened to hurt or harm her or others close to her, or insulted her. To each of these questions, women reported whether their spouse inflicted the form of abuse "often in the past twelve months", "sometimes in the past twelve months", "yes, but not in the past twelve months", or "never".

In our selected sample, we consider a woman to have suffered spousal violence if she reported facing at least one form of violence, physical, sexual, or emotional, either often or sometimes in the last 12 months at the time of survey. This is because our focus is on the effect of women's employment status on the probability of spousal violence, and data on the former is available for the past 12 months alone, making that the reference period for our analysis.

Tables 15.1 and 15.2 present survey weight-adjusted summary statistics of the variables that we use in this study. Table 15.1 depicts the statistics for the indicators of different kinds of spousal violence. It suggests that one out of every four married women in India reported facing some form of abuse from their husband sometimes or frequently over the 12 months prior to the survey. More specifically, 22.5 percent of women in our sample reported encountering physical abuse, 5.4 percent reported sexual violence, and 10.6 percent reported facing emotional violence. We use "any spousal violence" as the dependent variable in our analysis. It is represented as a binary variable that takes the value of 1 if a woman did experience spousal violence in any form, and 0 otherwise.

Table 15.2 presents the descriptive statistics of the explanatory variables and the instrumental variable (IV) that we use in the study. The employment status of the woman during the year before the survey is the explanatory variable of primary interest, and 32 percent of the women in our sample were ever employed during that period. The control variables include attributes of the woman and her spouse, and their household characteristics. The average age of women respondents is close to 33 years. 88 percent of them are younger than their husbands by 10 years or less, with the mean spousal

Table 15.1 Incidence of spousal violence against currently married and cohabiting women during the previous 12 months

Variable	*Percent*
Physical violence	22.54
Sexual violence	5.38
Emotional violence	10.56
Any spousal violence	26.47

Notes: Survey weight-adjusted percentages reported here.
Sample size: 41,928.
Source: Authors' calculations based on NFHS-4.

Table 15.2 Summary statistics of the explanatory variables and the instrumental variable

Variable	*Percent*	*Mean*	*SD*
Explanatory variables			
Wife and husband's characteristics			
Wife's age (15–49 years):		32.71	8.07
15–24 years	17.90		
25–34 years	39.68		
35–49 years	42.42		
Spousal age difference (in years):		4.83	3.85
Husband's age = wife's age	3.29		
Wife's age > husband's age	2.22		
Husband's age > wife's age by <= 10 years	87.72		
Husband's age > wife's age by > 10 years	6.77		
Wife's family history of violence:			
Her father ever beat her mother	21.69		
Husband's family history of violence:			
His father ever beat his mother	20.97		
Wife owns assets (house and/or land, solely or jointly)	40.43		
Husband owns assets (house and/or land, solely or jointly)	80.62		
Wife's education status:			
No education	31.63		
Primary education	14.42		
Secondary education	43.95		
Higher education	10.00		
Husband's education status:			
No education	18.13		
Primary education	15.64		
Secondary education	52.22		
Higher education	14.00		
Wife's employment status: Employed[a]	32.01		
Husband's employment status: Employed	96.01		
Husband drinks alcohol	27.82		
Husband has more than one wife	1.27		
Household characteristics			
Social identity:			
OBC	39.97		
SC	19.79		
ST	9.41		
Other	18.21		
Muslim	12.62		
Household wealth category:			
Poorest	16.32		
Poorer	19.29		
Medium	20.85		
Wealthier	21.52		
Wealthiest	22.02		
Region:			
Rural	65.16		
Urban	34.58		
Number of couple's children living at home		1.97	1.29

(*Continued*)

Table 15.2 Continued

Variable	*Percent*	*Mean*	*SD*
Number of other HH members:			
2	47.62		
3 to 5	36.70		
6 or more	15.68		
Instrumental variable			
Women's work participation rate per cluster		31.94	28.61

Notes: [a] denotes the explanatory variable that is of primary interest for our analysis.
Most of the explanatory variables are categorical variables, so we report their survey weight-adjusted percentages. For the variables that are quantitative (viz., number of couple's children residing with them and the instrumental variable), we report survey weight-adjusted mean and standard deviation. For wife's age and spousal age difference, we report percentages as well as mean and standard deviation, but we treat them as categorical variables (with 4 and 5 categories, respectively).
Our regression analyses also control for the state where a household is located. However, we do not present the summary statistics for states in the interest of space.
Sample size: 41,928.
Source: Authors' calculations based on NFHS-4.

age gap being slightly below five years. About one-fifth of both women and men report that their father physically abused their mother. However, there are vast differences between them in other variables: an overwhelming 96 percent of men were ever employed in the past 1 year as against a mere 32 percent of women; property ownership among men (80 percent) is twice as common as it is among women; and 66 percent of men have secondary education or higher as against 54 percent of women. Furthermore, 28 percent of men are reported by their wives to drink alcohol, and slightly over 1 percent have more than one wife.

In terms of household characteristics, only 35 percent of the couples were located in urban areas at the time of data collection. An average couple seems to have two children living with them. Almost half of the sample's households represent a nuclear family structure, and a majority of the remaining 50 percent represent small joint families. 13 percent of the respondents are married to Muslim men while 20, 9, 40, and 18 percent are wedded to men from Scheduled Castes (SC), Scheduled Tribes (ST), other "backward" classes (OBC), and a residual "others" category, respectively.[5] Finally, 16 percent of the households are in the poorest quintile and 22 percent in the richest. The relevance and validity of the IV that we use are discussed in the following section.

A caveat is in order here. Data on spousal violence can suffer from underreporting due to respectability politics or fear of social stigma, particularly among women from richer and forward caste households (Deshpande, 2002; Panda & Agarwal, 2005). While we cannot comment on the extent of this flaw in our sample without supporting qualitative data, we expect our intra-group analysis to be free from it. However, our inter-group examination may suffer from such data limitations and the corresponding results need to be treated with caution.

Methodology

To empirically examine the effect of women's employment status on spousal violence against them, we use the following linear regression:

$$V = \beta_0 + \beta_1 E + \beta_2 W + \beta_3 H + \beta_4 F + \varepsilon$$

where *V* is the indicator of spousal violence against a married woman, *E* stands for her employment status, *W* represents the other attributes of the woman, *H* represents the set of her husband's characteristics, *F* stands for the set of household characteristics, and ε represents unobserved factors. *V* is the outcome variable and *E* is the key regressor. As mentioned earlier, *V* takes the value of 1 if the woman reported encountering spousal violence in any form in the 12 months before the survey and 0 otherwise, and *E* takes the value of 1 if the woman reported herself to be employed in any capacity (in any occupation for any duration under any employer or as self-employed with or without pay) over the same period of 12 months and 0 otherwise.

The set of control variables represented by *W*, *H*, and *F* captures different socio-economic factors operating at the micro and macro levels that affect the incidence of spousal abuse against women. Our choice of these variables is based on the existing literature on intimate partner violence. While we do not present a detailed discussion of these in the interest of space, it is pertinent to elaborate on the variable "social identity" that we have constructed combining caste and religion, two of the most crucial historical markers of deprivation in India besides gender and class.

In India, the historically disadvantaged groups of the SCs (also known as *Dalits*) and STs (also called *Adivasis*) continue to face disparities and discrimination in socio-economic indicators (Borooah, 2005; Zacharias & Vakulabharanam, 2011; Thorat & Dubey, 2012). Among different religious communities that cohabit in the country, Muslims have been systematically marginalised along several dimensions of life and livelihood (Gayer & Jaffrelot, 2011; Shaban, 2018). Since men from these caste and religious groups may more actively resort to spousal abuse so as to reassert control in the domestic sphere (Anandhi & Jeyaranjan, 2002; Anandhi, 2017; Still, 2017), we include the variable on social identity in our study. Our study treats social identity as a qualitative explanatory variable with five categories as depicted in Table 15.2. This includes four deprived socio-religious categories: Muslims, and the SCs, STs, and OBCs belonging to all religious groups except Muslim. The rationale behind clubbing Muslims from various caste backgrounds under one category is twofold: one, given the continuing opposition to their inclusion in affirmative action policies, they are vastly under-represented in the official SC/ST/OBC categories; and two, the considerable shift of national and global politics to the right in recent times has made practically every Muslim susceptible to everyday discrimination in India (Hasan, 2011; Shaban, 2018). The fifth socio-religious group is a residual one comprising all those who are not covered under the deprived categories, with a majority of them expected to belong to the so-called "forward" castes (from all religious groups except Muslim).

We also use the wealth quintiles available in NFHS data generated from households' housing characteristics and their ownership of consumer goods to indicate the economic standing of households.

With respect to the estimation approach, given our regressand is a binary categorical variable, we use binary logit regression models in our study. We employ survey weight-adjusted logit estimations to account for the structure of the survey design. Controlling for *W*, *M*, and *H*, the marginal effect of a woman being employed from the logit estimations allows us to examine whether and how it is associated with the likelihood of her husband inflicting violence on her.

As discussed earlier, women's employment status is an endogenous explanatory variable. Following Lenze and Klasen (2017), we instrument it by women's workforce participation rate (WPR) per cluster, where cluster represents a Census enumeration block in urban areas and a village in rural areas consisting of 100–150 households (IIPS & ICF, 2017).[6, 7] This variable is used as a proxy measure for employment opportunities for married women in an area (including network efforts enabling them to find jobs) as well as for norms and attitudes that influence their decision to join the workforce. Based on the assumption that the probability of a woman being employed is positively correlated with favourable labour demand and supply conditions in her vicinity, we expect the average WPR of women per cluster to be a relevant IV. Diagnostic tests for the instrument from the first stage of IV estimation (presented in Tables 15.3, 15.4, and 15.5) confirm our expectation.[8] As the average WPR of women in a cluster goes up, the likelihood that a given woman from that cluster is employed increases significantly. Also, the magnitude of the F-test statistic for the significance of the IV in the first stage is much higher than 10, the benchmark for assessing the strength of an IV in an exact identification logistic model. These suggest that the variable is a suitable instrument for a married woman's employment status in India.

Given that the endogenous regressor is exactly identified in our case, we cannot conduct an empirical test for checking the validity of the IV. Nevertheless, there is no reason to assume that the cluster average of women's WPR ought to directly impinge on a man's violent behaviour, other than through its impact on his wife's employment status and other control variables. Thus, we expect the instrument to be a valid one for our purpose.

Since both our regressand and endogenous regressor are categorical variables, we use the two-stage residual inclusion (2SRI) estimation approach to account for endogeneity. For this, we follow Terza et al. (2008) who show the 2SRI approach to provide consistent estimates in case of such models, unlike the usual two-stage predictor substitution (2SPS) estimation approach. The first-stage regression of the 2SRI approach uses the IV and all control variables of the model to predict the endogenous explanatory

Table 15.3 Estimated marginal effect of women's employment status on spousal violence

Variable	*Logistic*	*2SRI*
Main explanatory variable		
Wife's employment status: Employed	0.028*** (0.007)	0.035*** (0.005)
Control variables		
Wife's age (15–49 years):	ref	ref
15–24 years	0.002 (0.010)	-0.017*** (0.007)
25–34 years	-0.017* (0.010)	-0.037*** (0.008)
35–49 years		
Spousal age difference (in years):	ref	ref
Husband's age = wife's age	0.043* (0.024)	0.030* (0.016)
Wife's age > husband's age	-0.005 (0.016)	-0.005 (0.010)
Husband's age > wife's age by <= 10 years	-0.004 (0.022)	-0.010 (0.013)
Husband's age > wife's age by > 10 years		
Wife's family history of violence: Her father ever beat her mother	0.195*** (0.009)	0.192*** (0.006)
Husband's family history of violence: His father ever beat his mother	0.044*** (0.008)	0.038*** (0.005)
Wife owns assets (house and/or land, solely or jointly)	0.018*** (0.007)	0.011*** (0.004)
Husband owns assets (house and/or land, solely or jointly)	0.007 (0.009)	0.011** (0.005)
Wife's education status:	ref	ref
No education	-0.005 (0.010)	-0.002 (0.006)
Primary education		
Secondary education	-0.031*** (0.009)	-0.023*** (0.006)
Higher education	-0.089*** (0.015)	-0.079*** (0.010)
Husband's education status:	ref	ref
No education	0.007 (0.010)	0.007 (0.007)
Primary education	-0.009 (0.009)	-0.009* (0.006)
Secondary education	-0.036** (0.014)	-0.031*** (0.009)
Higher education		
Husband's employment Status: Employed	0.005 (0.016)	0.009 (0.010)
Husband drinks alcohol	0.175*** (0.009)	0.171*** (0.005)
Husband has more than one wife	0.097*** (0.028)	0.072*** (0.018)
Social identity:	ref	ref
OBC	-0.002 (0.009)	0.007 (0.005)
SC	-0.019* (0.011)	-0.020*** (0.007)
ST	-0.009 (0.010)	-0.001 (0.006)
Other	0.029** (0.012)	0.035*** (0.008)
Muslim		
Household wealth category:	ref	ref
Poorest	-0.003 (0.010)	-0.012* (0.006)
Poorer	-0.036*** (0.012)	-0.036*** (0.007)
Middle	-0.068*** (0.013)	-0.057*** (0.008)
Wealthier	-0.095*** (0.015)	-0.087*** (0.009)
Wealthiest		

(*Continued*)

Table 15.3 Continued

Variable	*Logistic*	*2SRI*
Region:	ref	ref
Rural	0.006 (0.009)	0.013** (0.005)
Urban		
Number of couple's children living	0.014*** (0.003)	0.010*** (0.002)
at home	ref	ref
Number of other HH members:	-0.005 (0.007)	-0.010** (0.004)
2	-0.003 (0.011)	-0.019** (0.008)
3 to 5		
6 or more		
Number of observations	42,606	42,493
Instrumental variable (IV)		0.004*** (0.000)
First-stage estimate for the IV		699.14***
First-stage F-test for the IV		

Notes: [a] Standard errors in parentheses.
[b] Bootstrapped standard errors in parentheses.
***, **, and * denote statistical significance at 1, 5, and 10 percent levels, respectively.
We also control for the state where a household is located, but do not present the estimated marginal effect of states in the interest of space.
Source: NFHS-4.

variable, and the second-stage regression uses the original explanatory variable and the residual from the first stage along with all control variables.[9] We use binary logit models for both stages.[10]

Results

Tables 15.3, 15.4, and 15.5 present the estimated effects of women's employment status on the incidence of spousal violence. Table 15.3 shows the results for all women in our sample whereas Tables 15.4 and 15.5 record the estimated effects for women married into households from different economic statuses and different socio-religious communities, respectively.[11]

The 2SRI estimates in Table 15.3 show that, all else being equal, employed women are 3.5 percent more likely to face spousal abuse as compared to non-employed women.[12] This implies that being employed makes married women more susceptible to male aggression rather than enhance their intra-household bargaining power. Table 15.4 depicts that this association between women's workforce participation and the likelihood of spousal violence against them holds true in case of all economic sections barring the richest 20 percent. While the employment status of women belonging to households from the wealthiest quintile does not seem to influence their chances of facing spousal abuse, employed women from all other quintiles report encountering a significantly higher probability of violence than women who were not employed.[13] Furthermore, Table 15.5 shows that

Table 15.4 2SRI – Estimated marginal effect of women's employment status on spousal violence across economic groups

Explanatory variable (wife employed) ↓	*Poorest*	*Poorer*	*Medium*	*Wealthier*	*Wealthiest*
Marginal effect (S.E.[a])	0.049*** (0.012)	0.045*** (0.011)	0.037*** (0.010)	0.036*** (0.011)	0.004 (0.009)
Number of observations	7,821	8,847	8,928	8,640	8,155
First-stage estimate for the IV (S.E.)	0.004*** (0.000)	0.004*** (0.000)	0.004*** (0.000)	0.003*** (0.000)	0.003*** (0.000)
First-stage F-test for the IV	269.86***	199.43***	186.51***	128.46***	77.44***

Notes: [a] Bootstrapped standard errors in parentheses.
***, **, and * denote statistical significance at 1, 5, and 10 percent levels, respectively.
Source: NFHS-4.

Table 15.5 2SRI – Estimated marginal effect of women's employment status on spousal violence across socio-religious groups

Explanatory variable (wife employed) ↓	*Muslim*	*SC*	*ST*	*OBC*	*Other*
Marginal effect (S.E.[a])	0.057*** (0.015)	0.049*** (0.011)	0.035*** (0.010)	0.025*** (0.008)	0.029*** (0.010)
Number of observations	5,170	7,498	7,479	15,201	7,017
First-stage estimate for the IV (S.E.)	0.003*** (0.000)	0.004*** (0.000)	0.004*** (0.000)	0.003*** (0.000)	0.004*** (0.000)
First-stage F-test for the IV	73.88***	162.52***	139.26***	261.70***	126.15***

Notes: [a] Bootstrapped standard errors in parentheses.
***, **, and * denote statistical significance at 1, 5, and 10 percent levels, respectively.
Source: NFHS-4.

employed women across socio-religious groups report facing significantly higher risks of spousal abuse than women who did not participate in the workforce.

The estimates in these tables also indicate that the adverse effect of employment on spousal violence tends to be stronger for women who belong to deprived communities, economically or socially. The incidence of such violence seems to be progressively lower for employed women from higher wealth quintiles as compared to those from relatively poorer ones (Table 15.4). Employed women from Muslim, Dalit, and Adivasi communities, the sections that are documented to have been the most marginalised in India, report greater risks of spousal abuse than employed women from other groups (Table 15.5).

Our finding that married women's workforce participation is associated with a significantly higher incidence of spousal abuse supports the male backlash theory. We proceed to discuss some plausible explanations for such a backlash effect in the specific context of our study.

First, as feminist scholarship on the backlash theory postulates, the observed association may be a testament of the symbolic role that women's employment plays in challenging the socio-cultural norms of male supremacy and female dependency. This is especially true of India where gender hierarchy has been a fundamental organising principle of the caste-based social order, and marriage a primary institution to enforce such hierarchy through stringently defined gender roles and obligations (Chakravarti, 1993; Eswaran et al., 2013).[14] Among those are the husband's masculine role of a provider/protector and the wife's feminine role of a homemaker/recipient, which have together come to stigmatise the employment of married women in the Indian society. A low incidence of workforce participation among the women in our dataset is partly a reflection of this cultural tradition (see Figures 15.1 and 15.2).[15] In this context, it is highly probable for the women who do not adhere to such norms to be subjected to male aggression and abuse, which are non-material means used by men to compensate for their diminished or failed economic power and to re-establish control within the domestic space.

This "disciplining" mechanism is expected to affect employed women across social and economic groups in India, for married women's workforce participation rate is low throughout. As Figures 15.1 and 15.2 respectively show, the rate ranges from 21 percent in the wealthiest quintile to 41 percent in the poorest one, and from 17 percent in Muslim households to 49 percent in *Adivasi* families. These indicate how not taking part in the labour market is the dominant norm among Indian women from varied backgrounds, challenging which, as Tables 15.4 and 15.5 show, comes at the cost of heightened risk of domestic violence. However, a cross-sectional comparison of the employment rates and the corresponding incidence of spousal abuse highlights a puzzle: the probability of abuse is lower for employed women from groups that have historically discouraged and denounced women's

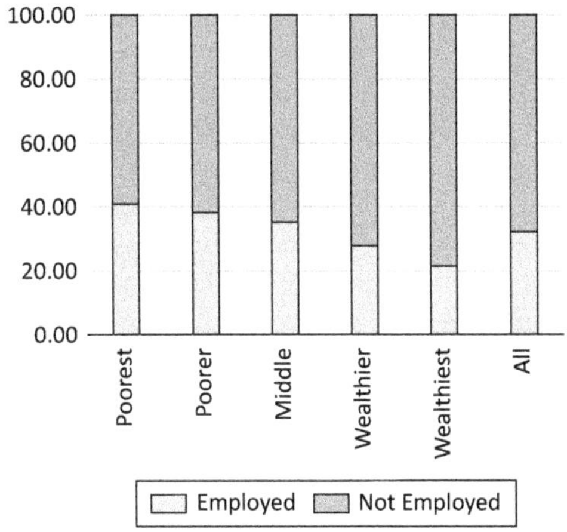

Figure 15.1 Share of employed and non-employed women across economic groups (in %)

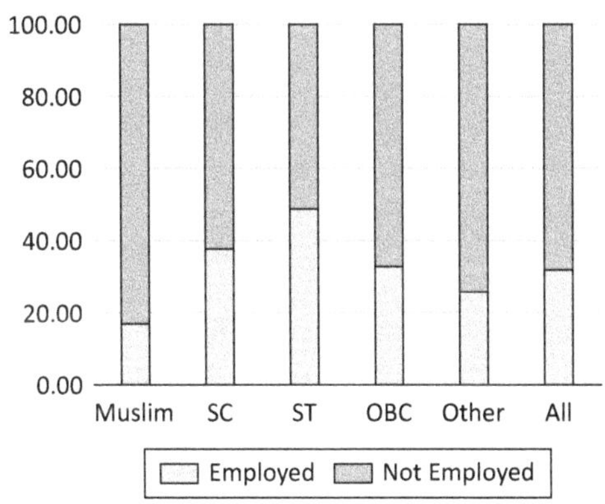

Figure 15.2 Share of employed and non-employed women across socio-religious groups (in %) *Source*: Authors' calculations based on NFHS-4.

employment most severely, namely, the upper-caste and wealthier sections (Liddle & Joshi, 1989; Eswaran et al., 2013). While attributable to under-reporting errors (that are expected to be more serious for women from relatively privileged groups) to some extent, are there additional factors that can possibly explain the observed tendency?

As Naidu (2016), Rao (2018), and Rao and Vakulabharanam (2019) argue, the Indian economy has been facing an intense crisis of social reproduction since the late 1980s. This has been a repercussion of a variety of neoliberal processes such as large-scale privatisation of rural and urban common property resources, displacement of marginalised populations from public lands and commons that they had inhabited for generations, and under-provisioning of essential facilities like water, electricity, and sanitation by the state in informal settlements.[16] Deepening the exigencies of reproduction at the household level, this crisis has mired large sections of Indian women in an ever-accelerating burden of everyday care activities. It is against this backdrop that we propose it is important to construe their employment as not only an indicator of economic means and symbolic value but also as that of compromised reproductive resources. This proposition leads us to hypothesise that the double burden of reproductive and market work may spur an additional source of backlash against employed women. To test this hypothesis, we use two proxy measures of care activities: having a very young child (i.e., less than or equal to 5 years) represents direct care responsibilities, and the need to go fetch drinking water from an outside source constitutes indirect care burden.[17] We adjust the proxy variables for the presence of another woman or teenage girl (between 15 and 49 years) at home to capture intensive work burden, meeting which may become particularly difficult for a woman who is also employed. Thus, we consider a woman to be dealing with intensive care burden if she has a very young child and if drinking water needs to be fetched from outside with no other female at home to share the workload, and not-so-intensive work burden otherwise.

Tables 15.6 and 15.7 present descriptive statistics on the incidence of spousal abuse among employed and non-employed women facing intensive and not-so-intensive care burden across economic and socio-religious groups. An intra-group comparison of the numbers offers two preliminary findings: one, irrespective of the intensity of care burden, employed women report facing greater risks of spousal violence than those who are not employed, and two, employed women report encountering a much

Table 15.6 Share of employed and unemployed women with intensive and not-so-intensive care burden reporting spousal violence across economic groups (in %)

Household wealth category (1)	*With intensive care burden*		*With not-so-intensive care burden*	
	Employed women (2)	*Non-employed women (3)*	*Employed women (4)*	*Non-employed women (5)*
Poorest	42.72	35.54	40.35	34.87
Poorer	44.62	31.66	36.76	29.13
Middle	38.17	26.50	32.55	25.83
Wealthier	33.04	24.59	27.64	20.37
Wealthiest	17.14	15.75	15.97	14.66
All	40.99	29.75	31.28	23.07

Source: Authors' calculations based on NFHS-4.

Table 15.7 Share of employed and unemployed women with intensive and not-so-intensive care burden reporting spousal violence across socio-religious groups (in %)

Household social identity *(1)*	*With intensive care burden*		*With not-so-intensive care burden*	
	Employed women (2)	*Non-employed women (3)*	*Employed women (4)*	*Non-employed women (5)*
Muslim	45.56	32.32	30.16	22.30
SC	40.34	29.24	35.61	28.26
ST	40.54	29.12	34.58	23.01
OBC	41.65	30.47	32.17	25.18
Other	38.26	27.09	20.03	15.24
All	40.99	29.75	31.28	23.07

Source: Authors' calculations based on NFHS-4.

greater likelihood of violence than non-employed women when they deal with intensive care burden vis-à-vis when they do not. For instance, being employed increases *Dalit* households' women's risks of spousal abuse by 11 percentage points when they deal with intensive care burden as compared to a 7-percentage point rise when they do not. These findings indicate that the double burden of reproductive and market work could contribute to a backlash effect against employed women. This could be due to the difficulties they face in handling care work or in meeting their husbands' expectations from them as caregivers, or due to conflicts over division of such work.

The incidence of spousal violence reported by employed women facing intensive care responsibilities decreases as we move up along the economic and social hierarchies (Tables 15.6 and 15.7). This may be because households from disadvantaged sections face greater limitations in substituting housework with paid domestic help. Additionally, reproductive burdens (direct, indirect, and both direct and indirect) appear to have been more intense for employed women from poorer and marginalised groups (Figures 15.3 and 15.4).[18] This could be because these communities have been more severely affected by the state's withdrawal from public provisioning and declining access to commons. Together, these observations offer a probable explanation as to why employed women from disadvantaged groups may be facing higher risks of spousal violence, and in the process, lends support to our hypothesis that employment, by jeopardising women's capacity to perform intensified care labour and/or meet their spouses' expectations around it, acts as an additional cause of male backlash against them.

Our findings on the effect of women's employment on spousal violence from the cross-sectional examination reinforce Anandhi and Jeyaranjan (2002), Anandhi (2017), and Still's (2017) thesis that men from socio-economically disadvantaged groups tend to be more prone to retaliate against their wives' economic independence through violence. This implies that

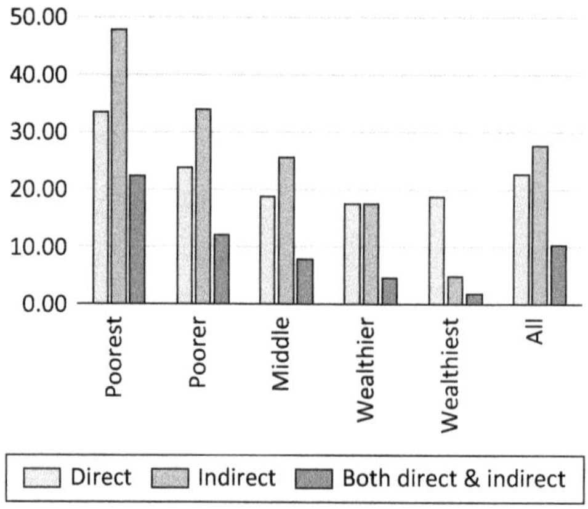

Figure 15.3 Share of employed women with intensive care burden across economic groups (in %)

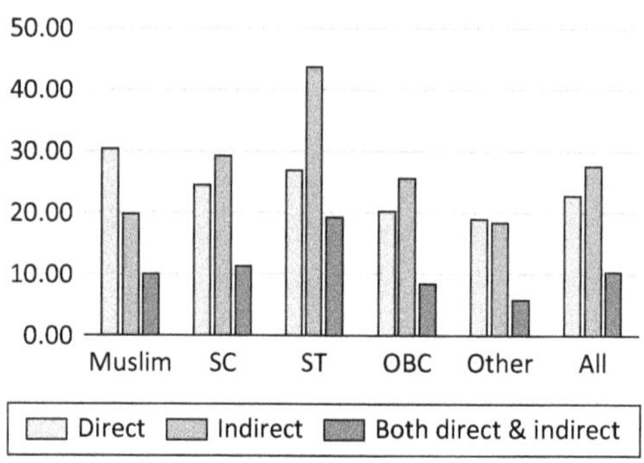

Figure 15.4 Share of employed women with intensive care burden across socio-religious groups (in %)

when historically entrenched patterns of deprivation and discrimination in the public space interact with their "failed masculinity" in terms of exerting control over their spouses and the family economy even within the private sphere, they feel especially provoked to display "manliness" through violence against their wives.

Conclusion

This chapter studies the incidence of spousal violence against women with reference to their employment status in the Indian context. Given the presence of vast socio-economic disparities in the country, it is important to examine how the association between a woman's workforce participation and the likelihood of violence is conditioned by her (marital) family's economic and social standing. We use nationally representative household survey data and a context-driven econometric model to investigate this link. Taking into account the potential endogeneity of this relationship, we instrument women's employment status by the cluster average of married women's workforce participation rate in our model.

Our findings show that women's employment in India is indeed associated with a significantly higher probability of spousal violence. We find this association to hold true for employed women across all wealth quintiles except the topmost and across all socio-religious communities. Engaging with insights from feminist scholarship, we argue that these could be explained through the backlash by men due to the perceived violation of socio-cultural norms by their wives. Moreover, the risks of spousal abuse are reported to be relatively higher for employed women from economically and socially disadvantaged sections. Our analysis indicates that such a pattern can be explained by recognising the double burden of reproductive and market work on employed women as another source of the backlash effect. Employed women – especially those with intensive reproductive burden – may witness an aggravated risk of backlash by their husbands due to difficulties in meeting the traditionally assigned responsibilities. We hypothesise that employed women from deprived communities witness greater risks of spousal abuse vis-à-vis employed women from relatively privileged backgrounds because they face higher incidence of intense care work resulting from the privatisation of common property resources and under-investment by the state in social welfare.

The exacerbation of the crisis of social reproduction is a critical feature of the contemporary regime that is founded on exclusionary processes of accumulation. The relationship between women's market work and the incidence of spousal violence is thereby mediated by the intensified care burden for which they are held responsible. Further feminist political economic analyses of the role of the reproductive burden of employed women in instigating spousal violence could strengthen the demand for renewal of reproductive responsibilities of the state in social movements and policy circles.

Finally, a discussion of the limitations of our study and the implications for future research is in order. First, our quantitative analyses use women's employment status as an explanatory variable for spousal abuse, which limits our understanding as to how differences in the kind of occupation or quality of employment affect the risks of such violence. An extension of the present models that incorporate more fine-grained classifications of women's employment can offer crucial insights in this regard. Additionally, it would be worthwhile to examine the association between relative spousal occupational prestige and intimate partner violence within and across socio-economic groups. Lastly, given the drawbacks of large surveys in capturing the intricacies of couple's intimate relations and the aetiology of violence, we would like to emphasise the importance of complementing quantitative studies with ethnographic research. Such exploration can also capture the complexities of the regional political economy more closely and help us better understand their implications for women's experience of violence.

Violence against women has been characterised as "a global public health problem of epidemic proportions" (WHO, 2013, p. 3). In the wake of another global public health crisis through the COVID-19 pandemic, reports suggest an increase in intimate partner violence across countries, including India. Action based on informed theory and evidence is all the more urgent at this juncture.

Acknowledgement

We would like to thank Smriti Rao, Vamsi Vakulabharanam, and Onupurba Das for helpful comments on earlier versions of this chapter.

Notes

1 In India, intimate partner violence can be well represented by spousal violence, for couples live together predominantly after marriage. So, this chapter uses the phrases interchangeably.

2 Both examples we mention are likely to have adverse effects on women's employment decision and spousal abuse against them and hence, can lead to a downward bias in the findings.

3 Here, the word "reproductive" follows social reproduction theory which recognises reproductive labour as all activities relating to the processes of reproducing and maintaining life (T. Bhattacharya, 2017). It can be further sub-divided into direct and indirect care work, with the former involving a process of personal and emotional care, and the latter comprising activities that provide support for direct care (Folbre, 2006; Mukherjee, 2012). The present study concerns with daily care work in the households and also terms it as reproductive labour or housework.

4 While the domestic violence schedule of our dataset (the National Family Health Survey) does not directly ask respondents about the reasons behind spousal violence, it does ask "yes" or "no" questions as to if they think the man is justified in beating his wife should she neglect the children or not cook food properly. 37 percent of currently married women and 19 percent of currently married men report these as valid reasons for physical abuse against the wife.

Note that a significantly smaller proportion of men as compared to women report any of the reasons given in the survey (viz., neglecting children, not cooking properly, going out without telling husband, arguing with him, and refusing to have sex with him) to be a justified one for beating one's wife, indicating a good chance of under-reporting from the men's end.

5 We use the husband's religion and caste in our analysis because we expect the household's social status as well as its members' everyday life, factors that may influence the incidence of spousal violence, to be determined by his social identity.

Note that even though OBCs are expanded as other backward *classes*, the Government of India uses the term to classify *castes* which are educationally or socially disadvantaged.

6 Note that we use the cluster average of *married* women's WPR as our instrument, where married refers to currently married women who are cohabiting with their husbands. As respectability norms associated with one's employment status and care work burden would vary between married and non-married women in India, the cluster average of married women's WPR serves as a suitable IV in our context. Thus, in the paper, women's WPR refers to married women's WPR and women's employment status refers to married women's employment status.

7 As in Lenze and Klasen (2017), we construct the instrument in a way that excludes the woman being considered in each observation to avoid an in-built correlation.

8 As can be seen from Tables 15.3, 15.4, and 15.5, diagnostic tests for all the regressions (i.e., for the whole sample population and for different economic and socio-religious groups) confirm the relevance and strength of the instrument.

9 In the 2SPS approach, the first stage remains the same whereas the second-stage regression uses the predicted values of the endogenous regressor and all control variables.

10 To check for robustness, we use different combinations of regression models in the two stages of 2SRI estimation: linear probability model in both stages, linear probability model in the first stage and binary logit model in the second stage, and binary logit model in the first stage and linear probability model in the second stage. These models provide similar results as those obtained from our main 2SRI model with binary logit model in both stages. The results are available on request.

11 Due to space considerations, only Table 15.3 presents the estimated marginal effects of the control variables on the risks of spousal violence against women. The complete sets of results for women from different economic and socio-religious groups are available on request.

12 Note that the qualitative result holds for the logistic model as well (i.e., when women's employment status is treated as exogenous), also shown in Table 15.3.

13 It is possible that employed women from the wealthiest quintile are not exposed to significantly higher risks of spousal violence than their non-employed counterparts because of the kind of employment they engage in. Figure A1 in the Appendix suggests that a majority of them (73 percent) have regular paid jobs which may enhance their bargaining power just enough to counter any backlash emanating specifically from their workforce participation. This figure (and figure A2) can also be taken to indicate that the nature of employment may be a reason why employed women from lower wealth quintiles (and varied social groups) cannot gain substantial economic security to protect themselves against spousal abuse.

14 Postcolonial theorists also attribute this strict division of gender roles in modern India to the nationalist response to (and struggle against) colonialism and, more generally, to the dominance of western culture. According to them, the discourse on nationalism has reinvented and reinforced the "new" Indian woman's primary responsibility of maintaining the home, the principal site for protecting and nurturing the sanctity of indigenous social life, as a significant marker of superior national culture. See Chatterjee (1989).

15 We say partly as recent literature on the low and falling female labour force participation rate in India underscores the deterioration of labour market conditions for women (consisting of reduction of employment opportunities as well as worsening quality of work for female workers) and implementation of neoliberal

policies (curtailing social provisioning of essential goods and services) as other important factors. See Colatei and Harris-White (2004); Ghosh (2008); Naidu (2016); Rao (2018).

16 See Roy (2007); Gidwani and Baviskar (2011); Coelho et al. (2013) for elaborate discussions on how these processes, vital for capitalist accumulation under the current regime, have caused a massive depletion of traditional sources, means, and mechanisms of social reproduction.

17 While our dataset provides information on time taken to fetch drinking water which could potentially make a better proxy for the intensity of indirect care work, it does not specify the number of trips one needs to make in a day. To avoid estimation biases, we use the variable on time taken as binary: 0 if the water source is on the household premises or if water is delivered at home, and 1 otherwise.

18 Naidu (2016) suggests that a similar tendency exists for women from different economic groups in both rural and urban India.

References

Agarwal, B. (1997). 'Bargaining' and gender relations: Within and beyond the household. *Feminist Economics*, *3*(1), 1–51.

Anandhi, S. (2017). Gendered negotiations of caste identity: Dalit women's activism in rural Tamil Nadu. In S. Anandhi, & K. Kapadia (eds.), *Dalit women: Vanguard of an alternative politics in India* (pp. 97–130). Oxon and New York: Routledge.

Anandhi, S., & Jeyaranjan, J. (2002). Masculinity and domestic violence in a Tamil Nadu village. In *Men, masculinity and domestic violence in India: Summary report of four studies* (pp. 16–26). Washington, DC: International Center for Research on Women.

Bhattacharya, H. (2015). Spousal violence and women's employment in India. *Feminist Economics*, *21*(2), 30–52.

Bhattacharya, T. (2013). Explaining gender violence in the neoliberal era. *International Socialist Review*, *91*. Retrieved from https://isreview.org/issue/91/explaining-gender-violence-neoliberal-era/index.html

Bhattacharya, T. (2017). Introduction: Mapping social reproduction theory. In T. Bhattacharya (ed.), *Social reproduction theory: Remapping class, recentering oppression* (pp. 1–20). London: Pluto Press.

Bhattacharyya, M., Bedi, A. S., & Chhachhi, A. (2011). Marital violence and women's employment and property status: Evidence from north Indian villages. *World Development*, *39*(9), 1676–1689.

Bloch, F., & Rao, V. (2002). Terror as a bargaining instrument: A case study of dowry violence in rural India. *The American Economic Review*, *92*(4), 1029–1043.

Borooah, V. K. (2005). Caste, inequality, and poverty in India. *Review of Development Economics*, *9*(3), 399–414.

Chakravarti, U. (1993). Conceptualising brahmanical patriarchy in early India: Gender, caste, class and state. *Economic & Political Weekly*, *28*(14), 579–585.

Chandrasekhar, C. P., & Ghosh, J. (2007, February 6). Women workers in urban India. *Macroscan*. Retrieved from https://www.macroscan.org/fet/feb07/fet060207Women_Workers.htm.

Chatterjee, P. (1989). Colonialism, nationalism, and colonialized women: The contest in India. *American Ethnologist*, *16*(4), 622–633.

Coelho, K., Chandrika, R., & Venkat, T. (2013). Housing, homes and domestic work: A study of paid domestic workers from a resettlement colony in Chennai. *Economic & Political Weekly*, *48*(43), 39–46.

Colatei, D., & Harriss-White, B. (2004). Social stratification and rural households. In B. Harriss-White, & S. Janakarajan (eds.), *Rural India facing the 21st century* (pp. 115–58). London: Anthem Press.

Crowne, S. S., Juon, H.-S., Ensminger, M., Burrell, L., McFarlane, E., & Duggan, A. (2011). Concurrent and long-term impact of intimate partner violence on employment stability. *Journal of Interpersonal Violence*, *26*(6), 1282–1304.

Deshpande, A. (2002). Assets versus autonomy? The changing face of the gender-caste overlap in India. *Feminist Economics*, *8*(2), 19–35.

Eswaran, M., Ramaswami, B., & Wadhwa, W. (2013). Status, caste, and the time allocation of women in rural India. *Economic Development and Cultural Change*, *61*(2), 311–333.

Farmer, A., & Tiefenthaler, J. (1997). An economic analysis of domestic violence. *Review of Social Economy*, *55*(3), 337–358.

Folbre, N. (2006). Measuring care: Gender, empowerment, and the care economy. *Journal of Human Development*, *7*(2), 183–199.

Fraser, N. (2016). Contradictions of capital and care. *New Left Review*, *100*(99), 99–117.

Gage, A. J. (2005). Women's experience of intimate partner violence in Haiti. *Social Science & Medicine*, *61*(2), 343–364.

Gayer, L., & Jaffrelot, C. (2011). Introduction: Muslims of the Indian city. From centrality to marginality. In L. Gayer & C. Jaffrelot (eds.), *Muslims in Indian cities: Trajectories of marginalisation* (pp. 1–22). New York: Columbia University Press.

Ghosh, J. (2008). Informalization and women's workforce participation: A consideration of recent trends in Asia. In S. Razavi (ed.), *The gendered impacts of liberalization: Towards "embedded liberalism"?* (pp. 163–190). New York and Oxon: Routledge.

Gibson-Davis, C. M., Magnuson, K., Gennetian, L. A., & Duncan, G. J. (2005). Employment and the risk of domestic abuse among low-income women. *Journal of Marriage and Family*, *67*(5), 1149–1168.

Gidwani, V., & Baviskar, A. (2011). Urban commons. *Economic & Political Weekly*, *46*(50), 42–43.

Goode, W. J. (1971). Force and violence in the family. *Journal of Marriage and the Family*, *33*(4), 624–636.

Gupta, A. (2014). *Reporting and incidence of violence against women in India*. Working paper. Research Institute for Compassionate Economics. Retrieved from https://riceinstitute.org/wordpress/wp-content/uploads/downloads/2014/10/Reporting-and-incidence-of-violence-against-women-in-India-working-paper-final.pdf.

Hadi, A. (2005). Women's productive role and marital violence in Bangladesh. *Journal of Family Violence*, *20*(3), 181–189.

Hasan, Z. (2011). *Politics of inclusion: Castes, minorities, and affirmative action*. New Delhi: Oxford University Press.

Himanshu. (2011). Employment trends in India: A re-examination. *Economic & Political Weekly*, *46*(37), 43–59.

IIPS and ICF. (2017). *National family health survey 4, 2015–16: India*. Mumbai: International Institute for Population Sciences [IIPS].

John, N. A. (2020). Exploring the linkages between women's paid and unpaid work and their experiences of intimate partner and non-partner violence in Nepal. *Feminist Economics*, *26*(4), 89–113.
Kalmuss, D. S., & Straus, M. A. (1982). Wife's marital dependency and wife abuse. *Journal of Marriage and the Family*, *44*(2), 277–286.
Katz, E. (1991). Breaking the myth of harmony: Theoretical and methodological guidelines to the study of rural third world households. *Review of Radical Political Economics*, *23*(3–4), 37–56.
Kessler, R. C., & McRae Jr., J. A. (1982). The effect of wives' employment on the mental health of married men and women. *American Sociological Review*, *47*(2), 216–227.
Kimerling, R., Alvarez, J., Pavao, J., Mack, K. P., Smith, M. W., & Baumrind, N. (2009). Unemployment among women: Examining the relationship of physical and psychological intimate partner violence and posttraumatic stress disorder. *Journal of Interpersonal Violence*, *24*(3), 450–463.
Lenze, J., & Klasen, S. (2017). Does women's labour force participation reduce domestic violence? Evidence from Jordan. *Feminist Economics*, *23*(1), 1–29.
Liddle, J., & Joshi, R. (1989). *Daughters of independence: Gender, caste, and class in India*. New Brunswick, NJ: Rutgers University Press.
Lundberg, S., & Pollak, R. A. (1994). Noncooperative bargaining models of marriage. *The American Economic Review*, *84*(2), 132–137.
MacMillan, R., & Gartner, R. (1999). When she brings home the bacon: Labour-force participation and the risk of spousal violence against women. *Journal of Marriage and the Family*, *61*(4), 947–958.
Mukherjee, A. (2012). Exploring inter-state variations of rural women's paid and unpaid work in India. *Indian Journal of Labour Economics*, *55*(3), 371–392.
Naidu, S. C. (2016). Domestic labour and female labour force participation: Adding a piece to the puzzle. *Economic & Political Weekly*, *51*(44 & 45), 101–108.
Oduro, A. D., Deere, C. D., & Catanzarite, Z. B. (2015). Women's wealth and intimate partner violence: Insights from Ecuador and Ghana. *Feminist Economics*, *21*(2), 1–29.
Owoo, N. S. (2020). Occupational prestige and women's experience of intimate partner violence in Nigeria. *Feminist Economics*, *26*(4), 56–88.
Panda, P., & Agarwal, B. (2005). Marital violence, human development and women's property status in India. *World Development*, *33*(5), 823–850.
Rao, S. (2018). Gender and class relations in rural India. *The Journal of Peasant Studies*, *45*(5–6), 950–968.
Rao, S., & Vakulabharanam, V. (2019). Migration, crises, and social transformation in India since the 1990s. In C. Menjívar, M. Ruiz, & I. Ness, (eds.), *The Oxford handbook of migration crises* (pp. 261–278). New York: Oxford University Press.
Roy, A. (2007). *Calcutta requiem: Gender and the politics of poverty*. New Delhi: Pearson Press.
Shaban, A. (2018). Introduction. In A. Shaban (ed.), *Lives of muslims in India: Politics, exclusion and violence* (pp. 1–24). Oxon and New York: Routledge.
Still, C. (2017). *Dalit women: Honour and patriarchy in south India*. London and New York: Routledge.
Tauchen, H. V., Witte, A. D., & Long, S. K. (1991). Domestic violence: A nonrandom affair. *International Economic Review*, *32*(2), 491–511.

Terza, J. V., Basu, A., & Rathouz, P. J. (2008). Two-stage residual inclusion estimation: Addressing endogeneity in health econometric modeling. *Journal of Health Economics*, *27*(3), 531–543.

Thoits, P. A. (1992). Identity structures and psychological well-being: Gender and marital status comparisons. *Social Psychology Quarterly*, *55*(3), 236–256.

Thorat, S., & Dubey, A. (2012). Has growth been socially inclusive during 1993–94 –2009–10? *Economic & Political Weekly*, *47*(10), 43–53.

Tolman, R. M., & Wang, H. C. (2005). Domestic violence and women's employment: Fixed effects models of three waves of women's employment study data. *American Journal of Community Psychology*, *36*(1–2), 147–158.

Villarreal, A. (2007). Women's employment status, coercive control, and intimate partner violence in Mexico. *Journal of Marriage and Family*, *69*(2), 418–434.

WHO. (2013). *Global and regional estimates of violence against women: Prevalence and health effects of intimate partner violence and nonpartner sexual violence.* Geneva: World Health Organization [WHO].

Zacharias, A., & Vakulabharanam, V. (2011). Caste stratification and wealth inequality in India. *World Development*, *39*(10), 1820–1833.

Appendix

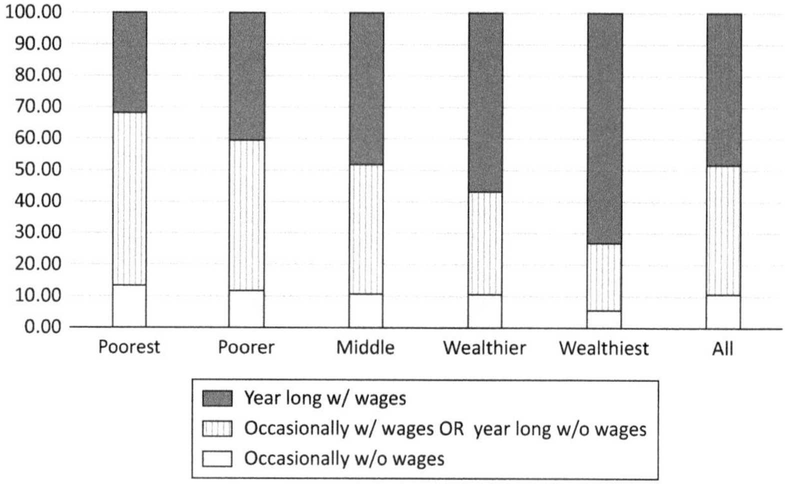

Figure 15A.1 Distribution of employed women as per the kind of work they were engaged in across economic groups (in %) Source: Authors' calculations based on NFHS-4.

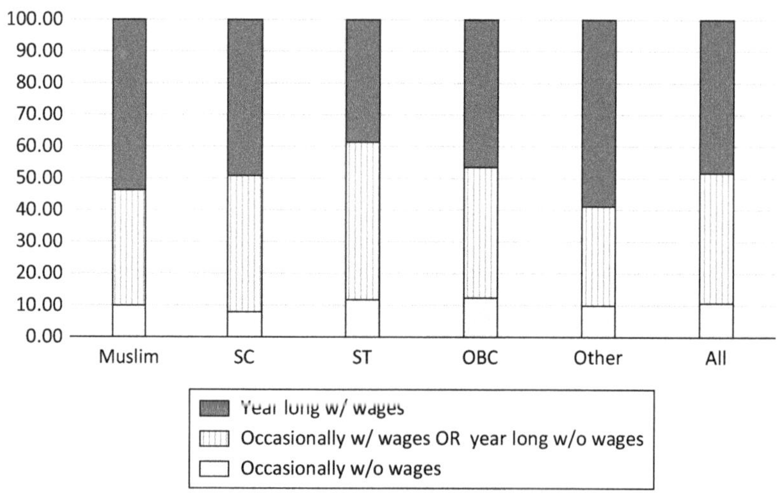

Figure 15A.2 Distribution of employed women as per the kind of work they were engaged in across socio-religious groups (in %) Source: Authors' calculations based on NFHS-4.

Index

Page numbers in **bold** and *italics* denotes tables and figures.